VOLUME

4

Obsessive-Compulsive Disorder

WPA Series
Evidence and Experience in Psychiatry

Other Titles in the *WPA Series* Evidence and Experience in Psychiatry

Volume 1—Depressive Disorders
Mario Maj and Norman Sartorius

Volume 2—Schizophrenia
Mario Maj and Norman Sartorius

Volume 3—Dementia
Mario Maj and Norman Sartorius

VOLUME

4

Obsessive-Compulsive Disorder

Edited by

Mario Maj
University of Naples, Italy

Norman Sartorius
University of Geneva, Switzerland

Ahmed Okasha
Ain Shams University, Cairo, Egypt

Joseph Zohar
Tel Aviv University, Israel

WPA Series
Evidence and Experience in Psychiatry

JOHN WILEY & SONS, LTD
Chichester • New York • Weinheim • Brisbane • Singapore • Toronto

Baffins Lane, Chichester,
West Sussex PO19 IUD, UK

National 01243 779777
International (+44) 1243 779777
e-mail (for orders and customer service enquiries): cs-books@wiley.co.uk
Visit our Home Page on: http://www.wiley.co.uk
or http://www.wiley.com

Other Wiley Editorial Offices

John Wiley & Sons, Inc., 605 Third Avenue,
New York, NY 10158-0012, USA

WILEY-VCH Verlag GmbH, Pappelallee 3,
D-69469 Weinheim, Germany

Jacaranda Wiley, Ltd., 33 Park Road, Milton,
Queensland 4064, Australia

John Wiley & Sons (Asia) Pte, Ltd., 2 Clementi Loop #02-01,
Jin Xing Distripark, Singapore 129809

John Wiley & Sons (Canada), Ltd., 22 Worcester Road,
Rexdale, Ontario M9W IL1, Canada

British Library Cataloguing in Publication Data

A catalogue record for this book is available from the British Library

ISBN 0-471-87163-X

Typeset in 10/12pt Times by Kolam Information Services Private Ltd, Pondicherry
Printed and bound in Great Britain by Biddles Ltd, Guildford and King's Lynn
This book is printed on acid-free paper responsibly manufactured from sustainable forestry, in which at least two trees are planted for each one used for paper production.

Contents

List of Review Contributors xi

Preface xiii

CHAPTER 1 DIAGNOSIS OF OBSESSIVE-COMPULSIVE DISORDER 1

Diagnosis of Obsessive-Compulsive Disorder: A Review 1
A. Okasha

COMMENTARIES

1.1 Obsessive-Compulsive Disorder: Towards a Diagnosis by Etiology 20
G. Nestadt

1.2 Assessment and Management of Obsessive-Compulsive Disorder 22
A. Rothenberg

1.3 Subtypes of Obsessive-Compulsive Disorder? 25
M.A. Riddle

1.4 Dissecting Obsessive-Compulsive Disorder into Subtypes 26
M.L. Berthier

1.5 The Diagnosis of Obsessive-Compulsive Disorder and Its Subtypes 29
E.C. Miguel and A.G. Hounie

1.6 Obsessive-Compulsive Symptoms: Implications for Treatment 32
L. Ravizza, U. Albert, G. Maina and F. Bogetto

1.7 Insight and Psychological Aspects of Obsessive-Compulsive Disorder 34
Y.G. Papakostas and G.N. Christodoulou

1.8 The Role of Overvalued Ideas and Biological Markers in the Diagnosis of Obsessive-Compulsive Disorder 37
F. Neziroglu

1.9 Research on Diagnosis of Obsessive-Compulsive Disorder in Latin America 39
H. Nicolini

CHAPTER 2 PHARMACOLOGICAL TREATMENT OF OBSESSIVE-COMPULSIVE DISORDER 43

Pharmacological Treatment of Obsessive-Compulsive Disorder: A Review 43
J. Zohar, Y. Sasson, M. Chopra, D. Amital and I. Iancu

COMMENTARIES

2.1 Pharmacotherapy of Obsessive-Compulsive Disorder: Accomplishment, Unanswered Questions and New Directions 62
T.A. Pigott

2.2 Beyond Serotonin Reuptake Inhibitors: Do We Have Our Second Wind? 65
C.J. McDougle

2.3 Future Pharmacotherapy for Obsessive-Compulsive Disorder: 5-HT_2 Agonists and Beyond 68
P.L. Delgado

2.4 Comments on the Pharmacological Treatment of Obsessive-Compulsive Disorder 71
M.R. Mavissakalian

2.5 The Expanding Obsessive-Compulsive Disorder Evidence Base 73
L.M. Koran

2.6 The Heterogeneity of Obsessive-Compulsive Disorder and Its Implications for Treatment 76
L. Bellodi

2.7 Pharmacotherapy of Obsessive-Compulsive Disorder: Questions for the Next Decade 79
M. Arato

2.8 Recent Progress and Open Issues in the Pharmacological Approach to Obsessive-Compulsive Disorder 82
J.A. Yaryura-Tobias

2.9 Treatment and Neurobiology of Obsessive-Compulsive Disorder 84
J.A. den Boer

2.10 Obsessive-Compulsive Disorder: Pharmacological Decision 86
J. Ananth

2.11 Serotonergic Antidepressants in Obsessive-Compulsive Personality Disorder 89
M. Ansseau

2.12 Drug Treatment of Obsessive-Compulsive Disorder: Dark Past, Bright Present, but Glowing Future 91
P. Blier

CHAPTER 3 PSYCHOTHERAPIES FOR OBSESSIVE-COMPULSIVE DISORDER **93**

Psychotherapies for Obsessive-Compulsive Disorder: A Review **93**
E.B. Foa and M.E. Franklin

COMMENTARIES

3.1 Effective Behavioural Therapy Constrained: Dissemination is the Issue 116
J.H. Greist

3.2 Can We Enhance the Effects of Cognitive-Behavioural Therapy in Obsessive-Compulsive Disorder? 119
P.M.G. Emmelkamp

3.3 Obsessive-Compulsive Disorder: Symptom-directed Behavioural Techniques and Beyond 122
I. Hand

3.4 Is the Combination of Antidepressants with Cognitive-Behavioural Therapy the Most Potent Treatment Possibility in Obsessive-Compulsive Disorder? 125
A.J.L.M. van Balkom

3.5 Cognitive Therapy and Behavioural Therapy in Obsessive-Compulsive Disorder: in Search of the Process 129
J. Cottraux

3.6 Obsessional Problems: Newer Cognitive-Behavioural Approaches Are a Work in Progress 131
P.M. Salkovskis

3.7 Current Issues in the Use of Behavioural Therapy for Obsessive-Compulsive Disorder 134
K.A. Kobak and B.C. Riemann

3.8 Cognitive-Behavioural Therapy and Integrated Approaches in the Treatment of Obsessive-Compulsive Disorder 136
F. Hohagen

3.9 Mindful Awareness: the Key to Successful Self-directed Treatment Strategies 139
J.M. Schwartz

3.10 The Role of Cognitive Therapy in the Treatment of Obsessive-Compulsive Disorder 142
L.M. Drummond

3.11 Psychodynamic Treatment of Obsessive-Compulsive Conditions 144
D. Shapiro

CHAPTER 4 CHILD AND ADOLESCENT OBSESSIVE-COMPULSIVE DISORDER 147

Child and Adolescent Obsessive-Compulsive Disorder: A Review 147
M.F. Flament and D. Cohen

COMMENTARIES

4.1 Theoretical and Clinical Implications of the Spectrum of Childhood Obsessionality 184
R.A. King

4.2 Developmental Perspectives in Pediatric Onset Obsessive-Compulsive Disorder 187
D.A. Geller

4.3 A Concept of Disorder in Some Disorder 190
D. Bolton

4.4 Obsessive-Compulsive Disorder: a Model for Closing the "Gap" between Adult and Pediatric Psychiatry 192
J. DeVeaugh-Geiss

4.5 The Spectrum of Obsessive-Compulsive Symptoms in Children and Adolescents 195
P.H. Thomsen

4.6 Obsessive-Compulsive Disorder in Children and Adolescents: Narrowing the Gap between Knowledge and Clinical Practice 196
J.G. Simeon

4.7 Obsessive-Compulsive Disorder in Children and Adolescents: Data from a Developing Country 198
C.E. Berganza

CHAPTER 5 OBSESSIVE-COMPULSIVE SPECTRUM DISORDERS **203**

Obsessive-Compulsive Spectrum Disorders: A Review **203**
E. Hollander and J. Rosen

COMMENTARIES

5.1 The Obsessive-Compulsive Spectrum: Promises and Pitfalls 225
K.A. Phillips

5.2 Understanding the Obsessive-Compulsive Spectrum: a Four-factor Model of Obsessive-Compulsive Symptoms 228
D. Watson and K. Wu

5.3 Extremes of Impulse Control and Serotonin/Frontal Lobe Pathophysiology 230
W. Kaye

5.4 The Obsessive-Compulsive Spectrum: Fact or Fancy? 233
D.W. Black

5.5 Blurry Spectrum Disorders 235
N.R. Swerdlow

5.6 Spectrum Disorders: Utilitarian Concepts or Utopian Fantasies? 238
J.W. Jefferson

5.7 Carving Nature at Its Joints: Different Approaches to the Obsessive-Compulsive Spectrum of Disorders 241
D.J. Stein

5.8 The Challenge of Deconvolving the Obsessive-Compulsive Disorder Spectrum into Its Component Diseases 244
M. George

5.9 Obsessive-Compulsive Spectrum Disorders: are Opposites Related? 246
R. Crino

5.10 The Spectrum of Obsessive-Compulsive-Related Disorders: State of the Art 249
D. Marazziti

CHAPTER 6 COSTS OF OBSESSIVE-COMPULSIVE DISORDER **253**

Costs of Obsessive-Compulsive Disorder: A Review **253**
M. Knapp, J. Henderson and A. Patel

COMMENTARIES
6.1 Considering the Full Economic Burden 276
M.M. Weissman
6.2 The Economics of Obsessive-Compulsive Disorder: Achieving the Potential Benefit 278
M. Aveline
6.3 In Search of Data on Costs of Obsessive-Compulsive Disorder 281
G. Steketee
6.4 Obsessive Slowness in Creating a Cost-Effectiveness Evidence Base for Obsessive-Compulsive Disorder 283
G. Thornicroft
6.5 Evaluations of Treatments for Obsessive-Compulsive Disorder: the Need for Health Economics Input 286
P. McCrone
6.6 Obsessive-Compulsive Disorder: a Psychiatric Disorder in Economic No Man's Land 288
P. Tyrer
6.7 Not Expensive and Cheap to Treat: New Evidence Leads to Different Conclusions 290
G. Andrews
6.8 Economics of Obsessive-Compulsive Disorder: on Safe Grounds? 293
W. Rössler
6.9 Obsessive-Compulsive Disorder: the Hidden Costs of a Hidden Epidemic 295
L. Salvador-Carulla
6.10 Obsessive-Compulsive Disorder: an Underestimated Disorder 297
M. Berger, U. Voderholzer and F. Hohagen

Acknowledgements 301

Index 303

Review Contributors

Dr Daniella Amital Division of Psychiatry, Sheba Medical Center, Tel Aviv University, Sackler School of Medicine, Tel Hashomer 52621, Israel

Dr Miriam Chopra Division of Psychiatry, Sheba Medical Center, Tel Aviv University, Sackler School of Medicine, Tel Hashomer 52621, Israel

Dr David Cohen CNRS UMR 7593, Pavillon Clérambault, Hôpital La Salpêtriere, 47 bd de l'Hôpital, 75013 Paris, France

Dr Martine F. Flament CNRS UMR 7593, Pavillon Clérambault, Hôpital La Salpêtriere, 47 bd de l'Hôpital, 75013 Paris, France

Professor Edna B. Foa Department of Psychiatry, University of Pennsylvania School of Medicine, 3535 Market Street, 6th Floor, Philadelphia, PA 19104, USA

Dr Martin E. Franklin Department of Psychiatry, University of Pennsylvania School of Medicine, 3535 Market Street, 6th Floor, Philadelphia, PA 19104, USA

Dr Juliet Henderson London School of Economics and Political Science, Department of Social Policy and Administration, Houghton Street, London WC2A, UK

Dr Eric Hollander Department of Psychiatry, Mount Sinai School of Medicine, Box 1230, One Gustave L. Levy Place, New York, NY 10029–6574, USA

Dr Iulian Iancu Division of Psychiatry, Sheba Medical Center, Tel Aviv University, Sackler School of Medicine, Tel Hashomer 52621, Israel

Professor Martin Knapp London School of Economics and Political Science, Department of Social Policy and Administration, Houghton Street, London WC2A, UK

Professor Ahmed Okasha Institute of Psychiatry, Ain Shams University, 3 Shawarby Street, Kasr El Nil, Cairo, Egypt

Dr Anita Patel London School of Economics and Political Science, Department of Social Policy and Administration, Houghton Street, London WC2A, UK

Dr Jennifer Rosen Department of Psychiatry, Mount Sinai School of Medicine, Box 1230, One Gustave L. Levy Place, New York, NY 10029–6574, USA

Dr Yehuda Sasson Division of Psychiatry, Sheba Medical Center, Tel Aviv University, Sackler School of Medicine, Tel Hashomer 52621, Israel

Professor Joseph Zohar Division of Psychiatry, Sheba Medical Center, Tel Aviv University, Sackler School of Medicine, Tel Hashomer 52621, Israel

Preface

Until relatively recently, obsessive-Compulsive disorder (OCD) was thought to be a rare disorder, with a prevalence of less than 5 per 1000 adults. Knowledge regarding the etiology was limited and no effective treatments were available. All of this has changed over the past two decades.

A number of studies have shown that OCD is much more frequent than was thought and, on the basis of these studies, it is estimated that its worldwide prevalence is about 2% of the adult population. Well-designed, double-blind, placebo controlled studies carried out in many countries have supported the notion that medium to high doses of serotonin reuptake inhibitors have a specific role in effectively treating OCD. Furthermore, there is increasing evidence that behavioural therapy, consisting of in-vivo exposure coupled with response prevention, is an effective treatment of the disorder.

Studies set up to investigate the pathophysiology of the disorder have produced intriguing findings, highlighting the role of serotonin and the frontal-basal-ganglia-thalamo-cortical (FBGTC) circuit in its pathogenesis. The use of new research tools, such as those stemming from molecular genetics, modern brain imaging techniques and advanced immunological procedures, has also resulted in findings contributing to our understanding of OCD. Some of these, used in combination with new approaches to the classification of the disorder (e.g. with or without tics, early vs late onset, etc.) may also soon lead to an improvement of the treatment strategies (e.g. by the addition of dopamine blockers for patients with tic disorders).

The work on OCD has also emerged as a bridge between psychiatry and neurology (e.g. in connection with Tourette's syndrome); between psychiatry and neuroimaging (through evidence of its distinctive neuronal circuitry); between psychiatry and immunology (through cases associated with streptococcal infection); and between psychiatry and neurosurgery (in view of the effectiveness of neurosurgical intervention in some forms of OCD).

On a different plane, interest in OCD has also contributed to the innovative conceptualization of links between OCD and impulse control disorders (e.g. trichotillomania, compulsive gambling) as part of the obsessive-compulsive spectrum which, in turn, has led to significant therapeutic advances resulting from the application of new therapeutic principles and strategies related to OCD in these disorders.

Two years ago, the World Psychiatric Association (WPA) undertook to produce a review of areas of psychiatry in which there have been significant advances of knowledge, and in which bringing together evidence and the experience of experts worldwide is likely to make a significant contribution to the improvement of care, reorientation of research and changes in training. There is every probability that OCD is such an area.

Mario Maj
Norman Sartorius
Ahmed Okasha
Joseph Zohar

CHAPTER

1

Diagnosis of Obsessive-Compulsive Disorder: A Review

Ahmed Okasha

Institute of Psychiatry, Ain Shams University, 3 Shawarby Street, Kasr El Nil, Cairo, Egypt

INTRODUCTION

A syndrome related to obsessive-compulsive disorder (OCD) has been recognized for more than 300 years [1]. Early descriptions focused on different aspects of the syndrome, and reflected the prevailing culture of the observers. English explanations stressed religious aspects and a relationship to melancholy [2]; French phenomenologists emphasized the importance of doubt and loss of will [3, 4]; the German view focused on the irrational nature of the thoughts, linking the disorder to psychosis [5].

Current epidemiological data [6] suggest that OCD is the fourth most common mental disorder. Only phobias, substance abuse, and depression are more common, and OCD is nearly as common as asthma and diabetes mellitus. Although this contradicts the original view that OCD is a rare psychiatric affliction, the latter notion (together with the often secretive nature of the disorder) continues to impede diagnosis.

PREVALENCE

OCD is an example of the positive impact of modern research on mental disorders. As recently as in the 1980s, it was considered an uncommon disorder, hardly responsive to treatment, whereas it is now recognized to be more prevalent than previously believed and often very responsive to treatment [6]. Lifetime prevalence rates of OCD vary considerably between countries. The lowest rates were observed in Taiwan [7], varying between 0.5% and 0.9%, and in India [8], where the prevalence was 0.6%. In North and Central Europe, the lifetime prevalence rates ranged between 2.6 and

Obsessive-Compulsive Disorder. Edited by Mario Maj, Norman Sartorius, Ahmed Okasha and Joseph Zohar.

3.2% [9], while the Epidemiological Catchment Area (ECA) study [10] found a 1-year prevalence rate of 1.65%. Okasha [11] found that the point prevalence rate of OCD, in a psychiatric outpatient Egyptian sample, was 2.3%.

Criticism has been levelled at these studies, because the Diagnostic Interview Schedule (DIS), used by most studies to assess symptoms, was designed for administration by lay interviewers rather than psychiatrists. Since studies using psychiatrists as interviewers have found lower rates of OCD, a more likely figure may be 1–2% [12–14]. Even so, it seems incontestable that OCD is a highly prevalent disorder in many countries. Further research is necessary, however, to ascertain the epidemiology of OCD in some countries, such as those on the African continent, for which few data exist.

DEMOGRAPHIC FEATURES

Early clinical reports suggested an almost even sex distribution in patients with OCD, as well as a higher than average intelligence [15]. The ECA study indicated that females are somewhat more prone to develop the disorder and that OCD is not associated with any level of educational attainment or marital status [10, 16]. However, another study reported that, while female OCD patients are as likely to be married as their non-psychiatric counterparts, male OCD patients are more likely to remain single [17]. The Cross-National Epidemiological Study confirmed that the female-to-male sex ratio varies between 1.2% and 1.6% [18]. Among children, however, more males than females present for treatment [19].

The mean age of onset of OCD has a wide range, between 21.9 and 35.5 years [18]. Most patients (65%) develop OCD before the age of 25 years, with only a small percentage (15%) after the age of 35 years [15]. Males seem to present with an earlier mean age of onset than females [15]. Such differences between male and female OCD patients may provide clues to investigating underlying neurobiological processes.

NOSOLOGY AND CLASSIFICATION

DSM-IV

For a diagnosis of OCD according to the Diagnostic and Statistical Manual of Mental Disorders, 4th edn (DSM-IV) [20], either obsessions or compulsions (or both) must be present. Obsessions are defined as recurrent and persistent thoughts, impulses, or images that are experienced—at some time during the disturbance—as intrusive and inappropriate, and that cause marked anxiety or distress. The thoughts, impulses or images are not simply excessive worries about "real-life" problems. The person attempts to ignore or suppress such thoughts, impulses or images, or to neutralize them with some other thought or action. The person recognizes that the obsessional thoughts, impulses or images are a product of his or her own mind (not imposed from without, as in thought insertion).

According to the DSM-IV, patients with OCD exhibit a broad range of obsessions, and many of them have multiple obsessions. Patients with obsessions are plagued by unwanted thoughts or impulses that they usually try to suppress or ignore. The recognition by the OCD sufferer that the obsessions are a product of his or her own mind differentiates them from the delusional thoughts characteristic of schizophrenia [20]. Common obsessions are repetitive thoughts concerning contamination, repetitive doubts, intense need for orderliness and symmetry, aggressive impulses and repeated sexual imagery.

In the DSM-IV, compulsions are described as repetitive behaviours (e.g. handwashing, ordering, checking) or mental acts (e.g. praying, counting, repeating words silently) that the person feels driven to perform in response to an obsession, or according to rules that must be applied rigidly. The behaviours or mental acts are aimed at preventing or reducing distress or preventing some dreaded event or situation; however, these behaviours or mental acts either are not connected in a realistic way with what they are designed to neutralize or prevent, or are clearly excessive [20].

Although people with OCD may exhibit a broad range of compulsions, the most common involve cleaning (handwashing), counting, checking (e.g. locks, ovens), putting objects in order, and asking for reassurance. Repetitive checking and other behaviours may be common, but are considered symptoms of OCD only when they are excessive and disruptive to daily living [20]. There may be symptom "shifts" in some patients—for instance, a washer may become a checker and vice versa.

In addition to the presence of obsessions and compulsions, DSM-IV requires that the following conditions be met: (a) at some point during the course of the disorder, the person has recognized that the obsessions or compulsions are excessive or unreasonable (this does not apply to children); (b) the obsessions or compulsions cause marked distress, are time-consuming (i.e. take more than 1 hour per day) or interfere with the person's normal routine, occupational (or academic) functioning, or usual social activities or relationships; (c) if another Axis I disorder is present, the content of the obsessions or compulsions is not restricted to it (e.g. preoccupation with food in the presence of an eating disorder; hair pulling in the presence of trichotillomania; concern with appearance in the presence of body dysmorphic disorder; preoccupation with having a serious illness in the presence of hypochondriasis; preoccupation with sexual urges or fantasies in the presence of paraphilia; or guilty ruminations in the presence of major depressive disorder); (d) the disturbance is not due to the direct physiological effects of a substance (e.g. a drug of abuse, a medication) or a general medical condition [20].

ICD-10

In the International Classification of Diseases, 10th edn (ICD-10) [21], the diagnostic criteria for OCD are as follows: (a) either obsessions or compulsions (or both) are present on most days for a period of at least 2 weeks; (b) obsessions (thoughts, ideas or images) and compulsions share the following features: (i) they are acknowledged as originating in the mind of the patient, and are not imposed by outside persons or influences; (ii) they are repetitive and unpleasant, and at least one obsession or compulsion must be present that is acknowledged as excessive or unreasonable; (iii) the subject tries to resist them (but if they are very long-standing, resistance to some obsessions and compulsions may be minimal) and at least one obsession or compulsion must be present which is unsuccessfully resisted; (iv) carrying out the obsessive thought or compulsive act is not in itself pleasurable (this should be distinguished from the temporary relief of tension or anxiety); (c) the obsessions or compulsions cause distress or interfere with the subject's social or individual functioning, usually by wasting time; (d) the most commonly used exclusion criteria are: not due to other mental disorders, such as schizophrenia and related disorders, or mood (affective) disorders [21].

Why Do We Not Diagnose OCD More Often?

Why is OCD not recognized more often? The answer to this question is found in the secretive nature of the condition. Studies have shown that it takes, on average, more than 8 years from onset of OCD to its correct diagnosis [22]. It has also been found that over 30% of patients presenting at dermatology clinics with dermatitis may be suffering from OCD [7]. Many OCD sufferers only recognize their condition following media coverage of the illness, or if they are asked a number of basic questions.

Five Questions to Identify an OCD Sufferer

In many cases, if patients are asked about their obsessive or compulsive symptoms, they will reveal their condition immediately. This readiness to "recognize" OCD is also illustrated by the fact that when the disorder is given public attention, for example by media exposure, this is invariably followed by an increase in patients presenting with it. Five simple questions are suggested to encourage OCD patients to reveal their obsessive or compulsive symptoms [23]: (a) Do you wash or clean a lot? (b) Do you check things a lot? (c) Are there any thoughts that keep bothering you and you would like to get rid of but cannot? (d) Do your daily activities take a very long time to finish? (5) Are you concerned about orderliness and symmetry?

Relationship between Obsessions and Compulsions

It is traditionally held that obsessions are covert mental events such as thoughts, images or impulses, whereas compulsions are observable, overt behaviours such as washing, checking, repeating actions or ordering. This distinction between obsessions and compulsions on the basis of their mode of expression contradicts a second, more current, view that emphasizes a dynamic functional relationship between obsessions and compulsions. According to this view, obsessions are mental events that elicit distress, such as thoughts of contamination, thoughts of being responsible for a disaster, unacceptable impulses, or blasphemous images. In contrast, compulsions are viewed as consisting of either overt behaviours or mental acts that are performed to reduce distress associated with the obsessions.

According to the more current concept of OCD, thoughts that are designed to neutralize other thoughts or impulses constitute compulsions. Compulsions can thus be overt behaviours, such as washing to offset distress about contamination, or covert rituals, such as silent praying to neutralize a blasphemous thought. Either behaviours or thoughts can function to reduce obsessional distress and, therefore, both can be considered compulsions. Distress-reducing thoughts are termed "cognitive compulsions".

Perhaps because the distinction between obsessions and compulsions has not been delineated clearly, studies of cognitive compulsions have been unavailable for a long time. The DSM-IV field trial [24] indicated the presence of mental compulsions in the majority of the assessed sample: 79.5% reported having both behavioural and mental compulsions; 20.3% had behavioural compulsions without mental compulsions; and only 0.2% had mental compulsions without behavioural compulsions. The results of the above study indicate that compulsions can be either behavioural or mental acts, and that mental rituals are quite prevalent among individuals with OCD. Consequently, in the DSM-IV, compulsions have been defined as "repetitive behaviours" (e.g. hand washing, ordering, checking) or mental acts (e.g. praying, counting, repeating words silently).

Recognizing Obsessions and Compulsions as Senseless

The DSM-III-R [25] was somewhat in conflict with both early and current views of OCD, since it stated that individuals with the disorder recognize obsessions as "intrusive and senseless" and compulsions as "excessive and unreasonable". Research indicates substantial variability between individuals in the extent to which they recognize their obsessions and compulsions as senseless.

In the DSM-IV field trial [24], subjects were interviewed to assess their insight into the senselessness of their obsessive fears. Data converged with previous results and with clinical observations that individuals with OCD exhibit a range of insight. Okasha *et al* [26] found that the affection of insight was mild in 26.6%, moderate in 50%, severe in 14.4% and extreme in 9% of OCD patients.

To alert clinicians to the range of insight that characterizes individuals with OCD, the subtype "with poor insight" was introduced into the DSM-IV. Inclusion of this subtype in the diagnostic criteria may also encourage researchers to explore the relationships between insight and other aspects of the psychopathology and treatment of OCD.

Comparison of DSM-IV and ICD-10

DSM-IV classifies OCD as one of a group of anxiety disorders, whereas ICD-10 classifies it as a stand-alone disorder within the area of neurotic, stress-related and somatoform disorders. Both systems require the presence of obsessions or compulsions (the ICD-10 requires the symptoms to be of at least 2 weeks' duration; there is no duration requirement in the DSM-IV). The DSM-IV does not require current insight but does require some history of insight. The ICD-10, on the other hand, requires that "at least one obsession or compulsion must be present that is acknowledged as excessive or unreasonable". Although there are formal differences in how the two systems handle insight, they converge in that both allow individuals who lack insight to be diagnosed with OCD.

The ICD-10 explicitly requires that "at least one obsession or compulsion must be present which is unsuccessfully resisted". No such requirement is specified in the DSM-IV, but the same idea is implied by the definition of obsessions as "intrusive" and by the requirement that the person "attempts to ignore or suppress" them. The ICD-10 devotes an entire criterion to specifying that pleasurable experiences cannot be obsessions or compulsions. In this way, the ICD-10 effectively excludes sexual deviations and addictions from the diagnosis of OCD. The DSM-IV does not have a general exclusion criterion for pleasurable activities. Rather, it handles this issue by listing a number of symptoms involving appetitive excesses that do not constitute OCD. The ICD-10 construes obsessions and compulsions as functionally equivalent, distinguishing them only according to their mode of expression: obsessions are covert, and compulsions overt symptoms. Consequently, there is no room for mental compulsions in the ICD-10. The DSM-IV has separate criteria for obsessions and compulsions, and compulsions can be either mental or behavioural. In the DSM-IV, there is only one subtype (the poor insight type) of OCD, while in the ICD-10 there are five subtypes: predominantly obsessional; predominantly compulsive; mixed obsessional thoughts and acts; other obsessive compulsive disorders; and OCD unspecified.

Because of an interest in promoting compatibility between the international and American classifications, the DSM-IV field trial [24] examined whether there are natural groupings of OCD symptoms that parallel the above ICD-10 subtypes. A large majority of the assessed patients (91%) fell into the "mixed obsessions and compulsions" category; a minority (8.5%) fell into the "predominantly obsessions" category; very few (0.5%) fell into the "predominantly compulsions" category. Okasha *et al* [26] found that 40% of their OCD patients presented with a mixture of obsessions and compulsions, 29% only with obsessions and 31% only with compulsions.

COURSE

OCD typically appears to be a chronic disorder with a waxing and waning course. Eighty-five per cent of patients experience chronic impairment [12]. A retrospective study of 62 patients fulfilling the ICD-8/9 criteria for OCD differentiated five courses: continuous and unchanging (27.4%); continuous with deterioration (9.7%); continuous with improvement (24.4%); episodic with partial remission (24.2%); and episodic with full remission (11.3%) [27].

Skoog and Skoog [28] observed improvement in 83% of cases, including recovery in 48% (complete recovery, 20%; recovery with subclinical symptoms, 28%). Among those who recovered, 38% had done so already in the 1950s. Forty-eight per cent had obsessive-compulsive disorder for more than 30 years. Early age of onset, having both obsessive and compulsive symptoms, low social functioning at baseline, and a chronic course at the examination between 1954 and 1956 were correlated with a worse outcome. Magical obsessions and compulsive rituals were correlated with a worse course. Qualitative symptom changes within the obsessive-compulsive disorder occurred in 58% of the patients. The probability of full remission from OCD over the 2-year period was 12%. The probability of partial remission was 47%. After achieving remission from OCD, the probability of relapse was 48%. Seventy-five per cent of the subjects received a serotonin reuptake inhibitor (SRI) for 12 weeks, and 68% ($n = 45$) received medium-to-high doses of SRIs for $\geq$ 12 weeks. Only 18% received a full trial of behavioural therapy [29].

Perugi *et al* [30] hypothesized that the episodic course of OCD is more likely to be related to bipolar mood disorder; 27.4% of OCD patients had an episodic and 72.6% a chronic course. Episodic OCD had a significantly lower rate of checking rituals and a significantly higher rate of a positive family history for mood disorder. Multivariate stepwise discriminant analysis revealed a positive and significant relationship between episodic course, family history of mood disorders, lifetime comorbidity for panic and bipolar II disorders, and late age at onset, and a negative correlation with comorbidity for generalized anxiety disorder. These data suggest that OCD with episodic course is related to cyclic mood disorders. This relationship may have implications for treatment and research strategies.

COMORBIDITY

High rates of comorbidity with major depression and other anxiety disorders have been consistently found in patients with OCD. An analysis of data from the ECA study showed that two-thirds of those with OCD had a comorbid psychiatric disorder [31]. Coexisting disorders included agoraphobia (39%), alcohol abuse (34%), major depression (32%), dysthymia (26%), drug abuse (22%), social phobia (19%), panic disorder (14%) and bipolar disorder (10%). The Cross-National Epidemiological Study found a higher rate of comorbidity with anxiety disorders than with major depression [18]. In individuals with OCD, the rates for anxiety disorders ranged from 24.5% to 69.6%, and those for major depression from 12.4% to 60.3%; the corresponding rates for individuals without OCD were 4.7–14.3% and 1.4–12.3%, respectively.

High rates for comorbid depression have also been reported in treatment-seeking OCD patients. For example, Rasmussen and Eisen [32] found major depressive disorder, with a prevalence of 67%, to be the most common comorbid lifetime diagnosis, followed by simple phobia (22%) and social phobia (18%). There are also reports of increased lifetime rates (10–17%) of anorexia nervosa in patients with OCD [33].

Clinical experience indicates that OCD and schizophrenia may coexist or alternate. It was suggested that some patients suffering from chronic obsessional symptoms are actually manifesting schizophrenia; others note that OCD may precede schizophrenia [34–36]. According to Okasha *et al* [37], patients may manifest obsessional perseveration or compulsive phenomena during the prodromal phase of schizophrenia, and OCD symptoms may appear at different stages of the schizophrenic process.

Studies using the Structured Clinical Interview for DSM-III (SCID) [38] report OCD and schizophrenic comorbidity to range from 10% to 12.2%. On the other hand, a 26% incidence of misdiagnosis of OCD with schizophrenia has been reported [39]. The very high prevalence (15–30%) of obsessive-compulsive symptoms in schizophrenic patients, as confirmed by additional studies [40, 41], may identify a subtype of schizophrenia.

In a study focusing on the comorbidity between OCD and personality disorders [42], 75% of the OCD patients fulfilled the DSM-III-R criteria for an axis II disorder, and 36% had an obsessive-compulsive personality disorder. In another study, the most prevalent personality disorder in OCD patients was found to be the "not otherwise specified" type, followed by the borderline, compulsive, avoidant, and histrionic [43, 44]. In a Brazilian investigation [45], the consensual Axis II diagnoses in the OCD group were: avoidant (52.5%), dependent (40%), histrionic (20%), paranoid (20%), obsessive-compulsive (17.5%), narcissistic (7.5%), schizotypal (5%), passive-aggressive (5%) and self-defeating (5%). At least one Axis II diagnosis was made in 70% of the patients.

Apparently, there is not a close relationship between OCD and obsessive-compulsive personality disorder. It seems that the comorbid personality disorder in OCD is most often not obsessive-compulsive personality.

TRANSCULTURAL ASPECTS OF THE DIAGNOSIS OF OCD

Culture and upbringing may alter the presentation of OCD. If we take Egypt as an example, we find that the religious nature of upbringing and education has a key role in OCD presentation. The emphasis on religious rituals, and the warding-off of blasphemous thoughts through repeated religious phrases, such as "I seek refuge with the Lord from the accursed Satan", can explain the high prevalence of religious obsessions and repeating compulsions among Egyptian OCD patients, even if they are not practising their religious duties.

The emphasis on cleanliness or ritual purity is the cornerstone of most of the compulsive rituals. The number of prayers and the verbal content can be the subject of scrupulousness, checking and repetition. The ritualistic cleansing procedures also can be a source of obsessions and compulsions about religious purity. Another evidence of the religious connotation inherent in OCD in Moslem culture lies in the term "*El Weswas*": this term is used in reference to the devil, and at the same time is used as a name for obsessions, which may lead patients to religious healers more than the medical profession.

A comparison in this context was also drawn between the most prevalent symptoms in Egypt, India, England and Jerusalem. Contamination obsessions were the most frequently occurring in all studies. However, the similarities of the contents of obsessions between Moslems and Jews as compared with Hindus and Christians signify the role played by cultural and religious factors in the presentation of OCD. The obsessional contents of the samples from Egypt and Jerusalem were similar, dealing mainly with religious matters related to cleanliness and dirt. Common themes between the Indian and British samples, on the other hand, were mostly related to orderliness and aggressive issues [26].

DIFFERENTIAL DIAGNOSIS

Distinguishing OCD from other disorders can be challenging. The differential diagnosis of OCD involves mood disorders, anxiety disorders, OCD spectrum disorders, impulsive spectrum disorders, obsessive-compulsive personality disorder, and delusional disorders.

A careful history, however, usually allows accurate diagnosis. For example, individuals with obsessive-compulsive personality disorder do not have obsessions or compulsions. Rather, there is a chronic and pervasive preoccupation which is essentially egosyntonic, although patients may be aware of the negative consequences of their trait [46].

Some OCD patients experience panic attacks, but these are usually secondary to their obsessional fears. Since spontaneous panic attacks are necessary to meet the DSM-IV criteria for panic disorder, and few panic patients exhibit rituals, the distinction from OCD can be readily made [47].

Major depressive episodes are often part of the differential diagnosis of OCD. Depression can certainly be accompanied by ruminations that may have an obsessive nature. However, these occur on the background of depressed mood, and within that context they differ from the senseless intrusions of OCD obsessions [48, 49].

Patients with trichotillomania do not present the multiple obsessions and compulsions often found in OCD [50]. Although hair-pulling and other impulsive symptoms are associated with a sense of relief, they typically are not closely related to obsessional thoughts, such as the prevention of a future event [46].

A recent case report describes the misdiagnosis of vivid, intrusive, obsessional images as "flashbacks" of repressed childhood trauma [51]. Conversely, patients with borderline personality disorder who experience strong thoughts and feelings about a particular theme may present complaining that these are symptoms of OCD.

While the delusions of schizophrenia can resemble particular obsessional concerns, there is typically markedly less insight in these patients. Similarly, the rituals of schizophrenia are often without purpose or in response to a force that is perceived as external. Other core positive and negative symptoms of schizophrenia are also not present in OCD.

ASSESSMENT TOOLS

Several scales are available to assist in the diagnosis of OCD and the measurement of treatment efficacy in that disorder. These include self-rating and rater-administered scales. Each group of scales has advantages and disadvantages.

Self-rating Scales

The most widely used self-rating scales are the Maudsley Obsessive Compulsive Inventory (MOCI), the Leyton Obsessional Inventory (LOI), the Hopkins Symptoms Checklist (HSCL and SCL-90), and the Self-rated Scale for Obsessive-Compulsive Disorder.

The MOCI consists of 30 questions designed to yield a total score and four subscale scores [52]. A patient with OCD according to DSM-IV criteria will usually have a score of at least 18 out of 30. Questions are balanced for true and false answers, and reliability can be partially assessed by looking at consistency of the patient's responses. Unfortunately, the MOCI has a disadvantage in that, because it relies on specific symptom sets, sometimes the chief obsessions of an individual are not listed. Furthermore, the MOCI cannot be graded. The subscales also seem to have no useful discriminative value [53].

The LOI was originally developed to differentiate between normal, house-proud housewives and obsessional patients. It consists of 69 yes/no questions [54]. These questions are divided into two sets: 46 on symptoms and 23 on traits. The scale would appear to have some construct validity and test–retest reliability, but the content validity may be compromised because the scale does not cover unpleasant obsessional thoughts and more florid bizarre symptoms [55]. The questions are also oriented more toward the home and cleaning [53]. The LOI seems acceptable as a screening tool, since it is relatively easy to administer, but it may not be a good indicator of severity [55].

The SCL-90 now consists of nine dimensions: obsessions-compulsions, anxiety, depression, somatization, interpersonal sensitivity, hostility, phobic anxiety, paranoid ideation, and psychoticism [56, 57]. Each item is rated according to a 0–4 scale. Although this instrument has shown good test–retest reliability and internal consistency, it may not be sufficiently robust to act as a measure of change in symptoms [58].

The Self-rated Scale for Obsessive-Compulsive Disorder is a 35-item questionnaire developed to measure the severity of OCD [6]. This scale evaluates distressing thoughts, rituals, perfectionism, and fear of contamination as separate dimensions. A cross-validation study found high internal consistency and significant correlation between this scale and two clinician-rated measures of OCD. Although this scale is advocated as being psychometrically sound for the measurement of severity in OCD [6], it probably has the same limitations as the MOCI.

An apparently reliable and low-cost alternative to pencil-and-paper measures is a computer-assisted telephone system. Such a system might use digitized human speech to administer rating for OCD. Scores derived with such systems are comparable to those obtained with human administration of the scales [59].

Rater-administered Scales

The Yale–Brown Obsessive Compulsive Scale (Y-BOCS)—the best instrument available for assessment of change in severity of OCD—consists of 16 items. The sum of the first 10 questions is ordinarily used. These 10 questions are divided into two sets of five questions, covering obsessions and compulsions. The questions assess time spent on obsessions or compulsions, interference, distress, resistance and control. Each is rated on a 0–4 scale correlating to severity (0 = no symptoms; 4 = extreme symptoms). Scores between 20 and 35 out of 40 are typical pretreatment values [60, 61].

The Y-BOCS differs from other rater-administered scales in how it assesses resistance. Instead of evaluating distress, resistance and control as a single item, it separates these entities and therefore affords a more sensitive measurement. Inter-rater reliability, internal consistency and test–retest reliability are good.

The Comprehensive Psychopathological Rating Scale (CPRS) is a factor-analysed scale, intended to cover a wide range of psychiatric symptoms and signs [62]. It consists of several subscales, with the OCD subscale containing eight items: rituals, inner tension, compulsive thoughts, concentration difficulties, worry over trifles, sadness, lassitude and indecision. Each item is scored on a 0–3 scale of severity. The fact that four of the items are also found in the depression subscale probably diminishes its discriminative validity. This is not as efficient a tool as the Y-BOCS for assessing OCD symptom severity.

The National Institute of Mental Health (NIMH)-Global Obsessive-Compulsive Scale (GOCS) is a rater-administered point scale (1–15 points). This scale comprises five severity categories (1–3, normal; 4–6, subclinical obsessive-compulsive syndrome; 7–9, clinical OCD; 10–12, severe; 13–15, very severe) [52].

The Clinical Global Impression (CGI) scales come in many varieties, including 1–7 number ratings and analogue scales. The CGI-OC has shown good correlation with the Y-BOCS and the NIMH-GOCS.

The Brown Assessment of Beliefs Scale has been developed to assess the degree of insight [63]. It is a semistructured interview consisting of 18 items, each with probes and anchors. The items focus on features of delusional content, e.g. conviction, perception of others' views, and fixity of beliefs. It also assesses the degree of preoccupation and impairment secondary to the beliefs. Degree of insight might be important in predicting the outcome of treatment [64].

The Overvalued Ideas Scale (OVIS) is an 11-item scale assessing overvalued ideas in OCD patients [65]. The impact of the ideas is evaluated on several different continua. The scale is available in four languages.

BIOLOGICAL ASPECTS IN DIAGNOSIS

Attempts have been made to identify a possible relationship of OCD to other mental disorders, mainly major depressive disorder and anxiety disorders. The special emphasis on the relation of OCD to major depressive disorder has been based on a number of biological investigations that pointed to a similarity in pathophysiology between the two disorders. Several of those investigations used the dexamethasone suppression test (DST). A 25% incidence of non-suppression among OCD patients [66] approximates the sensitivity of the DST for endogenous depression and is somewhat higher than the incidence of DST non-suppression in normal controls. However, the significance of this test in OCD is controversial. Monterio *et al* [67], for example, described normal DST responses in OCD.

Along another dimension, Weizman *et al* [68] showed that nine out of 10 drug-free OCD patients exhibited decreased thyroid-stimulating hormone (TSH) response to thyrotropin-releasing hormone (TRH) stimulation, indicating some dysfunction of the hypothalamic–pituitary–thyroid axis, and suggesting a link between OCD and mood disorders. However, similar results have also been found in other mental disorders, e.g. panic disorder, eating disorders, personality disorders, mania, alcoholism, schizophrenia and cocaine abuse [69], which again questions the specificity of the test.

Clonidine-stimulated release of growth hormone (GH) allows to evaluate dynamically the status of α_2-adrenoceptors. Siever *et al* [70] observed a significantly blunted GH response in nine out of 10 OCD patients following challenge with clonidine [67]. However, baseline GH levels were not significantly different between the two groups. Similar to the DST, the issue of specificity of the blunted GH response remains controversial, as non-depressed postmenopausal women and schizoaffective patients also show blunted response similar to that seen among depressives.

Using the somatosensory averaged evoked response, Shagass *et al* [71] have reported an abnormal pattern in the middle latency waves of the somatosensory averaged evoked response (ARE), that appears specifically in OCD and not in other mental disorders, including depression.

A decreased rapid eye movement (REM) sleep latency and a reduced platelet ^{3}H-imipramine binding have been reported both in major depression and in OCD. However, in major depression a decreased REM latency is coupled with an increased REM density, while in OCD the decrease in REM latency is not associated with an alteration in REM density. Similarly, the decreased ^{3}H-imipramine binding in major depression is accompanied by a reduced serotonin uptake, which is not the case in OCD. These discrepancies were taken to emphasize the biological difference, rather than the similarity, between major depressive disorder and OCD [72–74].

SUMMARY

Consistent Evidence

OCD is the fourth most common mental disorder and the fourth in producing disability expressed in DALYs (Disability Adjusted Life Years). It has high comorbidity with major depressive disorder, anxiety disorder and psychotic symptoms. There is no scientific evidence showing a high correlation between obsessive-compulsive personality and OCD, but there is a high co-occurrence of OCD with other personality disorders.

The tools for the assessment of OCD have been refined and can help a great deal in evaluating the severity of the disorder and the improvement after treatment. There are no biological markers for OCD, although alterations similar to major depression have been observed.

Given the high comorbidity of OCD and the existence of effective treatment, accurate diagnosis and thorough assessment of this disorder are essential. Because of the protean phenomenology of OCD, the frequent comorbidity and the discrete presentation, the diagnosis requires a high clinical acumen and a deep understanding of the symptomatology.

Incomplete Evidence

There is still a controversy about whether the lack of insight should be regarded as the hallmark of a delusional or psychotic subtype of OCD or as a dimension which is present in several OCD patients with different degrees of severity. It seems that the categorical diagnosis of OCD is not very satisfactory. The dimensional approach may account better for the variability of the degree of insight and resistance in OCD patients and for the relationship between OCD and OCD spectrum disorders, and can help a great deal in the management of OCD patients.

There is still incomplete evidence that OCD spectrum disorders are a separate cluster, as the similarity between them is greater than their similarity with OCD if we use proper diagnostic criteria. The fact that they may respond to selective serotonin reuptake inhibitors (SSRIs) is not a valid criterion for similarity.

Areas Still Open to Research

Further research is required to explore the biological and psychosocial correlates of OCD associated with depression, anxiety, psychosis, basal ganglia disorders, or streptococcal infection. Are they different diagnostic subtypes?

Further studies are necessary to solve the dispute regarding the relationship between obsessive-compulsive personality and disorder, as recent research showed that obsessive-compulsive personality is not a *forme fruste* of OCD.

Field studies to validate the classification of OCD into predominantly obsessional, predominantly compulsive and mixed types are necessary for fine tuning of the diagnostic criteria for OCD.

Finally, we should have reliable tools to differentiate between obsessive-compulsive symptoms, traits which are prevalent in many traditional societies where religious rituals play a major role in people's life, obsessive-compulsive personality and OCD. The Y-BOCS scale has a cut-off point to differentiate between obsessive-compulsive personality and OCD, but none for obsessive symptoms or traits.

REFERENCES

1. Hunter R., MacAlpine I. (1963) *Three Hundred Years of Psychiatry*, Oxford University Press, London.
2. Maudsley H. (1958) *The Pathology of the Mind*, Macmillan, London.

3. Ribot T. (1904) *Les Maladies de la Volontè*, Alcan, Paris.
4. Janet P. (1903) *Les Obsessions et la Psychasthenie*, Baillière, Paris.
5. Westphal K. (1878) Uber Zwangsvorstellungen. *Arch. Psychiatr. Nervenkrank.*, **8**: 734–750.
6. Kaplan H.I., Sadock B.J., Grebb J.A. (Eds) (1994) *Synopsis of Psychiatry*, 7th edn, pp. 598–606, Williams and Wilkins, Baltimore.
7. Yeh E.K., Hwu H.G., Chang L.Y., Yeh Y.L. (1985) Mental disorder in a Chinese metropolis: symptoms, diagnosis and lifetime prevalence. *Seishin Shinkeigaku Zasshi*, **87**: 318–324.
8. Khanna S., Garuray G., Sriram T.G. (1993) Epidemiology of obsessive compulsive disorder in India. Presented at the First International Obsessive-Compulsive Disorder Congress, Capri, March 9–12.
9. Degonda M., Wyss M., Angst J. (1993) The Zurich Study. XVIII. Obsessive-compulsive disorders and syndromes in the general population. *Eur. Arch. Psychiatry Clin. Neurosci.*, **243**: 16–22.
10. Karno M., Golding J.M. (1991) Obsessive-compulsive disorders. In *Psychiatric Disorders in America: the Epidemiological Catchment Area Study* (Eds L.N. Robins, D.A. Regier), pp. 204–219, Free Press, New York.
11. Okasha A. (1990) The biology of obsessive compulsive disorder. *Egypt. J. Psychiatry*, **13**: 3–4.
12. Rasmussen S.A., Eisen J.L. (1989) Clinical features and phenomenology of obsessive compulsive disorder. *Psychiatr. Ann.*, **19**: 67–73.
13. Flament M.F., Whitaker A., Rapoport J., Davies M., Berg C.Z., Kalikow K., Sceery W., Shaffer D. (1988) Obsessive-compulsive disorder in adolescence: an epidemiologic study. *J. Am. Acad. Child Adolesc. Psychiatry*, **27**: 764–771.
14. Nestadt G., Samuels J.F., Romanoski A.J., Folstein M.F., McHugh P.R. (1994) Obsessions and compulsions in the community. *Acta Psychiatr. Scand.*, **89**: 219–224.
15. Rasmussen S.A., Eisen J.L. (1990) Epidemiology and clinical features of obsessive compulsive disorder. In *Obsessive-Compulsive Disorders: Theory and Management* (Eds M.A. Jenike, L. Baer, W.E. Minichiello), pp. 10–27, Year Book Medical Publishers, Chicago.
16. Karno M., Golding J.M., Sorenson S.B., Burnam M.A. (1988) The epidemiology of obsessive compulsive disorder in five US communities. *Arch. Gen. Psychiatry*, **45**: 1094–1099.
17. Neziroglu F., Yariura-Tobias J.A., Lemli J.M., Yariura-Tobias R.A. (1994) Estudio demografico del trastorno obseso-compulsivo. *Acta Psiquiatr. Psicol. Am. Lat.*, **40**: 217–223.
18. Weissman M.M., Bland R.C., Canino G.J., Greenwald S., Hwu H.G., Lee C.K., Newman S.C., Oakley-Browne N.A., Rubio-Stipec M., Wichramaratne P.J. (1994) The cross-national epidemiology of obsessive compulsive disorder. *J. Clin. Psychiatry*, **55** (suppl. 3): 5–10.
19. Swedo S.E., Rapoport J.L., Leonard H., Lenane M., Cheslow D. (1989) Obsessive-compulsive disorder in children and adolescents: clinical phenomenology of 70 consecutive cases. *Arch. Gen. Psychiatry*, **46**: 335–341.
20. American Psychiatric Association (1994) *Diagnostic and Statistical Manual of Mental Disorders*, 4th edn, American Psychiatric Association, Washington, DC.
21. World Health Organization (1993) *The ICD-10 Classification of Mental and Behavioural Disorders. Clinical Descriptions and Diagnostic Guidelines*, World Health Organization, Geneva.

22. Pollitt J. (1956) Discussion: obsessive-compulsive states. *Proc. R. Soc. Med.*, **49**: 846.
23. International Council of OCD (1997) *Update on OCD Medical Action Communication. OCD Initiative*, Pfizer International Pharmaceuticals, New York.
24. Foa E.B., Kozak M.J., Goodman W.K., Hollander E., Jenike M.A., Rasmussen S.A. (1995) DSM IV field trial: obsessive-compulsive disorder. *Am. J. Psychiatry*, **152**: 90–96.
25. American Psychiatric Association (1987) *Diagnostic and Statistical Manual of Mental Disorders*, 3rd edn (revised), American Psychiatric Association, Washington, DC.
26. Okasha A., Saad A., Khalil A., Seif El Dawla A., Yehia N. (1994) Phenomenology of obsessive-compulsive disorder: a transcultural study. *Compr. Psychiatry*, **35**: 191–197.
27. Demal U., Lenz G., Mayrhofer A., Zapatoczky H.G., Zitterl W. (1993) Obsessive compulsive disorder and depression: a retrospective study on course and interaction. *Psychopathology*, **26**: 145–150.
28. Skoog G., Skoog I. (1999) A 40-year follow-up of patients with obsessive-compulsive disorder. *Arch. Gen. Psychiatry*, **56**: 121–132.
29. Eisen J.L., Goodman W.K., Keller M.B., Warshaw M.G., DeMarco L.M., Luce D.D., Rasmussen S.A. (1999) Patterns of remission and relapse in obsessive compulsive disorder: a 2-year prospective study. *J. Clin. Psychiatry*, **60**: 346–351.
30. Perugi G., Akiskal H.S., Gemignani A., Pfanner C., Presta S., Milanfranchi A., Lenzi P., Ravagli S., Maremmani I., Cassano G.B. (1998) Episodic course in obsessive-compulsive disorder. *Eur. Arch. Psychiatry Clin. Neurosci.*, **248**: 240–244.
31. Robins L.N., Helzer J.E., Weissman M.M., Orvaschel H., Guenberg E., Burke J.D., Jr, Regier D.A. (1984) Lifetime prevalence of specific psychiatric disorders in three sites. *Arch. Gen. Psychiatry*, **41**: 949–958.
32. Rasmussen S., Eisen D. (1991) Phenomenology of OCD: clinical subtypes, heterogeneity and coexistence. In *The Psychobiology of OCD* (Eds J. Zohar, T.R. Insel, S.A. Rasmussen), pp. 13–43, Springer, New York.
33. Rubenstein C.S., Pigott T.A., L'Heureux F., Hill J.L., Murphy D.L.A. (1992) Preliminary investigation of the lifetime prevalence of anorexia and bulimia nervosa in patients with obsessive-compulsive disorder. *J. Clin. Psychiatry*, **53**: 309–314.
34. Andreasen N.C. (1995) Introduction: Schizophrenia. In *Textbook of Psychiatry* (Eds N.C. Andreasen, D. Black), p. 212, American Psychiatric Press, Washington, DC.
35. Okasha A. (1970) Presentation and outcome of obsessional disorders in Egypt. *Ain Shams Med. J.*, **21**: 367–373.
36. Tibbo P., Narneke L. (1999) Obsessive compulsive disorder in schizophrenia: epidemiological and biologic overlap. *J. Psychiatry Neurosci.*, **24**: 15–24.
37. Okasha A., Seif El Dawla A., Youssef I. (1995) Obsessive-compulsive disorder: a transcultural comparison. *Ital. J. Psychiatry Behav. Sci.*, **3**: 109–115.
38. Spitzer R.L., Williams J.B.W., Gibbon M., First M.B. (1992) The Structured Clinical Interview for DSM-III-R (SCID). I: History, rationale and description. *Arch. Gen. Psychiatry*, **49**: 624–629.
39. Fenton W.S., McGlashan T.H. (1986) The prognostic significance of obsessive-compulsive symptoms in schizophrenia. *Am. J. Psychiatry*, **143**: 437–441.
40. Insel P.R., Akiskal H.S. (1986) Obsessive-compulsive disorder with psychotic features: a phenomenologic analysis. *Am. J. Psychiatry*, **143**: 1527–1533.

41. Eisen J.L., Rasmussen S.A. (1993) Obsessive-compulsive disorder with psychotic features. *J. Clin. Psychiatry*, **54**: 373–379.
42. Bejerot S., Ekselius L., von Knorring L. (1998) Comorbidity between OCD and personality disorders. *Acta Psychiatr. Scand.*, **97**: 398–402.
43. Okasha A., El Sayed M., Assad T., Seif El Dawla A., Okasha T. (1996) Sleep patterns in patients with OCD. *Neurosci. Spectrum*, **1**: 39–43.
44. Okasha A., Omar A.M., Lotaief F., Ghanem M., Seif El Dawla A., Okasha T. (1996) Comorbidity of axis I and Axis II diagnoses in a sample of Egyptian patients with neurotic disorders. *Compr. Psychiatry*, **37**: 95–101.
45. Rodrigues Torres A., Del Porto J.A. (1995) Comorbidity of obsessive-compulsive disorder and personality disorders. A Brazilian controlled study. *Psychopathology*, **28**: 322–329.
46. Simeon D., Hollander E., Cohen L. (1994) Obsessive compulsive related disorders. In *Current Insights in Obsessive-Compulsive Disorders* (Eds E. Hollander, I. Zohar, D. Marazziti, B. Olivier), pp. 53–63, Wiley, Chichester.
47. Kozak M.J., Foa E.B. (1994) Obsessions, overvalued ideas, and delusions in obsessive compulsive disorder. *Behav. Res. Ther.*, **32**: 343–353.
48. Peselow E.D., Robins C., Block P., Barouche F., Fieve R.R. (1990) Dysfunctional attitudes in depressed patients before and after clinical treatment and in normal control subjects. *Am. J. Psychiatry*, **147**: 439–444.
49. Vaughan M. (1976) The relationship between obsessional personality, obsessions in depression and symptoms of depression. *Br. J. Psychiatry*, **129**: 36–39.
50. Jenike M.A., Hyman S., Baer L. (1990) Clomipramine versus fluoxetine in obsessive compulsive disorder: a retrospective comparison of side effects and efficacy. *J. Clin. Psychopharmacol.*, **10**: 122–124.
51. Lipinski J.F., Jr, Pope H.G., Jr (1994) Do "flashbacks" represent obsessional imagery? *Compr. Psychiatry*, **35**: 245–247.
52. Rachman S.J., Hodgson R.J. (1980) *Obsessions and Compulsions*, Prentice-Hall, Englewood Cliffs.
53. Pato M.T., Eisen J.L., Pato C.N. (1994) Rating scales for obsessive compulsive disorder. In *Current Insights in Obsessive-Compulsive Disorder* (Eds E. Hollander, J. Zohar, D. Marazziti, B. Olivier), pp. 77–91, Wiley, Chichester.
54. Cooper J. (1970) The Leyton Obsessional Inventory. *Psychiatr. Med.*, **1**: 48–54.
55. Kim S., Dysken M., Kuskowski M. (1990) The Yale–Brown Obsessive Compulsive Scale: a reliability and validity study. *Psychiatry Res.*, **34**: 94–106.
56. Derogatis L., Lipman R., Covi L. (1973) The SCL-90: an outpatient psychiatric rating scale. *Psychopharmacol. Bull.*, **9**: 13–20.
57. Guy W. (1976) *ECDEU Assessment Manual for Psychopharmacology*, Publication 76–338. US Department of Health, Education and Welfare. US Government Printing Office, Washington, DC.
58. Steketee G., Doppelt H. (1986) Measurement of obsessive compulsive symptomatology: utility of the Hopkins symptom checklist. *Psychiatry Res.*, **19**: 135–145.
59. Baer L., Brown-Beasley M.W., Sorce J., Henriques A.I. (1993) Computer-assisted telephone administration of a structured interview for obsessive-compulsive disorder. *Am. J. Psychiatry*, **150**: 1737–1738.
60. Goodman W., Price L., Rasmussen S.A., Mazure C., Delgado P., Heninger G.R., Charney D.S. (1989) The Yale-Brown Obsessive Compulsive Scale. II. Validity. *Arch. Gen. Psychiatry*, **46**: 1012–1016.
61. Goodman W.K., Price L.H., Rasmussen S.A., Mazure C., Fleischmann R.L., Hill C.L., Heninger G.R., Charney D.S. (1989) The Yale–Brown Obsessive

Compulsive Scale. I. Development, use, and reliability. *Arch. Gen. Psychiatry*, **46**: 1006–1011.

62. Asberg M., Montgomery S., Perris C., Schalling D., Sedvall G. (1978) A comprehensive psychopathological rating scale. *Acta Psychiatr. Scand.*, **271** (suppl.): 5.
63. Eisen J.L., Phillips K.A., Beer D. (1993) Assessment of insight in obsessions and delusions. Presented at the American Psychiatric Association Meeting, San Francisco, May 15–20.
64. Foa E.B. (1979) Failures in treating obsessive compulsives. *Behav. Res. Ther.*, **17**: 169–176.
65. Neziroglu F., McKay D., Yariura-Tobias J.A., Stevens K.P., Todaro J. (1999) The Overvalued Ideas Scale: development, reliability and validity in obsessive compulsive disorder. *Behav. Res. Ther.*, **37**: 881–902.
66. Insel T.R., Gillin J.C., Moore A., Mendelson W.B., Loewenstein R.J., Murphy D.L. (1982) The sleep of patients with obsessive-compulsive disorder. *Arch. Gen. Psychiatry*, **39**: 1372–1377.
67. Monterio W., Noshiruani H., Marks I.M., Checkely S. (1986). Normal dexamethasone suppression test in OCD. *Br. J. Psychiatry*, **148**: 326–329.
68. Weizman A., Hermesh H., Gilad I., Aizenberg D., Tyano S., Laron Z. (1988) Blunted TSH response in obsessive compulsive disorder. Presented at the 70th Annual Meeting of the Endocrine Society, New Orleans, March 22–25.
69. Khan A.V. (1988) Sensitivity and specificity of TRH stimulation test in depressed and non-depressed adolescents. *Psychiatry Res.*, **25**: 11–17.
70. Siever L.J., Insel T.R., Jimerson D.C., Lake C.R., Uhde T.W., Aloi J., Murphy D.L. (1983) Growth hormone response to clonidine in obsessive compulsive patients. *Br. J. Psychiatry*, **142**: 184–187.
71. Shagass C., Roemer R.A., Straumanis J.J., Amadeo M. (1980) Topography of sensory evoked potentials in depressive disorders. *Biol. Psychiatry*, **15**: 183–207.
72. Meltzer H.Y., Arora R.C., Song P. (1982) Serotonin uptake in blood platelets as a biological marker for major depressive disorders. In *Biological Markers in Psychiatry and Neurology* (Eds E. Usdin, E. Costa), pp. 39–48, Pergamon, New York.
73. Weizman A., Carmi M., Hermesh H., Shahar A., Apter A., Tyano S., Rehavi M. (1986). High-affinity imipramine binding and serotonin uptake in platelets of eight adolescent and ten adult obsessive-compulsive patients. *Am. J. Psychiatry*, **143**: 335–339.
74. Insel T.R., Mueller E.A., Alterman I., Linnoila M., Murphy D.L. (1985) Obsessive-compulsive disorder and serotonin: is there a connection? *Biol. Psychiatry*, **20**: 1174–1188.

Commentaries

1.1
Obsessive-Compulsive Disorder: Towards a Diagnosis by Etiology

Gerald Nestadt[1]

Prof. Okasha reviews progress in the field of obsessive-compulsive disorder (OCD) using a lucid and practical approach. He concludes by summarizing the existing empirical evidence and suggests foci for future research. The diagnosis of OCD is relatively straightforward, requiring the presence of only one of two clinical phenomena, obsessions or compulsions (or both). However, it is abundantly clear that the contemporary nosological dilemma is the delineation of clinical boundaries, a concern not unique to OCD. Three axes, severity, breadth, and homogeneity, are at issue.

Severity may be adequately determined for individuals with OCD using instruments such as the Yale–Brown Obsessive Compulsive Scale (Y-BOCS). It remains unclear which other phenomena to include within the lower bounds. True obsessions and compulsions, which cause no discernible distress or impairment, are not included in the diagnosis by convention (DSM or ICD). These phenomena are more common than OCD, and certainly are not relevant from the perspective of treatment; nevertheless, they may share common pathophysiology with OCD.

Compulsive personality traits are particularly controversial with respect to their relationship to OCD. Despite indicating that there is "no scientific evidence showing a high correlation between obsessive-compulsive personality and OCD", Prof. Okasha recommends further investigation of this area. Our own research indicates an important relationship between the two conditions [1]. Notwithstanding this controversy, even careful clinical evaluation of certain patients may not yield an accurate differentiation between OCD and obsessive-compulsive personality disorder (OCPD). This may occur either as a result of an inability or unwillingness of the patient to reveal aspects of his mental life or due to the limitations of the clinical criteria themselves. The latter problem is illustrated by the

[1] *Department of Psychiatry, Johns Hopkins University, 600 N. Wolfe Street, Baltimore, MD 21287, USA*

difficulty of distinguishing whether hoarding behaviour is an obsession or an ego-syntonic trait of OCPD. Based on these complexities, I echo Prof. Okasha's sentiments that "diagnosis requires a high clinical acumen and a deep understanding of the symptomatology". These clinical and diagnostic concerns are applicable to the appreciation of other behaviours, such as "compulsive-like" habits and the differentiation of tics from compulsions.

The second area demanding clarification is the breadth of pathology appropriate to include in the OCD rubric. This involves consideration of the many Axis I disorders (e.g. depression and anxiety) that are found "co-morbid" with OCD, the so-called "OCD spectrum conditions", and even the normal personality dimension of neuroticism. The fundamental question that needs elucidation is whether these conditions are different expressions of the same pathophysiology, i.e. whether they share a common etiology with OCD. Alternatively, their co-occurrence, appearing with greater probability than chance, may be directly related to the presence of one another (i.e. secondary). It is most important to be sure to reject the possibility that they share phenomenological similarities without any underlying biological basis before considering them as part of the same spectrum of disorder.

The final area requiring investigation is that of homogeneity. Whereas the prior two areas involve the possibility of expanding the domain of OCD, several lines of investigation attempt to refine the disorder into more discrete homogeneous entities. These efforts to simultaneously embrace more psychopathology and to contract the condition into distinct subtypes are not mutually exclusive. It is conceivable, for instance, that patients with specific types of obsessions may be etiologically related to patients with generalized anxiety disorder and not to patients with other OCD symptoms. Pauls and Leckman [2] have pursued efforts to define subtypes by considering the coexistence of Tourette's syndrome as indicating a "type" of OCD. Factor analysis of OCD symptoms themselves is under investigation by several research groups for subtyping purposes [3].

Implicit in each of the aforementioned axes, is the understanding that the solutions will provide diagnostic entities that share a common underlying etiology. There are several known leads that could relate to a mechanism for the development of OCD, including basal ganglia diseases, encephalitis lethargica, Tourette's disorder, and streptococcal infections, among others. An important etiologic aspect of OCD is genetics. There is good evidence for the familial transmission of this disorder [4]; in addition, there is evidence for a genetic etiology from twin studies. Investigating the familial transmission of sub-clinical syndromes, subtypes and spectrum conditions is likely to yield important nosological contributions. Ultimately, knowledge regarding the genetic transmission, as well as other potential pathogenic mechanisms, will provide the basis for developing an etiologically-based taxonomy and hence a more rational approach to diagnosis.

Contemporary psychiatric diagnosis is, for the most part, based on descriptive criteria. This is an important advance compared to prior practice. Nevertheless, the goal of diagnosis is to categorize patients into rational groups that share a common course, outcome, prognosis, and treatment response. This promise may be better fulfilled when diagnosis is based on etiology.

REFERENCES

1. Nestadt G. Romanoski A.J., Brown C.H., Chahal R., Merchant A., Folstein M.F., Gruenberg E.M., McHugh P.R. (1991) DSM-III compulsive personality disorder: an epidemiological survey. *Psychiatry Med.*, **21**: 461–471.
2. Pauls D.L., Leckman J.F. (1986) The inheritance of Gilles de la Tourette's syndrome and associated behaviors. *N. Engl. J. Med.*, **315**: 993–997.
3. Summerfield L.J., Richter M.A., Antony M.M., Swinson R.P. (1999) Symptom structure in obsessive-compulsive disorder: a confirmatory factor-analytic study. *Behav. Res. Ther.*, **37**: 297–311.
4. Nestadt G., Samuels J., Riddle M., Bienvenu O.J., Liang K.-Y., LaBuda M., Walkup J., Grados M., Hoehn-Saric R. (2000) A family study of obsessive-compulsive disorder. *Arch. Gen. Psychiatry*, **57**: 358–363.

1.2
Assessment and Management of Obsessive-Compulsive Disorder

Albert Rothenberg[1]

A critically important clinical feature of obsessive-compulsive disorder (OCD) is the pervasive secrecy of patients suffering from the condition. As Prof. Okasha points out, this secrecy about OCD symptoms has been responsible for a long-standing marked underestimation of the true incidence of the illness. Although clinical recognition has increased, patients' secrecy, shame and denial continue to have an impact on assessment, treatment and the validity of research results.

More than with any other psychiatric disorder, possibly excepting severe forms of psychosis, OCD patients do not spontaneously or voluntarily report their symptoms to health providers or even intimate family members. Because the symptoms are wholly dominating and extreme and obsessional thinking may often be anti-social, e.g. repetitive obscene or blasphemous phrases, thoughts of attacking children or loved ones, removing one's clothes in public, OCD patients fear the censure and disapproval attendant

[1] *Department of Psychiatry, Harvard Medical School at Cambridge Hospital, Cambridge, MA, USA*

on revelation. Also, there is reason to believe that secrecy has its own function in the formation and perpetuation of OCD symptoms, all of which serve to protect against painful anxiety.

With respect to assessment of insight, both clinically and in investigative studies, the feelings of shame and desire for secrecy strongly influence patients' acknowledgement of the senselessness of symptoms. OCD patients are characteristically highly concerned with approval from other people, and their acknowledgement or denial of senselessness is often determined by assumptions about the expectations of interviewers, raters or administrators of self-report measures, rather than provision of veridical account. Moreover, there are very likely differences in profession of senselessness between those indulging in checking or cleanliness behaviours [1], the latter being more congruent with the values of Western middle class culture and therefore more individually and socially acceptable.

Attempts at diagnostic measurement, particularly studies of comorbid personality disorders, have been extensively confounded by the problem of shame and secrecy. These studies have shown markedly variable results (the reported association of OCD and compulsive or obsessive-compulsive personality disorder ranged from 0 to 71%) as well as a significant correlation after the partialing out of the effects of anxiety and depression [2]. Such wide variation in itself suggests unreliability of diagnostic instruments; these have consisted largely of paper-and-pencil self-reports, rating schedules and modified or unmodified standard structured interviews. Obsessive-compulsive personality disorder (OCPD) patients, however, also feel shameful, and they too are highly secretive about reporting excessive behaviour such as irrational control, hoarding, rigidity, miserliness and meticulous perfectionism. Paper-and-pencil self-report instruments, such as the Leyton Obsessive Inventory, the Maudsley Obsessive Compulsive Inventory, the Symptom Check List and the Personality Diagnostic Questionnaire, all lack both adequate corroboration procedures and safeguards against secrecy and withholding. Structured interviews carried out over delimited time periods, such as the Structured Interview for Personality Disorders, have been reported to yield a kappa coefficient of reliability with other instruments of only 0.25 for personality disorders overall [3] and a low 0.38 reliability with clinical interviews for OCD, probably because of the prescribed yes or no format for questions asked [4]. Rating procedures are primarily useful for assessing severity rather than establishing diagnoses. On the other hand, extended time evaluations carried out with persons suffering from OCPD do often reveal, because of the trust and familiarity developed, a full range of both OCPD and OCD patterns [5].

Although clinicians have historically avoided asking patients about OCD symptoms, patients will not now readily supply answers when asked the simple questions described by Prof. Okasha. All these questions rely on voluntary report and three of them require patients themselves to evaluate the excessiveness and inappropriateness of behaviour stipulated, an approach which invites self-criticism and shame, and relies completely on subjective response. How many times is "a lot"? It is up to the trained clinician to determine the answer.

An adequate clinical diagnostic assessment elicits information from the patient in a non-threatening and objective way. This orientation is also necessary for ongoing treatment and the following of specific features of the illness. In order to determine whether the patient engages in excessive checking behaviour, information may first be gathered about job history: does the patient go over paper-and-pencil work, repeat organizational tasks? If so, how often? At home, how many times is the lock on the door tested when the patient goes out, how often are the stove burners checked, how long does it take to dress in the morning? In order to assess cleanliness, the patient is asked about patterns of housekeeping, showering and hand-washing. Are particular places avoided because of possible contamination or dirt? For symmetry and order, questions are directed toward preferred placement of objects in the home, pictures on the wall, and about preferences about physical work environments.

For assessment of obsessional thinking, information is effectively evoked by identifying everyday difficulties in living and performing. Commonly reported problems in sleeping are followed by questions about the possibility of bothersome or repetitive thoughts that keep the patient awake. Similarly, if a patient reports distractions and inability to concentrate at work or at school, questions are asked about mental preoccupations.

We have begun to recognize and treat a condition that has long been hidden. In order to develop our knowledge about it properly and treat it effectively, we cannot rush to premature judgments and formulations but must continue to use our best clinical understanding and skills.

REFERENCES

1. Gibbs N.A., Oltmanns T.F. (1995) The relation between obsessive-compulsive personality traits and subtypes of compulsive behavior. *J. Anxiety Dis.*, **9**: 397–410.
2. Rosen K.V., Tallis F. (1995) Investigation into the relationship between personality traits and OCD. *Behav. Res. Ther.*, **33**: 445–450.
3. Perry J.C. (1993) Problems and considerations in the valid assessment of personality disorders. *Am. J. Psychiatry*, **150**: 1905–1906.
4. Steiner J.L., Tebes J.K., Sledge W.H., Walker M.L. (1995) A comparison of the structured clinical interview for DSM III-R and clinical diagnoses. *J. Nerv. Ment. Dis.*, **183**: 363–369.
5. Rothenberg A. (1986) Eating disorder as a modern obsessive-compulsive syndrome. *Psychiatry*, **49**: 45–53.

1.3
Subtypes of Obsessive-Compulsive Disorder?

Mark A. Riddle[1]

Prof. Okasha has provided a thoughtful and comprehensive overview regarding the phenomenology and diagnosis of obsessive-compulsive disorder (OCD). He notes the importance of identifying meaningful subtypes of OCD, which is the topic of this commentary.

Identification of homogeneous subtypes of psychiatric disorders is important, because it could facilitate the identification of etiologies. Unfortunately, progress in the explication of meaningful subtypes has been slow and relatively unproductive for psychiatric disorders. Recently, several preliminary studies have suggested possible approaches to identifying meaningful subtypes of OCD. Many of these studies have used factor analysis and other analytic techniques. Recently, data sets from OCD family studies have been used. Subtypes preliminarily identified to date include: familial vs. non-familial, tic-related vs. non-tic-related, association with certain comorbid psychiatric disorders, and specific symptom profiles.

Two recent family studies reported both familial and non-familial cases of OCD [1, 2]. Especially noteworthy was the strong association between early age of onset and familiality. For example, in the study by Nestadt *et al* [1], all OCD probands with a first-degree relative with OCD had an age of onset before age 18 years. These findings suggest that identification of families through probands with onset of OCD during childhood or adolescence will increase the likelihood of finding cases and families with a genetic etiology.

In both of these family studies, tics were identified in a subset of OCD probands. Preliminary data indicate that tics co-segregate with OCD in a subset of families, suggesting a tic-related subtype of OCD. Likewise, family studies of probands with tic disorders suggest that OCD runs with tics in some families.

Several studies of patients with OCD found a high frequency of comorbid anxiety disorders and obsessive-compulsive personality disorder (OCPD). A recent family study by Nestadt *et al* indicates that several anxiety disorders co-segregate with OCD in selected families [3]. The same is true for OCPD [4]. These findings are provocative and need to be replicated.

Perhaps the most research into subtyping of OCD has involved factor analyses of symptom profiles of individuals with OCD [5]. These studies have found adequate fit with two-factor, three-factor and four-factor

[1] *Children's Center CMSC 346, Johns Hopkins Hospital, 600 North Wolfe Street, Baltimore, MD 21287–3325, USA*

models. Several factors appear consistent across most, but not all, studies, indicating that a comprehensive model has not been identified.

To date, there have been no OCD subtype analyses that combined data regarding all four areas described above: familial vs. non-familial; tic-related vs. non-tic-related; association with certain comorbid psychiatric disorders; and specific symptom profiles. Unfortunately, such comprehensive analyses require larger data sets than have been available to date. An obvious next step would be for interested investigators to combine data sets to facilitate more complex analyses with the goal of identifying meaningful subtypes of OCD.

REFERENCES

1. Nestadt G., Samuels J., Riddle M.A., Bienvenu O.J. III, Liang K.-Y., LaBuda M., Walkup J.T., Grados M., Hoehn-Saric R. (2000) A family study of obsessive compulsive disorder. *Arch. Gen. Psychiatry* **57**: 358–363.
2. Pauls D.L., Alsobrook J.P., Goodman W., Rasmussen S., Leckman J.F. (1995) A family study of obsessive-compulsive disorder. *Am. J. Psychiatry,* **152**: 76–84.
3. Nestadt G., Samuels J., Riddle M.A., Liang K.-Y., Bienvenu O.J., Hoehn-Saric R., Grados M., Cullen B. The relationship between obsessive-compulsive disorder and anxiety and affective disorders: results from the Johns Hopkins OCD Family Study (submitted for publication).
4. Samuels J., Nestadt F., Bienvenu O.J., Costa P.T., Riddle M.A., Liang K.-Y., Hoehn-Saric R., Grados M., Cullen B. Personality disorders and normal personality dimensions in obsessive-compulsive disorder: results of the Johns Hopkins OCD Family Study (submitted for publication).
5. Summerfeldt L. J., Richter M. A., Antony M. M., Swinson R. P. (1999) Symptom structure in obsessive-compulsive disorder: a confirmatory factor-analytic study. *Behav. Res. Ther.,* **37**: 297–311.

1.4
Dissecting Obsessive-Compulsive Disorder into Subtypes

Marcelo L. Berthier[1]

Once described as "the hidden disease", obsessive-compulsive disorder (OCD) is now considered, as Prof. Okasha indicates in the opening paragraph of his review, the fourth most common mental disorder. Although the lifetime prevalence rates of OCD range from 2% to 3% of the population, OCD is still unrecognized by a variety of medical specialists other than

[1] *Unidad de Neurología Conductual, Servicio de Neurología, Hospital Clínico Universitario, Campus Universitario Teatinos, Apartado 3091 (29010), Málaga, Spain.*

psychiatrists, who commonly attend patients with non-psychiatric complications of OCD (e.g. dentists who treat gum lesions from excessive teeth cleaning). During the past two decades, the steady recognition of OCD as a common disorder has produced more accuracy and refinement in its diagnosis, yet assessment tools to rate obsessive-compulsive (OC) features peculiar to specific conditions (e.g. Tourette's syndrome) are scant [1]. In this regard, Prof. Okasha concludes his comprehensive review encouraging further research on cases of OCD associated with different conditions, to ascertain if different clinical subtypes really exist. There is widespread consensus that OCD is not a homogeneous condition, either in its clinical presentation or pathophysiological mechanisms. Therefore, in an attempt to reduce heterogeneity and improve diagnosis, clinical assessment, treatment strategies and prognosis, some researchers, including Prof. Okasha, have advocated the stratification of OCD patients into more homogeneous subtypes. The first steps in this direction have been taken, and subtypes of OCD based on either gender [2], age at onset [3], or nature of the associated medical [4] or neurological disorders [1,5–8] have been encountered.

Lensi *et al* [2] found gender-related differences in developmental history, clinical phenomenology of OC symptoms, and psychiatric comorbidity, with males showing significantly greater history of perinatal trauma, earlier onset of OC symptoms, higher frequency of sexual and symmetry/exactness obsessions and of odd rituals, and higher rates of bipolar II disorder than women, who instead showed later age at onset, higher frequency of aggressive obsessions and cleaning compulsions, and higher rates of panic attacks. On reviewing the literature on juvenile OCD, Geller *et al* [3] found important differences between juvenile-onset and adult-onset OCD, the former group being distinctly associated with strong familial aggregation, prepubertal onset, male preponderance, and frequent comorbidity with tics and development disorders in addition to anxiety, mood and disruptive disorders. In complementary terms, Berthier *et al* [6] reported similar patterns of OC symptoms and comorbidity in male patients with juvenile-onset OCD associated with developmental brain lesions (arachnoid cysts) involving the temporal and/or frontal cortices, thus supporting the development origin of this subtype of OCD.

Further phenomenological subdivisions come from the study of OCD associated with medical and neurological disorders. In fact, the growing evidence linking OCD with neurological disorders affecting the basal ganglia (Tourette's syndrome, Sydenham's chorea, Parkinson's disease, toxic and vascular lesions) and orbitofrontal and temporolimbic cortices (traumatic brain injury, tumours) has stimulated investigators to compare the clinical phenomenology of OCD cases associated with neurological disorders with cases of "idiopathic" or "pure" OCD [5]. To cite only one example, different groups of researchers independently found that the phenomenological characteristics of "pure" OCD are different as compared to tic-related OCD (i.e. Tourette's syndrome) [1, 7, 8]. Patients with Tourette's syndrome plus OCD report significantly more need for symmetry or exactness, sexual and aggressive obsessions, as well as more counting, repeating and touch/tap/rub compulsions than patients with "pure" OCD, who instead report more contamination obsessions and washing/cleaning and checking compulsions. The distinct clinical phenomenology of "pure" OCD and tic-related OCD is heuristically important, not only because it provides evidence for a different content of OC symptoms, but also because clinical differences may result from disorder-specific regional functional alterations of the cortico – striato–pallido–thalamic circuits [8–10].

Although further research is warranted, dissecting OCD into various subtypes may have implications for diagnosis, clinical assessment, pattern of comorbidity, underlying pathophysiological mechanisms and treatment. Potential advantages of this approach include: (a) a reduction of heterogeneity; (b) a better understanding of the phenomenological aspects of certain OC symptoms that are integral components of the subtype under scrutiny (e.g. compulsions induced by visual stimuli in Tourette's syndrome), but non-existent in other subtypes of OCD; (c) a better delineation of the profile of cognitive deficits and comorbid disorders of the subtype; (d) a better identification of the underlying functional mechanisms of the subtype; and (e) an improvement in treatment planning and prognosis.

REFERENCES

1. George M.S., Trimble M.R., Ring H.A., Sallee F.R., Robertson M.M. (1993) Obsessions in obsessive-compulsive disorder with and without Gilles de la Tourette's syndrome. *Am. J. Psychiatry*, **150**: 93–97.
2. Lensi P., Cassano G.B., Correddu G., Ravagli S., Kunovac J.L., Akiskal H.S. (1996) Obsessive-compulsive disorder. Familial-developmental history, symptomatology, comorbidity and course with special reference to gender-related differences. *Br. J. Psychiatry*, **169**: 101–107.
3. Geller D., Biederman J., Jones J., Park K., Schwartz S., Shapiro S., Coffey B. (1998) Is juvenile obsessive-compulsive disorder a developmental subtype of the disorder? A review of the pediatric literature. *J. Am. Acad. Child Adolesc. Psychiatry*, **37**: 420–427.
4. Swedo S.E., Leonard H.L., Garvey M., Mittleman B., Allen A.J., Perlmutter S., Dow S., Zamkoff J., Dubbert B.K., Lougee L. (1998) Pediatric autoimmune neuropsychiatric disorders associated with streptococcal infections: clinical descriptions of the first 50 cases. *Am. J. Psychiatry*, **155**: 264–271.
5. Berthier M.L., Kulisevsky J., Gironell A., Heras J.A. (1996) Obsessive-compulsive disorder associated with brain lesions: clinical phenomenology, cognitive function, and anatomic correlates. *Neurology*, **47**: 353–361.
6. Berthier M.L., Posada A., Puentes C., Gonzalez-Jiménez B. (1999) Obsessive-compulsive disorder (OCD) and related personality disorders associated with

supratentorial arachnoid cysts (SAC): behavioral, cognitive, and SPECT findings. *J. Neuropsychiat. Clin. Neurosci.*, **11**: 130.
7. Petter T., Richter M.A., Sandor P. (1998) Clinical features distinguishing patients with Tourette's syndrome and obsessive-compulsive disorder from patients with obsessive-compulsive disorder without tics. *J. Clin. Psychiatry*, **59**: 456–459.
8. Swerdlow N.R., Zinner S., Farber R.H., Seacrist C., Hartston H. (1999) Symptoms in obsessive-compulsive disorder and Tourette syndrome: a spectrum? *CNS Spectrums*, **4**: 21–33.
9. McGuire P.K., Bench C.J., Frith C.D., Marks I.M., Frackowiak R.S.J., Dolan R.J. (1994) Functional anatomy of obsessive-compulsive disorder. *Br. J. Psychiatry*, **164**: 459–468.
10. Wright C.I., Peterson B.S., Rauch S.L. (1999) Neuroimaging studies in Tourette syndrome. *CNS Spectrums*, **4**: 54–61.

1.5
The Diagnosis of Obsessive-Compulsive Disorder and Its Subtypes

Euripedes Constantino Miguel and Ana Gabriela Hounie[1]

Prof. Okasha's comprehensive description of contemporary concepts related to the diagnosis of obsessive-compulsive disorder (OCD) raises important questions concerning the limitations of current definitions and diagnostic classifications. In this commentary, we will try to discuss some of these issues suggesting that OCD is a heterogeneous disorder with a variety of clinical phenotypes.

It is interesting to note that the prevalence of OCD is found to be similar all over the world, although with a few exceptions. Okasha's transcultural study [1] on OCD found that some cultures influence the content of obsessions, specially religious ones. However, although the expression of specific symptoms can be shaped by the influence of culture, cross-cultural studies suggest the existence of a setting of nuclear symptoms, relatively independent of geographic, cultural and sociodemographic differences [2].

Prof. Okasha points out that males seem to present with an earlier age of onset. Interestingly, early-onset OCD cases tend also to be more frequently associated with tics [3]. Our group has recently concluded a study trying to compare the phenomenological characteristics of adults with early vs. late onset OCD. Tics and Tourette's syndrome (TS), as well as repeating, hoarding and tic-like compulsions, were significantly more frequent in the

[1] *Department of Psychiatry, University of São Paulo, Rua Ovidio Pires de Campos, 05430–010 São Paulo, Brazil*

early-onset group. Of relevance to clinical practice, the early-onset group had significantly higher scores on the Yale–Brown Obsessive Compulsive Scale (Y-BOCS) and a poorer response to a 3 month trial with clomipramine or a selective serotonin reuptake inhibitor (SSRI) [3]. In a recent single positron emission tomography (SPECT) study comparing OCD patients with early vs. late onset, we found regional cerebral blood flow differences in the two groups [4].

Okasha *et al* [1] found that 31% of their OCD patients reported only compulsions. We believe that most of those patients that report no obsessions preceding their compulsions would report other subjective experiences, such as sensory phenomena. These phenomena are inconsistently described in the literature and are usually defined as "generalized or focal uncomfortable feelings" [5]. Using an interview to assess these phenomena, we have recently investigated their presence in subgroups of OCD patients. Early-onset OCD and OCD plus TS patients reported a higher frequency of sensory phenomena preceding their repetitive behaviours compared to late-onset OCD and OCD without tics patients, respectively [3, 6]. Moreover, the presence of sensory phenomena was associated with a worse short-term response to clomipramine [3, 7]. Therefore, sensory phenomena may be valid and reliable phenotypic variables for grouping OCD patients.

There is now considerable evidence from family, genetic, phenomenological, neurophysiological and pharmacological studies suggesting that one candidate OCD subtype is related to chronic tics or TS. For instance, tic-related OCD, in comparison with non-tic-related OCD, is characterized by an earlier age of onset, is more frequently found in males, is associated with a positive family history of tic disorders, and has a distinct pattern of treatment response [7, 8].

The heterogeneity of OCD described above is also validated by genetic studies. Pauls *et al* [8] concluded that some cases of OCD are familial and related to tic disorders, some are familial and unrelated to tics, and in other cases there appears to be no family history of either OCD or tics. Prof. Okasha mentions the relationship between OCD and streptococcal infection as an area still open to research. In fact, the recent finding of higher rates of OCD in patients with Sydenham's chorea (SC) suggests that an abnormal immune process in patients recovering from a course of streptococcal infection with group A beta-hemolytic streptococci (GABHS) may play a role in OCD etiology [9]. Furthermore, OCD symptoms arising from or exacerbated in the context of GABHS infection may represent a distinct early-onset OCD subgroup [9]. Our group has recently assessed systematically patients with rheumatic fever (RF) with and without SC and found that OCD and OC symptoms were equally frequent in the two groups. OC symptoms were also more frequent in those groups when compared to controls [10].

The description of more precise clinical phenotypes is crucial for the discovery of the underlying etiologic factors involved in each OCD subtype. The phenotypes described above may have clinical implications. For instance, early-onset OCD patients may have a worse prognosis compared to late-onset cases. Tic-related OCD patients may require augmentation with neuroleptics to their treatment with serotonin reuptake inhibitors (SRIs). RF- or streptococcal-related OCD patients might benefit from immunomodulatory treatments.

ACKNOWLEDGEMENTS

This work was supported in part by grants from the Fundação de Amparo à pesquisa do Estado de São Paulo (FAPESP) and the Conselho National de Desenvolvimento Científico e Tecnológico (CNPq).

REFERENCES

1. Okasha A., Saad A., Khalil A., Seif El Dawla A., Yehia N. (1994) Phenomenology of obsessive-compulsive disorder: a transcultural study. *Compr. Psychiatry*, **35**: 191–197.
2. Del Porto J.A. (1994) Distúrbio obsessivo-compulsivo: fenomenologia clínica de 105 pacientes e estudo de aspectos trans-históricos e transculturais. Thesis, Escola Paulista de Medicina, São Paulo.
3. Rosário-Campos M.C., Leckman J.F., Prado H.S., Sada P., Zamignani D., Shavitt R.G., Miguel E.C. Early onset obsessive compulsive disorder as possible subgroup or subtype (submitted for publication).
4. Busatto D.F., Buchpiguel C.A., Zamignani D.R., Garrido G.E.J., Glabus M.F., Rosario-Campos M.C., Castro C.C., Maia A., Rocha E.T., McGuire P.K. *et al* Regional cerebral blood flow differences in obsessive-compulsive disorder subtype according to the age of illness onset (submitted for publication).
5. Miguel E.C., Rosário-Campos M.C., Prado H.S., Valle R.V., Rauch R.L., Coffey B.J., Baer L., Savage C., O'Sullivan R.L., Jenike M.A. *et al* (2000) Sensory phenomena in patients with obsessive-compulsive disorder (OCD) and/or Gilles de la Tourette Syndrome (TS). *J. Clin. Psychiatry*, in press.
6. Miguel E.C., Baer L., Coffey B.J., Rauch S.L., Savage C.R., O'Sullivan R.L., Phillips K., Moretti C., Leckman J.F., Jenike M.A. (1997) Phenomenological differences of repetitive behaviors in obsessive-compulsive disorder and Tourette's Syndrome. *Br. J. Psychiatry*, **170**: 140–145.
7. Miguel E.C., Rosário-Campos M.C., Shavitt R.G., Hounie A.G., Mercadante M.T. (2000) The tic-related obsessive-compulsive disorder phenotype. *Adv. Neurol.*, in press.
8. Pauls D.L., Alsobrook J.P., Goodman W., Rasmussen S., Leckman J.F. (1995) A family study of obsessive-compulsive disorder. *Am. J. Psychiatry*, **152**: 76–84.
9. Swedo S., Leonard H., Mittelman B., Allen A, Rapoport J., Dow K., Kanter M.E., Chapman F., Zabriskie J. (1997) Children with PANDAS (pediatric autoimmune

neuropsychiatric disorders associated with streptococcal infections) are identified by a marker associated with rheumatic fever. *Am. J. Psychiatry*, **154**: 110–112.
10. Mercadante M.T., Busatto G., Lombroso P.J., Prado L., Campos M.C.R., Valle R., Marques-Dias M.J., Kiss M.H., , Leckman J.F., Miguel E.C. The psychiatric symptoms of rheumatic fever (submitted for publication).

1.6 Obsessive-Compulsive Symptoms: Implications for Treatment

Luigi Ravizza, Umberto Albert, Giuseppe Maina and Filippo Bogetto[1]

Okasha's review on the diagnosis of obsessive-compulsive disorder (OCD) stimulates some thoughts, mainly on two major problematic areas: (a) where to put the cut-off between a true OCD and a subclinical disorder, and what is the significance of the subthreshold OC syndrome; and (b) whether symptomatological characterization can guide the choice of treatment.

Obsessive and/or compulsive symptoms whose severity is not sufficient to fulfil DSM-IV diagnostic criteria (subclinical OCD or subthreshold OC syndrome) have been detected in a high proportion of first-degree relatives of both OCD patients and subjects without mental disorders [1]. Moreover, OC symptoms were highly prevalent (12%) in a community sample of 1883 male adolescents in the area of Turin (Italy), suggesting that subthreshold OC syndromes may be a normal phenomenon in youths and that only "vulnerable" subjects will go on to develop a full-blown OCD [2]. Two studies [3, 4] looked at the prognostic significance of a diagnosis of subthreshold OCD in the adolescent population; both of them concluded that the probability for a subject with subclinical OCD to develop the clinically significant disorder in the following 1 or 2 years was low (1.5% and 10%, respectively). This low predictive value may depend on our inability to diagnose the subclinical disorder correctly, mainly because of the difficulty in defining the boundaries between OCD, the subclinical disorder (OC symptoms) and obsessive traits. Nevertheless, the presence of obsessive and/or compulsive symptoms has an importance, as: (a) a proportion of patients with obsessive or compulsive symptoms will be impaired from these symptoms and will thus be diagnosed with OCD in few years, and (b) the vast majority of patients with OCD in clinical samples had obsessive and/or compulsive symptoms a long time before developing OCD. These considerations fuel interest in: (a) producing a consensus statement on how we could appropriately differentiate (based on rating scales, for example) OCD from its subclinical variants and subclinical OCD from

[1] *Department of Neuroscience, Psychiatric Unit, University of Turin, Via Cherasco 11, 10126 Turin, Italy.*

obsessional traits; and (b) studying those factors that enable a subject with subclinical symptoms to function relatively well without developing OCD, or, on the other hand, identifying those factors that trigger the onset of the disorder in a subject that was functioning relatively well until that moment.

The question is whether or not those subjects with OC symptoms but without the full-blown disorder should be treated; if we could identify the small proportion of subjects who will develop OCD, we could perhaps treat only these subjects, in order to prevent them from becoming completely impaired by the symptoms of the disorder.

The dimensional rather than the categorical approach to OC syndromes may allow to include subclinical variants of the disorder within the OC spectrum. Moreover, this approach might be useful in the study of the genetic loading in the families of OCD probands.

The dimensional approach might prove useful also in the characterization of OCD patients aimed to the choice of treatment. There is some preliminary evidence that patients with symmetry and unusual somatic obsessions may preferentially respond to monomine oxidase inhibitors (MAOIs) [5]; patients with cleaning and checking symptoms may respond best to exposure and response prevention [6]; the predominance of compulsive symptoms and cleaning rituals has been found to negatively affect response to serotonin reuptake inhibitors (SRIs) [7] while anecdotal evidence seems to suggest that patients with predominantly obsessive symptoms (ruminations) might respond better to medication and worse to behavioural techniques. Recently, several authors independently used the same factor analysis methodology to identify symptom dimensions [8, 9], and a group of researchers applied this methodology to identify factor-analysed symptom dimensions predictive of outcome with SRIs: they demonstrated that higher scores on the hoarding dimensions are predictive of a poorer outcome and that the same may be true for the somatic dimension [10].

Future studies will probably focus on predictors to specific drugs. The main merit of works performed to date is, according to our opinion, that they stressed the importance of characterizing the subtype of OCD: while 10 years ago it was sufficient for a clinician to appropriately diagnose OCD in order to select an appropriate treatment strategy, today we should also consider whether there are peculiar features that may be helpful in targeting the treatment to the single patient.

REFERENCES

1. Pauls D.L., Alsobrook J.P., Goodman W., Rasmussen S., Leckman J.F. (1995) A family study of obsessive-compulsive disorder. *Am. J. Psychiatry*, **152**: 76–84.

2. Maina G., Albert U., Bogetto F., Ravizza L. (1999) Obsessive-compulsive syndromes in older adolescents. *Acta Psychiatr. Scand.*, **100**: 447–450.
3. Berg C.Z., Rapoport J.L., Whitaker A., Davies M., Leonard H., Swedo S., Braiman S., Lenane M. (1989) Childhood obsessive-compulsive disorder: a two-year prospective follow-up of a community sample. *J. Am. Acad. Child Adolesc. Psychiatry*, **28**: 528–533.
4. Valleni-Basile L.A., Garrison C.Z., Waller J.L., Addy C.L., Mckeown R.E., Jackson K.L., Cuffe S.P. (1996) Incidence of obsessive-compulsive disorder in a community sample of young adolescents. *J. Am. Acad. Child Adolesc. Psychiatry*, **35**: 898–906.
5. Jenike M.A., Baer L., Minichiello W.E., Rauch S.L., Buttolph M.L. (1997) Placebo-controlled trial of fluoxetine and phenelzine for obsessive-compulsive disorder. *Am. J. Psychiatry*, **154**: 1261–1264.
6. Ball S.G., Baer L., Otto M.W. (1996) Symptom subtypes of obsessive-compulsive disorder in behavioral treatment studies: a quantitative review. *Behav. Res. Ther.*, **34**; 47–51.
7. Alarcon R.D., Libb J.W., Spitler D. (1993) A predictive study of obsessive-compulsive disorder response to clomipramine. *J. Clin. Psychopharmacol.*, **13**: 210–213.
8. Baer L. (1994) Factor analysis of symptom subtypes of obsessive compulsive disorder and their relation to personality and tic disorder. *J. Clin. Psychiatry*, **55**: (suppl. 3): 18–23.
9. Leckman J.F., Grice D.E., Boardman J., Zhang H., Vitale A., Bondi C., Alsobrook J., Peterson B.S., Cohen D.J., Rasmussen S.A. *et al* (1997) Symptoms of obsessive-compulsive disorder. *Am. J. Psychiatry*, **154**: 911–917.
10. Mataix-Cols D., Rauch S.L., Manzo P.A., Jenike M.A., Baer L. (1999) Factor-analyzed symptom dimensions to predict outcome with serotonin reuptake inhibitors and placebo in the treatment of obsessive-compulsive disorder. *Am. J. Psychiatry*, **156**: 1409–1416.

1.7
Insight and Psychological Aspects of Obsessive-Compulsive Disorder

Yiannis G. Papakostas and George N. Christodoulou[1]

The remarkable explosion in research that we have been witnessing during the last two decades on obsessive-compulsive disorder (OCD), comprehensively reviewed by Prof. Okasha, raises many ideas and possibilities. We will focus on the issue of insight and the potentials of psychological theorizing in the diagnostic process of OCD.

Insight. The way the patients judge their obsessions and compulsions (intrusive, senseless, inappropriate, unreasonable, excessive, etc.), i.e. the

[1] *Department of Psychiatry, Athens University, Eginition Hospital, 72–74 Vas. Sophias Ave., 115 28 Athens, Greece.*

degree of insight, is of crucial importance in the diagnosis and treatment of OCD and related disorders. From a categorical point of view, we may simply state that the insight is either present (indisputable OCD cases) or absent (indisputable delusional cases). However, things do not work that way clinically. The degree of insight not only varies among people with OCD, but it often varies within the patient, i.e. it fluctuates depending on the patient's emotional state and proximity to an anxiety-provoking situation. Therefore, this either/or categorization of insight may not be as suitable, and many diagnostic dilemmas occur in distinguishing, for example, OCD from delusional disorders and schizophrenia. Prof. Okasha acknowledges these difficulties and raises the possibility of employing dimensional approaches. Thus, we may consider these two conditions as holding the opposite ends of a continuum. In the middle of the continuum we might place the notion of "overvalued ideas" (a concept established long ago by Wernicke) as suggested by several authors (1–3). As an example, the patient may say, "I know that it's foolish to wash my hands, but..." (obsessions), or "I constantly wash may hands because others try to transmit germs to me and I shall get sick" (delusions). Or, he/she might insist that "even if the possibilities are very remote, the price of contracting a dangerous illness is too high to take the risk of not washing" (overvalued idea). Based on their findings as well as findings from other studies, Eisen *et al* [2] concluded that (a) insight does exist on a continuum, and (b) as many as a quarter of patients with OCD may have poor insight, but only a few are frankly delusional. It is obvious, therefore, that most OCD patients with poor insight are patients with overvalued ideas. This finding is important from many aspects. For example, while behavioural interventions are considered appropriate in pure obsession cases, formidable difficulties, at least theoretically, may arise when applying exposure and response prevention to patients with overvalued ideas. However, there are no instruments for reliable assessment of this construct. The Brown Assessment of Beliefs Scale (BABS) is essentially a measure of "delusionality". The recent development of an instrument specifically designed to assess overvalued ideas (the Overvalued Ideas Scale, OVIS [3]) seems to us to be in the right direction. In conclusion, the standard introduction of the construct of overvalued ideas to the diagnostic procedures regarding OCD seems to be needed, justified and promising.

Potential of psychological approaches to diagnosis. There is no question that the earlier, psychological (mostly Freudian) models of OCD have been recently replaced by neurobiological approaches, in spite of the fact that highly elaborated mental phenomena—such as guilt, hypermorality and hyperreligiosity—predominate in the clinical picture of the disorder. But, as Cohen *et al* [4] remind us, although psychology emerges from biology, it cannot be reduced to biology and, on the other hand, psychological factors do not necessarily point towards a psychogenic model of OCD. From a cognitive-behavioural point of view, the criteria established by DSM-IV are more psychologically "friendly" and compatible than those of ICD-10, since DSM-IV (as Prof. Okasha stresses) clearly accepts (a) a dynamic functional relationship between obsessions and compulsions, and (b) the existence of covert (cognitive) compulsions, which are positions adopted earlier by behavioural and cognitive theories and practices [5].

Recent cognitive-behavioural approaches suggest that certain beliefs and assumptions play a role in the pathogenetic chain of the events that lead to and/or maintain OCD [6]. Among them, two belief domains most relevant to OCD are inflated responsibility assumptions, that can make the patient believe that he/she is responsible for the intrusion and for its perceived dangerous consequences, and dysfunctional assumptions regarding the perceived relationship between thoughts and actions. The latter concept is called "thought–action fusion" (TAF) and is presented either as moral TAF (the belief that the thoughts are morally equivalent to actions) or likelihood TAF (the belief that thinking about something increases its likelihood of occurrence, either to oneself or to others).

Admittedly, these ideas are at a preliminary stage of development, as their proper assessment and clinical significance is currently under investigation. However, they are promising, not only as possible targets of novel interventions, but also because they might offer diagnostic help in distinguishing OCD from other disorders.

REFERENCES

1. Kozak M.J., Foa E.B. (1994) Obsessions, overvalued ideas, and delusions in obsessive-compulsive disorder. *Behav. Res. Ther.*, **32**: 343–353.
2. Eisen J.L., Phillips K.A., Rasmussen S.A. (1999) Obsessions and delusions: the relationship between obsessive-compulsive disorder and the psychotic disorders. *Psychiatr. Ann.*, **29**: 515–522.
3. Neziroglu F., McKay D., Yaryura-Tobias J.A., Stevens K.P., Todaro J. (1999) The Overvalued Ideas Scale: development, reliability and validity in obsessive-compulsive disorder. *Behav. Res. Ther.*, **37**: 881–902.
4. Cohen L.J., Stein D., Galynker I., Hollander E. (1997) Towards an integration of psychological and biological models of obsessive-compulsive disorder: phylogenetic considerations. *CNS Spectrums*, **2**: 26–44.
5. Salkovskis P.M., Forrester E., Richards C. (1998) Cognitive-behavioural approach to understanding obsessional thinking. *Br. J. Psychiatry*, **173** (suppl. 35): 53–63.
6. Obsessive Compulsive Cognitions Working Group (1997) Cognitive assessment of obsessive-compulsive disorder. *Behav. Res. Ther.*, **35**: 667–681.

1.8
The Role of Overvalued Ideas and Biological Markers in the Diagnosis of Obsessive-Compulsive Disorder

Fugen Neziroglu[1]

Prof. Okasha's authoritative and comprehensive review of diagnostic issues in obsessive-compulsive disorder (OCD) encompasses many areas of importance. Although OCD was described very eloquently as early as the seventeenth century, our knowledge of it was limited. Until the early 1980s there was a scarcity of information available on the disorder; in fact, most psychiatric books devoted only two or three pages to it. When several researchers suggested that OCD prevalence may be greater than previously assumed, the pharmaceutical industry began to invest research money into the discovery of specific medications. In the United States, the investigation of clomipramine led to the serotonin hypothesis of OCD [1]. Later, blood serotonin levels in OCD patients were found to be significantly lower than those in controls [2]. The hypothesis gave rise to many biological investigations. The results of many of these studies substantiated the role of serotonin in OCD and this in return generated the development of specific serotonin reuptake inhibitors (SSRIs). Cerebrospinal fluid 5-hydroxyindoleacetic acid (5-HIAA) [3] and platelet serotonin levels [4] were inversely correlated to symptom severity and positively correlated to treatment response. Although some did not find platelet serotonin levels to be different between OCD patients and healthy controls, patients with higher serotonin concentrations responded better to clomipramine [5]. Challenge with the serotonergic agonist *m*-chlorophenylpiperazine (*m*-CPP) aggravated OCD symptoms [6], whereas administration of the 5-hydroxytryptophan antagonist metergoline decreased OCD symptoms [7]. Because the amino acid L-tryptophan is the precursor of serotonin, whole blood serotonin was measured before and after the administration of L-tryptophan. Results indicated an elevation of serotonin levels in blood without modification of urinary 5-HIAA [8]. Even behavioural therapy has been reported to alter serotonin activity [9]. Although the data supporting the serotonergic hypothesis have been challenged, it is still possible to speak of a dysregulation of the serotonergic system. Prof. Okasha discusses some of these biological aspects in diagnosis, although, as he points out, there are no specific biological markers. Studies investigating receptor subtypes will perhaps answer more of these questions.

The biological aspects of OCD were mentioned in the review to understand their impact on diagnosis. Perhaps for this reason no mention was made of the social learning components in the development of the disorder,

[1] *Bio-Behavioral Institute, 935 Northern Blvd., Great Neck, NY 11021, USA*

since there are no known social variables that assist in diagnosing OCD or its spectrum. There are components that may trigger or exacerbate the disorder, but it was not the purpose of the review to discuss these aspects.

The issue of insight and, even more important, overvalued ideas needs to be taken into consideration in any discussion of diagnosis. Does OCD belong under anxiety disorders, is it an entity of its own, or can it at times reach psychosis? Prof. Okasha presents self- and clinician-administered tools assessing delusionality, overvalued ideas and insight, and he indicates that the categorical diagnosis of OCD is not very satisfactory. The strength of belief is on a continuum from very weak to very strong, completely reasonable to completely unreasonable, totally sensible to totally senseless. In previous diagnostic manuals, an obsession had to be perceived as senseless by the patient. In DSM-IV the term "with poor insight" was added to indicate that an obsession may be perceived as sensible. However, the term "with poor insight" does not connote the concept of overvalued ideas. Poor insight is only one characteristic of an overvalued idea. Overvalued ideas have been measured not only in OCD but also in other spectrum disorders, where they have been found to be stronger than in OCD. Perhaps it is because of strong overvalued ideas in other spectrum disorders, such as body dysmorphic disorder, that response to treatment is not as good. Prof. Okasha suggests investigating the degree of insight and resistance in OCD and spectrum disorders in order to better manage the patients.

REFERENCES

1. Yaryura-Tobias J.A. (1977) Obsessive compulsive disorder: a serotonergic hypothesis. *J. Orthomol. Psychiatry*, **6**: 317–326.
2. Yaryura-Tobias J.A., Bebirian R.J., Neziroglu F., Bhagavan H. (1977) Obsessive-compulsive disorders as a serotonergic defect. *Res. Commun. Psychol. Psychiatry Behav.*, **2**: 279–286.
3. Thoren P., Asberg M., Bertilsson L., Mellström B., Sjoqvist, F., Träskman L. (1980) Clomipramine treatment of obsessive-compulsive disorder, II: Biochemical aspects. *Arch. Gen. Psychiatry*, **37**: 1289–1295.
4. Flament M.F., Rapoport J.L., Berg C.J., Sceery W., Kilts C., Mellström B., Linnoila M. (1985) Clomipramine treatment of childhood obsessive compulsive disorder: a double-blind controlled study. *Arch. Gen. Psychiatry*, **42**: 977–983.
5. Flament M.F., Rapoport J.L., Murphy D.L., Berg C.J., Lake R. (1987) Biochemical changes during clomipramine treatment of childhood obsessive-compulsive disorder. *Arch. Gen. Psychiatry*, **44**: 219–225.
6. Zohar J., Mueller E.A., Insel T.R., Zohar-Kadouc R.C., Murphy D.L. (1987) Serotonergic responsivity in obsessive-compulsive disorder. Comparison of patients and healthy controls. *Arch. Gen. Psychiatry*, **44**: 946–951.
7. Zohar J., Insel T.R., Zohar-Kadouch R.C., Hill J.L., Murphy D.L. (1988) Serotonergic responsivity in obsessive-compulsive disorder. Effects of chronic clomipramine treatment. *Arch. Gen. Psychiatry*, **45**: 167–172.

8. Yaryura-Tobias J.A., Neziroglu F., Fuller B. (1979) An integral approach in the management of the obsessive compulsive patient. *Pharm. Med.*, **1**: 155–167.
9. Neziroglu F., Steele J., Yaryura-Tobias J.A., Hitri A., Diamond B. (1990) Effect of behavior therapy on serotonin level in obsessive compulsive disorder. In *Psychiatry: A World Perspective*, Vol 1. (Eds C.N. Stefanis, A.D. Rabavilas, C.R. Soldatos), pp. 707–710, Elsevier, Amsterdam.

1.9 Research on Diagnosis of Obsessive-Compulsive Disorder in Latin America

Humberto Nicolini[1]

This commentary begins by providing some data on the prevalence of obsessive-compulsive disorder (OCD) in Latin America. OCD lifetime prevalence has been found to be 3% in Argentina [1], 2.5% in Brazil [2, 3], 2.8% in México [4, 5], 2.5% among Mexican-Americans in the USA [6] and 3.2% in Puerto Rico [7]. These reports show a range of 2.5–3% lifetime prevalence, similar to that found elsewhere in the world.

In addition, gender and age of onset have been shown to have an effect in Latin Americans with OCD: females were slightly overpresented (60% of the sample) and males had a higher severity and an earlier age of onset. Also, among those with an earlier age of onset, a higher number of symmetry compulsions was found [8–10].

High rates of comorbidity with major depression and other anxiety disorders have been consistently found in Hispanic patients with OCD. Additionally, motor tics were frequently found in Mexican OCD patients and their relatives [3, 10–12].

Culture was reflected also in the presentation of OCD in Mexico. We found a higher number of sexual obsessions and compulsions (31%) among females with OCD. This fact is probably due to social limitations for Mexican females concerning sexuality [5].

Several scales are available in Spanish to assist in the evaluation of OCD. This is the list of the scales which have been translated and assessed in terms of reliability and validity in Spanish: the SCL-90, The Yale–Brown Obsessive Compulsive Scale (Y-BOCS), The National Institute of Mental Health (NIMH) Global Obsessive-Compulsive Scale (GOCS) and the Clinical Global Impression (CGI) scales [13, 14].

[1] *Mexican Institute of Psychiatry, Carracci 107, col. Insurgentes Extremadura, C.P. 03740, México City, México*

Genetic research has provided some interesting results in trying to understand some biological subtypes of the disorder. Family and twin studies have clearly shown that OCD is a familial disease [15]. Segregation analysis data have lent some support to the notion of the probable existence of a single gene mechanism in the etiology of OCD [15, 16]. Using this same type of analysis, some forms of OCD, such as OCD with predominant symmetry and ordering symptoms, have been described as the possible single gene subtype [17]. Association studies of OCD candidate genes, in spite of the methodological difficulties, have highlighted some loci as candidates for OCD subtypes. Among these findings are the association between the low activity allele of the catechol-O-methyltransferase enzyme (COMT) gene and OCD in males [15] and the association between an allele of the mono-amino-oxidase enzyme gene and OCD in females [18].

REFERENCES

1. Yaryura-Tobias J., Neziroglu F. (1994) *La Epidemia Oculta: Trastorno Obsesivo-Compulsivo*, Cangrejal, Buenos Aires.
2. Almeida F., Mari J., Coutinho E., Franca J., Fernandes J., Andreoli S., Busnello E. (1992) Estudio multicentrico de morbidade psiquiatrica em areas urbanas brasileiras (Brasilia, Porto Alegre e Sao Paulo). *Rev. da ABP-APAL*, **14**: 93–104.
3. Miguel E. (1996) *Trastornos de Espectro Obsessivo-Compulsivo: Diagnostico e Tratamento*, Guanabara Koogan, Rio de Janeiro.
4. Caraveo J. (1996) La prevalencia de los trastornos psiquiátricos en la población Mexicana. Estado actual y perspectivas. *Salud Mental*, **19**: 8–13.
5. Nicolini H., Benilde O., Mickalonis L., Sánchez de Carmona M., Mejía J.M., Páez F., De la Fuente J.R. (1998) Etude familial du trouble obsessionnel-compulsif. *Neuropsychiatrie de l'Infance et de l'Adolescence*, **46**: 164–172.
6. Karno M., Golding J., Sorenson S., Burnam M. (1988) The epidemiology of obsessive-compulsive disorder in five U.S. communities. *Arch. Gen. Psychiatry*, **45**: 1094–1099.
7. Canino G., Bird H., Shrout P., Rubio-Stipec M., Bravo M., Martínez R., Sesman M., Guevara L. (1987) The prevalence of specific psychiatric disorders in Puerto Rico. *Arch. Gen. Psychiatry*, **44**: 727–735.
8. Burke K., Burke J., Rae D., Regier D. (1991) Comparing age at onset of major depression and other psychiatric disorders by birth cohorts in five U.S. community populations. *Arch. Gen. Psychiatry*, **48**: 789–795.
9. Nicolini H., Páez F., Sánchez de Carmona M., Herrera K., Mejía J., Giuffra L., De la Fuente J.R., Sidenberg D. (1997) Age of onset, gender and severity in obsessive-compulsive disorder. *Salud Mental*, **20**: 1–4.
10. Yaryura-Tobias J., Bertoldi A., Suárez M., Rey R. (1999) Estudio sobre la opinión de psiquiatras sobre el trastorno obseso-compulsivo. In *Psiquiatría Biológica, 25°* Aniversario (Ed. Colegio Argentino de Neuropsicofarmacologia), pp. 113–125, Fernández-Labriola y Kalina, Buenos Aires.
11. Cruz C., Camarena B., Orozco B., Páez F., De la Fuente J.R., Nicolini H. (1997) DRD4 gene polymorphism in OCD with and without tics. *Neurosci. Lett.*, **231**: 1–4.

12. Nicolini H, Camarena B., Cruz C., Orozco B., Weissbecker K., De la Fuente J.R., Sidenberg D. (1996) DRD2, DRD3 and 5HT2 genes polymorphisms in obsessive-compulsive disorder. *Mol. Psychiatry*, **16**: 461–465.
13. Apiquiàn R., Fresán-Orellana A., Nicolini H. (2000) *Escalas de Valoraciòn de la Psicopatologìa In Español*, Editorial Ciencia y Cultura Latinoamericana, Mexico City, in press.
14. Nicolini H., Orozco B., Sánchez de Carmona M., Páez F., Loreido G., De la Fuente J.R. (1996) Estudio de traducción y confiabilidad de la escala Yale-Brown in Español para trastorno obsesivo-compulsivo. *Salud Mental*, **19** (suppl. 3): 13–16.
15. Nicolini H., Cruz C., Camarena B., Páez F., De la Fuente J.R. (1999) Understanding the genetic basis of obsessive-compulsive disorder. *CNS Spectrums*, **4**: 32–48.
16. Cavallini M.C., Macciardi F., Pasquale L., Bellodi L., Smeraldi E. (1999) Complex segregation analysis of obsessive-compulsive and spectrum related disorder. *Am. J. Med. Genet. (Neuropsychiatric Genetics)*, **88**: 38–43.
17. Alsobrook J.P., Leckman J.F., Goodman W.K., Rasmussen S.A., Pauls D.L. (1999) A mendelian form of OCD derived from symptom based factors. *Am. J. Med. Genet. (Neuropsychiatic Genetics)*, **88**: 669–675.
18. Camarena B., Cruz C., De la Fuente J.R., Nicolini H. (1998) A higher frequency of a low activity-related allele of the MAO-A gene in females with obsessive-compulsive disorder. *Psychiatr. Genet.*, **8**: 255–257.

CHAPTER

2

Pharmacological Treatment of Obsessive-Compulsive Disorder: A Review

Joseph Zohar, Yehuda Sasson, Miriam Chopra, Daniella Amital and Iulian Iancu

Division of Psychiatry, Sheba Medical Center, Tel Aviv University, Sackler School of Medicine, Tel Hashomer 52621, Israel

INTRODUCTION

The well-established finding that patients with obsessive-compulsive disorder (OCD) respond to a particular group of drugs—serotonin reuptake inhibitors (SRIs)—which have a specific effect on the activity of the serotonergic neurotransmitter system, has changed the outlook for OCD sufferers. Since the early 1980s, several potent SRIs have been studied extensively in OCD. Aggregate statistics for all SRIs suggest that 70% of treatment-naïve patients will improve at least moderately. With the specific response of OCD patients to compounds with serotonin reuptake blocking activity, an understanding of the biochemical nature and origins of OCD begins to unfold.

One of the ways to demonstrate the specific serotonergic response in OCD has been by using comparative studies with serotonergic vs. non-serotonergic medications. The serotonergic drug clomipramine (CMI) was compared to the noradrenergic antidepressant desipramine (DMI) in two double-blind studies in a randomized, cross-over fashion. In the first study [1], CMI was found to have significant antiobsessive effects, while DMI was completely ineffective in this regard. In the second study, conducted among 48 children and adolescents with OCD, CMI was again shown to be significantly more effective [2].

CMI has also been compared to other non-serotonergic antidepressants, such as nortriptyline and imipramine, with much the same results [3, 4]. Moreover, other non-tricyclic selective serotonin reuptake inhibitors

Obsessive-Compulsive Disorder. Edited by Mario Maj, Norman Sartorius, Ahmed Okasha and Joseph Zohar.

(SSRIs), such as fluvoxamine, fluoxetine, paroxetine, sertraline and citalopram, have also been reported to be effective antiobsessional drugs [5–8].

ANTIDEPRESSANT OR ANTIOBSESSIONAL?

One of the first controversies regarding the treatment of OCD patients with antiobsessive medications, such as CMI, was whether the patients benefited from the antidepressant effect of those medications, or whether improvement was actually due to an antiobsessional effect. In an early study, Marks *et al* [9] reported on the efficacy of CMI in depressed OCD patients. However, subsequent studies showed the antiobsessive effectiveness of CMI and SSRIs to be independent of their antidepressant activity [3, 10–14]. For example, it has been demonstrated with the SSRI fluvoxamine that severity of depression at the beginning of the study was not related to outcome [15] and that depressive symptoms improved in conjunction to the OC symptoms [16, 17]. Moreover, if the antiobsessional effect were due to an antidepressant action, then the entire range of antidepressants, including DMI, would be expected to prove effective in OCD, which is not the case [2, 14, 18, 19]. Hence, depression is not a prerequisite for an antiobsessional response to serotonergic antidepressants. In this regard, OCD resembles other non-affective disorders, such as panic disorder, bulimia, enuresis, migraine and chronic pain syndrome, in which tricyclic antidepressants (TCAs) are effective in the absence of depression [20].

CLOMIPRAMINE (CMI)

CMI was the first effective drug treatment reported for OCD [21]. Several placebo-controlled studies have clearly shown its effectiveness as compared to placebo [9–13, 22].

A multicenter trial with CMI that included 21 centers in two studies ($n = 520$) examined the efficacy, safety and tolerability of up to 300 mg/day of CMI [23]. CMI was significantly more effective than placebo on the Yale–Brown Obsessive Compulsive Scale (Y-BOCS) and the National Institute of Mental Health Global Obsessive Compulsive Scale (NIMH–GOCS). After 10 weeks of treatment, 58% of patients treated with CMI rated themselves much or very much improved, vs. only 3% of placebo-treated patients.

SELECTIVE SEROTONIN REUPTAKE INHIBITORS (SSRIs)

As serotonin appears to play an important role in OCD, SSRIs are an obvious treatment option. SSRIs lack important pharmacological activity on other neurotransmitter systems and thus offer effective and well-tolerated treatment that is generally acceptable to patients.

Fluoxetine

In a double-blind, fixed-dose study [7], 217 OCD patients were treated with fluoxetine (20, 40 or 60 mg/day) or with placebo for 8 weeks; 161 patients continued the drug until the 16th week. Fluoxetine, at a dose of 40 and 60 mg/day, but not at 20 mg/day, was significantly superior to placebo, suggesting that medium-to-high doses are required. The rate of discontinuation due to adverse effects was low and not significantly different between groups.

In another multicenter investigation of fixed-dose fluoxetine [24], 355 OCD outpatients participated in two randomized, double-blind, parallel, 13-week trials, receiving either fluoxetine (20, 40 or 60 mg/day) or placebo. Patients treated with fluoxetine (all doses) obtained significantly lower ratings on the Y-BOCS and on other efficacy measures. However, a trend suggesting greater efficacy at 60 mg/day was noted. The authors reported few side effects and most patients (79.2%) completed the study.

Fluvoxamine

Fluvoxamine has been compared to placebo in several studies and has been shown to be superior [15, 16, 25]. It was found to be as potent as CMI in several double-blind trials, including the study of Koran *et al* [26]. Long-term efficacy was reported by Mallya *et al* [27]: 21 patients continued in an open extension study of a controlled trial for 2–12 months; 12 of them (57%) showed improvement. Seven out of nine patients relapsed within a few days to weeks following discontinuation of fluvoxamine.

Sertraline

Sertraline was found to be more effective than placebo and was well tolerated in an earlier study [28]. Only 2% of patients discontinued treatment with the drug due to adverse reactions. The most common side effects were nausea (30%), insomnia (26%), dyspepsia (21%) and ejaculatory failure (19%).

Sertraline was also compared to placebo in a fixed-dose study of 325 non-depressed OCD patients, who were randomized to 12 weeks of double-blind treatment with either placebo or 50, 100 or 200 mg/day of the drug [6]. Sertraline was significantly efficacious at all doses. Sertraline-treated patients fared better on all measures of efficacy compared to those on placebo. Although no significant differences were noted between the three doses, 100 mg appeared to be less efficacious than 50 mg, and 200 mg tended to be slightly more effective than the other two doses.

The long-term efficacy of sertraline in OCD has been examined in a follow-up study of 1 year duration [29]. Patients continued to improve with time, and the treatment was well tolerated. With the exception of headache, the occurrence of side effects decreased significantly throughout the year of treatment.

Paroxetine

Wheadon *et al* [8] and Steiner *et al* [30] reported the results of a 12-week, fixed-dose, multicenter study with 348 OCD patients. The subjects were randomized in a double-blind fashion to receive 20, 40 or 60 mg/day of paroxetine or placebo. Analysis of the results revealed improvement for the two higher paroxetine doses as compared to placebo. Steiner *et al* [30] also reported that male gender, no comorbidity and longer duration of illness were related to greater improvement with paroxetine. Patients with moderate OCD symptoms responded to 40 mg of paroxetine, whereas patients with severe OCD symptoms (Y-BOCS $\geq$ 26) showed a greater response to a dose of 60 mg. The authors concluded that paroxetine is effective in the treatment of OCD and that some baseline characteristics are predictive of response to therapy.

These findings are in line with the results of a European study, in which paroxetine was compared with clomipramine and found to be an effective antiobsessive agent [31].

Citalopram

Early open case studies suggested efficacy for citalopram in OCD. The preliminary results from a recently completed placebo-controlled study in acute treatment have shown this drug to be effective. Efficacy was seen at doses of 20, 40 and 60 mg/day, although the effect appeared most convincing at 60 mg [32].

Choice among SSRIs

Since "head-to-head" comparisons between SSRIs have not yet been carried out, the rationale for choosing one SSRI rather than another has more to do with the side effect profile, the potential for interaction with other medications (via effect on cytochrome P450), pharmacokinetic properties (different half-lives: 4–6 days for fluoxetine, and 15, 21 and 26 hours for fluvoxamine, paroxetine and sertraline, respectively), and last, but not least, the personal acquaintance of the prescribing physician with the compound. Relevant data regarding such factors as safety during pregnancy, sexual side effects and interaction with other medications should also be considered.

DRUG DOSAGE

In OCD, a trend exists for higher efficacy at higher doses. The perception that higher doses are needed in OCD may be partly related to the nature of the response, which for the most part is slow and incremental over some weeks before the maximum is attained. If the dose is raised in this early period, as is customary in a flexible dosage regime, response may be attributed to a higher dose than was necessary.

Fixed-dose studies were carried out with fluoxetine, paroxetine and sertraline. Based on these studies, the recommended daily dose of fluoxetine or paroxetine is 40–60 mg/day. The titration towards this dose might take 1–2 weeks. Before considering a patient a non-responder, he should be given 60–80 mg per day (if tolerated) for 10 weeks.

In a fixed-dose study with sertraline, 50 mg/day appeared to be more effective than 100 mg, whereas 200 mg was somewhat more effective than either. Although the data for this compound does not suggest that higher doses are more effective, the authors believe that, as with other SSRIs, increasing the dosage in resistant cases might help.

No fixed-dose studies have been carried out for fluvoxamine and citalopram. However, by way of extrapolation from other studies, the recommended dosage is 200–300 mg/day for fluvoxamine and 40–60 mg/day for citalopram.

Due to their safe therapeutic index, some psychiatrists use even higher doses of SSRIs in the treatment of resistant OCD. However, data on the efficacy of these very high doses in resistant OCD patients is not yet available.

Although no fixed-dose studies have been carried out, it seems that high doses of CMI are needed in order to obtain response in OCD patients. The titration to these doses should last for 1–3 weeks. If possible, therapeutic drug monitoring should be performed in order to ascertain blood levels (200–500 ng/ml) for the parent drug plus the desmethyl derivative, to avoid side effects that result from very high blood levels. If tolerated, a dose of 200–300 mg/day is considered efficacious in OCD; this dose should be administered for 10 weeks before determining lack of response.

SIDE EFFECTS OF ANTIOBSESSIONAL MEDICATIONS

Using higher doses of medication for OCD complicates treatment, as more side effects can be expected. The need for well-tolerated drugs becomes particularly important. The tolerability of medication is also an important issue for a condition such as OCD, a long-term disorder, for which patients will be required to take medication over very long periods of time. The side effect issue is important, as poorly-tolerated drugs will likely reduce a patient's willingness to continue taking medication and thus adversely effect the chance of improvement.

Due to its action on neurotransmitter systems other than the serotonergic one, CMI has more significant side effects than SSRIs. As the older TCAs, CMI has a significant anticholinergic action, giving rise to dry mouth, blurred vision, constipation, tachycardia, urinary retention or hesitancy, sedation and orthostatic hypotension. These unwanted and unpleasant side effects limit the willingness of many patients to use this medication.

CMI should be given after an adequate work-up that includes an electrocardiogram and ruling out ophthalmological problems (i.e. closed angle glaucoma).

The side effects of SSRIs are characteristically transient and short-lived (1–3 weeks). They include nausea, vomiting, transient nervousness, insomnia and drowsiness. Persistent side effects include sexual problems and headache. However, side effects are generally relatively mild and well tolerated by patients.

Data analyses that compared treatment withdrawal rates of depressed patients taking TCAs with those of patients taking SSRIs showed that the latter were less likely to withdraw prematurely from treatment [33, 34]. This better tolerability profile also holds true for OCD patients, who have a better chance of continuing treatment with an SSRI, as reported for sertraline [35] and paroxetine [31] compared with CMI.

ONSET OF TREATMENT RESPONSE

A relatively long period of time is needed before CMI can be clearly shown to be significantly effective in OCD treatment. Thoren *et al* [11] reported that only at the fifth week did the differences between CMI and other treatments become evident. Volavka *et al* [4] postulated that at least 12 weeks are required for CMI to exceed imipramine's effects. However, quicker responses were found by the CMI Collaborative Study Group [23], which noted statistically significant improvement in Y-BOCS scores in all post-randomization office visits in Study 1, and at weeks 2–10 in Study 2. Altogether, it seems that it may take as long as 10–12 weeks for OCD patients to show initial response, and several months, half a year, or even longer to achieve maximum response.

LONG-TERM APPROACH

Available data suggests that in most cases the beneficial effects of SSRIs and CMI are maintained as long as the treatment continues. Therefore, patients should be encouraged to continue taking medication for extensive periods of time. Although no definitive, evidence-based answer is yet available regarding the duration of treatment, it appears that at least 1 year is generally necessary. However, based on a double-blind discontinuation study [36], it seems that in many cases one should consider an even longer duration (several years) before down-titration is attempted.

While attempting down-titration of medication, one should bear in mind that it may take longer than 1 month (and, in the case of fluoxetine, even more than several months) from the titration of the dose until changes (i.e. exacerbation) in OC symptoms will be observed. It is therefore recommended that doses be down-titrated slowly, in 6–10-week steps, and that symptomatic changes be evaluated 6–10 weeks following the actual decrease in the dose.

SPECIAL CONDITIONS

Tic Disorder and OCD

Comorbidity studies have consistently found elevated rates of tic disorder in OCD patients, varying from 37% [37] to 59% [38]. There are also increased rates of OCD and OC symptoms in patients with Tourette's syndrome, with rates varying from 12% to 90% [39, 40]. Tic disorder and OCD share phenomenological similarities: both are perceived by patients as irresistable, and after performing either compulsions or tics patients experience relief. Additionally, both are often exacerbated by stress. However, there are important differences between tic disorder and OCD. Unlike OCD, tic disorder is more common among males, has an earlier age of onset and tends to diminish during adolescence. Other differences relate to cognitive and autonomic anxiety, which are less frequent in tic disorder than in OCD, while impulsive behaviour, including outbursts of rage, are more typical in tic disorder.

If the diagnosis is OCD and tic disorder, it has been reported in a double-blind study [41] that only patients who received a combination of antiobsessive medication and a dopamine blocker experienced reduction of both

OC and tic symptoms. If only antiobsessive medications were received, there was no reduction of OC or tic symptoms. Small doses of pimozide, haloperidol or risperidone, in addition to the serotonergic drug, are associated with a higher therapeutic response in this subset of patients.

Schizophrenia and OCD

During the course of OCD, some patients lose the egodystonic component of their obsessions. A relatively higher prevalence of OCD in schizophrenic patients (15%) has been documented, as compared with that in the general population (2%) [42]. This finding has raised some intriguing questions regarding the association between OCD and schizophrenia. Yet, despite this high prevalence, few studies have addressed the issue of comorbidity of schizophrenia and OC symptoms. One such study, by Fenton and McGlashan [43], reported that schizophrenic patients with OC symptoms demonstrated poorer long-term outcome than schizophrenic patients without such symptoms.

In the past, antidepressants were reputed to exacerbate psychosis in schizophrenic patients [44]. Three double-blind placebo-controlled studies examined the effects of adding antidepressant medication to the ongoing neuroleptic regimen in schizophrenic patients with depressive symptoms and with active psychosis [45–47]. These studies demonstrated that the addition of antidepressants *did not* exacerbate psychosis, nor was there a significant increase in side effects with the combination treatment.

Based on these findings, we designed an open study aimed at exploring the possible benefits of adding CMI to the ongoing neuroleptic regimen in schizophrenic patients with OC symptoms [48]. The distinction between obsessions, compulsions and delusions was obtained through focused interviewing techniques: patients reported obsessive symptoms as persistent, intrusive thoughts which they attempted, at least part of the time, to suppress or ignore; compulsions, when present, were repetitive goal-oriented behaviours designed to neutralize or prevent the discomfort associated with the obsessions; psychotic symptoms were perceived by patients as originating from outside themselves and as egosyntonic, in contrast with OC symptoms, perceived as originating from within themselves and as egodystonic.

Twelve of the 18 patients in this study showed substantial reduction in previously persistent OC symptoms, 3–6 weeks after the addition of CMI (250–300 mg/day) to their ongoing neuroleptic treatment. Psychotic exacerbation was observed in only two cases during CMI addition. Cessation of CMI was associated with a relapse in OC symptoms. In all patients for whom reinstitution of CMI treatment was possible, improvement in OC symptoms was once again observed.

This finding, along with the findings of another recent study [49], illustrates that clinical benefit can be derived from the addition of CMI to the ongoing neuroleptic regimen in a subset of schizophrenic patients with OC symptoms. These results can only be considered preliminary, pending replication in controlled double-blind trials. However, given the currently poor prognosis of these patients, the adoption of a symptom-oriented multipharmacy approach, as described by van Praag *et al* [50], seems justified.

In summary, if a schizophrenic patient has OC symptoms, the addition of antiobsessive treatment to the ongoing neuroleptic treatment might be useful. This combination has been associated with somewhat better outcome in some of these patients, who are otherwise difficult to treat. The role of mixed dopaminergic and serotonergic blockers such as risperidore in this subset of patients has not been studied systematically, but their pharmacological profile and some open reports suggest that they may be useful.

Post-Streptococal Autoimmunity

The study of autoimmune factors has been prompted by the association of OCD and an autoimmune disease of the basal ganglia, Sydenham's chorea (SC), a complication of rheumatic fever that is accompanied by OC symptoms in over 70% of cases. In a study of children with SC, Swedo *et al* [51] found antibodies directed against human caudate tissue in 10 of 11 cases. These children had a history of OC symptoms which started prior to the onset of movement disorder, reached a peak in line with the motor symptoms and declined before their resolution. This association has raised speculation that childhood-onset OCD may represent the sequela of an antineuronal antibody-mediated response to an infectious agent, such as group A haemolytic streptococcus. A study following this autoimmune line of enquiry found raised serum antibodies for somatostatin and prodynorphin, two of the principal neuromodulatory peptides of the basal ganglia, in patients with OCD [52]. The therapeutic and clinical implications of these OC subtypes might include administration of intravenous immunoglobulin and plasma exchange [53].

TREATMENT-RESISTANT OCD

While about 70% of OCD patients respond to appropriate treatment for the disorder, i.e. medium-to-high doses of antiobsessive medication for at least 10 weeks, a substantial number of patients respond only partially or experience minimal changes in their OC symptoms. Possible pharmacological interventions for these patients are outlined in the following sections. In addition, comprehensive psychological and familial assessments may be important in such cases for initiating effective non-pharmacological interventions.

Switching

If a patient is unable to tolerate adequate doses of SSRIs or has not responded to SSRIs administered in the upper range of the relevant dose, a trial of CMI is recommended (and vice versa).

Caution is necessary if CMI is administered immediately after fluoxetine; in this case, lower initial doses of CMI should be the rule, due to fluoxetine's long half-life and the fact that it inhibits cytochrome P450 enzymes (thus increasing the availability of CMI). Switching from SSRIs with shorter half-lives and less inhibition of cytochrome P450 enzymes (such as fluvoxamine and sertraline) to CMI is less problematic. However, the common procedure of slow-down titration is recommended.

Augmentation

Augmentation is called for when there is partial or no response to the above-mentioned approaches. Combination of SSRIs (or SRIs) with other medications, such as risperidone, pindolol, buspirone, lithium, fenfluramine, trazodone, tryptophan, olanzapine or thyroid hormones, has been reported. To date, only two augmenting agents have been found to be effective in double-blind studies, i.e. risperidone and pindolol. However, many other augmenting agents have been tried.

Risperidone

Risperidone in small doses (1–2 mg twice a day) was found in one double-blind and three open studies to be effective in alleviating OC symptoms in some partial responders or non-responders [54].

Pindolol

Pindolol (2.5 mg three times daily) is the second augmenting agent which has been found in double-blind studies to be effective, and thus might be placed quite high on the list of augmenting agents [55]. However, it appears to give an extra "push" to partial responders, rather than actually turning non-responders into responders.

Lithium

Several open reports suggested an efficacy of lithium in OCD. However, the only double-blind placebo-controlled study that was conducted with this combination did not find significant differences between placebo and lithium augmentation [56].

Buspirone

The value of buspirone augmentation in OCD is unclear, as reports of its efficacy are conflicting. If attempted, buspirone is started with doses of 5 mg t.i.d. and increased as tolerated to 30–60 mg/day, usually given in three divided doses.

CMI

An augmentation of SSRIs with CMI (or vice versa) is a common practice with non-responders, although formal documentation of the efficacy of this approach is lacking. In these cases, it is important to bear in mind the possible pharmacokinetic interaction between SSRIs and CMI, as the co-administration of these drugs may lead to a substantial increase in the level of CMI in the blood.

Fenfluramine

Fenfluramine releases serotonin into the synapse and blocks its reuptake, thus potentially augmenting the effect of SSRIs by increasing the concentration of serotonin in the synaptic cleft. Fenfluramine augmentation (20–60 mg/day for several weeks) is no longer used, due to its potential cardiac side effects.

Trazodone

Several case reports described the efficacy of trazodone for OCD, but a controlled study was terminated prematurely because the investigators could see no response [57]. Doses of 100–200 mg/day are recommended.

Tryptophan

L-tryptophan, the amino acid precursor of serotonin, has been reported to be effective in OCD. However, one should be careful with this augmentation, due to the safety issue (association between tryptophan and eosinophilia–myalgia syndrome). The recommended dose of tryptophan is 2–10 g/day.

Thyroid hormones

L-triodothyronine has been reported to be efficacious in open trials as an adjunctive agent to an SRI. However, a controlled study did not confirm its efficacy in OCD [58]. The recommended dose is 25–50 μg/day.

Olanzapine

The mixed serotonergic-dopaminergic profile of this compound draws attention to its potential role in the treatment of severe OCD. OCD patients with poor insight, partial responders or non-responders, and "schizo-obsessive" patients are of special interest. Open reports appear to be encouraging (as they usually do). However, only well-controlled double-blind studies will supply us with conclusive evidence.

Clozapine

Several open reports have been published concerning a transient exacerbation of OCD symptoms due to clozapine. These reports suggest that, based on the hypersensitivity hypothesis of OCD, chronic treatment might have beneficial effects. However, a study in which clozapine was administered to 20 treatment-resistant OCD patients for 10 weeks reported a lack of efficacy.

Other Options

Intravenous CMI

Several studies have reported the efficacy of intravenous CMI in intractable OCD. This strategy includes daily infusions of CMI for circa 14 days, the maximum dose being 325 mg.

Monoamine Oxidase Inhibitors (MAOIs)

A placebo-controlled trial of fluoxetine and phenelzine provided no evidence to support the use of phenelzine in OCD, except possibly for patients with symmetry-related or other atypical obsessions. An earlier controlled, comparative study of CMI and clorgyline, a reversible MAO-A inhibitor, also failed to show any beneficial effect of the MAOI. Only one small, controlled study, which compared phenelzine and CMI (without placebo), suggested that they are equally effective. Doses of phenelzine up to 90 mg/day should be used for at least 10 weeks.

As some OCD patients may be hypersensitive to the activation of their serotonergic systems, specific attention should be paid to the dangerous combination of SSRIs and MAOIs, and to the longer washout periods for serotonergic medication needed by OCD patients before initiating MAOI treatment. The washout period needed for discontinuation of CMI and SSRIs with a relatively short half-life (such as fluvoxamine and sertraline) should be at least 4 weeks, whereas with fluoxetine it should be even longer (at least 6 weeks).

Clonazepam

Several case reports suggest the efficacy of clonazepam as monotherapy and augmentation in OCD. As this benzodiazepine also has effects on the serotonergic system, its reported efficacy might be related to this specific pharmacological profile. However, negative results were reported in one controlled study.

Inositol

An improvement in OCD was reported in one double-blind study using 6–12 g of inositol in treatment-refractory OCD patients. A replication of this result by another group might help to promote the importance of this novel and essentially safe approach.

Clonidine

Clonidine, an α-2 adrenergic agonist, has been reported to be effective for OCD symptoms in the context of Tourette's syndrome. Despite reports of improvement in typical OCD patients with intravenous clonidine and one case report of success with this drug when given alone orally, the range of side effects associated with this drug and the lack of controlled studies hinder its use for OCD patients.

SUMMARY

Consistent Evidence

Several large multicenter, double-blind, placebo-controlled studies have demonstrated again and again that SRIs, such as CMI and SSRIs, are therapeutically effective in OCD, with or without depression. Moreover, OCD is unique among anxiety and affective disorders with regard to its specific response to SRIs: currently, only serotonergic medications appear to be therapeutically effective in OCD, while non-serotonergic medications (such as DMI), although potent antidepressant and antipanic agents, are entirely ineffective with obsessive-compulsive symptoms and OCD.

Several researchers have compared CMI to SSRIs and have shown that there is little difference between them in terms of efficacy. Based on these results, and considering that SSRIs have fewer side effects and are safer in case of overdose, it is reasonable to regard them as the first choice for treatment. Moreover, if CMI is contraindicated due to a medical condition (such as closed angle glaucoma, prostatic hypertrophy or a cardiac illness), the choice of SSRIs is obvious.

Incomplete Evidence

Several, although not all, fixed-dose studies have found that medium-to-high doses of SSRIs are effective in OCD. In one study, only fluoxetine at doses of 40 and 60 mg/day was different from placebo, while dosage of 20 mg/day was not. The same results were found with paroxetine—again, 20 mg/day of paroxetine did not differ from placebo in OCD, while 40 and 60 mg/day did. However, other studies—one with sertaline, and the other with fluoxetine—did not replicate these findings, although in the fluoxetine study a trend for higher doses to be more effective was observed. It seems, therefore, although there is incomplete evidence, that doses in the medium to high range are indicated. Data on the efficacy of "mega-doses" of SSRIs in resistant OCD (i.e. doses higher than 80 mg/day of fluoxetine or above 400 mg/day of fluvoxamine) are still missing; therefore, such "mega-doses" should be carefully studied before any clinical recommendation is given.

The data regarding maintenance treatment are sketchy; only a couple of studies have examined this issue with a double-blind study design. The emerging data suggest that patients need to stay on their medication for extensive periods of time—at least 1 year—and most probably longer.

Another area in which we need to sharpen our knowledge is the combination of cognitive-behavioural therapy and psychopharmacological intervention. Although clinical wisdom suggests that the combination of these two methods should be clinically more effective than the administration of either alone, emerging data are not as consistent as one might expect. Additional and better designed studies may serve to shed a different light on this widely used clinical approach.

Areas Still Open to Research

The dramatic progress in the understanding of OCD in the last 20 years has definite clinical implications for about 60–70% of patients. However, for those 30–40% of refractory OCD, there are very little "red" data (i.e. data derived from large, placebo-controlled, double-blind studies) to suggest what steps should be taken by clinicians once a patient has not responded to the initial attempted SRI, assuming, of course, that the strategy and dose were suitable and sufficient. One study has shown that, in the case of patients who have OCD and tic disorder, a combination of a dopamine blocker and an antiobsessive medication is recommended. Apart from this study on this specific subtype (OCD + tic disorder), double-blind studies on augmentation strategies have given negative results. One small trial found pindolol augmentation to be helpful in resistant OCD patients, but two other pindolol augmentation studies were negative. Two other options that have been studied in a double-blind fashion, and appear to be promising, are risperidone augmentation and intravenous pulse loading CMI administration in resistant OCD patients.

All other options and suggestions, such as augmentation of SSRIs with CMI, fenfluramine, trazodone, tryptophan, thyroid hormones, olanzapine and clozapine, although possibly effective in one patient or another, are currently considered to be "potentially useful interventions" that need to be studied. The same status holds true for clonazepam, inositol and clonidine. Neurosurgery, the last resort for very refractory OCD patients, has been difficult to study until the introduction of the "gamma knife". This technique, which involves a surgical operation without physically penetrating the scalp, introduces the possibility of performing double-blind studies, allowing clinicians to get a better idea of the usefulness of this procedure, which many experts in the field consider to be effective in severely refractory patients.

It seems, therefore, that the entire field of treating resistant OCD patients will not only benefit from, but badly needs, more research.

It may be that dividing OCD into subtypes, such as early vs. late onset, autoimmune vs. non-autoimmune, hoarding vs. non-hoarding, etc., would be one way to direct future explorations in the field. One example is related to the high prevalence of OCD among schizophrenic patients: exciting areas for future research include whether or not these "schizo-obsessive" patients are a subtype of schizophrenia, or whether they merely reflect the high co-morbidity of the two disorders. A research issue that is still wide open is that of therapy for this specific subset of patients. Will they respond better to the new, atypical antipsychotics with their mixed dopamine and serotonin properties? This issue and many others related to the surprisingly high prevalence of OCD in schizophrenia, such as the relationship between fixed delusions and obsessions, promise to keep OCD the focus of intriguing research in years to come.

REFERENCES

1. Zohar J., Mueller E.A., Insel T.R., Zohar-Kadouch R.C., Murphy D.L. (1987) Serotonergic responsivity in obsessive-compulsive disorder. Comparison of patients and healthy controls. *Arch. Gen. Psychiatry*, **44**: 946–951.
2. Leonard H., Swedo S., Lenane M., Rettew D.C., Cheslow D.L., Hamburger S.D., Rapoport J.L., (1991) A double-blind desipramine substitution during long-term clomipramine treatment in children and adolescents with obsessive-compulsive disorder. *Arch. Gen. Psychiatry*, **50**: 922–927.
3. Ananth J. Pecknold J.C., Van Den Steen N., Engelsman F. (1981) Double-blind comparative study of clomipramine and amitriptyline in obsessive neurosis. *Progr. Neuropsychopharmacol.*, **5**: 257–262.
4. Volavka J., Neziroglu F., Yaryura-Tobias J.A. (1985) Clomipramine and imipramine in obsessive-compulsive disorder. *Psychiatry Res.*, **14**: 85–93.
5. Insel T.R., Mueller E.A., Alterman I., Linnoila M., Murphy D.L. (1985) Obsessive-compulsive disorder and serotonin: is there a connection? *Biol. Psychiatry*, **20**: 1174–1188.
6. Greist J.H., Chouinard G., DuBoff E., Halaris A., Kim S.W., Koran L., Liebowitz M., Lydiard R.B., Rasmussen S., White K. *et al* (1995) Double-blind parallel comparison of three doses of sertraline and placebo in outpatients with obsessive-compulsive disorder. *Arch. Gen. Psychiatry*, **52**: 289–295.
7. Montgomery S.A., McIntyre A., Osterheider M., Sarteschi P., Zitterl W., Zohar J., Birkett M., Wood A. (1993) A double-blind, placebo controlled study of fluoxetine in patients with DSM-III-R obsessive-compulsive disorder. *Eur. Neuropsychopharmacol.*, **3**: 143–152.
8. Wheadon D.E., Bushnell W.D., Steiner M. (1993) A fixed dose comparison of 20, 40 or 60 mg paroxetine to placebo in the treatment of OCD. Presented at the Annual Meeting of the American College of Neuropsychopharmacology, Honolulu, December 13–17.
9. Marks I.M., Stern R.S., Mawson D., Cobb J., McDonald R. (1980) Clomipramine and exposure for obsessive-compulsive rituals. *Br. J. Psychiatry*, **136**: 1–25.
10. Montgomery S.A. (1980) Clomipramine in obsessional neurosis: a placebo controlled trial. *Pharmacol. Med.*, **1**: 189–192.

11. Thoren P., Asberg M., Gronholm B., Jornestedt L., Traskman L. (1980) Clomipramine treatment of obsessive-compulsive disorder. A controlled clinical trial. *Arch. Gen. Psychiatry*, **37**: 1281–1285.
12. Flament M.F., Rapoport J.L., Berg C.J., Sceery W., Kilts C., Mellstrom B., Linnoila M. (1985) Clomipramine treatment of childhood obsessive-compulsive disorder: a double-blind controlled study. *Arch. Gen. Psychiatry*, **42**: 977–983.
13. Mavissakalian M., Turner S.M., Michelson L., Jacob R. (1985) Tricyclic antidepressants in obsessive-compulsive disorder: antiobsessional or antidepressant agents? *Am. J. Psychiatry*, **142**: 572–576.
14. Zohar J., Insel T. (1987) Obsessive compulsive disorder: psychobiological approaches to diagnosis, treatment and pathophysiology. *Biol. Psychiatry*, **22**: 667–687.
15. Goodman W.K., Price L.H., Rasmussen S.A. (1989) Efficacy of fluvoxamine in obsessive-compulsive disorder: a double-blind comparison of fluvoxamine and placebo. *Arch. Gen. Psychiatry*, **46**: 36–40.
16. Perse T.L., Greist J.H., Jefferson R.H., Rosenfeld R., Dar R. (1987) Fluvoxamine treatment of obsessive-compulsive disorder. *Am. J. Psychiatry*, **144**: 1543–1548.
17. Price L.H., Goodman W.K., Charney D.S., Rasmussen S.A., Heninger G.R. (1987) Treatment of severe obsessive-compulsive disorder with fluvoxamine. *Am. J. Psychiatry*, **144**: 1059–1061.
18. Insel T.R., Alterman I., Murphy D.L. (1982) Antiobsessional and anti-depressant effects of clomipramine in the treatment of obsessive-compulsive disorder. *Psychopharmacol. Bull.*, **18**: 115–117.
19. Goodman W.K., Price L.H., Delgado P.L., Palumbo J., Krystal J.H., Nagy L.M., Rasmussen S.A., Heninger G.R., Charney D.S. (1990) Specificity of serotonin reuptake inhibitors in the treatment of obsessive-compulsive disorder. Comparison of fluvoxamine and desipramine. *Arch. Gen. Psychiatry*, **47**: 577–585.
20. Murphy D.L., Siever L.J., Insel T.R. (1985) Therapeutic responses to tricyclic antidepressants and related drugs in non-affective disorder patient population. *Progr. Neuropsychopharmacol. Biol. Psychiatry*, **9**: 3–13.
21. Fernandez C.E., Lopez-Ibor J.J. (1967) Monochlorimipramine in the treatment of psychiatric patients resistant to other therapies. *Actas Luso Esp. Neurol. Psiq. Cienc. Afines*, **26**: 119–147.
22. DeVeaugh Geiss J., Landau P., Katz R. (1989) Treatment of obsessive-compulsive disorder with clomipramine. *Psychiatr. Ann.*, **19**: 97–101.
23. Clomipramine Collaborative Study Group (1991) Clomipramine in the treatment of patients with obsessive-compulsive disorder. *Arch. Gen. Psychiatry*, **48**: 730–738.
24. Tollefson G.D., Rampey A.H., Potvin J.H. (1994) A multicenter investigation of fixed-dose fluoxetine in the treatment of obsessive-compulsive disorder. *Arch. Gen. Psychiatry*, **51**: 559–567.
25. Jenike M.A., Hyman S., Baer L., Holland A., Minichiello W.E., Buttolph L., Summergrad P., Seymour R., Ricciardi J. (1990) A controlled trial of fluvoxamine in obsessive-compulsive disorder: implications for a serotonergic theory. *Am. J. Psychiatry*, **147**: 1209–1215.
26. Koran L.M., McElroy S.L., Davidson J.R.T., Rasmussen S.A., Hollander E., Jenike M.A. (1996) Fluvoxamine versus clomipramine for obsessive-compulsive disorder: a double-blind comparison. *J. Clin. Psychopharmacol.*, **16**: 121–129.
27. Mallya G.K., White, K., Waternaux C., Quay S. (1992) Short and long-term treatment of OCD with fluvoxamine. *Ann. Clin. Psychiatry*, **4**: 77–80.

28. Chouinard G., Goodman W., Greist J., Jenike M., Rasmussen S., White K., Hackett E., Gaffney M., Bick P. (1990) Results of a double-blind placebo controlled trial of a new serotonin uptake inhibitor, sertraline, in the treatment of obsessive-compulsive disorder. *Psychopharmacol. Bull.*, **26**: 279–284.
29. Greist J.H., Jefferson J.W., Kobak K.A., Chouinard G., DuBoff E., Halaris A., Kim S.W., Koran L., Liebowitz M.R., Lydiard B. *et al* (1995) A 1 year double-blind placebo-controlled fixed dose study of sertraline in the treatment of obsessive-compulsive disorder. *Int. Clin. Psychopharmacol.*, **10**: 57–65.
30. Steiner M., Oakes R., Gergel I.P., Wheadon D.E. (1994) Predictors of response to paroxetine therapy in OCD. Presented at the American Psychiatric Association Annual Meeting, Philadelphia, May 21–26.
31. Zohar J., Judge R. (1996) Paroxetine versus clomipramine in the treatment of obsessive-compulsive disorder. *Br. J. Psychiatry*, **169**: 468–474.
32. Montgomery S.A. (1998) Citalopram treatment of obsessive-compulsive disorder: results from a double-blind, placebo-controlled trial. Presented at the Annual Meeting of the American College of Neuropsychopharmacology, Puerto Rico, December 14–18.
33. Montgomery S.A., Henry J., McDonald G., Dinan T., Lader M., Hinmarch I., Clare A., Nutt D. (1994) Selective serotonin reuptake inhibitors: meta-analysis of discontinuation rates. *Int. Clin. Psychopharmacol.*, **9**: 47–53.
34. Kasper S., Note I.D., Montgomery S.A. (1999) Citalopram treatment of obsessive-compulsive disorder: results from a double-blind placebo-controlled study. *Eur. Neuropsychopharmacol.*, **9** (suppl. 5): S217–S218.
35. Bisserbe J.C., Lane R.M., Flament M., and the Franco-Belgian Study Group (1997) A double-blind comparison of sertraline and clomipramine in outpatients with obsessive-compulsive disorder. *Eur. Psychiatry*, **12**: 82–93.
36. Pato M.T., Zohar-Kadouch R., Zohar J., Murphy D.L. (1988) Return of symptoms after discontinuation of clomipramine in patients with obsessive-compulsive disorder. *Am. J. Psychiatry*, **145**: 1521–1525.
37. Pitman R.K., Green R.C., Jenike M.A., Mesulam M.M. (1987) Clinical comparison of Tourette's disorder and obsessive-compulsive disorder. *Am. J. Psychiatry*, **144**: 1166–1171.
38. Leckman J.F., Grice D.E., Barr L.C., deVries A.L.C., Martin C., Cohen D.J., McDougle C.J., Goodman W.K., Rasmussen S.A. (1995) Tic-related vs. non-tic-related obsessive-compulsive disorder. *Anxiety*, **1**: 208–215.
39. Leckman J.F., Goodman W.K., North W.G., Chappell R.B., Price L.H., Pauls D.L., Anderson G.M., Riddle M.A., McSwiggan-Hardin M., McDougle C.J. *et al* (1994) Elevated cerebrospinal fluid levels of oxytocin in obsessive-compulsive disorder: comparison with Tourette's syndrome and healthy controls. *Arch. Gen. Psychiatry*, **51**: 782–792.
40. Como P. (1995) Obsessive-compulsive disorder in Tourette's syndrome. In *Behavioral Neurology of Movement Disorders* (Eds W.J. Weiner, A.E. Lang), pp. 281–291, Raven Press, New York.
41. McDougle C.J., Goodman W.K., Price L.H., Delgado P.L., Krystal J. H., Charney D.S., Heninger G.R. (1990) Neuroleptic addition in fluvoxamine-refractory obsessive-compulsive disorder. *Am. J. Psychiatry*, **147**: 652–654.
42. Berman I., Kalinowski A., Berman S.M., Lengua J., Green A.L. (1995) Obsessive and compulsive symptoms in chronic schizophrenia. *Compr. Psychiatry*, **36**: 6–10.
43. Fenton W.S., McGlashan T.H. (1986) The prognostic significance of obsessive-compulsive symptoms in schizophrenia. *Am. J. Psychiatry*, **43**: 437–441.

44. Siris S.G., van Kammen D.P., Docherty G.P. (1978) Use of antidepressant drugs in schizophrenia. *Arch. Gen. Psychiatry.*, **35**: 1368–1377.
45. Dufresne R.L., Kass D.J., Becker R.E. (1988) Bupropion and thiothixene versus placebo and thiothixene in the treatment of depression in schizophrenia. *Drug Develop. Res.*, **12**: 259–266.
46. Siris S.G., Morgan V., Fagerstrom R., Rifkin A., Cooper T.B. (1987) Adjunctive imipramine in the treatment of post-psychotic depression in schizophrenia: a controlled trial. *Arch. Gen. Psychiatry*, **44**: 533–539.
47. Siris S.G., Bermanzohn P.C., Mason S.E., Shuwall M.A. (1994) Maintenance imipramine for secondary depression in schizophrenia: a controlled trial. *Arch. Gen. Psychiatry*, **51**: 109–115.
48. Zohar J., Kaplan Z., Benjamin J. (1993) Clomipramine treatment of obsessive-compulsive symptomatology in schizophrenic patients. *J. Clin. Psychiatry*, **54**: 385–388.
49. Berman I., Sapers B.H., Chang H.H.G., Losonczy M.F., Schmilder J., Green A.I. (1995) Treatment of obsessive-compulsive symptomatology in schizophrenic patients with clomipramine. *J. Clin. Psychopharmacol.*, **15**: 206–210.
50. van Praag H., Kahn R.S., Asnis G.M., Wetzler S., Brown S.L., Bleich A., Korn M.L. (1987) Denosologization of biological psychiatry. *J. Affect. Disord.*, **13**: 1–8.
51. Swedo S.E., Leonard H., Shapiro M.B., Casey B.J., Mannheim G.B., Lenane M., Rettew D.C. (1993) Sydenham's chorea: physical and psychological symptoms of St. Vitus' dance. *Paediatrics*, **91**: 706–713.
52. Roy B.F., Benkelfat C., Hill J.L., Pierce P.F., Dauphin M.M., Kelly T.M., Sunderland T., Weinberger D.R., Breslin N. (1994) Serum antibody for somatostatin 14 and prodynorphin 209–240 in patients with obsessive-compulsive disorder, schizophrenia, Alzheimer's disease, multiple sclerosis and advanced HIV infection. *Biol. Psychiatry*, **35**: 335–344.
53. Perlmutter S.J., Leitman S.F., Garvey M.A., Hamburger S., Feldman E., Leonard H.L., Swedo S.E. (1999) Therapeutic plasma exchange and intravenous immunoglobulin for obsessive-compulsive disorder and tic disorders in childhood. *Lancet*, **354**: 1153–1158.
54. Ravizza L., Barzega G., Bellino S., Bogetto F., Maina G. (1996) Therapeutic effect and safety of adjunctive risperidone in refractory obsessive-compulsive disorder (OCD). *Psychopharmacol. Bull.*, **32**: 677–682.
55. Dannon P.N., Zohar J., Hirschmann S., Iancu I., Grunhaus L.J., Sasson Y. (2000) Pindolol augmentation in treatment resistant obsessive-compulsive disorder: a double-blind placebo controlled trial. *Eur. Neuropsychopharmacol.*, in press.
56. McDougle C.J., Price L.H., Goodman W.K., Charney D.S., Heninger F.R. (1991) A controlled trial of lithium augmentation in fluvoxamine-refractory obsessive-compulsive disorder: lack of efficacy. *J. Clin. Psychopharmacol.*, **11**: 175–181.
57. Pigott T.A., L'Heureux F., Rubenstein C.S., Bernstein S.E., Hill J.L., Murphy D.L. (1992) A double-blind, placebo controlled study of trazodone in patients with obsessive-compulsive disorder. *J. Clin. Psychopharmacol.*, **12**: 156–162.
58. Pigott T.A., Pato M., L'Heureux F. (1991) A controlled comparison of adjuvant lithium carbonate or thyroid hormone in clomipramine-treated OCD patients. *J. Clin. Psychopharmacol.*, **11**: 245–248.

Commentaries

2.1
Pharmacotherapy of Obsessive-Compulsive Disorder: Accomplishment, Unanswered Questions and New Directions

Teresa A. Pigott[1]

As aptly summarized in Zohar *et al*'s excellent review, a relatively astonishing metamorphosis in the treatment of OCD has transpired over the last 10–15 years. Historically considered extremely rare and often treatment-refractory, a wealth of data now confirms that OCD is a much more common illness than originally appreciated. Fortunately, considerable progress has also occurred in identifying effective and readily available treatments for OCD.

As accurately summarized in the review, separate multi-center, placebo-controlled studies have convincingly established the selective serotonin reuptake inhibiting (SSRI) antidepressants fluoxetine, sertraline, paroxetine and fluvoxamine, as well as the tricyclic antidepressant (TCA) clomipramine, as first-line medication for OCD. In contrast to the treatment of depression and most anxiety disorders, tricyclic (except for clomipramine) and monoamine oxidase inhibiting (MAOI) antidepressants are largely ineffective for OCD. Similarly, non-antidepressant anxiolytics, such as benzodiazepines and the azipirone buspirone, fail to effectively reduce OCD symptoms. Antiobsessional effects, as duly noted in the review, are clearly independent of antidepressant or anxiolytic properties.

Unfortunately, effective treatment for OCD is associated with relatively modest symptom reduction (25–40%); not surprisingly, significant impairment persists in most OCD patients even after they receive effective treatment. Behavioural therapy may convey more lasting benefits than medication but, as noted in the review, it is not widely available.

Remarkably little data is available concerning the comparative efficacy or tolerability of the medications found to be effective for OCD. A meta-analysis conducted from the data collected during the multicenter OCD trials of clomipramine, fluoxetine, sertraline and fluvoxamine, respectively, suggested that clomipramine may have some advantage in efficacy and similar tolerability when compared to the SSRI antidepressants [1]. Results

[1] *Clinical Trials Division, Comprehensive NeuroScience Inc., Chevy Chase, MD 20815, USA*

from the few head-to-head comparisons, however, suggest similar efficacy but improved tolerability for the SSRIs in comparison to clomipramine treatment. Although Zohar *et al* argue that this data offers strong support for the contention that SSRIs represent first-line treatment for OCD, this recommendation may be somewhat premature. Identification of response predictors for medication treatment, as well as estimates of expected "cross-response" between the specific SSRI medications, should be extensively investigated before we conclude that the SSRIs are interchangeable for the treatment of OCD.

Thus far, most investigators have failed to detect any associations between medication response and numerous baseline variables, including age, age of OCD onset, gender or race. Several studies have suggested that concomitant schizotypal personality disorder [2] and perhaps longer illness duration [2, 3] may predict non-response to medication treatment. Information concerning "cross-response" between OCD medications is even more limited. There is some evidence that SSRI response is a strong (60–70%) predictor of subsequent clomipramine response in OCD, whereas the association between clomipramine response and subsequent SSRI response is less robust (40–50%) [4]. Although most patients treated for OCD will receive more than one trial of an SSRI, systematic data concerning "cross-response" between the individual SSRI agents is conspicuously absent.

Zohar *et al*'s review succinctly outlines the evidence correlating relatively high doses with greater antiobsessional efficacy. Indeed, a relatively robust dose, in comparison to a standard antidepressant dose, appears to be optimal for the treatment of OCD. However, there is also evidence that substantial reductions in daily dose may be instituted without a substantial loss in efficacy during the long-term or maintenance treatment of OCD. Relapse is reportedly the rule after medication discontinuation in OCD, as noted by Zohar *et al*. However, this conclusion is primarily based upon studies conducted at academic or tertiary care centers, where the selection bias often favours the treatment of patients with more severe or treatment-refractory illness. Anecdotal evidence suggests that the long-term prognosis of patients with OCD may be much more variable than previously appreciated. Behavioural therapy may represent a particularly promising "protective" strategy for patients contemplating medication discontinuation.

In addition to behavioural therapy, novel pharmacological strategies must be identified for patients with OCD who are partial or non-responders to treatment. Since the majority of patients treated for OCD will fall within these categories, this may well represent the most critical area of OCD research for the next decade. Since serotonin-selective agents appear preferentially effective in the treatment of OCD, most of the early augmentation strategies focused on enhancing serotonin tone. Despite extensive investigation of such agents, results have been largely discouraging. Although Zohar and colleagues correctly note that initial reports supported the benefit of pindolol as an augmentation strategy for OCD, results from a subsequent controlled trial were negative [5].

The only agents that have demonstrated significant improvement in placebo-controlled augmentation trials have been clonazepam and haloperidol. An initial trial suggested that only OCD patients with concomitant tics or Tourette's syndrome would benefit from haloperidol augmentation. However, a subsequent controlled trial revealed that neuroleptic augmentation could benefit OCD in the absence of concomitant tic disorder [6]. Moreover, addition of an atypical neuroleptic (risperidone or olanzapine) to ongoing SSRI therapy may represent an effective strategy for OCD patients previously refractory to treatment [7, 8]. The neuroleptic augmentation studies, coupled with the emerging data well summarized by Zohar *et al* supporting genetic and pathophysiological links between OCD and schizophrenia, suggest that further study of dopaminergic mechanisms for enhancing response in OCD are indicated.

Recent research findings have also demonstrated intriguing evidence of neuropeptide (arginine vasopressin, corticotropin-releasing hormone, oxytocin and somatostatin) abnormalities in OCD. Initial open case reports suggest that certain neuroendocrine strategies may prove beneficial as augmentation strategies for OCD, although others have failed to demonstrate benefit [9]. Autoimmune factors (group A beta-hemolytic streptococcal infection) have also been implicated in the onset of a subtype of pediatric OCD. Preliminary results suggest that therapies aimed at treating the underlying autoimmune or infectious process may be successful [10]. With these issues in mind, future investigations aimed at exploring novel, non-serotonergic mechanisms appear to be a particularly promising path.

REFERENCES

1. Greist J., Jefferson J., Koback K., Katzelnick D., Serlin R. (1995) Efficacy and tolerability of serotonin transport inhibitors in obsessive-compulsive disorder: meta-analysis. *Arch. Gen. Psychiatry*, **52**: 53–60.
2. Ravizza L., Barzega G., Bellino S., Bogetto F., Maina G. (1995) Predictors of drug treatment response in obsessive-compulsive disorder. *J. Clin. Psychiatry*, 56: 368–373.
3. DeVeaugh-Geiss J., Katz R., Landau P., Goodman W., Rasmussen S. (1990) Clinical predictors of treatment response in obsessive-compulsive disorder: exploratory analyses from multicenter trials of clomipramine. *Psychopharmacol. Bull.*, **26**: 54–59.
4. Pigott T., L'Heureux F., Dubbert B. (1994) Obsessive-compulsive disorder: comorbid conditions. *J. Clin. Psychiatry*, **55**: 15–27.

5. Mundo E., Guglielmo E., Bellodi L. (1998) Effect of adjuvant pindolol on the antiobsessional response to fluvoxamine: a double-blind, placebo-controlled study. *Int. Clin. Psychopharmacol.*, **13**: 219–224.
6. McDougle C.J., Goodman W., Leckman J., Lee N., Heninger G., Price L. (1994) Haloperidol addition in fluvoxamine-refractory obsessive-compulsive disorder. A double-blind, placebo-controlled study in patients with and without tics. *Arch. Gen. Psychiatry*, **51**: 302–308.
7. McDougle C.J. (1997) Update on pharmacologic management of OCD: agents and augmentation. *J. Clin. Psychiatry*, **58**: 11–17.
8. Potenza M., Wasylink S., Longhurst J., Epperson C., McDougle C. (1998) Olanzapine augmentation of fluoxetine in the treatment of refractory obsessive-compulsive disorder. *J. Clin. Psychopharmacol.*, **18**: 423–424.
9. den Boer J., Westenberg H. (1992) Oxytocin in obsessive compulsive disorder. Peptides, **13**: 1083–1085.
10. Leonard H. (1997) New developments in the treatment of obsessive-compulsive disorder. *J. Clin. Psychiatry*, **58**: 39–45.

2.2
Beyond Serotonin Reuptake Inhibitors: Do We Have Our Second Wind?

Christopher J. McDougle[1]

Zohar *et al* present a comprehensive and thoughtful review of the state of the art of drug treatment for obsessive-compulsive disorder (OCD). As they point out, there have been tremendous advances in this area during the past 25 years. To a large extent, the establishment of serotonin reuptake inhibitors (SRIs) as the primary drug treatment for OCD has been at the forefront of this progress. In fact, this class of drugs is the only one, to date, that has proven efficacy as a monotherapy for the disorder. The development of SRIs as a treatment for OCD, in conjunction with the application of exposure and response prevention behavioural therapy, has resulted in a significant reduction in morbidity for a large number of OCD sufferers. Despite these therapeutic strides, up to 40–60% of patients experience minimal to no improvement with these treatments. Furthermore, for those patients who do "respond" to SRI or behavioural modification intervention, the degree of improvement is typically incomplete; few patients experience full symptom remission [1].

The consistent finding that SRIs have significant therapeutic advantages over other anxiolytic and antidepressant drug treatments in OCD is unparallelled in anxiety and mood disorders research. For example, numerous drugs with very different mechanisms of pharmacological action, such as

[1] *Riley Hospital for Children, 702 Barnhill Drive, Room 3701, Indianapolis, IN 46202–5200, USA*

tricyclic agents, including those with potent norepinephrine uptake blocking properties, monoamine-oxidase inhibitors and selective norepinephrine and mixed serotonin-norepinephrine reuptake inhibitors, have been shown to be efficacious for the treatment of other anxiety disorders and depression. In addition, benzodiazepines and electroconvulsive therapy have demonstrated efficacy for treating anxiety and mood disorders, respectively. However, this multitude of somatic treatments has generally been ineffective in OCD. It has been shown convincingly that the acute blockade of serotonin transport into nerve terminals by a drug appears to be a necessary initial action for efficacy in OCD. Nevertheless, the implications of this unique drug response for the underlying pathobiology of OCD is muted by the lack of significant clinical improvement in many SRI-treated patients [2].

The fact that a large minority of OCD patients experience only a partial or no response to adequate trials of SRIs suggests that the disorder, as currently defined, is pathophysiologically heterogeneous. Why don't all patients with OCD show improvement with SRI treatment? Currently, the diagnosis of OCD depends upon the clinician's assessment of signs and symptoms, as well as the subjective report of the patient. Repetitive thoughts and behaviours that appear similar at this clinical level may have widely divergent neurobiological underpinnings. Thus, all interfering thoughts and behaviours that are repetitive in nature are unlikely to respond to a single class of drugs. To continue to rely upon clinical phenotype to guide pharmacotherapy will not advance the drug treatment of OCD. For instance, where should the nosologic boundaries be drawn for different types of repetitive thoughts? How are obsessions with dirt and germs different from preoccupations with gambling or body image, the ruminations of major depression, the overvalued ideas of body dysmorphic disorder or the delusions of schizophrenia? And what about repetitive behaviour? How good are we as clinicians at clearly differentiating the complex motor tics of Tourette's syndrome from the compulsions of OCD? Where do the stereotypies of autism, repetitive motor movements secondary to extrapyramidal dysregulation, and the automatisms of temporal lobe epilepsy fit into our diagnostic schema? Is response to SRIs influenced by the degree of insight the patient has into the irrational nature of repetitive thoughts and behaviours?

Using our current assessment and diagnostic approaches, the field has identified some clinical signs that appear to be related to reduced response to SRIs in OCD. For example, we have demonstrated that OCD patients with a chronic tic disorder respond less well to SRI monotherapy compared to those without such comorbidity. A clinically meaningful improvement in obsessive-compulsive symptoms occurred in only 21% of OCD patients with comorbid chronic tics compared to a 52% response rate in OCD patients without chronic tics [3]. Moreover, it has been further demonstrated that OCD patients with a past personal or current diagnosis of chronic tic disorder or a first-degree relative with Tourette's syndrome are preferentially responsive to the addition of low doses of a dopamine antagonist to ongoing SRI therapy compared to OCD patients without this tic-relatedness [4]. Similarly, as Zohar *et al* describe in their review, preliminary studies suggest that the addition of the anti-obsessional drug clomipramine to ongoing antipsychotic treatment in patients with schizophrenia and co-morbid obsessive-compulsive symptoms may result in clinical benefit.

Yet, despite these examples of some association between clinical phenotype and drug responsivity, a number of patients do not respond as predicted, based upon their clinical presentation. In what direction should our research proceed to begin to more objectively identify patients who will be most likely to respond to SRIs or particular combination drug treatment strategies? A recent report described results which provide preliminary evidence for linkage disequilibrium between OCD and the serotonin transporter protein gene (SLC6A4) "long" allele [5]. This finding lends support to a model of disease which links a variation in a gene, SLC6A4, which encodes a medication target, the serotonin transporter protein, with a disorder, OCD, in which drugs that act at the serotonin transporter protein (the potent SRIs) are the preferred therapeutic agents. Such an approach may have practical clinical applications. For instance, Smeraldi *et al* [6] recently found that a polymorphism within the promoter region of the serotonin transporter gene was related to response to fluvoxamine in patients with major depressive disorder. Although these results need to be replicated, they may pave the way for using genetic findings to assist clinicians in the appropriate choice of medication for an individual patient.

The past three decades of research have generated effective treatments for many patients with OCD. Rather than search for yet another SRI, the field needs to develop methods to objectively determine which patients are most likely to respond to this class of drugs; alternative treatment strategies will need to be pursued for those patients identified as being unlikely to improve.

REFERENCES

1. McDougle C.J. (1999) The neurobiology and treatment of obsessive-compulsive disorder. In *Neurobiology of Mental Illness* (Eds D.S. Charney, E.J. Nestler, B.S. Bunney), pp. 518–533, Oxford University Press, New York.
2. Goodman W.K., Price L.H., Delgado P.L., Palumbo J., Krystal J.H., Nagy L.M., Rasmussen S.A., Heninger G.R., Charney D.S. (1990) Specificity of serotonin reuptake inhibitors in the treatment of obsessive-compulsive disorder. *Arch. Gen. Psychiatry*, **47**: 577–585.

3. McDougle C.J., Goodman W.K., Leckman J.F., Barr L.C., Heninger G.R., Price L.H. (1993) The efficacy of fluvoxamine in obsessive-compulsive disorder: effects of comorbid chronic tic disorder. *J. Clin. Psychopharmacol.*, **13**: 354–358.
4. McDougle C.J., Goodman W.K., Leckman J.F., Lee N.C., Heninger G.R., Price L.H. (1994) Haloperidol addition in fluvoxamine-refractory obsessive-compulsive disorder: a double-blind, placebo-controlled study in patients with and without tics. *Arch. Gen. Psychiatry*, **51**: 302–308.
5. McDougle C.J., Epperson C.N., Price L.H., Gelernter J. (1998) Evidence for linkage disequilibrium between serotonin transporter protein gene (SLC6A4) and obsessive compulsive disorder. *Mol. Psychiatry*, **3**: 270–273.
6. Smeraldi E., Zanardi R., Benedetti F., Di Bella D., Perez J., Catalano M. (1998) Polymorphism within the promoter of the serotonin transporter gene and antidepressant efficacy of fluvoxamine. *Mol. Psychiatry*, **3**: 508–511.

2.3
Future Pharmacotherapy for Obsessive-Compulsive Disorder: 5-HT_2 Agonists and Beyond

Pedro L. Delgado[1]

There have been dramatic changes in our view of the etiology and treatment of obsessive-compulsive disorder (OCD) over the past 15–20 years. It now appears highly likely that OCD is a condition caused by one or more of many biological factors that lead to dysfunction in the brain circuits connecting frontal cortex with basal ganglia or in these brain regions themselves [1, 2]. OCD was once thought to represent an example of intrapsychic defense mechanisms gone awry. It was believed that obsessive thoughts and compulsions were an attempt to defend oneself from intolerable inner conflicts dealing with aggression or sexuality. The growing awareness that OCD symptoms are specifically reduced in most patients by antidepressants that potently block reuptake of serotonin (5-HT) has led to a new set of hypotheses.

Zohar *et al*'s review admirably summarizes the historical context and recent data showing that people suffering from OCD respond to specific pharmacological agents. The authors review the empirical data showing that the presence of concurrent depression is not required for successful treatment response to antiobsessional drugs and that many drugs that are proven antidepressants are not antiobsessional. They review the efficacy data for clomipramine, fluoxetine, fluvoxamine, sertraline, paroxetine and citalopram. They review issues of dose and duration of treatment and side

[1] *Department of Psychiatry, University of Arizona College of Medicine, 1501 N. Campbell Ave. Tucson, AZ 85724, USA*

effects, summarize the recent data on treatment of medication-resistant OCD and review the treatment of OCD symptoms concurrent with schizophrenia or tic disorders.

In reading this apt review of the pharmacological treatment of OCD, one cannot help but come to the conclusion that the field may have reached "the end of the road" as it relates to the use of available pharmacological classes of drugs. Great strides have been made, but most patients continue to have less than satisfactory results with available pharmacological treatments. The results of the studies reviewed in regard to augmentation strategies are disappointing, and it seems that the field seems lacking a clear direction for future drug development.

How can the new and provocative data showing an association between OCD and Tourette's syndrome or post-streptococcal autoimmunity be understood in the context of the putative mechanism of action of the current medications? Perhaps the answer to this question is that 5-HT neurotransmission may be normal in OCD, in spite of the fact that the current treatments may in fact mediate their therapeutic effects by enhancement of 5-HT neurotransmission. While seemingly contradictory, this statement can be understood by analogy to the mechanism of action of some other medications. For example, one would not assume that the pathophysiology of a cutaneous rash was due to a deficiency of corticosteroids, simply because the rash was alleviated by administration of corticosteroids.

It is unlikely that the improvement in symptoms of OCD with potent 5-HT reuptake inhibitors is simply due to achieving a sufficient synaptic level of 5-HT. If treatments for OCD are not simply restoring 5-HT levels, what are they doing? What are the pharmacological consequences of potent enhancement of 5-HT on brain areas modulated by 5-HT? Data on the behavioural effects of selective 5-HT_2 agonists are extremely relevant to these questions. Intriguing reports of the acute effects of hallucinogens in patients with OCD [3, 4] suggest that some patients may experience rapid relief of OCD symptoms during and after intoxication with psychedelic drugs such as psilocybin, mescaline or lysergic acid diethylamide (LSD).

A large body of data suggest that agonist activity at 5-HT_2 receptors underlies the majority of the behavioural effects of psychedelic drugs [5]. Psilocybin, LSD and mescaline are extremely potent agonist at 5-HT_{2A} and 5-HT_{2C} receptors, and they potently and rapidly downregulate 5-HT_2 receptor function. Their *in vitro* binding potency to these receptors is highly correlated with their human potency as hallucinogens [6, 7], and it seems likely that these effects are at least the first step in the process of initiating psychedelic activity. While potent 5-HT reuptake inhibitors inconsistently reduce radioligand binding indices of 5-HT_2 receptor numbers, they more consistently lead to a downregulation of 5-HT_2 receptor-mediated behavioural responses, as do most hallucinogens [8]. 5-HT_2 receptor agonist activity also enhances the release of brain derived neurotrophic factor (BDNF) [9] and this compound leads to neuronal remodeling.

These pieces of information suggest novel directions for future research. While it is not practical to consider psychedelic drugs as treatments for OCD, much more work with selective agonists at specific 5-HT receptor subtypes needs to be done to understand whether this effect may be beneficial to patients with OCD. More importantly, we need to begin to focus on the many neurochemical factors that regulate the function of neurons in the frontal cortex and basal ganglia, as well as increasing our understanding of the way in which these brain areas interact. If the pathophysiology of OCD is not directly related to 5-HT, then understanding the regulation and function of the brain areas (and interconnecting circuits) implicated in OCD will lead to new and more effective treatments.

REFERENCES

1. Baxter L.R., Schwartz J.M., Bergman K.S., Szuba M.P., Guze B.H., Mazziotta J.C., Alazraki A., Selin C.E., Ferng H.-K., Munford P., Phelps M.E. (1992) Caudate glucose metabolic rate changes with both drug and behavior therapy for obsessive-compulsive disorder. *Arch. Gen. Psychiatry*, **49**: 681–689.
2. Cummings J.L. (1993) Frontal-subcortical circuits and human behavior. *Arch. Neurol.*, **50**: 873–880.
3. Moreno F.A., Delgado P.L. (1997) Hallucinogen-induced relief of obsessions and compulsions. *Am. J. Psychiatry*, **154**: 1037–1038.
4. Delgado P.L., Moreno F.A. (1998) Hallucinogens, serotonin, and obsessive compulsive disorder. *J. Psychoactive Drugs*, **30**: 359–366.
5. Aghajanian G.K. (1994) Serotonin and the action of LSD in the brain. *Psychiatr. Ann.*, **24**: 137–141.
6. Glennon R.A., Titeler M., McKennay J.D. (1984) Evidence for 5-HT_2 involvement in the mechanism of action of hallucinogenic agents. *Life Sci.*, **35**: 2505–2511.
7. Glennon R.A., Raghupathi R., Bartyzel P., Teitler M., Leonhardt S. (1992) Binding of phenylalkylamine derivatives at 5-HT_{1C} and 5-HT_2 serotonin receptors: evidence for a lack of selectivity. *J. Med. Chem.*, **35**: 734–740.
8. Bonson K.R., Buckholtz J.W., Murphy D.L. (1996) Chronic administration of serotonergic antidepressants attenuates the subjective effects of LSD in humans. *Neuropsychopharmacology*, **14**: 425–436.
9. Duman R.S., Heninger G.R., Nestler E.J. (1997) A molecular and cellular theory of depression. *Arch. Gen. Psychiatry*, **54**: 597–606.

2.4 Comments on the Pharmacological Treatment of Obsessive-Compulsive Disorder

Matig R. Mavissakalian[1]

It is firmly established that antidepressants with serotonin reuptake inhibiting action are effective in the treatment of obsessive-compulsive disorder (OCD) and that their antiobsessional effects are independent of their antidepressant effects. The effectiveness of selective serotonin reuptake inhibiting drugs (SSRIs), and the virtual absence of medical contraindications for their use, satisfy both the biochemical rationale and the safety concerns as first line treatment of choice for OCD. Approximately 50% of patients treated with SSRIs show clinically significant improvement, and one-third of patients become marked responders at the end of 3 months of treatment. Because of the consolidation of therapeutic gains that takes place over time, the minimum duration of acute treatment is usually considered to be 6 months. Maintenance treatment for longer periods of time is recommended, because it is rare to have complete remission in OCD and the risk of relapse appears to be quite high under these conditions. Here, I briefly comment on some issues still requiring clinicians to draw on their own experience and interpretation of the literature to make important decisions for the particular patient under their care.

Choice. SSRIs are more expensive compared to tricyclics. In the absence of medical contraindications or suicidality, there is no good reason not to start treatment with clomipramine (CMI), but if financial concerns are present, imipramine (IMI) may be a viable alternative. In the early 1980s we participated in a multicenter double-blind study comparing IMI and CMI. The results of the entire study were not published, because they did not reveal significant differences in improvement in OCD symptoms between the two drugs and did not contribute to the effort of introducing CMI for commercial use in the United States. Of the two small pieces published from that study, one [1] suggested a slight but unimpressive trend in favour of CMI, the other [2] suggested no differences between the treatments. The point is that clinicians should not feel limited to the selective or very powerful serotonergic agents if circumstances make these agents unavailable or impractical.

Switching. Differences among SSRIs are overwhelmed by the similarities between them. It is a clinical fact that some individuals can tolerate some

[1] *Anxiety Disorders Program, University Hospitals of Cleveland, 11100 Euclid Avenue, Cleveland, OH 44106, USA*

SSRIs better than others and, given the proliferation of SSRIs in recent years, it is a rare patient who cannot have an adequate trial with one of these drugs. However, there is no good justification for switching from one SSRI to another if the patient has not responded to an adequate trial with a previous SSRI. This raises false hopes unnecessarily. Switching to a biochemically different antidepressant, in particular to CMI, makes sense because of the suggestions, admittedly still unsettled, of greater antiobsessional effectiveness with CMI compared to SSRIs [3] and of relatively more preferential response to CMI than SSRIs in patients treated sequentially with both types of drugs [4]. Finally, whereas the side effects of both SSRIs and tricyclics decrease and become more tolerable over time, sexual side effects generally persist and interfere with long-term maintenance treatment. In these cases shifting to nefazodone has been a very helpful strategy in our clinical experience.

Dose. The oft-repeated suggestion that higher doses of SSRIs are specifically required in OCD needs to be seriously questioned, because the evidence from dose-ranging studies is not convincing in this regard. Fluoxetine 40–60 mg/day is not necessarily better, and maybe worse, than 20 mg/day [5]. Moreover, similar dose–response patterns have been observed in panic disorder and OCD with paroxetine and sertraline, respectively. For both disorders, paroxetine performed better at higher doses (40 mg), while sertraline performed the same at the lowest (50 mg) and at higher doses. It may be as important to emphasize the duration of the acute trial on an adequate dose. In a recent study, we demonstrated that nearly 50% of panic disorder with agoraphobia patients who were non-responders by week 8 to imipramine treatment became marked responders at week 16 without dose increase [6]. This is most likely to be the case for the treatment of OCD with serotonergic drugs.

Augmentation and combination treatment. Unsatisfactory response and at times non-response to antidepressants is a clinical reality in OCD. Not infrequently, this may be the joint outcome of neglecting diagnostic hierarchical principles of classification and of undermining the primary phenomenological importance of obsessions in this disorder. It serves no good practical or heuristic purpose to blur the boundaries between psychotic and neurotic conditions or the difference between compulsive behaviours that are functionally linked to obsessions and repetitive or even ritualistic behaviours in general, even when patients say they want to stop them but they cannot. Specific pharmacological augmentation strategies of antidepressants in OCD have been disappointing to date. Antipsychotics, mood stabilizers, etc., are best used as primary treatment targeting their own specific symptom clusters. However, when the diagnosis of OCD conforms to what was once one of the best delineated syndromes in clinical psychiatry, behavioural treatments based on the principles of exposure and response prevention still offer the most reliable augmenting strategy to antidepressants [7].

REFERENCES

1. Volavka J., Neziroglu F., Yaryura-Tobias J.A. (1985) Clomipramine and imipramine in obsessive-compulsive disorder. *Psychiatry Res.*, **14**: 85–93.
2. Mavissakalian M.R., Turner S.M., Michelson L., Jacob R. (1986) The relationship of antiobsessional and antidepressant effects of tricyclic and antidepressants. *Psychopharmacol. Bull.*, **22**; 161–166.
3. Greist J.H., Jefferson J.W., Kobak K.A., Katzelnick D.J., Serlin R.C. (1995) Efficacy and tolerability of serotonin transport inhibitors in obsessive-compulsive disorder: a metanalysis. *Arch. Gen. Psychiatry*, **52**: 53–60.
4. Tamimi R.R., Mavissakalian M.R. (1991) Are effective antiobsessional drugs interchangeable? *Arch. Gen. Psychiatry*, **48**: 857–858.
5. Dominguez R.A. (1992) Serotonergic antidepressants and their efficacy in obsessive compulsive disorder. *J. Clin. Psychiatry*, **53** (suppl. 10): 56–59.
6. Mavissakalian M.R. (1998) Gauging the effectiveness of extended imipramine treatment for panic disorder with agoraphobia. *Biol. Psychiatry*, **43**: 848–854.
7. Mavissakalian M.R., Jones B. (1989) Antidepressant drugs plus exposure treatment of agoraphobia/panic and obsessive-compulsive disorders. *Int. Rev. Psychiatry*, **1**: 275–282.

2.5
The Expanding Obsessive-Compulsive Disorder Evidence Base

Lorrin M. Koran[1]

Prof. Zohar and his colleagues review the strongest evidence concerning the effectiveness of clomipramine (CMI) and the selective serotonin reuptake inhibitors (SSRIs) for treating obsessive-compulsive disorder (OCD). They also cite data regarding the slow onset of treatment response and the need for long-term treatment, and briefly describe the side effects of primary medications. They discuss the published data on treating OCD in patients with schizophrenia and add novel data of their own. Finally, they suggest pharmacological approaches to helping patients whose OCD is resistant to standard, single medications. The expanding OCD evidence base allows certain additional points and minor corrections to be made.

The study of Montgomery *et al* [1] was too short (8 weeks) to support a conclusion that fluoxetine 20 mg/day is ineffective; the longer study by

[1] *Department of Psychiatry, Stanford University Medical Center, Stanford, CA 94305, USA*

Tollefson *et al* [2] (12 weeks) found this dose effective. Sertraline 100 mg/day appeared to be less effective than 50 and 200 mg/day [3] because of the higher drop-out rate in the 100 mg/day group; clinically, 100 mg/day is effective for some patients.

Sertraline has shown continued efficacy for as long as 2 years of continuous use, with continued, albeit small, improvement in the second year [4]. The decrease in side effect rates with long-term use probably reflects not only decreased incidence, but also some patients dropping out because of side effects.

Prof. Zohar and colleagues' statement that "it may take as long as 10–12 weeks for OCD patients to arrive at an initial response" can be clarified: the onset of improvement from SSRI treatment is frequently within the first 4–6 weeks; a substantial response, however (i.e. a $\geq$ 25% drop in Yale–Brown Scale score), usually takes 8–12 weeks [5].

Patients who discontinue pharmacotherapy after achieving a response are indeed at high risk of relapse. Ravizza *et al* [6], for example, found that three-quarters or more of patients who had responded for 6 months to CMI, fluoxetine or fluvoxamine relapsed within 2 years of discontinuing medication, as compared to one-quarter to one-third of those randomly assigned to continue full- or half-dose treatment.

Although the safety of SSRIs has not been established in pregnancy, a study of 109 infants whose mothers took fluoxetine during pregnancy [7] and a study of 128 pregnancies in which fluoxetine exposure was limited to the first trimester [8] each found no excess rate of major anomalies.

The authors mention that patients may discontinue SSRIs because of sexual side effects (reduced desire, impaired arousal or erection and delayed or absent orgasm). Many medications have been described as helpful in counteracting these side effects in case series and case reports [5], including amantadine, bupropion, buspirone, cyproheptadine, mirtazapine, nefazodone, sildenafil, stimulants and yohimbine.

In treatment-resistant cases, we have had success with pulse-loaded intravenous CMI (150 mg on day 1, 200 mg on day 2) followed after a 5-day drug holiday by oral CMI treatment [9]. We are following up our double-blind pilot study with a large-scale, double-blind trial. Pulse-loaded CMI appears to be much more rapidly effective than the gradual dosing regimen utilized by others [10]. We have also seen good results in nine of nine treatment-resistant patients randomized to CMI plus citalopram vs. only one of seven randomized to oral citalopram alone [11].

When augmenting CMI with fluvoxamine or vice versa, the clinician should monitor plasma CMI levels, since fluvoxamine can raise these levels four-fold [12]. I usually aim at a CMI level of 225 ng/ml or more, while keeping the total plasma concentration of CMI and desmethyl-CMI (DCMI) below 450 ng/ml to minimize the seizure risk. CMI reaches steady-state in 2 weeks and DCMI in 3 weeks.

Future research into pharmacotherapies for OCD will undoubtedly explore neurotransmitters other than serotonin. Promising areas include opioid, substance P, glutamatergic systems and perhaps, in the case of OCD hoarders, cholinergic systems. We have noted significant improvement in several hoarders when donepezil was added to an SSRI.

REFERENCES

1. Montgomery S.A., McIntyre A., Osterheider M., Sarteschi P., Zitterl W., Zohar J., Birkett M., Wood A. (1993) A double-blind, placebo controlled study of fluoxetine in patients with DSM-III-R obsessive-compulsive disorder. The Lilly European OCD study Group. *Eur. Neuropsychopharmacol.*, **3**: 143–152.
2. Tollefson G.D., Rampey A.H., Potvin J.H. (1994) A multicenter investigation of fixed-dose fluoxetine in the treatment of obsessive-compulsive disorder. *Arch. Gen. Psychiatry*, **51**: 559–567.
3. Greist J.H., Chouinard G., DuBoff E., Halaris A., Kim S.W., Koran L., Liebowitz M., Lydiard R.B., Rasmussen S., White K. *et al* (1995) Double-blind, parallel comparison of three doses of sertraline and placebo in outpatients with obsessive-compulsive disorder. *Arch. Gen. Psychiatry*, **52**: 289–295.
4. Koran L.M., Robinson D., Hackett E., Rubin A., Wolkow R. Efficacy of sertraline in long-term treatment (submitted for publication).
5. Koran L.M. (1999) *Obsessive-Compulsive and Related Disorders in Adults: A Comprehensive Clinical Guide*, Cambridge University Press, Cambridge.
6. Ravizza L., Barzega G., Bellino S., Bogetto F., Maina G. (1996) Drug treatment of obsessive-compulsive disorder (OCD): long-term trial with clomipramine and selective serotonin reuptake inhibitors (SSRIs). *Psychopharmacol. Bull.*, **32**: 167–173.
7. Rosa F. (1994) Medicaid antidepressant pregnancy exposure outcomes. *Reprod. Toxicol.*, **8**: 444.
8. Pastuszak A., Schick-Boschetto B., Zuber C., Feldkamp M., Pinelli M., Sihn S., Donnenfeld A., McCormack M., Leen-Mitchell M., Woodland C. *et al* (1993) Pregnancy outcome following first-trimester exposure to fluoxetine (Prozac). *JAMA*, **269**: 2246–2248.
9. Koran L.M., Sallee F.R., Pallanti S. (1997) Rapid benefit of intravenous pulse loading of clomipramine in obsessive-compulsive disorder. *Am. J. Psychiatry*, **154**: 396–401.
10. Koran L.M., Pallanti S., Paiva R.S., Quercioli L. (1998) Pulse loading versus gradual dosing of intravenous clomipramine in obsessive-compulsive disorder. *Eur. Neuropsychopharmacol.*, **8**: 121–126.
11. Pallanti S., Quercioli L., Paiva R.S., Koran L.M. (1998) Citalopram plus clomipramine for treatment resistant obsessive-compulsive disorder. *Eur. Psychiatry*, **8**: 121–126.
12. Szegedi A., Wetzel H., Leal M., Hartter S., Hiemke C. (1996) Combination treatment with clomipramine and fluvoxamine: drug monitoring, safety, and tolerability data. *J. Clin. Psychiatry*, **57**: 257–264.

2.6
The Heterogeneity of Obsessive-Compulsive Disorder and Its Implications for Treatment

Laura Bellodi[1]

Only 60–70% of patients with obsessive-compulsive disorder (OCD) significantly improve with current pharmacological approaches, mainly based on the manipulation of serotonergic function in the central nervous system.

The widely accepted threshold for a significant clinical improvement is a 35–40% reduction from baseline of the total score on the Yale–Brown Obsessive Compulsive Scale (Y-BOCS), induced by a 10–12 week treatment. Some patients may further improve after longer periods of treatment, but generally they do not have a complete remission of symptoms.

Different pharmacological strategies, described by Zohar *et al* in terms of switching and/or augmenting strategies for treatment-resistant OCD, have been applied to ameliorate the clinical response and to increase the rate of "good responders".

Among the augmenting strategies, the efficacy of pindolol in shortening the long latency to antiobsessional response would have had a relevant theoretical and practical value if unequivocally verified. Pindolol, a known beta-blocker, also blocks 5-HT_{1A} receptors, thereby increasing the available amount of serotonin in the synaptic cleft [1].

The ability of pindolol to enhance the antidepressant response to selective serotonin reuptake inhibitors (SSRIs) is generally ascribed to a blockade of the feedback inhibition of serotonergic neuronal activity mediated by somatodendritic 5-HT_{1A} autoreceptors. Pindolol has been successfully employed in shortening the latency of antidepressant response to different SSRIs and increasing the response rate in affective patients [2]. Nevertheless, in OCD patients results have been inconsistent. At least one double-blind controlled trial [3], evaluating the effect of pindolol in OCD patients, indicated that pindolol did not shorten the latency of the antiobsessional response to fluvoxamine. Despite the fact that SSRIs produce both antiobsessional and antidepressant effects, the mechanisms involved may be different.

However, the episodic course of OCD in some patients seems to suggest that depression and OCD have a common etiopathogenetic background, as sometimes evidenced by the presence of familial loading for affective disorders in patients with OCD.

Mood disorders, with depressive and/or manic episodes, co-occur frequently in OCD patients and represent a therapeutic challenge. OCD patients treated with SSRIs can develop a clinical syndrome characterized

[1] *Clinical and Research Unit for Anxiety Disorders, Department of Psychiatry, S. Raffaele Hospital, University of Milan, Via Prinetti 29, 20127 Milan, Italy*

by insomnia, expansive or dysphoric mood, claiming ideation, aggression, reckless acts, impulse discontrol, inflated self-esteem and loss of insight [4]. The incidence of drug-induced manic or hypomanic episodes is about 30%. During the manic or hypomanic phase, the obsessive-compulsive symptoms tend to improve. If the manic or hypomanic episode is a drug-induced phenomenon, withdrawal of the drug is sufficient for resolution of the episode in a few days. However, in some cases, withdrawal alone is not an adequate intervention to control this phenomenon and patients require a specific antimanic treatment, such as lithium or carbamazepine. This treatment should be maintained after the remission of the manic episode. In fact, obsessive-compulsive symptoms reappear, requiring the reintroduction of an antiobsessional drug.

When a depressive syndrome appears in OCD patients already on treatment with an SSRI, the therapeutical strategy becomes more complicated. In fact, the depressive syndrome may be just considered a secondary expression of the impairment caused by the severity of OC symptoms, so it probably will disappear after their improvement, without any other pharmacological addition. Moreover, in these cases, an integrated approach with a psychotherapeutic programme may be suggested. Otherwise, the presence of a depressive syndrome with "core" endogenous features suggests a true comorbidity with a mood disorder, so that a better approach would be to add an antidepressant drug with a different pharmacological profile, i.e. a noradrenergic drug and/or lithium.

The lack of response to antiobsessional drug treatment in some patients urged researchers to single out factors predicting drug efficacy, or in other words to select which characteristics of patients predict their good response to drug treatment.

Previous studies have identified several negative predictors of response to antiobsessional agents: earlier onset [5, 6], comorbid tic disorder [7], comorbid social phobia [8], comorbid schizotypal personality disorder [9, 10], comorbid obsessive-compulsive personality disorder [11], presence of hoarding obsessions [12, 13], and higher baseline severity of obsessive-compulsive symptoms [14]. On the other hand, one study [15] suggested a gender effect for antiobsessional response.

In a recent study [16], 159 OCD patients, treated with fluvoxamine, clomipramine, citalopram or paroxetine, were divided into responders and non-responders, depending on the extent of the reduction in obsessive-compulsive symptoms as scored on the Y-BOCS at the end of the 12-week standardized treatment. Ninety patients responded to treatment (56.6%). No significant differences in the percentages of responders when divided by treatment group were found. Responders had a higher frequency of a positive family history (FH) for OCD. Non-responders showed an earlier age at onset and a higher frequency of the poor insight subtype.

Somatic obsessions were more frequent in the group of non-responders, suggesting that OCD patients with symptoms akin to dysmorphophobia and/or hypochondriasis are more likely to be resistant to classical serotonergic drugs. In a stepwise logistic regression analysis, "poor insight" was the most significant predictor of poor response. In subsequent steps, positive FH-OCD proved to be a predictor of good response, whereas earlier age at onset predicted a poor response to antiobsessional drugs. The presence of somatic obsessions was not included in the model, probably because it was a redundant variable, with a worse insight score in patients with those obsessions.

The observation of a positive predictive value of positive FH-OCD in antiobsessional drug response is particularly interesting. The relationship between familial OCD and response to drug treatment focuses on the heterogeneity of the disorder, at least from a genetic point of view.

In conclusion, prospective long-term follow-up studies have to be done and they will be useful in identifying specific subgroups of OC patients that respond to drugs differently, and in defining specific treatment strategies that improve the long-term outcome of OCD.

REFERENCES

1. Hjorth S., Auerbach S.B. (1994) Further evidence for the importance of 5-HT_{1A} autoreceptors in the action of the selective serotonin reuptake receptors. *Eur. J. Pharmacol.*, **260**: 251–255.
2. Artigas F., Perez V., Alvarez E. (1994) Pindolol induces a rapid improvement of depressed patients treated with serotonin reuptake inhibitors. *Arch. Gen. Psychiatry*, **248**: 248–251.
3. Mundo E., Guglielmo E., Bellodi L. (1998) Effect of adjuvant pindolol on the antiobsessional response to fluvoxamine: a double-blind placebo-controlled study. *Int. Clin. Psychopharmacol.*, **13**: 219–224.
4. Diaferia G., Mundo E., Bianchi Y., Ronchi P. (1994) Behavioral side effects in obsessive-compulsive patients treated with fluvoxamine: a clinical description. *J. Clin. Psychopharmacol.*, **14**: 78–79.
5. Ackerman D.L., Greenland S., Bystritsky A., Morgenstern H., Katz R.J. (1994) Predictors of treatment response in obsessive-compulsive disorder: multivariate analyses from a multicenter trial of clomipramine. *J. Clin. Psychopharmacol.*, **14**: 247–254.
6. Ravizza L., Barzega G., Bellino S., Bogetto F., Maina G. (1995) Predictors of drug treatment response in obsessive-compulsive disorder. *J. Clin. Psychiatry*, **56**: 368–373.
7. McDougle C.J., Goodman W.K., Leckman J.F., Lee N.C., Heninger G.R., Price L.H. (1994) Haloperidol addition in fluvoxamine-refractory obsessive-compulsive disorder. *Arch. Gen. Psychiatry*, **51**: 302–308.
8. Carrasco J.L., Hollander E., Schnefer F.R., Liebowitz M.R. (1992) Treatment outcome of obsessive-compulsive disorder with comorbid social phobia. *J. Clin. Psychiatry*, **53**: 387–391.

9. Baer L., Jenike M.A., Black D.W., Treece C., Rosenfeld R., Greist J. (1992) Effect of axis II diagnoses on treatment outcome with clomipramine in 55 patients with obsessive-compulsive disorder. *Arch. Gen. Psychiatry*, **49**: 862–866.
10. Mundo E., Erzegovesi S., Bellodi L. (1995) Follow-up of obsessive-compulsive patients treated with proserotonergic agents. *J. Clin. Psychopharmacol.*, **15**: 288–289.
11. Cavedini P., Erzegovesi S., Ronchi P., Bellodi L. (1997) Predictive value of obsessive-compulsive personality disorder in antiobsessional treatment. *Eur. Neuropsychopharmacol.*, **7**: 45–49.
12. Black D.W., Monahan P., Gable J., Blum N., Clancy G., Baker P. (1998) Hoarding and treatment response in 38 nondepressed subjects with obsessive-compulsive disorder. *J. Clin. Psychiatry*, **59**: 420–425.
13. Mataix-Cols D., Rauch S.L., Manzo P.A., Jenike M.A., Baer L. (1999) Use of factor-analyzed symptom dimensions to predict outcome with serotonin reuptake inhibitors and placebo in the treatment of obsessive-compulsive disorder. *Am. J. Psychiatry*, **156**: 1409–1416.
14. Alarcon R.D., Libb J.W., Spitler D. (1993) A predictive study of obsessive-compulsive disorder response to clomipramine. *J. Clin. Psychopharmacol.*, **13**: 210–213.
15. Mundo E., Bareggi S., Pirola R., Bellodi L. (1999) Effect of intravenous clomipramine and antiobsessional response to proserotonergic drugs: is gender a predictive variable? *Biol. Psychiatry*, **45**: 290–294.
16. Erzegovesi S., Cavallini M.C., Cavedini P., Diaferia G., Locatelli M., Bellodi L. Clinical predictors of drug response in obsessive-compulsive disorder (submitted for publication).

2.7
Pharmacotherapy of Obsessive-Compulsive Disorder: Questions for the Next Decade

Mihaly Arato[1]

After a glorious decade for obsessive-compulsive disorder (OCD), we have to soberly realize that the "glass is half empty". Based on various assessments, most of them only short-term studies, approximately 50% of patients show a 50% symptom reduction—more precisely at least a 25–35% drop in scale scores [1]. The use of the potent serotonergic reuptake inhibitors (PSRIs) has resulted in a real breakthrough in the treatment of the hidden epidemic. Furthermore, the elegant and convincing cross-over studies with clomipramine vs. desipramine [2, 3] pointed to the pivotal role of serotonin. The postulated serotonergic abnormality, however, seems to be elusive, in spite of significant efforts to pinpoint the faulty receptors or pathways. The

[1] *Department of Psychiatry, University of Calgary, 1403 29th St. NW, Calgary, Alberta, Canada T2N 2T9*

PSRIs seem to be like Jolly Jokers, are "specifically and selectively" effective in many conditions, but are the aspirin-responsive conditions related to aspirin deficiency?

By now there is a fairly good consensus regarding the separation of the antidepressant effect and the anti-OCD effect of the PSRIs. If we assume a similar serotonergic pathophysiology in the background of depressions and OCD, why is the time course of the treatment response so different in these two illnesses? In depression, with a 10–20-day latency, a yes or no response is rather typical; in OCD, a very slow, gradual, but steady, long-term symptom reduction is characteristic. They are separate disorders, but their comorbidity is so common that the overlap is obvious, creating just further controversy. Using DSM criteria, pure OCD is almost an exception compared with the majority of the cases with numerous comorbid conditions [4].

Another intriguing issue is the use of higher dosage of the PSRIs in OCD compared with other "serotonin-related" mood and anxiety disorders. Although there is very little scientific evidence behind it (see for example [5]), it is the general recommendation (and clinical practice?) that PSRIs should be given in a higher dose than in depression. Is it just the consequence of the impatience of the patients and the doctors, that they want to speed up the slow recovery, or to enhance the very common partial response? The simplistic rationale behind this strategy is that with increased dosage the probability of success is also increased. The question is, do we really have to use the higher dose for an optimal response, or is it rather that the extension of the treatment duration is the key element, when we use this long-term up-titration strategy? Do we have data about the net outcome, considering the poorer compliance due to the higher doses?

During long-term treatment, when we inevitably have to face a large portion of treatment-refractory or partial responder patients, we have to speculate about the heterogeneity of OCD. When the use of some combination, augmentation, adjunct or non-conventional treatment becomes necessary, we have to consider the various possible, other than serotonergic, pathophysiologic components. How far can we stretch the obsessive-compulsive-impulsive spectrum? Patients with OCD and multiple tics benefit from adjunct neuroleptic treatment, but usually the neuroleptic combination is not helpful in OCD, although the continuous schizo-obsessive spectrum theory implicates dopamine in the pathomechanism of these disorders. The augmentation strategies successfully used in depression do not necessarily enhance the anti-OCD effect of the PSRIs. What would be the rationale behind the use of mood stabilizers? Unfortunately, even in pure OCD the treatment response is unpredictable. The usual clinical characteristics (such as acute onset of illness, chronic course, symptom profile, etc.) are hardly helpful. We have no scientific basis for the selection of the right medication in each patient. Usually we just want to avoid some specific side effects in a given case when we choose anti-OCD medication. The situation is not very different from depression or other anxiety disorders, but in OCD it is more justified to assume the contribution of different pathogenic factors (viral and bacterial infection, autoimmune mechanisms, neuropeptides, hormones). Consideration of these possible factors, in the light of some further research in this area, may help in treatment selection and response prediction in the future.

Because of the paucity of face-to-face, comparative PSRI studies, it is hard to pick the most promising first-choice medication. The efficacy/side effect ratio seemed to be a simple, useful estimate in the evaluation of the long-term pharmacotherapy in our OCD clinic [6]. We have analyzed retrospectively the treatment of the 134 patients with OCD (out of 212) who were on the same medication at least for 1 year. Fluvoxamine therapy (100–400 mg/day) resulted in the best "compliance": 80% of the patients started and stayed on this medication for at least 1 year. For clomipramine (100–300 mg/day), the chronic, persisting side effects resulted in only 61% compliance, while for fluoxetine (20–80 mg/day), 47% were compliant for 1 year. Our clinical experience with intravenous clomipramine (24 subjects, for 10 days, up to 250 mg/day) supports the original observation of Warneke [7] that this treatment can be effective and tolerated in 40% of those patients who did not respond to the oral PSRI treatment. We have found it specially helpful in anxious, agitated inpatients, in whom the onset of action seemed to occur earlier than with oral medication.

In summary, further research on these questions could fill the other half of the glass.

REFERENCES

1. Ballenger J.C. (1999) Current treatment of the anxiety disorders in adults. *Biol. Psychiatry*, **46**: 1579–1594.
2. Zohar J., Insel T. (1987) Obsessive compulsive disorder: psychobiological approaches to diagnosis, treatment and pathophysiology. *Biol. Psychiatry*, **22**: 667–687.
3. Leonard H., Swedo S., Koby E., Rapoport J.L., Lenane M., Cheslow D., Hamburger S. (1989) Treatment of obsessive-compulsive disorder with clomipramine and desmethylimipramine in children and adolescents: a double-blind crossover comparison. *Arch. Gen. Psychiatry*, **46**: 1088–1092.
4. Nemeth A., Szadoczky E., Arato M. (1998) Epidemiology and comorbidity of OCD in Hungary. Presented at the Third International OCD Conference, Madeira, September 11–13.
5. Greist J., Chouinard G., DuBoff E., Halaris A., Kim S.W., Koran L., Liebowitz M., Lydiard B., Rasmussen S., White K. *et al.* (1995) Double-blind parallel

comparison of three dosages of sertraline and placebo in outpatients with obsessive-compulsive disorder. *Arch. Gen. Psychiatry*, **52**: 289–295.
6. Arato M., Nemeth A. (1996) Retrospective study on the long-term pharmacotherapy in OCD. Presented at the Second International OCD Conference, Guadeloupe, Feburary 14–16.
7. Warneke L. (1989) Intravenous chlorimipramine therapy in obsessive-compulsive disorder. *Can. J. Psychiatry*, **34**: 853–859.

2.8
Recent Progress and Open Issues in the Pharmacological Approach to Obsessive-Compulsive Disorder

José A. Yaryura-Tobias[1]

Zohar *et al*'s review is a well-qualified contribution to the study of the pharmacological treatment for obsessive-compulsive disorder (OCD). Historiography of OCD indicates a paucity of specific pharmacological treatments before 1975, as correctly shown in the review. Revising past literature on the treatment of OCD one encounters three drugs or groups of drugs of choice: diazepam, tricyclic antidepressants and neuroleptics. These substances have been given with the hope that OCD is a form of anxiety disorder (diazepam), a type of depression (tricyclics), or a pseudoneurotic schizophrenia (neuroleptics). These medications were prescribed alone or in combination, in small or in larger doses, and for various lengths of time. However, OCD is a distinct disorder *per se*, as has been well established by the old school of psychiatry in England [1], France [2] and Germany [3]. Hence, this concept of uniqueness made it necessary to find a drug with specific properties focused on OCD symptomatology. Clomipramine (CMI), a potent serotonin (5-HT) reuptake blocker, seemed to be the answer proposed in the 1970s. It seems to operate as an anti-OCD agent, independently from its antidepressant activity. Moreover, it has been clearly determined that anxiolytics have no action on obsessions or compulsions.

In the 1980s, the introduction of selective serotonin reuptake inhibitors (SSRIs) corroborated previous findings that 5-HT is the major factor in OCD physiopathology. Nowadays, 20 years later, this idea is arguable. Norepinephrine, amino acids, folic acid, co-enzymes and neuropeptides, to name but a few, may conceivably participate in the pathology of OCD. One must remember that about 50% of patients with OCD respond well to pharmacotherapy; yet one needs to account for the other 50% of non-responders. One fascinating observation is that similar positive results may be seen in

[1] *Institute for Bio-Behavioral Therapy, 935 Northern Blvd., Great Neck, NY 11021, USA*

those patients undergoing behavioural therapy. Finally, the combination of drugs with behavioural therapy, and recently with the addition of cognitive therapy, have yielded even better results [4].

As specified in Zohar *et al*'s review, wider pharmacological choices are available for the clinician. Undesirable side effects reported may require a decrease in dosage or switching to another anti-OCD agent. Patients having cardiovascular conditions may benefit from SSRIs; patients who plan to become pregnant may select fluoxetine. It is in the best interest of the patient to gradually step up the dose, hopefully to by-pass untoward effects in intensity and frequency.

Additional options are augmentation therapy, consisting of drugs that potentiate the action of the main drug by increasing the availability of 5-HT. One such a drug is L-tryptophan (LTRY), a precursor of 5-HT, and another is 5-hydroxytryptophan, a metabolite of LTRY. The administration of substances to potentiate the action of the main medication has a partial therapeutic effect.

A subject of reflection is the placebo effect. Placebo has a definite therapeutic activity, notably during the first 4–6 weeks of therapy, as has been our observation in a meta-analysis of placebo in OCD [5].

Two fundamental questions addressed by Zohar *et al* are onset of treatment response, and for how long should the patient be kept under treatment. Considerable treatment response should be observable between 12 and 16 weeks; otherwise, it is ineffective to keep a patient for so many weeks without satisfactory results. I suggest counting the onset of treatment from the point when the largest tolerable dosage has been achieved.

One still needs to explain cases of OCD which are refractory to drug treatment. An OCD expert consensual opinion indicates that several variables, such as comorbidities, personality disorders, structural cerebral pathology, drug dependence and abnormal electroencephalographic findings, constitute serious obstacles in the outcome prospect [6]. Our research indicates comorbid major depression and personality disorders as the two greatest barriers for an efficacious outcome.

Because there is not a unique etiology, drug therapy is aimed to a target symptom approach. This is a common practice in neuropsychiatry.

In conclusion, one is pleased with Zohar *et al*'s review, expecting that better classifications of OCD, and a return to record descriptive psychopathology, will enable researchers to develop more targeted approaches.

REFERENCES

1. Tuke D.H. (1894) Imperative ideas. *Brain*, **17**: 179–197.

2. Luys M. (1883) Des obsessions pathologiques dans leurs rapports avec l'activité automatique des elements nerveux. *Encephale*, **3**: 20–61.
3. Westphal C. (1877) Über Zwangsvorstellungen. *Arch. Psychiatr. Nervenkr.*, **8**: 734–750.
4. Yaryura-Tobias J.A., Neziroglu F. (1997) *Biobehavioral Treatment of Obsessive Compulsive Spectrum Disorder*, Norton, New York.
5. Yaryura-Tobias J.A., Hsia C., Lancaster J. Placebo effects in psychopharmacological research on OCD: a short report (submitted for publication).
6. March J.S., Frances A., Carpenter D., Kahn D.A. (1997) The Expert Consensus Guideline Series, Treatment of Obsessive-Compulsive Disorder. *J. Clin. Psychiatry*, **58** (suppl. 4).

2.9
Treatment and Neurobiology of Obsessive-Compulsive Disorder

Johan A. den Boer[1]

In their comprehensive overview, Zohar *et al* describe the latest developments in pharmacological approach to obsessive-compulsive disorder (OCD). There is reason for both optimism and pessimism with respect to current pharmacotherapeutic possibilities in OCD. The optimistic view shared by many researchers is that the treatment outlook for OCD has changed in a relatively short time since the introduction of selective serotonin reuptake inhibitors (SSRIs). On the other hand, the picture is complicated by the relatively modest treatment response: a maximum reduction of the Yale–Brown Obsessive Compulsive Scale (Y-BOCS) score of 50% can be achieved with SSRIs, justifying the need to search beyond the serotonin (5-HT) hypothesis and investigate new compounds for this disorder. In the review by Zohar *et al*, some examples are given of the search for new compounds.

The search for novel compounds is, however, hampered by the fact that (a) very often patients with OCD suffer from comorbid conditions, and (b) the neurobiology of OCD is still unclear. Moreover, 5-HT disturbances have been identified in a variety of disorders. So far SSRIs have been found to be effective in depression, OCD, panic disorder and social phobia and we can hardly assume that SSRIs in OCD constitute a *rational* pharmacotherapy based upon a solid understanding of the underlying pathophysiology.

Challenge studies, for example, in which the functional state of 5-HT_{2c} receptors was assessed using *m*-chlorophenylpiperazine (*m*-CPP), yielded controversial results [1]. Neuroimaging studies revealed hyperactivity in the orbitofrontal cortex and basal ganglia in OCD and, in view of the fact

[1] *Department of Biological Psychiatry, University of Groningen, P.O. Box 30001, 9700 RB Groningen, The Netherlands*

that the basal ganglia include areas with a high density of 5-HT_{1D} receptors, this receptor subtype became a focus of interest. In recent challenge studies with the 5-$HT_{1B/D}$ agonist sumatriptan, Zohar [2] observed a significant increase in obsessive-compulsive symptoms, but a double-blind placebo-controlled study failed to corroborate this [3]. Since sumatriptan does not cross the blood–brain barrier, we recently performed a placebo-controlled study using the 5-$HT_{1B/D}$ agonist zolmitriptan, which does cross the barrier. No behavioural effects of any kind were observed, which argues against involvement of this receptor subtype in OCD [4]. A problem often encountered in this type of research is the heterogeneity of the OCD population, and we cannot exclude the possibility that a subtype of OCD patients exists which does present an abnormality at the level of the 5-HT_{1D} receptor. Therefore, future research should focus on identifying specific subgroups of OCD in challenge studies. Hopefully this will enable us the create a theory-driven search for novel anti-OCD compounds.

Zohar *et al* describe in their review a variety of augmentation strategies that have been employed in OCD, with equally mixed results. There is circumstantial evidence that individual patients may benefit from adding buspirone, tryptophan, fenfluramine and even dopamine blockers to SSRIs, but well-designed studies are scarce or give little support to the use of these combinations.

Adding pindolol to SSRI treatment yielded varying results in depression, and Zohar *et al.* acknowledge that this combination might improve the response of partial responders in OCD, but does not turn non-responders into responders. The background of pindolol augmentation is based upon the hypothesis that desensitization of presynaptic 5-HT_{1A} receptors can be mimicked by administration of the 5-HT_{1A} antagonist pindolol. A recent study, however, found evidence that even at very low doses of an SSRI (where pindolol no longer potentiates 5-HT release), 5-$HT_{1B/1D}$ antagonists are still able to potentiate central 5-HT release after administration of an SSRI [5]. These findings may open exciting avenues for new augmentation strategies in OCD and other anxiety disorders.

REFERENCES

1. den Boer J.A., Westenberg H.G.M. (1997) Challenge studies in obsessive compulsive disorder. In *Focus on Obsessive Compulsive Spectrum Disorders* (Eds J.A. den Boer, H.G.M. Westenberg), pp. 123–134, Syn-Thesis Publishers, Amsterdam.
2. Zohar J. (1996) Is 5-HT_{1D} involved in obsessive compulsive disorder? *Eur. Neuropsychopharmacol.*, **6**: S44–S54.
3. Ho Pian K.L., Westenberg H.G.M., den Boer J.A., De Bruin W.I., Van Rijk P.P. (1998) Effects of *meta*-chlorophenylpiperazine on cerebral blood flow in obsessive-compulsive disorder and controls. *Biol. Psychiatry*, **44**: 367–370.

4. Boshuisen M.L., den Boer J.A. Zolmitriptan (a 5-HT_{1D} receptor agonist with central action) does not increase symptoms in obsessive compulsive disorder (submitted for publication).
5. Cremers T.I.F.H., De Boer P., Liao Y., Bosker F.J., den Boer J.A., Westerink B.H.C., Wikström H.V. Augmentation with a 5-HT_{1A} antagonist, but not a 5-HT_{1B} antagonist critically depends on the dose of citalopram. A pharmacodynamic and pharmacokinetic study (submitted for publication).

2.10 Obsessive-Compulsive Disorder: Pharmacological Decision

Jambur Ananth[1]

Zohar *et al*'s paper provides a sound review of the use of serotonin reuptake inhibitors (SRIs) in obsessive-compulsive disorder (OCD). The biochemistry of OCD is yet to be elucidated, and both serotonin and dopamine may play a role in the pathogenesis of the disorder. While all SRIs are effective in OCD patients, dopamine antagonists, particularly haloperidol and pimozide, have been used with positive results in resistant patients.

Are all SRIs equally effective? Greist *et al* [1] performed a meta-analysis of four large multicenter placebo-controlled studies of SRI treatment of OCD. All the SRIs were superior to placebo and produced a 25–35% decrease in symptoms in about 60% of the patients. Clomipramine (CMI) was superior to other SRIs. The limitation of this finding is that CMI was available early and the patients included in other studies were treatment failures to CMI. In a double-blind placebo-controlled 12-week study comparing paroxetine to CMI, the former was found to be as effective as the latter, but with a superior side effect profile [2]. Therefore, the superiority of CMI is an inconclusive finding. With respect to the relative efficacy of selective serotonin reuptake inhibitors (SSRIs), the published studies indicate that they are all equal in efficacy. Patients not responding to one agent may be responsive to the other.

There are differences in several parameters when SRIs are used for anti-obsessional or antidepressant treatment. First, an SRI trial for OCD requires a longer duration of treatment. Second, the anti-obsessive effect is seen in about 12 weeks, whereas the antidepressant effect occurs in 3–4 weeks. Third, in treating depression, a flat dose-response curve is noted: most

[1] *Department of Psychiatry, Harbor/UCLA Medical Center, 1000 West Carson Street, Torrance, CA 90509, USA*

depressed patients improve with about 20 mg of fluoxetine, citalopram or paroxetine. The dosage recommended for OCD is two to three times higher [3]. While the reason for this is not clear, clinically it is important not to label a patient as non-responder until a higher dose is tried. In order to minimize the side effects, the dosage of SRIs should be gradually increased in about 2–3 weeks. Gains made via behavioural therapy may facilitate dose reductions and even permit discontinuation of medication altogether in some patients. If response is satisfactory, the dose of the SRI can be titrated downwards in the context of maintenance therapy. Three adequate trials with SRIs are necessary before concluding their ineffectiveness.

What is improvement? About 25–35% decrease in symptoms is what can be expected in the majority of patients. It is important to advise the patients at the outset that 100% improvement is rare. OCD psychopathology includes anxiety, depression, obsessions and compulsions. In some patients phobias as well as panic symptoms are noted. Anxiety improves first, allowing the person to resist the obsessions and compulsions. Compulsions improve better than obsessions. Even when the obsessions are still present, the patient does not have the severe tension and, therefore, it is easier than before to control the compulsions. The decrease in tension improves the quality of life even with a 30–50% decrease of symptoms. The Yale–Brown Obsessive Compulsive Scale is necessary to quantify the improvement and decide on dose increase and switching if there is no response.

Pure OCD vs. OCD spectrum disorder Response of OCD spectrum disorders, such as eating disorder, body dysmorphic disorder, sexual deviations, trichotillomania, compulsive buying and pathological gambling, to SRIs is less dramatic than in clear-cut OCD. For example, patients with trichotillomania do not respond as well. Some respond well initially, with a recurrence of symptoms after a few months. Body dysmorphic disorder patients with symptoms of delusional proportions may require additional pimozide or an atypical antipsychotic agent.

The psychotic spectrum requires a special consideration. Do the new antipsychotic drugs affect schizophrenic patients with OC symptoms? A recent study [4] indicated that 28% of the first-break schizophrenic patients manifested OC symptoms. Recent studies suggest that patients who have schizophrenia with OCD symptoms tend to have a poorer global functioning and long-term outcome and suffer from greater neuropsychological impairments compared with those who have only schizophrenic symptoms. These patients need to be treated with a combination of an SRI and an antipsychotic drug. Choice of the appropriate drugs is important. CMI has an advantage as it can be combined with antipsychotic drugs without an interactional effect. Schizophrenic symptoms have been reported to improve with the addition of CMI or an SSRI [5–7] to neuroleptic therapy. Some reports indicate worsening of the OC symptoms with the administration of risperidone or clozapine [8] as well as successful treatment of OC symptoms with risperidone [9]. Ghaemi *et al* [10] failed to find any evidence of an increase in or appearance of new OC symptoms with clozapine. In combining the antipsychotic medications with an SSRI, both the pharmacokinetic and pharmacodynamic interactions have to be considered. SSRIs can increase antipsychotic levels. Such an increase may at times be beneficial, with further improvement of psychotic symptoms, or may induce severe extrapyramidal symptoms. A slow titration is indicated to avoid mishaps.

Personality plays an important role in predicting the response. For example, those with schizoid personality do not generally respond well to SRIs [11], but respond to the addition of pimozide or haloperidol and possibly new antipsychotic agents.

REFERENCES

1. Greist J.H., Jefferson J.W., Kobak K.A., Katzelnick D.J., Serlin R.C. (1995) Efficacy and tolerability of serotonin transport inhibitors in obsessive-compulsive disorder. *Arch. Gen. Psychiatry*, **52**: 53–60.
2. Pigott T.A., Seay S.M. (1999) A review of the efficacy of selective serotonin reuptake inhibitors in obsessive-compulsive disorder. *J. Clin. Psychiatry*, **60**: 101–106.
3. Montgomery S.A., McIntyre A., Osterheider M., Sarteschi P., Zitterl W., Zohar J., Birckett M., Wood A. (1993) A double-blind placebo-controlled study of fluoxetine in patients with DSM-IIIR obsessive-compulsive disorder. *Eur. Neuropsychopharmacol.*, **3**: 143–152.
4. Poyurovsky M., Fuchs C., Weizman A. (1999) Obsessive-compulsive disorder in patients with first episode schizophrenia. *Am. J. Psychiatry*, **156**: 1998–2000.
5. Pulman J., Yassa R., Ananth J. (1984) Clomipramine treatment of repetitive behavior. *Can. J. Psychiatry*, **29**: 254–255.
6. Berman L., Sapers B.L., Chang H.H.J., Losonzy M.F., Schmilder J., Green A.L. (1995) Treatment of obsessive-compulsive symptoms in schizophrenic patients with clomipramine. *J. Clin. Psychopharmacol.*, **15**: 206–210.
7. Hwang M.Y., Rho J., Opler L.A., Wolfsohn R., Wolkin A., Rotrosen J. (1995) Treatment of obsessive compulsive and schizophrenia patients with clomipramine. *Neuropsychiat. Neuropsychol. Behav. Neurol.*, **8**: 231–233.
8. Baker R.W., Bermanzohn P.C., Wirsching D.A., Chengappa K.N.R. (1997) Obsessions, compulsions, clozapine and risperidone. *CNS Spectrums*, **2**: 26–36.
9. McDougle C.J., Goodman W.K., Leckman J.F., Price L.H. (1993) The psychopharmacology of obsessive compulsive disorder: implications for treatment and pathogenesis. *Psychiatr. Clin. North Am.*, **16**: 749–766.
10. Ghaemi S.N., Zarate C.A., Jr, Popli A.P., Pillay S.S., Cole J.O. (1995) Is there a relationship between clozapine and obsessive-compulsive disorder? A retrospective chart review. *Compr. Psychiatry*, **36**: 267–270.
11. Baer L., Jenike M.A. (1992) Personality disorders in obsessive compulsive disorder. *Psychiatr. Clin. North Am.*, **15**: 803–812.

2.11 Serotonergic Antidepressants in Obsessive-Compulsive Personality Disorder

M. Ansseau[1]

The essential feature of obsessive-compulsive personality disorder (OCPD) is a preoccupation with orderliness, perfectionism and mental and interpersonal control, at the expense of flexibility, openness and efficiency. These personality traits have been the subject of study since the early days of psychoanalysis. In 1894, Freud pointed out that defence mechanisms of isolation and displacement underlie obsession and in 1908 added that anal eroticism plays a role in the formation of compulsive personality; he described the triad of orderliness, obstinacy and parsimony as the central features of the anal character [1]. Those three traits and six others have been repeatedly cited in the literature of both psychoanalysis and descriptive psychiatry, in rough order of importance: emotional constriction, orderliness, parsimony, rigidity, strict superego, perseverance, obstinacy, indecisiveness, and a lack of provocativeness [2].

In the literature, OCPD has often been confused with obsessive-compulsive disorder (OCD), which is currently viewed as a separate and distinct illness. In the traditional psychoanalytic explanation of obsessional disorders, OCPD has been seen as a predisposing feature of OCD, with the two conditions existing side-by-side along a continuum [3]. On this continuum, persons with OCD differ from those with OCPD only in that they are symptomatic [4].

Pharmacological Treatment of OCPD. In contrast to OCD, symptoms of OCPD have generally not been regarded as responsive to pharmacological interventions. Recently, based on a possible relationship between OCPD and OCD, we hypothesized that OCPD could be associated with some form of serotonergic dysfunction and improved by serotonergic agents, such as clomipramine or selective serotonin reuptake inhibitors (SSRIs).

In a pilot open study, we included four outpatients who fulfilled DSM-III-R criteria for OCPD [5]. All were men, aged 34–51 years (mean = 43.7 ± 6.5) and devoid of any significant depressive symptomatology, as evidenced by scores less than 7 on the 17-item Hamilton Depression Scale. The subjects received fluvoxamine at the initial dose of 50 mg during the first week and 100 mg throughout the reminder of a 3-month study period. Initial and final assessments were performed by rating each of the nine features of DSM-III-R OCPD on a five-point scale (0 = absent, 1 = mild, 2 = moderate, 3 = severe, 4 = very severe). All four patients completed the trial. The mean total score of

[1] *Department of Psychiatry, University of Liege, C.H.U. du Sart Tilman, B35, B-4000 Liege, Belgium*

OCPD features improved statistically during the study, from an initial score (SD) of 16.2 (2.9) to a final score of 11.7 (3.6) ($t = 7.0$, $p = 0.006$). Side effects were limited and mainly gastrointestinal (three cases). The results of this preliminary open study supported a beneficial activity of SSRIs in OCPD. Therefore, we decided to validate this result in a controlled study.

In the second study, 24 outpatients who fulfilled DSM-IV criteria for OCPD were included, 15 males and 9 females, aged 24–62 years (mean = 44.3 ± 11.7). Again, all patients were devoid of significant depressive symptomatology, as evidenced by scores less than 7 on the 17-item Hamilton Depression Scale. The patients were randomly assigned to either fluvoxamine (50 mg during the first week, then 100 mg) ($n = 12$) or placebo ($n = 12$) in double-blind conditions. The duration of the study was 3 months. Initial and final assessments were performed by rating each of the eight features of DSM-IV OCPD on a five-point scale (0 = absent, 1 = mild, 2 = moderate, 3 = severe, 4 = very severe). Three patients did not complete the study, two in the fluvoxamine group and one in the placebo group. Changes over time in OCPD scores showed a significant superiority of fluvoxamine over placebo: from 18.6 to 13.7 in the fluvoxamine group vs. from 18.5 to 17.7 in the placebo group ($t = 4.39$, $p = 0.0003$). Side effects were more frequent with fluvoxamine (13 vs. 3), mainly of the gastrointestinal type (7 vs. 2). These results support a beneficial activity of SSRIs in OCPD. They favour the possibility that at least some elements of personality disturbances have a biological component. In the case of OCPD, serotonergic dysfunction could play a role. These findings should, however, be confirmed in further studies.

OCPD as a predictor of outcome in OCD. Two studies have evaluated the influence of an underlying compulsive personality disorder on the outcome of OCD patients following pharmacotherapy with serotonergic antidepressants. The first study used clomipramine [6]. Among a total sample of 54 patients, 10 (17%) exhibited a DSM-III compulsive personality disorder. This subgroup did not exhibit any significant correlation with outcome, measured by the Yale–Brown Obsessive Compulsive Scale (Y-BOCS) ($r = 0.11$) or the National Institute of Mental Health Global Improvement Scale ($r = 0.21$). In contrast, schizotypal personality disorder was found to be negatively related to outcome on both dependent variables; avoidant, borderline, and paranoid personality disorders were also negatively related to outcome on several variables.

The second study used fluoxetine [7]. Among 67 patients, only three (4%) exhibited a DSM-III compulsive personality disorder. Again, this subgroup was not significantly related to any of the outcome measures ($r = -0.18$ for the Y-BOCS and $r = 0.01$ for the Maudsley Obsessional Compulsive Inventory). Surprisingly, in this study, the presence of avoidant personality disorder was related to greater improvement on Y-BOCS.

In summary, the presence of an underlying obsessive-compulsive personality does not seem to represent a predictor of outcome to serotonergic antidepressants in patients with OCD. In contrast, a comorbid schizotypal disorder or a borderline personality disorder, and to a lesser extent an avoidant personality disorder, could have a negative impact on outcome [6, 8, 9].

REFERENCES

1. Freud S. (1908/1959) Character and anal erotism. In *Standard Edition of the Complete Psychological Works of Sigmund Freud*, vol. 9, pp. 193–197, Hogarth, London.
2. Perry J.C., Vaillant G.E. (1989) Personality disorders. In *Comprehensive Textbook of Psychiatry*, 5th edn. (Eds H. I. Kaplan, B. J. Sadock) vol. 2, pp. 1352–1395, Williams and Wilkins, Baltimore.
3. Salzman L. (1968) *The Obsessive Personality*, Science House, New York.
4. Ingram I.M. (1961) The obsessional personality and obsessional illness. *Am. J. Psychiatry*, **117**: 1016–1019.
5. Ansseau M., Troisfontaines B., Papart P., von Frenckell R. (1993) Compulsive personality and serotonergic drugs. *Eur. Neuropsychopharmacol.*, **3**: 288–289.
6. Baer L., Jenike M.A., Black D.W., Treece C., Rosenfeld R., Greist J. (1992) Effects of axis II diagnoses on treatment outcome with clomipramine in 55 patients with obsessive-compulsive disorder. *Arch. Gen. Psychiatry*, **49**: 862–866.
7. Baer L., Jenike M.A. (1990) Personality disorders in obsessive-compulsive disorder. In *Obsessive-Compulsive Disorders: Theory and Management* (Eds M.A. Jenike, L. Baer, W.E. Minichiello), pp. 76–88, Year Book Medical Publishers, Chicago.
8. Minichiello W.E., Baer L., Jenike M.A. (1987) Schizotypal personality disorder: a poor prognostic indicator for behavior therapy in the treatment of obsessive-compulsive disorder. *J. Anxiety Disord.*, **1**: 273–276.
9. Hermesh H., Shahar A., Munitz H. (1987) Obsessive-compulsive disorder and borderline personality disorder. *Am. J. Psychiatry*, **144**: 120–121.

2.12
Drug Treatment of Obsessive-Compulsive Disorder: Dark Past, Bright Present, but Glowing Future

Pierre Blier[1]

Until the early 1980s, obsessive-compulsive disorder (OCD) was generally believed to be an extremely rare psychiatric disorder. However, at that time,

[1] *Neurobiological Psychiatry Unit, Faculty of Medicine, McGill University, 1033 Avenue des Pins Ouest, Montreal, Canada H3A 1RA*

large epidemiology catchment area studies established that the lifetime prevalence of OCD was about 2%, that is, higher than either schizophrenia or bipolar affective disorder. Fortunately though, in that period, the first placebo-controlled studies established the effectiveness of the tricyclic drug clomipramine for OCD, thereby providing clinicians with a useful tool to treat a condition which was, until then, known to be drug-resistant. The subsequent demonstration that it is the capacity of clomipramine to block the serotonin (5-HT) reuptake which is responsible for its anti-OCD effect triggered a significant research endeavour into the function of the 5-HT system in OCD. The next major advance was the introduction of the non-tricyclic selective 5-HT reuptake inhibitors, the side effect profile of which made the treatment of OCD amenable to most patients. In their review Zohar *et al.* summarize in a comprehensive fashion for clinicians the pharmacological principles for the use of standard drugs to treat OCD. The clarity of their description is no doubt due to the fact that they personally carried out several of the pivotal studies that rigorously examined the clinical characteristics of these agents in OCD.

Given that many patients do not respond adequately, and some not at all, to 5-HT reuptake inhibitors, there remains an unmet need for augmentation strategies. The major approaches commonly used in specialized clinics are also briefly described and referenced in Zohar *et al*'s review. This field is constantly evolving as new approaches are being devised and tested, while others are being demonstrated to be effective in controlled trials. For instance, risperidone, under placebo-controlled conditions, has recently been shown to be an effective augmentation strategy in patients resistant to a 5-HT reuptake inhibitor not necessarily presenting tics or Tourette's syndrome [1].

Although considerable progress has been made in the therapy of OCD, continued advancements in understanding the pathophysiology of this disorder have been somewhat hampered by a clear demonstration of a crucial role for 5-HT in its treatment. Indeed, anomalies of the 5-HT system cannot account entirely for the pathogenesis of OCD. The field is now exploring the role of other neurotransmitters in the well-identified neurocircuitry involved in generating OCD symptoms. While there certainly remain major therapeutic advances to be made by developing selective 5-HT receptor ligands to treat OCD more rapidly and effectively, novel targets in other neurotransmitter systems constitute future generations of anti-OCD agents.

REFERENCE

1. McDougle C. (personal communication).

CHAPTER

3

Psychotherapies for Obsessive-Compulsive Disorder: A Review

Edna B. Foa and Martin E. Franklin

Department of Psychiatry, University of Pennsylvania School of Medicine, 3535 Market Street, 6th Floor, Philadelphia, PA 19104, USA

INTRODUCTION

In the last 30 years, much progress has been made in the development and empirical evaluation of psychotherapies for obsessive-compulsive disorder (OCD). We will first review some of the early behavioural interventions that, although they did not prove to be especially potent, set the stage for the development of more effective treatments. Next, we will discuss the treatment outcome literature pertaining to cognitive-behavioural therapy (CBT) involving exposure and ritual prevention (EX/RP), a program of established efficacy for reducing OCD symptoms. We will then describe the EX/RP treatment variables that may affect outcomes, such as session frequency and therapist-assisted exposures. Next, we will compare the relative efficacy of EX/RP to other therapies, including cognitive therapies and medication. Finally, we will review the findings on prediction of treatment outcome and then provide a summary of the empirical literature as it stands now.

EARLY PSYCHOTHERAPIES

OCD was considered a treatment refractory condition until the middle of the 1960s. Behavioural techniques derived from learning theory were then brought to bear on OCD, and initial reports on these treatments were generally encouraging. These interventions usually included either a

Obsessive-Compulsive Disorder. Edited by Mario Maj, Norman Sartorius, Ahmed Okasha and Joseph Zohar.

form of exposure (e.g. systematic desensitization) or reinforcement procedures (e.g. aversion). Methodological flaws rendered the findings of these studies difficult to interpret, and there was considerable variability reported with respect to patient outcomes. For instance, systematic desensitization was examined only in case studies and small case series, yet for the most part its efficacy appeared to be very modest [1]. Cooper *et al* [2] found that only three of 10 patients treated with systematic desensitization improved. One finding that did emerge from the early research on systematic desensitization for OCD was that *in vivo* desensitization appeared to be more effective than imaginal [3].

Paradoxical intention, i.e. *in vivo* confrontation with stimuli that evoke the obsessions coupled with instructions to elaborate the obsessional material, was also attempted with OCD. Gertz [4] reported 66% of responders in a small case series; Solyom *et al* [5] reported that five of 10 treated patients were markedly improved at post-treatment. In practical terms, this paradoxical technique resembles current forms of imaginal and *in vivo* exposure, which may explain its benefits.

Other exposure procedures have been examined in single case reports. Noonan [6] reported that after seven sessions of implosive therapy the patients were symptom-free; McCarthy [7] found that prolonged imaginal exposure to feared consequences produced symptom remission in another patient. Broadhurst [8] found that imaginal exposure to menstrual blood resulted in mild improvement for one patient at post-treatment, with further improvement at long-term follow-up.

Exposure did not prove particularly effective in a study of non-ritualizers conducted by Emmelkamp and Kwee [9], with only one of three patients showing improvement after five 1-hour sessions. Similarly, satiation, which involves having patients verbalize their obsessive ruminations in 1-hour sessions, resulted in improvement for only two of seven treated patients [10].

A series of studies examining exposure in combination with aversion relief demonstrated evidence for the partial efficacy of this program. Treatment consisted of exposure to taped narratives of obsessive thoughts, which were periodically interrupted by 20-second silences followed by a mild electric shock. Shock was terminated by the patient, at which point the taped narratives resumed. Results indicated improvement for patients with a variety of obsessive concerns [11, 12].

Several studies reported that procedures aimed at reducing compulsions also appeared to be at least partly effective. For example, Rabavilas *et al* [13] instructed four patients with checking rituals to continue checking beyond their urge to do so. Patients reportedly did not comply with the instructions, yet still showed a substantial decrease in ritualizing at follow-up. Perhaps the mechanism underlying this intervention is similar to that involved in paradoxical intention, which was also effective in several case studies.

Reinforcement procedures have also been utilized to treat OCD. An aversion relief paradigm was examined in which OCD washers received electric shocks when they began ritualizing; these shocks were terminated upon contact with the contaminant. Patients in two studies evidenced some improvement in compulsive behaviour with this technique [14, 15]. Aversion procedures without relief upon contact with feared stimuli were also examined, with improvement noted in three of five treated patients in one study [16] and in one compulsive washer [17]. A patient with ordering rituals receiving another variant of aversion therapy, covert sensitization, was also treated successfully [18].

Other types of blocking procedures have aimed to reduce obsessions, with some positive case outcomes reported for delivery of shock following obsessional thoughts [19, 20]. Thought-stopping, which involves shouting "Stop!" in response to obsessive intrusions, was also found effective in case examples [21–23]. However, when treatment by relaxation training alone was compared to relaxation plus thought-stopping conducted during tape-recorded presentations of obsessional scenes, only four of 11 patients improved in the combined treatment [24]. Similarly, a study using therapist presentation of scenes was also ineffective, with two of seven patients showing only slight improvement [10]; Emmelkamp and Kwee [9] found that one of two patients treated with thought-stopping as a first treatment improved.

In summary, the literature on these early behavioural treatments for OCD is equivocal. As is routine with innovations in treatment development, most of these reports were either case studies or uncontrolled case series, and long-term outcome data were typically not available. The primary impression to be gleaned from these reports is that the procedures used were not very powerful, except perhaps to the extent that they employed actual exposure, as in the paradoxical intention studies. Also, the treatments that used reinforcement procedures to inhibit ritualizing showed some promise. Despite their limitations, these early studies served to generate new hypotheses about treatment efficacy and mechanisms of change, advancing the development of the treatment procedures that have since proven highly effective, such as exposure and ritual prevention.

EXPOSURE AND RITUAL PREVENTION (EX/RP)

Meyer's [25] report on two patients treated successfully with a treatment that included prolonged exposure to obsessional cues and strict prevention of rituals was the first of several small uncontrolled investigations that suggested the efficacy of this treatment program. This treatment, known then as exposure and response prevention, was later found to be extremely successful in 10 of 15 cases and partly effective in the remainder. Moreover, maintenance of gain appeared to be common, with only two of 15 patients evidencing relapse at 5-year follow-up [26, 27]. In the years that followed these groundbreaking reports, the EX/RP procedure has been modified somewhat and tested against a variety of active and control treatments. As will be described below, the core procedures of exposure to feared stimuli and simultaneous prevention of rituals appear to be at the heart of those psychological treatment programs that have yielded the best treatment responses.

Current EX/RP programs typically include *in vivo* exposures to feared stimuli, such as having the patient who fears contamination from germs touch toilets and sinks. Feared consequences, which are reported by the majority of OCD patients [28], are often addressed via imaginal exposure. Both forms of exposure are designed specifically to prompt obsessional distress; repeated, prolonged exposure without ritualizing or avoiding is thought to provide information that disconfirms mistaken associations and evaluations held by the patients and promotes habituation to previously fearful thoughts and situations [29]. Exposure is typically gradual, with situations provoking moderate distress confronted before more upsetting ones. Exposure homeworks to be conducted between treatment sessions are also assigned. Additionally, patients are asked to refrain from rituals between sessions and to record any violations of ritual abstinence on self-monitoring sheets to be discussed with the therapist in the next treatment session.

Since Meyer's initial reports of the efficacy of EX/RP, numerous uncontrolled and controlled studies have shown that the majority of EX/RP treatment completers are responders at post-treatment and remain so at follow-up. Foa and Kozak [30] reviewed 12 EX/RP outcome studies ($n = 330$), and found that an average of 83% of treatment completers were classified as responders immediately after treatment. In 16 studies reporting long-term outcome ($n = 376$; mean follow-up interval of 29 months) 76% were responders. Several meta-analytic studies [31–34] have detected large effect sizes for EX/RP with OCD in adults (> 1.0), regardless of the study selection criteria utilized for the various meta-analytic procedures.

The meta-analytic studies described above did not, however, exclude studies of EX/RP that failed to utilize some form of control treatment, so their reported effect sizes may overestimate the benefit of EX/RP. Convergent evidence for the efficacy of EX/RP is derived from several randomized controlled trials (RCTs) that have demonstrated the superiority of EX/RP in comparison to various control treatments, including relaxation [35], pill placebo [36] and anxiety management training [37]. On the whole, the empirical evidence indicates clearly that EX/RP is superior to control treatments, produces substantial and clinically meaningful symptom reductions at post-treatment, and provides durable symptom reduction at long-term follow-up. These findings appear to be particularly robust: they are largely consistent across different sites and procedural variations. Because there are many variants of EX/RP treatment, we will review the literature of the relative efficacy of the ingredients that comprise EX/RP.

EX/RP TREATMENT VARIABLES

Exposure vs. Ritual Prevention vs. EX/RP

Most studies that have examined the efficacy of exposure therapy for OCD also included ritual prevention techniques [38–40], thus confounding the effects of these procedures. To separate these effects, Foa *et al* [41] randomly assigned patients with washing rituals to either treatment by exposure only (EX), ritual prevention only (RP), or their combination (EX/RP). Each treatment was conducted intensively (15 daily 2-hour sessions conducted over 3 weeks) and followed by a home visit. Results indicated that the combined treatment was superior to the single-component treatments on almost every symptom measure at post-treatment and follow-up. Notably, patients who received exposure alone reported lower anxiety when confronting feared contaminants than did patients who had received only ritual prevention, whereas the RP alone group reported greater decreases in their urge to ritualize than did the EX alone group. Thus, it appears that EX and RP affect symptoms differently, and that treatments that do not include exposure and ritual prevention yield inferior outcome.

Frequency of Exposure Sessions

EX/RP programs that have achieved excellent results [42] typically involve daily sessions, but favourable outcomes have also been achieved with more widely spaced sessions [43]. Pilot data gathered with a pediatric OCD sample suggests that children and adolescents who received weekly sessions responded very favourably and similarly to those treated intensively [44], but the lack of random assignment to these treatments renders the findings inconclusive. Our clinical impression is that less frequent sessions may suffice for patients whose OCD symptoms are mild, who readily understand the importance of daily exposure homeworks, and adhere strictly to ritual abstinence instructions. We have also observed that patients with severe symptoms or those who exhibit considerable difficulty complying with exposure homework or ritual prevention benefit from a more intensive regimen.

Therapist-assisted vs. Self-exposure

The importance of therapist-aided exposure in EX/RP is unclear. Although one study found that modeling of exposure by the therapists did not enhance overall treatment efficacy [45], patients in this study did prefer modeling. Moreover, clinical experience suggests that patients appear more willing to confront feared situations in the presence of the therapist, and some patients find modeling helpful. Empirical evaluations of the presence of a therapist during exposure have yielded inconsistent results. In one study, patients with OCD who received therapist-aided exposure were more improved immediately post-treatment than those receiving clomipramine and self-exposure, but this difference disappeared by 1-year follow-up [46]. However, the design of the study introduced confounds and therefore the results are difficult to interpret. In a second study with OCD, no differences between therapist-assisted treatment and self-exposure were detected either at post-treatment or at follow-up [47]. In this study, the number of patients in each condition was too small to render these results conclusive. Meta-analytic findings have suggested that therapist-assisted exposure is more potent than self-exposure [31].

In contrast to the generally negative findings described above, therapist presence enhanced the efficacy of a single 3-hour exposure session for persons with specific phobia compared to self-exposure of equal length [48]. Since specific phobias are on the whole less debilitating and easier to treat than OCD, one might surmise that therapist presence could also enhance OCD exposures. The effect of therapist-assisted exposure on treatment outcome awaits a well-controlled study with a sufficiently large sample to afford the necessary power to detect group differences. In our clinical practice, we routinely include therapist-assisted exposure during treatment sessions, and ask patients to conduct self-directed exposure exercises between sessions.

Duration of Exposure

Prolonged continuous exposure is superior to short interrupted exposure [13]. How much time is adequate? Although there is no hard and fast rule, clinical observations suggest that exposure should continue at least until the patient notices a decrease in obsessional distress. Indeed, reduction in anxiety (habituation) within the exposure session to the most distressing item, as well as reduction in the peak anxiety across sessions, were associated with improvement following EX/RP treatment [49]. Studies have indicated that continuous exposure of approximately 90 minutes duration is needed for reduction of anxiety [50] and for a decrease in urges to ritualize [51]. Although this time period is a useful rule of thumb, exposure should be continued beyond 90 minutes if the patient has not felt some relief within that time, or terminated before 90 minutes if substantial reduction in distress occurs.

Gradual vs. Abrupt Exposures

Patients who confront the most distressing situations from the start of therapy have achieved the same gains as patients who confront less distressing situations before confronting the most distressing one [52]. However, most patients appear to be more satisfied with a gradual approach. Because patients' willingness to comply with treatment procedures is such a critical aspect of successful EX/RP, situations of moderate difficulty are usually confronted first, followed by several intermediate steps before the most distressing exposures are accomplished. This may be especially important in conducting EX/RP with younger patients, as treatment experts have emphasized the need for hierarchy-driven exposure and a collaborative approach between the therapist and the child in the development of exposure exercises [53].

Use of Imaginal Exposure

The addition of imaginal exposure to a program that includes *in vivo* exposure and ritual prevention appeared to enhance maintenance of treatment gains for OCD patients [54, 55]. However, no such effect was found in another similar study [43]. This discrepancy may be explained by differences in the treatment program utilized by Foa *et al* [54, 55] in comparison to that of de Araujo *et al* [43] (e.g. 90-minute vs. 30-minute imaginal exposures, respectively).

Clinically, we find imaginal exposure to be useful, especially for patients whose obsessional fears include disastrous consequences (e.g. killing one's child) and/or for those patients whose fears are not readily translated into *in vivo* exposure exercises (e.g. burning in hell for failure to neutralize blasphemous thoughts). Also, the addition of imagery to *in vivo* exposure may circumvent the cognitive avoidance strategies used by patients who evade thinking about the consequences of exposure while confronting feared situations *in vivo*. Thus, although imaginal exposure does not appear to be essential for successful outcome at post-treatment, it may enhance long-term maintenance and is often a useful adjunct to *in vivo* exercises for patients with fears focusing on disastrous consequences. For patients who do not report any feared disasters consequent to refraining from rituals (other than being extremely distressed), imaginal exposure may not be necessary.

Implementation of Ritual Prevention

In Meyer's [25] treatment program, hospital staff actually stopped the patients from performing rituals (e.g. turning off water supply in patient's room). However, physical intervention by others to prevent patients from ritualizing is no longer typical or recommended. In addition to concerns that actual physical prevention is too coercive to be acceptable, it is believed that reliance upon this technique may limit generalizability to non-therapy situations in which staff are not present to prevent rituals. Instead of physical prevention, instructions and encouragement to refrain from ritualizing and avoidance are much more common procedures in implementing ritual prevention [40]. As noted earlier, although exposure reduces obsessional distress, in itself it is not so effective in reducing compulsions. To maximize improvement, the patient needs to voluntarily refrain from ritualizing while engaging in programmatic exposure exercises. Therapists should assist with this difficult task by providing support, encouragement and suggestions about how to refrain from ritualizing in particular situations. Self-monitoring of rituals may also serve to promote ritual abstinence by increasing patient awareness of rituals and by providing an alternative activity to ritualizing when the urges to do so are high.

FAMILY INVOLVEMENT VS. STANDARD EX/RP TREATMENT

Emmelkamp *et al* [56] examined whether assistance by a family member would enhance the efficacy of EX/RP for OCD. Patients who were married or living with a romantic partner were randomly assigned to receive EX/RP either with or without partner involvement in treatment. Each treatment lasted 5 weeks and consisted of eight 45–60 min sessions with the therapist; exposures were not practiced in session. Results indicated that OCD severity was significantly reduced immediately after treatment for both groups, and that no group differences were detected. Moreover, initial marital distress was unrelated to outcome. Notably, although mean symptom reduction reached statistical significance, the reduction in anxiety/distress reported for the sample as a whole was modest (33%). This may have resulted from the shorter treatment and absence of *in vivo* exposure in treatment sessions.

Mehta [57] also examined the adjunctive role of family involvement in EX/RP treatment in a study conducted in India. In order to adapt the treatment to serve the large numbers of young unmarried people seeking OCD treatment and the "joint family system" prevalent in India, a family-based rather than spouse-based treatment approach was utilized. Patients previously non-responsive to pharmacotherapy were randomly assigned to receive treatment by systematic desensitization and EX/RP, either with or without family assistance. Sessions in both conditions were held twice per week for 12 weeks; response prevention was gradual. In the family condition, a designated family member (parent, spouse or adult child) assisted with homework assignments, supervised relaxation therapy, participated in response prevention, and was instructed to be supportive. On self-reported OCD symptoms, a greater improvement was found for the family-based intervention at post-treatment and 6-month follow-up. While the study had methodological problems that complicate interpretation of findings (e.g. use of self-report OCD measures only, unclear description of treatment procedures), it offers evidence that family involvement may enhance OCD treatment.

In our clinic we typically identify a "support person" from the patient's family or social circle, and provide psychoeducation to the family member about OCD and how best to assist the patient between sessions as he/she attempt to confront his/her fears without ritualizing or avoiding. With our youngest patients, we will often enlist a parent to serve essentially as a co-therapist between sessions. Exceptions to the active involvement of parents in the treatment process are made when clinical observation suggests that the parent–child interactions around OCD are too contentious for the parent to fulfill this role effectively.

INDIVIDUAL VS. GROUP EX/RP

Intensive individual EX/RP, although of demonstrated efficacy, can pose practical problems such as high cost for treatment and difficulty scheduling daily therapy sessions. Additionally, because experts in EX/RP treatment are scarce, individual patients may need to wait for long periods of time, or travel substantial distances, in order to receive treatment.

Uncontrolled explorations of group therapy for OCD [58] prompted a controlled trial by Fals-Stewart *et al* [35]. OCD patients were randomly assigned to EX/RP conducted individually, group EX/RP treatment, or a psychological control condition (relaxation). Each of the active treatments was 2 weeks long, with sessions held twice weekly, and included daily exposure homework assignments. Reductions in OC symptoms were obtained only with the two active treatments. Moreover, no differences between individual and group EX/RP were detected immediately post-treatment or at 6-month follow-up, although profile analysis of OCD symptom ratings collected throughout treatment indicated a faster reduction in symptoms for patients receiving individual treatment.

These results offer evidence for the efficacy of group treatment. However, patients were excluded from this study if they were diagnosed with *any* personality disorder or with comorbid major depression based on Beck Depression Inventory (BDI) score [59] greater than 22. These exclusion criteria, together with the relatively low pre-treatment OCD severity scores and the fact that all 93 patients had received no previous treatment of any kind for OCD, renders the sample somewhat atypical. Thus, inferences about the efficacy of group procedures with a broader population of more severe and more comorbid OCD patients should be made with caution.

EX/RP VS. COGNITIVE THERAPIES

Dissatisfaction with formulations of treatment as mediated by autonomic processes, such as extinction [60] or habituation [61], and the increased interest in cognitive therapy [62] prompted researchers to examine the efficacy of cognitive procedures for OCD. Emmelkamp *et al* [63] compared Self-instructional Training [64] plus EX/RP to EX/RP alone. Treatment was conducted twice weekly and sessions were of 2 hours duration. Both groups improved on all outcome measures; on assessor-rated avoidance associated with main compulsion, a superiority of EX/RP alone emerged. Thus, self-instructional training may have slightly hindered, rather than enhanced, efficacy.

The failure to find an additive effect for self-instructional training led Emmelkamp *et al* [65] to examine the efficacy of Rational Emotive Therapy (RET), a cognitive therapy program that focuses on irrational beliefs. Patients were randomly assigned to EX/RP or RET. Treatment consisted of 10 sessions (60 minutes each) conducted over 8 weeks. In the EX/RP condition, exposure exercises were not practiced during treatment sessions. Instead, patients were assigned exposure exercises from their treatment hierarchy to perform at home twice per week for at least 90 minutes. RET involved determining the irrational thoughts that mediated negative feelings, confronting these thoughts via cognitive techniques, and modifying them with the aim of reducing anxiety and thereby decreasing the need to ritualize. In the RET condition, irrational beliefs were challenged socratically by the therapist during sessions; patients were instructed to continue challenging their irrational thinking for homework. Patients receiving RET were not instructed to expose themselves to feared situations, nor were they explicitly instructed to refrain from such exposure. Results indicated that both groups were improved at post-treatment and no group differences emerged. On ratings of anxiety/discomfort associated with the main OCD problem, the RET group showed an average post-treatment improvement of 40% and the EX/RP an improvement of 51%. Long-term comparisons were confounded by the large number of individuals who received additional treatment during the follow-up period.

Emmelkamp and Beens [66] sought to replicate the findings of Emmelkamp *et al* [65] and also to examine whether a combined package of cognitive therapy plus EX/RP would enhance the effects of EX/RP. They compared a program that included six sessions of RET alone followed by six sessions of RET plus self-controlled EX/RP to a program that included 12 sessions of self-controlled EX/RP. In both programs the first six sessions were followed by 4 weeks of no treatment, after which the additional six sessions were delivered. As in Emmelkamp *et al*'s [65] study, treatment sessions were conducted approximately once per week, and lasted for 60 minutes each. EX/RP sessions did not include therapist-assisted exposure, and patients were assigned twice-weekly exposure homework exercises. The first six sessions of the RET program were equivalent to that employed in the Emmelkamp *et al* [65] study and did not include exposure homework. When self-controlled EX/RP was introduced following the first six RET-only sessions, the latter was focused on irrational thoughts that occurred in response to exposure homework exercises. Immediately following the completion of six sessions of cognitive therapy without exposure and EX/RP (week 9), the mean reduction of anxiety associated with main OC problem was 25% for RET and 23% for EX/RP. Following six more sessions (RET + EX/RP in one condition and EX/RP only in the other), both groups continued to improve on most measures compared to pre-treatment; no significant group differences emerged. Notably, approximately 30% of the sample dropped out during treatment, which is higher than reported in several other studies and may limit generalizability of the findings.

van Oppen *et al* [67] compared the efficacy of self-controlled EX/RP and a cognitive intervention developed to correct specific cognitive distortions hypothesized by Salkovskis [68] to underlie OCD. Patients were randomly assigned to receive 16 sessions of cognitive therapy or EX/RP. In order to examine the effects of "purer" versions of cognitive therapy and EX/RP, behavioural experiments (exposures) were not introduced into the cognitive treatment until after session six and, conversely, in the first six EX/RP sessions, care was taken by the therapist to specifically avoid any discussion of disastrous consequences. Sessions in both treatment conditions lasted for 45 minutes.

Results were similar to the studies of cognitive therapy reviewed above. After six sessions of cognitive therapy without behavioural experiments and

EX/RP without discussion of disastrous consequences, OCD symptom reductions of 20% were observed for cognitive therapy vs. 23% for EX/RP. At post-treatment, both groups continued to improve on almost all measures, with trends favouring cognitive therapy over EX/RP. However, inspection of the reduction in Yale–Brown Obsessive Compulsive Scale (Y-BOCS) scores [69] for the EX/RP condition suggests that outcome for EX/RP at post-treatment (32% for EX/RP) was inferior to that typically achieved in other studies of EX/RP [43, 70]. It also appears that there was very little effect for adding discussion of disastrous outcomes in EX/RP at mid-treatment (10% reduction from mid-test to post-treatment).

Hiss *et al* [70] investigated whether adding a formal relapse prevention program following intensive EX/RP enhanced maintenance of therapeutic gains. In this study, all components typically included to address relapse prevention (e.g. discussion of lapse vs. relapse, post-treatment exposure instructions, themes of guilt and personal responsibility) were removed from the 15 daily sessions of the intensive phase. All patients received the modified EX/RP, followed by either a relapse prevention treatment or a psychosocial control treatment (associative therapy). All patients were responders to EX/RP at post-treatment (defined as 50% or greater reduction in OCD symptoms). At 6-month follow-up, gains were better maintained in the relapse prevention group than in the associative therapy condition. Using the criterion of 50% OCD symptom reduction as measured by the Y-BOCS, the percentage of responders at follow-up was 75% and 33%, respectively.

As can be seen from the above review, the results of studies examining the relative and combined efficacy of EX/RP and cognitive interventions have been mixed: one study found that the addition of self-instructional training to EX/RP hindered outcome compared to EX/RP only [63] and one found no difference between RET and EX/RP [65]. A third study comparing cognitive therapy that excluded any exposure, with EX/RP that excluded discussions of feared consequences, found no significant differences between these procedures [67]. Notably, the EX/RP treatments used in these studies were compromised versions (e.g. shorter sessions, fewer sessions, absence of therapist-assisted exposure) of the procedures that have been found to yield the largest improvements. These diluted programs resulted in attenuated outcome compared to programs that used intensive regimens (e.g. 80% reduction on assessors ratings of rituals in Foa *et al* [42]; 60% and 66% reduction on the Y-BOCS in Hiss *et al* [70]). The relevance of studies comparing attenuated versions of EX/RP to variants of cognitive therapy is unclear. Notably, recent meta-analytic findings [71] indicate that cognitive therapies that include "behavioural experiments" are more potent than those that do not, suggesting that the efficacy of these therapies may be explained at least in part by the inclusion of exposure exercises.

The issue of whether or not cognitive therapy improves the efficacy of EX/RP is of theoretical interest but may be practically moot because most EX/RP specialists customarily discuss dysfunctional thinking and mistaken beliefs during exposure sessions. The need for cognitive change is an essential component of the rationale for exposure therapy and is routinely discussed with the patient throughout treatment. Notably, Foa and Kozak [29] argued that a crucial mechanism underlying the efficacy of exposure is the disconfirmation of erroneous associations and beliefs. For example, a patient and therapist sitting on the bathroom floor in a public rest room conducting an exposure to contaminated surfaces often discuss risk assessment, probability overestimation, etc., as the therapist helps the patient achieve the cognitive modification necessary for improvement. In our clinic, therapists routinely discuss patients' mistaken beliefs, but these discussions anticipate and accompany exposure, rather than compete with it. Thus, studies that examine the efficacy of "stripped-down" versions of cognitive therapies (e.g. without behavioural experiments) or EX/RP (e.g. without discussion of mistaken beliefs) cannot help us to ascertain what combination of treatment techniques would yield greater symptom reduction than what we already achieve with EX/RP. Perhaps the best route for future research is to develop cognitive procedures to prepare reluctant patients to engage in EX/RP, i.e. readiness programs, or to develop cognitive theories of OCD and companion treatments to treat OCD subtypes (e.g. patients with poor insight or personality disorders) who are less likely to respond to standard EX/RP programs.

EX/RP VS. PHARMACOTHERAPY

It seems that serotonin reuptake inhibitors (SRIs) are the drugs of choice for OCD in both children and adults, and that there is not a clear advantage for one compound over another with respect to symptom reduction [72]. Generally speaking, studies examining the efficacy of EX/RP and pharmacotherapy with SRIs have indicated that both forms of treatment are individually neither completely nor universally helpful, which has prompted interest in their combined efficacy. However, there is little compelling evidence from empirical investigations for the superiority of such combined treatment over the individual treatments. Several studies have combined antidepressants with EX/RP [42, 46, 73–77]. However, methodological issues with these studies preclude strong conclusions about: (a) the relative efficacy of the individual treatments; (b) the combined efficacy vs. each treatment individually; or (c) whether the addition of EX/RP to pharmacotherapy reduces the problem of relapse after drug discontinuation.

A multicenter study in progress at the University of Pennsylvania and Columbia University is examining the relative and combined efficacy of clomipramine (CMI) and intensive EX/RP [36]. In this study, an EX/RP program that includes an intensive phase (15 2-hour sessions conducted over 3 weeks) and follow-up phase (six brief sessions delivered over 8 weeks) is compared to CMI, EX/RP + CMI, and pill placebo (PBO). Preliminary findings with treatment completer data as well as intent-to-treat data suggest that the active treatments are superior to placebo; EX/RP appears superior to CMI, and the combination of the two treatments does not appear superior to EX/RP alone. However, the design used in this multicenter collaborative study may not have been optimal for promoting an additive effect of CMI, because the intensive portion of the EX/RP program was largely completed before the medication effects could be realized.

In summary, there is ample evidence for the efficacy of both pharmaceutical and EX/RP treatments, but information about their relative and combined efficacy is scarce, because most of the studies that have addressed these issues have been methodologically limited. With this caveat in mind, no study has found clear long-term superiority for combined pharmacotherapy plus EX/RP over EX/RP alone. The absence of conclusive supportive findings notwithstanding, many experts continue to advocate combined procedures as the treatment of choice for OCD (78).

In our view, the results of the outcome studies on the whole lead to a conclusion that EX/RP is the best available treatment for patients who are willing or able to complete it. Whether EX/RP is superior for patients overall, and whether an adequate pharmacotherapy trial followed by EX/RP would be generally superior in the short and long-term, is yet unclear. Monotherapy by certain serotonergic medications is also of established efficacy. If the patient refuses EX/RP, or if it is unavailable, serotonergic medications are a reasonable alternative.

PREDICTORS OF TREATMENT OUTCOME

Pretreatment Depression

Several early reports in the literature suggested that patients with severe depression responded poorly to behavioural interventions [79, 80]. However, a controlled prospective study revealed that both depressed and non-depressed groups responded favourably to EX/RP and that the reduction of depression by imipramine prior to EX/RP did not enhance EX/RP outcome [42]. Generally, the literature is inconclusive about whether pretreatment depression predicts outcome of either EX/RP or medication. In six of 10 available studies, depression was not predictive of outcome; in the remaining four studies it predicted poor outcome [81] (for a review, see [82]). We have recently examined the effects of depression on EX/RP treatment outcome, and found that only patients with severe depressive symptoms (BDI > 30) appeared to have an attenuated treatment response [83]. Thus, when patients' pre-treatment level of depression is very severe, it may be preferable to refer the patient for treatment of these symptoms before attempting the time and labour-intensive EX/RP program.

Pretreatment OCD Severity

The overall pretreatment OCD severity has not emerged as a predictor of EX/RP outcome [76, 84–87]. In contrast, severity of *specific* OCD symptoms (e.g. behavioural avoidance, rituals, obsessions) does predict poor EX/RP outcome [88, 89]. With respect to the relationship between EX/RP outcome and type of ritual (washing vs. checking), findings have been inconsistent. No relationship was found in two studies [84, 45]; one study found that checking predicted better outcome [90]; and three studies found that washing predicted better outcome [88, 91, 81]. In summary, it appears that overall OCD severity may not be predictive, but certain specific OCD symptoms may be related to outcome.

Personality Disorders (PD)

Comorbid PD of any kind was predictive of poor behavioural therapy outcome in two studies [92, 93], while specific PD diagnoses have also been found related to poor response to SRIs [94–97]. Only one study failed to find a relationship between presence of PDs and medication treatment outcome [98]. Thus, the presence of PDs, especially schizotypal and borderline, predicts poor outcome for *both* SRIs and EX/RP.

Expectancy of Outcome

Patients' expectations of treatment benefits were found to influence EX/RP outcome in one study [89], but not in another [99]. It may also be the case that patients with the lowest expectations of EX/RP treatment benefit refuse to enter EX/RP; thus, the predictive value of expectancy may be underestimated in studies that do not consider treatment refusal as an outcome variable.

Motivation and Compliance with BT

Several studies found that motivation (and compliance) influenced EX/RP outcome [84, 85, 100]. However, one study [99] failed to find such a relationship. Clinically, we have found that motivation and compliance with treatment procedures are important mediators of EX/RP success.

SUMMARY

Consistent Evidence

The OCD treatment outcome literature indicates clearly that EX/RP is a highly effective treatment for adult OCD. The majority of patients who complete the course of treatment show substantial, clinically significant improvement, which for most patients is maintained at follow-up assessments. Meta-analytical studies reveal that EX/RP is more effective than control conditions (e.g. relaxation) or other psychological treatments (e.g. cognitive therapy). Two studies revealed that the outcome of combining exposure and ritual prevention exceeds that of exposure or ritual prevention alone.

The overall pre-treatment OCD symptom severity does not predict outcome of EX/RP, but some symptoms such as avoidance do. Comorbid personality disorders, such as schizotypal and borderline, hinder treatment efficacy.

Incomplete Evidence

Although meta-analytic studies find EX/RP superior to cognitive therapy that does not involve behavioural experiments, some individual studies found cognitive therapy with behavioural experiments to be as effective as EX/RP and other did not. This inconsistency is likely due to variability of treatment protocols across studies.

Studies that compare the effects of medication to those of psychological treatments also produce inconsistent results. All studies that used intensive EX/RP revealed its superiority over medication. On the other hand, studies that used watered-down EX/RP programs have failed to show a consistent advantage for EX/RP.

With respect to predictors of outcome, depression was found to hinder outcome on some but not all studies. This inconsistency may be due to a non-linear relationship between depression and treatment outcome, where only extreme depression hinders treatment response.

Areas Still Open to Research

A relatively high number of patients refuse to participate in intensive EX/RP treatment programs for various reasons, one of which is that EX/RP is perceived as threatening and demanding. More studies are needed to elucidate patient's reasons for rejecting treatment and to develop programs that will increase their motivation. Perhaps the optimal treatment for patients who are too frightened to try EX/RP should involve medication at the start, followed by EX/RP implemented after medication has lessened the OCD symptoms and thereby increased the acceptability of EX/RP. Cognitively-focused readiness programs that include psychoeducation, cognitive therapy techniques, and feedback of former OCD patients who completed EX/RP may also prove helpful in increasing the acceptance rate for EX/RP.

Although intensive EX/RP in the hands of experts is extremely powerful, the centers of expertise that conducted most of the available studies may be non-representative, not only with respect to their level of expertise but also in the kinds of patients they attract and accept for treatment. Findings from a large effectiveness study conducted at our center indicated that patients who received EX/RP on a fee-for-service basis outside of carefully controlled research trials were comparable to patients treated in RCTs [101]. However, the question of whether centers not specializing in EX/RP can obtain similar success has yet to be determined. Effectiveness studies that examine the effects of EX/RP expert supervision on OCD patient outcomes in more typical clinical settings are needed to determine the transportability of EX/RP to community-based treatment facilities.

Another issue that must be addressed is the effect of decreasing session frequency while holding other EX/RP variables constant, such as ritual prevention instructions and therapist-assisted exposure. Meta-analytic studies have suggested a relationship between session frequency and symptom reduction, but other differences between the treatment programs (e.g. strictness of ritual prevention instructions, use of therapist-assisted exposure) confound these observations. Market pressures and patients' reluctance often preclude the intensive treatment regimen, so studies comparing twice-weekly EX/RP to the virtually identical program provided in an intensive format may allow us to determine whether the decreased session frequency attenuates outcome substantially. Such an investigation is underway at our center, and similar studies should be conducted before we shift to less intensive (and perhaps less effective) programs simply on practical grounds.

As we discussed in this review, several factors have been found associated with poor outcome. Further investigation on factors that moderate and mediate treatment response is needed to help clinicians determine what type of treatment is likely to help a given patient. A related issue is the influence of treatment choice on outcome. Because most carefully controlled outcome studies use random assignment to treatment conditions, the effect of patients' treatment choices on outcome is obscured. We also have no knowledge of whether a patient who does not respond to his/her first choice (e.g. EX/RP) is likely to respond to a subsequent application of a different treatment modality (e.g. medication). These questions are best addressed using a naturalistic design that includes patient choice of treatment. Because patients treated outside expert clinical research settings typically end up choosing their treatment, studies that incorporate choice will inform us about the generalizability of findings from well-controlled treatment outcome studies to the applied clinical settings where many OCD sufferers receive care.

ACKNOWLEDGEMENTS

This review was supported in part by grant # MH45404 awarded to Dr Foa. The authors would like to thank Constance Hamlin for her assistance with the preparation of the manuscript.

REFERENCES

1. Foa E.B., Steketee G.S., Ozarow B.J. (1985) Behavior therapy with obsessive-compulsives: from theory to treatment. In *Obsessive-Compulsive Disorders: Psychological and Pharmacological Treatments* (Ed. M. Mavissakalian), pp. 49–129, Plenum, New York.
2. Cooper J.E., Gelder M.G., Marks I. M. (1965) Results of behaviour therapy in 77 psychiatric patients. *Br. Med. J.*, **1**: 1222–1225.
3. Beech H. R., Vaughn M. (1978) *Behavioral Treatment of Obsessional States*, Wiley, New York.
4. Gertz H.O. (1966) Experience with the logotherapeutic technique of paradoxical intention in the treatment of phobic and obsessive-compulsive patients. *Am. J. Psychiatry*, **123**: 548–553.
5. Solyom L., Garza-Perez B.L., Ledwidge L., Solyom C. (1972) Paradoxical intention in the treatment of obsessive thoughts: a pilot study. *Compr. Psychiatry*, **13**: 291–297.
6. Noonan J.R. (1971) An obsessive-compulsive reaction treated by induced anxiety. *Am. J. Psychother.*, **25**: 293–295.
7. McCarthy B.W. (1972) Short term implosive therapy: case study. *Psychol. Rep.*, **30**: 589–590.
8. Broadhurst A. (1976) It's never too late to learn: an application of conditioned inhibition to obsessional ruminations in an elderly patient. In *Case Studies in Behaviour Therapy* (Ed. H.J. Eysenck), pp. 173–183, Routledge & Kegan Paul, London.

9. Emmelkamp P.M.G., Kwee K.G. (1977) Obsessional ruminations: a comparison between thought-stopping and prolonged exposure in imagination. *Behav. Res. Ther.*, **15**: 441–444.
10. Stern R.S. (1978) Obsessive thoughts: the problem of therapy. *Br. J. Psychiatry*, **132**: 200–205.
11. Solyom L., Kingstone E. (1973) An obsessive neurosis following morning glory seek ingestion treated by aversion relief. *J. Behav. Ther. Exp. Psychiatry*, **4**: 293–295.
12. Solyom L., Zamanzadeh D., Ledwidge B., Kenny F. (1971) Aversion relief treatment of obsessive neurosis. In *Advances in Behavior Therapy* (Ed. R.D. Rubin), pp. 93–109, Academic Press, New York.
13. Rabavilas A.D., Boulougouris J.C., Stefanis C. (1977) Compulsive checking diminished when over-checking instructions were disobeyed. *J. Behav. Ther. Exper. Psychiatry*, **8**: 111–112.
14. Marks I.M., Crowe E., Drewe E., Young J., Dewhurst W.G. (1969) Obsessive-compulsive neurosis in identical twins. *Br. J. Psychiatry*, **15**: 991–998.
15. Rubin R.D., Merbaum M. (1969) Self-imposed punishment versus desensitization. In *Advances Behavior Therapy* (Eds R.D. Rubin, H. Gensterheim, A.A. Lazarus, C.M. Franks), pp. 85–91, Academic Press, New York.
16. Kenny F.T., Mowbray R.M., Lalani S. (1978) Faradic disruption of obsessive ideation in the treatment of obsessive neurosis: a controlled study. *Behav. Ther.*, **9**: 209–221.
17. LeBoeuf A. (1974) An automated aversion device in the treatment of a compulsive handwashing ritual. *J. Behav. Ther. Exp. Psychiatry*, **5**: 267–270.
18. Wisocki P.A. (1970) Treatment of obsessive-compulsive behavior by covert sensitization and covert reinforcement: a case report. *J. Behav. Ther. Exp. Psychiatry*, **1**: 233–239.
19. Kenny F.T., Solyom L., Solyom C. (1973) Faradic disruption of obsessive ideation in the treatment of obsessive neurosis. *Behav. Ther.*, **4**: 448–451.
20. McGuire R.J., Vallance M. (1964) Aversion therapy by electric shock: a simple technique. *Br. Med. J.*, **1**: 151–153.
21. Gullick E.L., Blanchard E.B. (1973) The use of psychotherapy and behavior therapy in the treatment of an obsessional disorder: an experimental case study. *J. Nerv. Ment. Dis.*, **156**: 427–431.
22. Leger L.A. (1978) Spurious and actual improvement in the treatment of preoccupying thoughts by thought-stopping. *Br. J. Soc. Clin. Psychol.*, **17**: 373–377.
23. Stern R.S. (1970) Treatment of a case of obsessional neurosis using thought-stopping technique. *Br. J. Psychiatry*, **117**: 441–442.
24. Stern R.S., Lipsedge M.S., Marks I.M. (1975) Obsessive ruminations: a controlled trial of thought-stopping technique. *Behav. Res. Ther.*, **11**: 650–662.
25. Meyer V. (1966) Modification of expectations in cases with obsessional rituals. *Behav. Res. Ther.*, **4**: 273–280.
26. Meyer V., Levy R. (1973) Modification of behavior in obsessive-compulsive disorders. In *Issues and Trends in Behavior Therapy* (Eds. H.E. Adams, P. Unikel), pp. 77–136, Thomas, Springfield.
27. Meyer V., Levy R., Schnurer A. (1974) The behavioural treatment of obsessive-compulsive disorders. In *Obsessional States* (Ed. H.R. Beech), pp. 233–258, Methuen, London.
28. Foa E.B., Kozak M.J., Goodman W.K., Hollander E., Jenike M., Rasmussen S. (1995) DSM-IV field trial: obsessive-compulsive disorder. *Am. J. Psychiatry*, **152**: 90–94.

29. Foa E.B., Kozak M.J. (1986) Emotional processing of fear: exposure to corrective information. *Psychol. Bull.*, **99**: 20–35.
30. Foa E.B., Kozak M.J. (1996) Psychological treatment for obsessive-compulsive disorder. In *Long-term Treatments of Anxiety Disorders* (Eds M.R. Mavissakalian, R.F. Prien), pp. 285–309, American Psychiatric Press, Washington, DC.
31. Abramowitz J.S. (1996) Variants of exposure and response prevention in the treatment of obsessive-compulsive disorder: a meta-analysis. *Behav. Ther.*, **27**: 583–600.
32. Christenson H., Hadzi-Pavlovic D., Andrews G., Mattick R. (1987) Behavior therapy and tricyclic medication in the treatment of obsessive-compulsive disorder: a quantitative review. *J. Consult. Clin. Psychol.*, **55**: 701–711.
33. Cox B.J., Swinson R.P., Morrison B., Lee P.S. (1993) Clomipramine, fluoxetine, and behavior therapy in the treatment of obsessive-compulsive disorder: a meta-analysis. *J. Behav. Ther. Exp. Psychiatry*, **24**: 149–153.
34. van Balkom A.J.L., van Oppen P., Vermeulen A.W.A., van Dyck R., Nauta M.C.E., Vorst H.C.M. (1994) A meta-analysis on the treatment of obsessive-compulsive disorder: a comparison of antidepressants, behavior, and cognitive therapy. *Clin. Psychol. Rev.*, **5**: 359–381.
35. Fals-Stewart W., Marks A.P., Schafer J. (1993) A comparison of behavioral group therapy and individual behavior therapy in treating obsessive-compulsive disorder. *J. Nerv. Ment. Dis.*, **181**: 189–193.
36. Kozak M.J., Liebowitz M.R., Foa E.B. (2000) Cognitive behavior therapy and pharmacotherapy for OCD: the NIMH-Sponsored Collaborative Study. In *Treatment Challenges in Obsessive Compulsive Disorder* (Eds W.K. Goodman, M. Rudorfer, J. Maser), pp. 501–530, Erlbaum, Mahwah.
37. Lindsay M., Crino R., Andrews G. (1997) Controlled trial of exposure and response prevention in obsessive-compulsive disorder. *Br. J. Psychiatry*, **171**: 135–139.
38. Foa E., Goldstein A. (1978) Continuous exposure and complete response prevention in the treatment of obsessive-compulsive neurosis. *Behav. Ther.*, **9**: 821–829.
39. Rachman S., Cobb J., Grey S., McDonald B., Mawson D., Sartory G., Stern R. (1979) The behavioural treatment of obsessional-compulsive disorders, with and without clomipramine. *Behav. Res. Ther.*, **17**: 467–478.
40. Rachman S., Hodgson R., Marks I.M. (1971) The treatment of chronic obsessive-compulsive neurosis. *Behav. Res. Ther.*, **9**: 237–247.
41. Foa E.B., Steketee G., Grayson J.B., Turner R.M., Latimer P. (1984) Deliberate exposure and blocking of obsessive-compulsive rituals: immediate and long-term effects. *Behav. Ther.*, **15**: 450–472.
42. Foa E.B., Kozak M.J., Steketee G.S., McCarthy P.R. (1992) Treatment of depressive and obsessive-compulsive symptoms in OCD by imipramine and behavior therapy. *Br. J. Clin. Psychol.*, **31**: 279–292.
43. de Araujo L.A., Ito L.M., Marks I.M., Deale A. (1995) Does imagined exposure to the consequences of not ritualising enhance live exposure for OCD? A controlled study. I. Main outcome. *Br. J. Psychiatry*, **167**: 65–70.
44. Franklin M.E., Kozak M.J., Cashman L., Coles M., Rheingold A., Foa E.B. (1998) Cognitive behavioral treatment of pediatric obsessive compulsive disorder: an open clinical trial. *J. Am. Acad. Child Adolesc. Psychiatry*, **37**: 412–419.
45. Rachman S., Marks I.M., Hodgson R. (1973) The treatment of obsessive-compulsive neurotics by modelling. *Behav. Res. Ther.*, **8**: 383–392.

46. Marks I.M., Lelliott P.T., Basoglu M., Noshirvani H., Monteiro W., Cohen D., Kasvikis Y. (1988) Clomipramine, self-exposure and therapist-aided exposure for obsessive-compulsive rituals. *Br. J. Psychiatry*, **152**: 522–534.
47. Emmelkamp P.M.G., van Kraanen J. (1977) Therapist-controlled exposure *in vivo*: a comparison with obsessive-compulsive patients. *Behav. Res. Ther.*, **15**: 491–495.
48. Ost L.-G. (1989) One-session treatment for specific phobias. *Behav. Res. Ther.*, **27**: 1–7.
49. Kozak M.J., Foa E.B., Steketee G. (1988) Process and outcome of exposure treatment with obsessive-compulsives: psychophysiological indicators of emotional processing. *Behav. Ther.*, **19**: 157–169.
50. Foa E.B., Chambless D.L. (1978) Habituation of subjective anxiety during flooding in imagery. *Behav. Res. Ther.*, **16**: 391–399.
51. Rachman S., DeSilva P., Roper G. (1976) The spontaneous decay of compulsive urges. *Behav. Res. Ther.*, **14**: 445–453.
52. Hodgson R.J., Rachman S., Marks I.M. (1972) The treatment of chronic obsessive-compulsive neurosis: follow-up and further findings. *Behav. Res. Ther.*, **10**: 181–189.
53. March J.S., Mulle K. (1998) *OCD in Children and Adolescents: a Cognitive-Behavioral Treatment Manual*, Guilford, New York.
54. Foa E.B., Steketee G., Turner R.M., Fischer S.C. (1980) Effects of imaginal exposure to feared disasters in obsessive-compulsive checkers. *Behav. Res. Ther.*, **18**: 449–455.
55. Steketee G.S., Foa E.B., Grayson J.B. (1982) Recent advances in the treatment of obsessive-compulsives. *Arch. Gen. Psychiatry*, **39**: 1365–1371.
56. Emmelkamp P.M.G., de Haan E., Hoogduin C.A.L. (1990) Marital adjustment and obsessive-compulsive disorder. *Br. J. Psychiatry*, **156**: 55–60.
57. Mehta M. (1990) A comparative study of family-based and patients-based behavioural management in obsessive-compulsive disorder. *Br. J. Psychiatry*, **157**: 133–135.
58. Enright S.J. (1991) Group treatment for obsessive-compulsive disorder: an evaluation. *Behav. Psychother.*, **19**: 183–192.
59. Beck A.T., Ward C.H., Mendelson M., Mock J.E., Erbaugh J.K. (1961) An inventory for measuring depression. *Arch. Gen. Psychiatry*, **4**: 561–571.
60. Stampfl T.G., Levis D.J. (1967) Essentials of implosive therapy: a learning-theory-based psychodynamic behavioral therapy. *J. Abnorm. Psychol.*, **72**: 496–503.
61. Watts F.N. (1973) Desensitization as an habituation phenomenon: II. Studies of interstimulus interval length. *Psychol. Rep.*, **33**: 715–718.
62. Beck A.T. (1976) *Cognitive Therapy and the Emotional Disorders*, International Universities Press, New York.
63. Emmelkamp P.M.G., van der Helm M., van Zanten B.L., Plochg I. (1980) Treatment of obsessive-compulsive patients: the contribution of self-instructional training to the effectiveness of exposure. *Behav. Res. Ther.*, **18**: 61–66.
64. Meichenbaum D. (1974) Self-instructional methods. In *Helping People Change* (Eds F.H. Kanfer, A.P. Goldstein), pp. 357–392, Pergamon Press, New York.
65. Emmelkamp P.M.G., Visser S., Hoekstra R.J. (1988) Cognitive therapy vs. exposure *in vivo* in the treatment of obsessive-compulsives. *Cogn. Ther. Res.*, **12**: 103–114.
66. Emmelkamp P.M.G., Beens H. (1991) Cognitive therapy with obsessive-compulsive disorder: a comparative evaluation. *Behav. Res. Ther.*, **29**: 293–300.

67. Van Oppen P., de Haan E., Van Balkom A.J.L.M., Spinhoven P., Hoogduin K., van Dyck R. (1995) Cognitive therapy and exposure *in vivo* in the treatment of obsessive compulsive disorder. *Behav. Res. Ther.*, **33**: 379–390.
68. Salkovskis P.M. (1985) Obsessional compulsive problems: a cognitive behavioral analysis. *Behav. Res. Ther.*, **23**: 571–583.
69. Goodman W.K., Price L.H., Rasmussen S.A., Mazure C., Fleischmann R.L., Hill C.L., Heninger G.R., Charney D.S. (1989) The Yale-Brown Obsessive Compulsive Scale: I. Development, use, and reliability. *Arch. Gen. Psychiatry*, **46**: 1006–1011.
70. Hiss H., Foa E.B., Kozak M.J. (1994) Relapse prevention program for treatment of obsessive-compulsive disorder. *J. Consult. Clin. Psychol.*, **62**: 801–808.
71. Abramowitz J.S., Franklin M.E., Foa E.B. (2000) Empirical status of cognitive methods in the treatment of OCD. In *Cognitive Approaches to Treating Obsessions and Compulsions: A Clinical Casebook* (Eds M.H. Freeston, S. Taylor), Erlbaum, Mahwah.
72. March J.S., Leonard H.L. (1998) Obsessive-compulsive disorder in children and adolescents. In *Obsessive-Compulsive Disorder: Theory, Research, and Treatment* (Eds R.P. Swinson, M.M. Antony, S. Rachman, M.A. Richer), pp. 367–394, Guilford, New York.
73. Amin M.D., Ban T.A., Pecknold J.C., Klingner A. (1977) Clomipramine (Anafranil) and behavior therapy in obsessive-compulsive and phobic disorders. *J. Int. Med. Res.*, **5**: 33–37.
74. Cottraux J., Mollard E., Bouvard M., Marks I., Sluys M., Nury A.M., Douge R., Cialdella P. (1990) A controlled study of fluvoxamine and exposure in obsessive-compulsive disorder. *Int. Clin. Psychopharmacol.*, **5**: 17–30.
75. Hembree E.A., Cohen A., Riggs D., Kozak M.J., Foa E.B. (1992) The long-term efficacy of behavior therapy and serotonergic medications in the treatment of obsessive-compulsive ritualizers (unpublished manuscript).
76. Marks I.M., Stern R.S., Mawson D., Cobb J., McDonald R. (1980) Clomipramine and exposure for obsessive-compulsive rituals—I. *Br. J. Psychiatry*, **136**: 1–25.
77. Neziroglu F. (1979) A combined behavioral-pharmacotherapy approach to obsessive-compulsive disorder. In *Biological Psychiatry Today* (Eds J. Oriols, C. Ballus, M. Gonzalez, J. Pujol) pp. 591–596, Elsevier, Amsterdam.
78. Greist J.H. (1992) An integrated approach to treatment of obsessive compulsive disorder. *J. Clin. Psychiatry*, **53** (suppl. 4): 38–41.
79. Foa E.B. (1979) Failure in treating obsessive-compulsives. *Behav. Res. Ther.*, **17**: 169–176.
80. Marks I.M. (1973) New approaches to the treatment of obsessive-compulsive disorder. *J. Nerv. Ment. Dis.*, **156**: 420–426.
81. Buchanan A.W., Meng K.S., Marks I.M. (1996) What predicts improvement and compliance during the behavioral treatment of obsessive compulsive disorder? *Anxiety*, **2**: 22–27.
82. Steketee G., Shapiro L.J. (1995) Predicting behavioral treatment outcome for agoraphobia and obsessive compulsive disorder. *Clin. Psychol. Rev.*, **15**: 317–346.
83. Abramowitz J.S., Franklin M.E., Street G.P., Kozak M.J., Foa E.B. (2000) Effects of pretreatment depression on treatment outcome in OCD. *Behav. Ther.*, in press.
84. Foa E.B., Grayson J.B., Steketee G.S., Doppelt H.G., Turner R.M., Latimer P.R. (1983) Success and failure in the behavioral treatment of obsessive-compulsives. *J. Consult. Clin. Psychol.*, **51**: 287–297.

85. Hoogduin C.A.L., Duivenvoorden H.J. (1988) A decision model in the treatment of obsessive-compulsive neurosis. *Br. J. Psychiatry*, **152**: 516–521.
86. O'Sullivan G., Noshirvani H., Marks I., Monteiro W., Lelliott P. (1991) Six-year follow-up after exposure and clomipramine therapy for obsessive compulsive disorder. *J. Clin. Psychiatry*, **52**: 150–155.
87. Steketee G. (1993) Social support and treatment outcome of obsessive compulsive disorder at 9-month follow-up. *Behav. Psychother.*, **21**: 81–95.
88. Basoglu M., Lax T., Kasvikis Y., Marks I.M. (1988) Predictors of improvement in obsessive-compulsive disorder. *J. Anxiety Disord.*, **2**: 299–317.
89. Cottraux J., Mollard E., Bouvard M., Marks I. (1993) Exposure therapy, fluvoxamine, or combination treatment in obsessive-compulsive disorder: one-year followup. *Psychiatry Res.*, **49**: 63–75.
90. Drummond L.M. (1993) The treatment of severe, chronic, resistant obsessive compulsive disorder: an evaluation of an inpatient program using behavioral psychotherapy in combination with other treatments. *Br. J. Psychiatry*, **163**: 223–229.
91. Boulougouris J. (1977) Variables affecting the behaviour modification of obsessive-compulsive patients treated by flooding. In *The Treatment of Phobic and Obsessive-Compulsive Disorders*, (Eds J.C. Boulougouris, A.D. Rabavilas), pp. 73–84, Pergamon, Oxford.
92. AuBuchon P.G., Malatesta V.J. (1994) Obsessive compulsive patients with comorbid personality disorder: associated problems and response to a comprehensive behavior therapy. *J. Clin. Psychiatry*, **55**: 448–453.
93. Fals-Stewart W., Lucente S. (1993) An MCMI cluster typology of obsessive-compulsives: a measure of personality characteristics and its relationship to treatment participation, compliance and outcome in behavior therapy. *J. Psychiatr. Res.*, **27**: 139–154.
94. Baer L., Jenike M.A., Black D.W., Treece C., Rosenfeld R., Greist J. (1992) Effect of axis II diagnoses on treatment outcome with clomipramine in 55 patients with obsessive-compulsive disorder. *Arch. Gen. Psychiatry*, **49**: 862–866.
95. Jenike M.A., Baer L., Carey R.J. (1986) Coexistent obsessive-compulsive disorder and schizotypal personality disorder: a poor prognostic indicator. *Arch. Gen. Psychiatry*, **43**: 296.
96. Minichiello W.E., Baer L., Jenike M.A. (1987) Schizotypal personality disorder: a poor prognostic indicator for behavior therapy in the treatment of obsessive-compulsive disorder. *J. Anxiety Disord.*, **1**: 273–276.
97. Ravizza L., Barzega G., Bellino S., Bogetto F., Maina G. (1995) Predictors of drug treatment response in obsessive-compulsive disorder. *J. Clin. Psychiatry*, **56**: 368–373.
98. Mavissakalian M., Hamann M.S., Jones B. (1990) DSM-III personality disorders in obsessive-compulsive disorder: changes with treatment. *Compr. Psychiatry*, **31**: 432–437.
99. Lax T., Basoglu M., Marks I.M. (1992) Expectancy and compliance as predictors of outcome in obsessive-compulsive disorder. *Behav. Psychother.*, **20**: 257–266.
100. Keijsers G.P.J., Hoogduin C.A.L., Schaap C.P.D.R. (1994) Predictors of treatment outcome in the behavioural treatment of obsessive-compulsive disorder. *Br. J. Psychiatry*, **165**: 781–786.
101. Franklin M.E., Abramowitz J.S., Kozak M.J., Levitt J.T., Foa E.B. (2000) Effectiveness of exposure and ritual prevention for obsessive compulsive disorder: randomized versus non-randomized samples *J.Consult. Clin. Psychol.*, in press.

Commentaries

3.1
Effective Behavioural Therapy Constrained: Dissemination is the Issue

John H. Greist[1]

Foa and Franklin have written a stellar review of psychological treatments of obsessive-compulsive disorder (OCD). The view that exposure and ritual prevention (ERP) is the present treatment of choice for OCD is inescapable. Although there are gaps in what we know from available studies, several attributes of ERP are clear: (a) onset of improvement is at least as rapid as with potent serotonin reuptake inhibitors (SRIs), the other efficacious treatment for OCD; (b) acute treatment response is at least as great as with SRIs; (c) maintenance of gains is substantially longer than with SRIs.

Other issues are less clear: (a) How many hours of therapist contact are needed to achieve good outcomes? (b) What is the role of therapist assistance? (c) Does combination of behavioural therapy (BT) and SRI provide additive benefit? (d) What has retarded dissemination of BT? (e) Reasons for and corrections of limited availability of ERP.

Amount of therapist contact needed? While amount of therapist contact correlates with benefit in some studies [1], others [2] have not found that therapist contact enhances outcome. In the end, habituation occurs in the patient—not in the therapeutic dyad—and the main role of the therapist may be to persuade the patient to do ERP. Most of us have seen the occasional patient who, given an understanding of the principles of ERP, applies them successfully with little or no additional therapist contact. Some attribute such improvement to a positive transference or identification with the therapist. Regardless of mechanisms, therapist time is expensive and the 45-hour standard treatment of some centers of excellence is not public health practical. Beyond cost barriers, excellent therapists are in short supply and most of what masquerades as BT is a pale facsimile of the real thing.

Combination therapy. Foa's and Liebowitz' ongoing controlled trial of clomipramine (CMI) and BT, alone and in combination, has found no

[1] *Health Care Technology Systems, LLC, 7617 Mineral Point Road, Madison, WI 53717, USA*

significant benefit of combined therapy over BT alone (they also found their BT produced almost twice as much improvement as CMI). Other studies have found the combination beneficial [3–5], raising the possibility that the BT Foa and Liebowitz provide is so robust that medication cannot improve on its gains, while something is lacking in the BT when added medications improve outcome. Of course, many other factors may be involved (sample differences, medications employed, etc.) and the intensive and expensive Foa and Liebowitz study ERP method is probably not financially feasible on a broad scale and has not been widely disseminated more than 15 years after it was elaborated.

What has retarded dissemination of ERP? Many explanations have been offered for the failure of uptake of ERP despite its dramatic efficacy and effectiveness. I have had some success persuading clinicians that SRIs are efficacious for OCD over the 11 years of their availability in the USA, but have failed miserably in spreading the word about ERP's greater benefits over the last 23 years. Misery loves company, but there is meager comfort in knowing I am not alone in this failing. Possible explanations for this disappointing state of affairs include the following: (a) psychotherapists are reluctant to increase patient discomfort in the short term even to gain substantial improvements over the long term; (b) in the era of managed cost (there's very little managed caring going on), a course of psychotherapy costing thousands of dollars is not bottom-line friendly; (c) many patients want ERP but can't find competent behavioural therapists to provide it; (d) enough therapists do enough incompetent ERP that many patients have understandably written off BT; (e) what the heart loves becomes truth. Those imbued with dynamic psychotherapy continue to look for underlying causes, enjoy interpretations of intrapsychic or interpersonal conflicts and distrust symptomatic treatment. Planck was right that in shifting paradigms one does not persuade the older generation to change its ideas, but rather wait until the older generation dies off and a new generation grows up that is familiar with the new concepts.

Reasons for and corrections of limited availability of ERP. Put simply, despite its proven superior efficacy, skilled BT for OCD in the form of ERP is seldom available. It is too costly as presently provided by both excellent and quack behavioural therapists; too frightening for new therapists to learn because it can increase anxiety/discomfort; and it also frightens some patients. We cannot alleviate the last concern for those who fear too much, but we can address the issues of cost and scarcity of effective therapists.

BT STEPS™ is one approach to disseminating standardized yet personalized and interactive ERP. A series of open and controlled trials has found it effective [6–10]. Dissemination is limited only by the availability of the touch-tone telephone system, and patients have already been treated in the USA, Canada, UK and Switzerland, all from a single small computer in Madison, Wisconsin. While slightly less effective in an intent-to-treat analysis than expert behavioural therapists, with whom it was compared in an eight-site trial, BT STEPS™ was as effective as the therapists once patients did even one ERP session, and both treatments were significantly more effective than relaxation control. The dissemination of low-cost ERP for OCD is feasible and, while BT STEPS will not help everyone, it obtains an excellent behavioural assessment from 80% of users that would manifestly assist a behavioural therapist, if one can be found. Another striking advantage of an approach such as BT STEPS™ is that it collects data to evaluate change as the patient participates and is susceptible to systematic manipulations of technique (e.g. adding or deleting specific treatment elements) in ways impossible with human therapists.

Foa and Franklin are to be commended for their clear and compelling exposition describing the excellence of ERP for OCD. They identify issues of technique needing further study. But the larger issue for the field is how to disseminate the benefits proven over the past 35 years.

REFERENCES

1. Abramowitz J.S. (1996) Variants of exposure and response prevention in the treatment of obsessive-compulsive disorder: a meta-analysis. *Behav. Ther.*, **27**: 583–600.
2. van Balkom A.J.L., van Oppen P., Vermeulen A.W.A., van Dyck R., Nauta M.C.E., Vorst H.C.M. (1994) A meta-analysis on the treatment of obsessive-compulsive disorder: a comparison of antidepressants, behavior, and cognitive therapy. *Clin. Psychol. Rev.*, 5: 359–381.
3. Simpson H.B., Gorfinkle K.S., Liebowitz M.R. (1999) Cognitive-behavioral therapy as an adjunct to serotonin reuptake inhibitors in obsessive-compulsive disorder: an open trial. *J. Clin. Psychiatry*, **60**: 584–590.
4. Hohagen F., Winkelmann G., Rasche-Rauchle H., Hand I., Konig A., Munchau N., Hiss H., Geiger-Kabisch D., Kappler C., Schramm P., *et al* (1998) *Br. J. Psychiatry*, **173**: 71–78.
5. Neziroglu F. (1998) Integration of behavior therapy with medications. Presented at the Third International Obsessive-Compulsive Disorder Conference, Madeira, September 11–13.
6. Bachofen M., Nakagawa A., Marks I.M., Park J.M., Greist J.H., Baer L., Wenzel K.W., Parkin J.R., Dottl S.L. (1999) Home self-assessment and self-treatment of obsessive-compulsive disorder using a manual and a computer-conducted telephone interview: replication of a UK–US study. *J. Clin. Psychiatry*, **60**: 545–549.
7. Greist J.H., Marks I.M., Baer L., Parkin J.R., Manzo P.A., Mantle J.M., Wenzel K.W., Spierings C.J., Kobak K.A., Dottl S.L. *et al* (1998) Self-treatment for obsessive compulsive disorder using a manual and a computerized telephone interview: a US–UK study. *MD Comput.*, **15**: 149–157.

8. Greist J.H. (1998) Treatment for all: the computer as a patient assistant. *Psychiatr. Serv.*, **49**: 887–889.
9. Marks I.M., Baer L., Greist J.H., Park J.M., Bachofen M., Nakagawa A., Wenzel K.W., Parkin J.R., Manzo P.A., Dottl S.L. *et al* (1998) Home self-assessment of obsessive-compulsive disorder. *Am. J. Psychiatry*, **172**: 406–412.
10. Baer L., Greist J.H. (1997) An interactive computer-administered self-assessment and self-help program for behavior therapy. *J. Clin. Psychiatry*, **58** (suppl. 12): 23–28.

3.2
Can We Enhance the Effects of Cognitive-Behavioural Therapy in Obsessive-Compulsive Disorder?

Paul M.G. Emmelkamp[1]

The scholarly review of Foa and Franklin attests to the effectiveness of cognitive-behavioural therapy (CBT) in patients with obsessive-compulsive disorder (OCD). However, on the negative side, not all patients improve with CBT, a number of patients drop out of CBT treatment, and some patients relapse after successful treatment. The ability to predict post-treatment response on indices of pre-treatment condition is likely to have considerable clinical utility. Unfortunately, as described by Foa and Franklin, prediction of outcome at the moment is far from impressive.

Does personality disorder predict worse outcome? Research reviewed by Foa and Franklin suggests that comorbid personality disorder of any kind is predictive of poor outcome of CBT. In a recent study [1] there was some evidence that only cluster A personality disorder predicted success of treatment. However, personality disorder status was based on self-report, rather than on a structured interview. In the best study to date, Dreessen *et al* [2] found that OCD patients with a personality disorder measured by means of the Structured Clinical Interview for DSM-III-R (SCID)-II improved after CBT to an equal extent as patients without a personality disorder.

Does the relationship with the therapist affect treatment outcome? Findings of treatment efficacy could be enhanced by the identification of early treatment variables which might act as predictors of success of treatment. In this respect, research into the therapeutic relationship is of some importance.

[1] *University of Amsterdam, Department of Clinical Psychology, Roetersstraat 15, 1018 WB Amsterdam, The Netherlands*

Within the area of CBT, the therapeutic relationship has received little attention. Hoogduin *et al* [3] reported two studies on OCD patients in which significant correlations were found between the therapeutic relationship, assessed with the Barrett–Lennard Relationship Questionnaire (BLRQ) and outcome of exposure and response prevention. However, the BLRQ was based on a therapeutic relationship other than the behavioural orientation, i.e. the client-centered point of view. Another study [4] examined to what extent the Therapist Client Rating Scale (TCRS) could predict outcome of exposure and response prevention in OCD patients. The TCRS was constructed to assess the therapeutic relationship in behavioural therapy. A significant relationship was found between positive regard and patients' improvement in feelings of discomfort and anxiety when entering a (previously) anxiety-provoking situation. These findings indicate that patient–therapist interpersonal behaviour—even in standardized exposure/response prevention programs—is of some importance in regard to a favourable therapy outcome with CBT for OCD complaints, although it does not explain much of the variance in outcome.

Can we enhance treatment outcome by individualized treatment? A related issue is whether it is necessary to provide individualized treatment. Despite the generally good response to exposure and response prevention, some clinicians are reluctant to treat patients with a standardized program. A number of behavioural therapists rely heavily on the importance of a functional behavioural analysis. However, in the outcome research described by Foa and Franklin, a functional analysis was not made, but patients were randomly assigned to treatment conditions. Emmelkamp *et al* [5] investigated the value of an individualized treatment approach based on a functional behavioural analysis, as compared to that of a standardized exposure and response prevention program. Results revealed that both treatment formats resulted in highly significant improvements on obsessive-compulsive problems, and the tailor-made treatment was not more effective than the standardized exposure and response prevention program. The results confirm previous findings that exposure and response prevention is not only effective in reducing obsessive-compulsive problems, but may also result in generalized improvements in depressed mood, social anxiety and psychopathology, even though therapy focuses exclusively on obsessive-compulsive targets.

Can we prevent drop-out and relapse? One of the challenges for the future is to prevent drop-out and relapse. We have reasons to believe that patients who are improved with respect to anxiety and ritualizing, but not to their underlying cognitions, are vulnerable to relapse. In the relapse prevention model of OCD [6] it is assumed that, although OCD patients may have become symptom-free after successful CBT treatment, sooner or later they will be confronted with stressful situations that pose a threat to their sense of control. The model predicts that the more stress the patient experiences after treatment, the more he lacks adequate social support, and the more he is exposed to high levels of expressed emotion, the more likely he will relapse. Coping strategies, life events and daily hassles, and expressed emotion by relatives were all found to be significantly related to relapse at follow-up [6].

A recent study [7] found that expressed emotion, especially hostility, by the relative of a patient was related to dropout of treatment and to worse outcome. When relatives were hostile, the odds were six times greater that patients would drop out than when relatives were not hostile. Taking the results of these studies [6, 7] together, it might be therapeutically wise to involve hostile relatives early in the treatment. Although the inclusion of the spouse has not led to improved treatment outcome [8, 9], the more recent results of studies into expressed emotion in OCD [6, 7] suggest that with patients living with a hostile relative, it might be therapeutically wise to provide the couple with training in communication skills in order to prevent drop-out, enhance treatment response and prevent relapse.

Finally, it is becoming increasingly clear that meta-cognition is of paramount importance in OCD, and there is also some evidence that specific beliefs are related to specific obsessive-compulsive behaviour [10]. As noted by Foa and Franklin, cognitive therapy has not been found to be superior to exposure and response prevention. However, it is tempting to assume that cognitive therapy may have an additional value. By changing the irrational cognitions and dysfunctional assumptions, cognitive therapy may make OCD patients less vulnerable to relapse. Further studies along these lines are clearly needed.

REFERENCES

1. De Haan E., van Oppen P., van Balkom A.J.L.M., Spinhoven P., Hoogduin K.A.L., van Dyck R. (1997) Prediction of outcome and early vs. late improvement in OCD patients treated with cognitive behaviour therapy and pharmacotherapy. *Acta Psychiatr. Scand.*, **96**: 354–361.
2. Dreessen L., Hoekstra R., Arntz A. (1997) Personality disorders do not influence the results of cognitive and behavior therapy for obsessive compulsive disorder. *J. Anxiety Disord.*, **11**: 503–521.
3. Hoogduin K.A.L., De Haan E., Schaap C. (1989) The significance of the patient–therapist relationship in the treatment of obsessive-compulsive neurosis. *Br. J. Clin. Psychol.*, **28**: 185–186.
4. Blaauw E., Emmelkamp P.M.G. (1994) The therapeutic relationship: a study on the value of the Therapist Client Rating Scale. *Behav. Cogn. Psychother.*, **22**: 25–35.

5. Emmelkamp P.M.G., Bouman T.K., Blaauw E. (1994) Indvidualized versus standardized therapy: a comparative evaluation with obsessive-compulsive patients. *Clin. Psychol. Psychother.*, **1**: 95–100.
6. Emmelkamp P.M.G., Kloek J., Blaauw E. (1992) Obsessive-compulsive disorder. In *Principles and Practice of Relapse Prevention* (Ed. P.H. Wilson), pp. 213–234, Guilford, New York.
7. Chambless D., Steketee, G. (1999) Expressed emotion and behavior therapy outcome: a prospective study with obsessive-compulsive and agoraphobic patients. *J. Consult. Clin. Psychol.*, **67**: 658–665.
8. Emmelkamp P.M.G., De Haan E., Hoogduin K.A.L. (1990) Marital adjustment and obsessive-compulsive disorder. *Br. J. Psychiatry*, **156**: 55–60.
9. Emmelkamp P.M.G., Gerlsma C. (1994) Marital functioning and the anxiety disorders. *Behav. Ther.*, **25**: 407–429.
10. Emmelkamp P.M.G., Aardema A. (1999) Metacognition, specific obsessive-compulsive beliefs and obsessive-compulsive behaviour. *Clin. Psychol. Psychother.*, **6**, 139–145.

3.3 Obsessive-Compulsive Disorder: Symptom-directed Behavioural Techniques and Beyond

Iver Hand[1]

Obsessive-compulsive disorder (OCD) has always been a major research topic in behavioural therapy. More than 90% of the published studies have dealt with the development and refinement of *symptom-directed techniques*, usually regarded as the essence of behavioural treatments for OCD. Foa and Franklin give a comprehensive review of this process, from the very first individual treatment attempts to the most recent variations of exposure–response prevention (EX/RP; in the literature usually ERP), including family involvement, group application, and the combination with drug treatment. This commentary will address specific aspects of the symptom-directed approach, with additional clinical recommendations based on our own *multi-modal, systemic-strategic behavioural approach to* OCD [1].

The quoted responder rates of 76% and 83% for EX/RP should be interpreted with some caution: most publications are vague regarding content and intensity of additional "unspecific" interventions (other than EX/RP) during the treatment and follow-up periods; the operationalization of "response" varies between studies; outcome and follow-up studies rarely give sufficient information about the drop-outs from intake assessment to last follow-up; research programs require patients to comply with

[1] *Behaviour Therapy Unit, Clinic for Psychiatry and Psychotherapy, University Hospital Eppendorf/ Hamburg, Martinistrasse 52, D-20246 Hamburg, Germany*

complex assessments (which many OCD patients cannot or will not do). In our follow-up study with unselected OCD patients, we found a responder rate of 50% of the follow-up participants. A re-analysis of data only from those patients who had complied with all assessments increased our responder rate to around 75% ![2]. This may imply that OCD patients who fit all research requirements are a less disturbed subgroup.

We have developed a modification of EX/RP. During exposure (with "prevention" of the motor avoidance response), patients often experience increasing emotional, cognitive or physiological responses. In our approach, this may then be used for a more in-depth analysis of "underlying causes" and/or for a training in active coping with intense emotions (exposure response-management, ERM). Depending on the individual patient's condition, exposure may thus go beyond the extinction paradigm.

In severely disturbed patients, additional interventions—as part of multimodal behavioural therapy for OCD—typically concern one or more of the following problems: early social deficits and social phobia, with low self-esteem; reduced tolerance for intense emotions; reduced emotional awareness (anhedonia, alexithymia); deficits in problem solving; deficits in self-initiated alternative behaviour (often a life-long problem); interactional and other traumata in the biography.

Foa and Franklin emphasize the importance of "daily exposure homework" to achieve optimal effects with EX/RP. This is a very important point, and the following additional measures during self-exposure are strongly recommended: providing the possibility for immediate telephone contact with the therapist; use of self-help manuals [3]; use of a CD-ROM computer-dialogue program, animated with voice-feedback and cartoons [4]; video-documentation of self-exposure for subsequent joint discussion with the therapist in his office. Most recently, a self-help computer program, accessible via the home telephone, has been found to be very effective [5, 6].

The importance of spouse or family involvement in the context of exposure treatment cannot be evaluated from the currently available research data, as Foa and Franklin conclude. Yet, suffering in couples or families with a long history of OCD is very high. In classical behavioural therapy, family members are regarded as potential "co-therapists" in exposure homework. For some couples/families (especially when a child is the patient) this is helpful. For others it is clearly counterproductive, particularly when there are negative interpersonal consequences of OCD or when the other family members themselves suffer from severe impairments. These are then rather to be treated as "co-patients". In families with chronic OCD it is often useful to combine individual, couple and family interventions (see clinical examples in [7]).

Foa and Franklin's review of group treatment with ERP implies that this has not been widely employed in OCD. Its effectiveness probably depends on the selection of patients who are less disturbed—without severe social deficits, personality disorders, or severe comorbid depression. Yet, a variety of other group approaches to OCD are now available. Some include training of social competence and problem solving (sometimes with partial integration of relatives), additionally to ERP. Others aim at improving the quality of life in chronically ill patients (for a recent review of published group treatments, see [8]). Finally, there are now efficient (often behaviourally-oriented) self-help groups for OCD in several countries. "Clinical judgement" and experts' availability do currently guide the recommendations to participate in one or the other mode.

Does "cognitive therapy" enhance the effectiveness of EX/RP? Foa and Franklin's criticism regarding faulty designs in the comparative studies are fully supported: there is no convincing evidence for additional benefits [1].

Does drug treatment enhance the effects of behavioural therapy? A recent multicentre study (for details, see Hohagen, this volume) supports Foa and Franklin's conclusion that there is little evidence for a general superiority of combined treatments. Results indicate that even patients with severe, chronic OCD profit profoundly from intensive, inpatient, multimodal behavioural therapy. Additional medication only enhances effectiveness in patients with predominant obsessions or with compulsions complicated by severe initial depression. Short-term intensive behavioural therapy is expensive—but so is the necessarily long-term selective serotonin reuptake inhibitor (SSRI) treatment!

Further improvement in the treatment of OCD probably depends on the identification of OCD subgroups for specific modifications of the current behavioural (and drug) interventions. Ongoing research in the following areas may be helpful: (a) comorbidity on Axis I and Axis II; personality variables; biological variables (brain imaging techniques or neuropsychological tests); chronic vs. intermittent course of OCD [9]; (b) specification of intra-individual consequences of OCD and OC-spectrum disorders (many patients "confess" positive expected immediate consequences of OCD behaviour, in spite of long-term negative consequences [10]); (c) specification of treatment-relevant inter-individual (interactional) consequences of OCD (the most common is the "use" of OC behaviour as a weapon in marital or family feuds, whenever the patient feels unable to defend his or her autonomy otherwise); (d) the role of "magical thinking" as a basic coping mechanism with anxiety or other negative emotions in the normal population and in religions (particularly patients with touching, counting and repeating rituals have strong magical beliefs that maintain their compulsions).

The necessary intensity, complexity, and duration of behavioural interventions for OCD vary greatly from patient to patient. Our current clinical guidelines still need more research evidence as to "when to apply what to whom". Hopefully, this research will lead to a more "evidence-based" tailoring of individual, multimodal treatment strategies for OCD patients and their social surroundings. This will also increase the effectiveness of ERM or EX/RP and its various modifications.

REFERENCES

1. Hand I. (1998) Outpatient, multi-modal behavior therapy for obsessive-compulsive disorder. *Br. J. Psychiatry*, **173** (suppl. 35): 45–52.
2. Lacher M. (1989) Langzeiteffekte von Kurzzeit-Verhaltenstherapie bei Zwangsneurotikern. Diploma thesis, Institute of Psychology, University of Hamburg.
3. Foa E., Wilson R. (1991) *Stop Obsessing. Self-help for Obsessions and Compulsions*, Bantam Books, New York.
4. Wölk C. (1999) "Brainy"—a Talking, Virtual Co-therapist for Exposure Homework. CD-ROM (in German).
5. Clark A., Kirkby K.C., Daniels B.A., Marks I.M. (1998) A pilot study of computer-aided vicarious exposure for obsessive-compulsive disorder. *Austral. N. Z. J. Psychiatry*, **32**: 268–275.
6. Marks I.M. (1999) Computer aids to mental health care. *Can. J. Psychiatry*, **44**: 548–555.
7. Hand I. (1988) Obsessive-compulsive patients and their families. In *Handbook of Behavioral Family Therapy* (Ed. Falloon I.R.H.), pp. 231–256, Guildford, New York.
8. Grabe H.J., Welter-Werner E., Freiberger H.J. (1999) Obsessive-compulsive disorder and comorbidity—results from a 12-months behavioral group therapy. *Verhaltenstherapie*, **9**: 132–139.
9. Nelson E., Rice J. (1997) Stability of diagnosis of obsessive-compulsive disorder in the Epidemiological Catchment Area study. *Am. J. Psychiatry*, **154**: 826–831.
10. Hand I. (1988) Pathological gambling: a negative state model and its implication for behavioral treatments. *CNS Spectrums*, **3**: 58–71.

3.4
Is the Combination of Antidepressants with Cognitive-Behavioural Therapy the Most Potent Treatment Possibility in Obsessive-Compulsive Disorder?

Anton J.L.M. van Balkom[1]

Confronted with a patient suffering from obsessive-compulsive disorder (OCD), it is important for the clinician to know which treatment he should

[1] *Department of Psychiatry, Vrije Universiteit, Valeriusplein 9, 1075 BG Amsterdam, The Netherlands*

offer. Due to the numerous randomised controlled trials on treatment outcome in OCD that have been published in the last decades, the clinician is now able to base this clinical decision on scientific knowledge. Effective treatments for OCD consist mainly of cognitive-behavioural therapy (CBT) and antidepressants. Although many patients do improve, few actually become asymptomatic. In order to maximize the treatment effect, clinicians frequently combine antidepressants and CBT. But, as Foa and Franklin point out, the scientific grounds for the use of this combination as the treatment of choice in OCD are surprisingly thin. Up to now, six combination studies have been carried out [1–6], which are briefly summarized in Table 3.4.1.

The short-term results of three studies [1, 2, 5] indicate some superior effect of the combination treatment. In contrast, three studies [3, 4, 6] concluded that the effect of CBT was not augmented by the addition of antidepressants.

One study with inpatients concluded that the combination of CBT with fluvoxamine was superior to the combination with placebo [5]. In a study with clomipramine, the combination was superior for the subgroup of depressed OCD patients only [1]. In another study with clomipramine, however, no association with a concomitant depression was found [2]; patients treated with the combination improved more quickly, but after 4 months of treatment the difference with CBT alone disappeared. This study found a superior effect of the combination over clomipramine alone. Thus, the effect of antidepressants in OCD may be increased by the addition of CBT, but the effect of CBT is not increased by the addition of antidepressants.

Five studies have presented naturalistic follow-up data, ranging from 0.5 to 6 years [4, 7–10]. In all these follow-up studies any differences that were found at post-test disappeared. The improvement measured at post-test was maintained at follow-up, even after tapering off the medications. Since OCD has a relapse rate of almost 100% after stopping antidepressants, these data indicate that relapse after stopping pharmacological treatment may be prevented by the addition of CBT before tapering off the medication.

We can conclude that the combination treatment has no great advantages over treatment with CBT alone in the long run. In our opinion, based on these data, the clinician should treat his non-depressed OCD patient initially with CBT. However, we need more research into the most optimal treatment for our patients. First, it should be noted that most research into the combination treatment has been performed with patients suffering from compulsions. This means that we do not know whether patients with obsessions *alone* might benefit more from the combination treatment (e.g. antidepressants with cognitive therapy). Second, research into treatment

Table 3.4.1 Design and results of combination (cognitive-behavioural therapy + antidepressants) studies in obsessive-compulsive disorder

Study	Patients included/ completed (*n*)	Design	Duration (weeks)	Results
Marks *et al* [1]	48/40	CLM + EX/RP CLM + REL PLA + EX/RP PLA + REL	36	CLM > PLA for most depressed patients EX/RP > REL
Marks *et al* [2]	55/49	CLM + Anti-EX/RP CLM + Self-EX/RP CLM + Ther-EX/RP PLA + Self-EX/RP	27	CLM + EX/RP = PLA + EX/RP CLM + EX/RP > CLM + Anti-EX/RP CLM + Self-EX/RP = CLM + Ther-EX/RP
Cottraux *et al* [3]	60/44	FLU + Anti-EX/RP FLU + EX/RP PLA + EX/RP	24	No differences
Foa *et al* [4]	48/38	IMI + EX/RP HD IMI + EX/RP MD PLA + EX/RP HD PLA + EX/RP MD	22	No differences
Hohagen *et al* [5]	60/58	FLU + EX/RP + COG PLA + EX/RP + COG	10	FLU + EX/RP + COG > PLA + EX/RP + COG
van Balkom *et al* [6]	99/70	FLU + COG FLU + EX/RP COG EX/RP	16	No differences

CLM, clomipramine; PLA, placebo; FLU, fluvoxamine; IMI, imipramine; EX/RP, exposure *in vivo* with response prevention; REL, relaxation; Anti-EX, anti-exposure instructions; Self-EX, self-controlled exposure; Ther-EX, therapist-controlled exposure; COG, cognitive therapy; HD, highly depressed; MD, mildly depressed.

specific predictors must be carried out. We do not know whether OCD subgroups should be treated with special treatments. Finally, we must have data on the efficacy of treatment protocols. We do not know how best to treat non-responders. Such research would identify the logical order of treatments, so as to ensure an optimal treatment for our patients.

REFERENCES

1. Marks I.M., Stern R.S., Mawson D., Cobb J., McDonald R. (1980) Clomipramine and exposure for obsessive-compulsive rituals. *Br. J. Psychiatry*, **136**: 1–25.
2. Marks I.M., Lelliott P., Basoglu M., Noshirvani H., Monteiro W., Cohen D., Kasvikis Y. (1988) Clomipramine, self-exposure and therapist-aided exposure for obsessive-compulsive rituals. *Br. J. Psychiatry*, **152**: 522–534.
3. Cottraux J., Mollard E., Bouvard M., Marks I.M., Sluys M., Nury A.M., Douge R., Cialdella P. (1990) A controlled study of fluvoxamine and exposure in obsessive-compulsive disorder. *Int. Clin. Psychopharmacol.*, **5**: 17–30.
4. Foa E.B., Kozak M.J., Steketee G.S., McCarthy P.R. (1992) Treatment of depressive and obsessive-compulsive symptoms in OCD by imipramine and behaviour therapy. *Br. J. Clin. Psychol.*, **31**: 279–292.
5. Hohagen F., Winkelmann G., Rasche-Räuchle H., Hand I., König A., Münchau N., Hiss H., Geiger-Kabisch C., Käppler C., Schramm P. *et al* (1998) Combination of behaviour therapy with fluvoxamine in camparison with behaviour therapy and placebo. Results from a multicentre study. *Br. J. Psychiatry*, **173** (suppl. 35): 71–78.
6. van Balkom A.J.L.M., de Haan E., van Oppen P., Spinhoven P., Hoogduin C.A.L., van Dyck R. (1998) Cognitive-behavioural therapy versus the combination with fluvoxamine in the treatment of obsessive-compulsive disorder. *J. Nerv. Ment. Dis.*, **186**: 492–499.
7. O'Sullivan G., Noshirvani H., Marks I.M., Monteiro W., Lelliott P. (1990) Six-year follow-up after exposure and clomipramine therapy for obsessive-compulsive disorder. *J. Clin. Psychiatry*, **52**: 150–155.
8. Kasvikis Y., Marks I.M. (1988) Clomipramine, self-exposure, and therapist-accompanied exposure in obsessive-compulsive ritualizers: two-year follow-up. *J. Anxiety Disord.*, **2**: 291–298.
9. Cottraux J., Mollard E., Bouvard M., Marks I.M. (1993) Exposure therapy, fluvoxamine, or combination treatment in obsessive-compulsive disorder: one year follow-up. *Psychiatry Res.*, **49**: 63–75.
10. de Haan E., van Oppen P., van Balkom A.J.L.M., Spinhoven P., Hoogduin C.A.L., van Dyck R. (1997) Prediction of outcome and early versus late improvement in OCD patients treated with cognitive behaviour therapy and pharmacotherapy. *Acta Psychiatr. Scand.*, **96**: 354–362.

3.5 Cognitive Therapy and Behavioural Therapy in Obsessive-Compulsive Disorder: in Search of the Process

Jean Cottraux[1]

It has been a pleasure for me to read the review by Foa and Franklin. One first remark concerns the absence of any kind of reference to psychodynamic treatments: an unpredictable omission 25 years ago. This may represent the ultimate victory of Janet over Freud. Janet [1, 2] was the first to describe exposure and response prevention (ERP) in obsessive-compulsive disorder (OCD), and also proposed a psychological model with cognitive interventions.

Nowadays, behavioural therapy (BT) is firmly established. A recent meta-analysis [3], including 77 studies with 4651 patients, showed that BT was superior to selective serotonin reuptake inhibitors (SSRIs) as a class. Nevertheless, this difference should be taken with caution, as BT is limited by the problem of availability, accessibility and third-party payment in many countries. The status of cognitive therapy (CT) is still under investigation. Some new studies recently came out (Table 3.5.1), completing the picture presented by Foa and Franklin.

The French multicenter study [8] compared CT with intensive BT. Sixty-five ambulatory patients with DSM-IV OCD and without major depression were randomized into two groups for a 16-week psychological treatment in

TABLE 3.5.1 Controlled studies of cognitive therapy (CT) in obsessive-compulsive disorder

- *CT vs. BT*
  Emmelkamp *et al* [4]: self-instructional training + ERP = ERP (follow-up 6 months)
  Emmelkamp *et al* [5]: CT = ERP on rituals; CT > ERP on depression (follow-up 6 months)
  Emmelkamp and Beens *et al* [6]: CT = ERP (follow-up 6 months)
  Van Oppen *et al* [7]: CT > ERP (post-test)
  Cottraux *et al* [8]: CT = ERP on rituals; CT > ERP on depression (post-test)
- *CT vs. a waiting list*
  Freeston *et al* [9]: CBT > waiting list (follow-up 6 months) in pure obsessions
  Jones *et al* [10]: CT > waiting list at post-test only. No difference at 3-month follow-up.
- *CT vs. fluvoxamine*
  Van Balkom *et al* [11]: ERP, CT or fluvoxamine combined with ERP or CT: same positive outcomes at 16 weeks. Active treatments are better than a waiting list at week 8.

BT, behavioural therapy; ERP, exposure and response prevention.

[1] *Unité de Traitement de l'Anxiété, Hôpital Neurologique, 59 Boulevard Pinel, 69394 Lyon, France*

three centres. Group 1 received CT; group 2 received ERP over a 4-week intensive treatment period, followed by a maintenance phase of 12 weeks. No medication was prescribed. Both groups had 20 hours of therapist contact time. A first analysis showed that baseline variables were balanced in the two groups, except for outcome expectations, which were higher in CT ($p = 0.05$). Sixty-two patients were evaluated at week 16, and 48 were present at week 52. At week 16, the rates of responders were similar in the two groups. Depression (as assessed by the Beck Depression Inventory) was significantly more improved in the group which received CT ($p = 0.005$). Improvement in depression was correlated with expectations in BT but not in CT. At weeks 26 and 52, improvement was retained in both groups without between-group difference. In conclusion, CT and BT were equally effective on OCD. Cognitive measures of obsessions changed equally in the two groups. CT had specific effects on depression, which were stronger than those of BT at post-test. This study replicates on a larger scale Emmelkamp *et al*'s [5] findings. Further analyses will include a 2-year follow-up and a study of process and predictive variables.

REFERENCES

1. Janet P. (1903) *Les Obsessions et la Psychasthénie*, Alcan, Paris.
2. Janet P. (1919) *Les Médications Psychologiques*, Alcan, Paris.
3. Kobak K.A., Greist J.H., Jefferson J.W., Katzlenick D.J., Henk H.J. (1998) Behavioral versus pharmacological treatments of obsessive-compulsive disorder. *Psychopharmacology*, **136**: 205–216.
4. Emmelkamp P., Van der Helm M., Van Zanten B., Plochg I. (1980) Contribution of self-instructional training to the effectiveness of exposure *in vivo*: a comparison with obsessive-compulsive patients. *Behav. Res. Ther.*, **18**: 61–66.
5. Emmelkamp P., Visser S., Hoekstra R.J. (1988) Cognitive therapy versus *in vivo* exposure in the treatment of obsessive-compulsive patients. *Cogn. Ther. Res.*, **12**: 103–114.
6. Emmelkamp P., Beens H. (1991) Cognitive therapy with obsessive-compulsive disorder: a comparative evaluation. *Behav. Res. Ther.*, **29**: 293–300.
7. Van Oppen P., de Hann E., van Balkom A.J., Spinhoven P., Hogduin K., Van Dyck R. (1995) Cognitive therapy and exposure *in vivo* in the treatment of obsessive-compulsive disorder. *Behav. Res. Ther.*, **33**: 379–390.
8. Cottraux J., Note I., Dartigues J.F., Note B., Sauteraud A., Mollard E., Dubroca B., Bourgeois M. (1998) A multicenter controlled trial of cognitive therapy versus intensive behaviour therapy. Presented at the Third International Obsessive-Compulsive Disorder Conference, Madeira, September 10–12.
9. Freeston M.H., Ladouceur R., Gagnon F., Thibodeau N., Rhéaume J., Letarte H., Bujold A. (1997) Cognitive-behavioral treatment of obsessive thoughts: a controlled study. *J. Consult. Clin. Psychol.*, **65**: 405–413.
10. Jones M.K., Menzies R.G. (1998) Danger ideation reduction therapy (DIRT) for obsessive compulsive washers. Controlled trial. *Behav. Res. Ther.*, **36**: 959–970.

11. van Balkom A.J.L.M, De Haan E., Van Oppen P., Spinhoven P., Hogduin K.A.L., Van Dyck R. (1998) Cognitive and behavioral therapies alone or in combination with fluvoxamine in the treatment of obsessive-compulsive disorder. *J. Nerv. Ment. Dis.*, **186**: 492–498.

3.6
Obsessional Problems: Newer Cognitive-Behavioural Approaches Are a Work in Progress

Paul M. Salkovskis[1]

The crucial importance of exposure and response prevention (ERP) is clear from Foa and Franklin's comprehensive review of treatment of obsessional problems. As they point out, the behavioural techniques which are now so widely practised originally emerged from the somewhat haphazard admixture of treatment techniques and theory which characterized early attempts at behavioural treatment of obsessive-compulsive disorder (OCD). ERP subsequently became the mainstay of psychological treatment in the mid-1970s, as behavioural theory developed and matured, driven by the systematic synthesis of experimental and outcome studies. There was also some interplay with the parallel development occurring in pharmacological treatment for obsessional problems. The signs are that we again find ourselves at a similar stage, with the development of the new and integrated cognitive-behavioural approaches to the understanding of OCD (which have emerged from and overtaken older "cognitive restructuring" approaches) offering not only a much clearer theoretical understanding but also the possibility of yet more effective and efficient treatments. These developments are in turn fuelled by high quality clinical-experimental studies, which also echo the earlier development of ERP. The final similarity with developments occurring in the mid-1970s lies in the possible integration with new neuroscience approaches which do not depend on simple "lesion" models of obsessional problems.

ERP as currently practised had its clear experimental justification in an elegant series of clinical experimental studies carried out by Rachman and his colleagues [1]. These studies were designed to test the two-process conditioning theory, which still forms the guiding principle for standard ERP. Obsessional patients were asked to provoke the urge to ritualize in the laboratory; it was then demonstrated that ritualizing was, as expected, associated with an immediate reduction in anxiety. A similar degree of

[1] *University of Oxford Department of Psychiatry, Warneford Hospital, Oxford, OX3 7JX, UK*

anxiety reduction was noted over a longer period in patients who refrained from ritualizing. This latter phenomenon, known as spontaneous decay, firmly established the clinical and scientific basis of ERP. Rachman, Marks and others (including Foa) went on to clarify these experimental effects in the context of treatment. ERP as a treatment was refined and developed, culminating in the excellent results summarized in Foa and Franklin's review. However, even in its present refined form, and even when exposure is at maximal levels and response prevention is virtually total, not only are engagement and compliance major problems, but also the extent and endurance of improvement is incomplete. Furthermore, treatment is time-consuming and therefore expensive. Clearly, if ERP has reached limits, the need is for theoretical and clinical refinement.

Other experiments from Rachman's group (using similar methodology to the spontaneous decay experiments, but in the patients' own homes rather than the laboratory) demonstrated that the elicitation of discomfort by obsession-triggering stimuli was substantially blocked by the presence of the experimeter during the provocation phase. It was concluded that it is probably crucial for the patient to carry out a large variety of self-directed and self-monitored tasks outside the treatment sessions. This suggestion anticipated the current emphasis on self-directed exposure, and provides a clear empirical basis for such procedures. It also highlighted the possible importance of responsibility beliefs as a mediator between the occurrence of obsessional thinking and the development of ritualizing. Building on this work, cognitive researchers have developed cognitive-behavioural approaches to understanding and treating obsessional problems. Such an approach, which is in its infancy, suggests that, to be fully effective, cognitive-behavioural treatment requires a fully integrated procedure. Therapy begins with a detailed formulation in which patient and therapist reach a shared understanding of the problem in a way which provides the patient with a credible alternative view of his problems, couched in normalizing terms. The therapist then helps the patient to actively test this alternative, less threatening explanation of his problems by carefully interwoven discussion techniques and behavioural experiments [2].

To exclude behavioural components of such a treatment would be entirely inappropriate, as would the mechanistic addition of "cognitive restructuring" to an essentially behavioural treatment. Discussing dysfunctional thinking and mistaken beliefs during exposure sessions is unlikely to have any additional impact without the framework which would allow the patient to take advantage of these techniques. It is instructive to note the evolution of cognitive-behavioural treatments for panic, which has followed a similar course, with initial work focusing on adding a component of "cognitive restructuring" meeting relatively little success prior to the development of fully integrated cognitive-behavioural approaches [3].

Special considerations apply to the specific cognitive theory of obsessional problems. It is hypothesized that OCD results from the way in which the person interprets the occurrence and/or content of *intrusive thoughts, images, impulses and doubts*, and that obsessional thoughts often focus on fears for which the focus may be far in the future (e.g. that blasphemous thoughts will result in one burning in hell for the rest of eternity), and that these are therefore not subject to disconfirmation in ways which might be possible for other anxiety disorders, such as panic. Such considerations mean that therapy has to be conducted with a major emphasis on validation of a less threatening explanation of the person's problems as opposed to exposure to corrective information intended to disconfirm his fears. Doing this requires that both therapist and patient develop a thorough (and normalizing) shared understanding of the cognitive-behavioural theory as it applies to the specific obsessional problems experienced.

Two conclusions might be drawn from the present analysis of the understanding and treatment of obsessional problems. Firstly, cognitive-behavioural approaches to OCD are still at an early stage of evolution from behavioural approaches, and may follow a similar course. Secondly, an emphasis on the central role of cognitive factors in the maintenance of obsessional problems offers the exciting prospect of integration with the emerging field of cognitive neuroscience (as opposed to more traditional lesion based biological psychiatry approaches).

REFERENCES

1. Rachman S.J., Hodgson R.J. (1980) *Obsessions and Compulsions*, Prentice Hall, Englewood Cliffs.
2. Salkovskis P.M. (1999) Understanding and treating obsessive-compulsive disorder. *Behav. Res. Ther.*, **37**: 29–52.
3. Clark D.M. (1994) Cognitive therapy for panic disorder. In *Treatment of Panic Disorder: A Consensus Development Conference* (Eds B.E. Wolfe, J.D. Maser), pp. 121–132, American Psychiatric Press, Washington, DC.

3.7 Current Issues in the Use of Behavioural Therapy for Obsessive-Compulsive Disorder

Kenneth A. Kobak and Brad C. Riemann[1]

Foa and Franklin's review on psychological treatments of obsessive-compulsive disorder (OCD) inspires many thoughts, some of which we will elaborate on below. First, exposure and ritual prevention (ERP) has been found to be an effective and robust treatment for OCD for nearly 35 years [1]. However, its availability is still surprisingly scarce. It has been estimated that it would take over 54 000 behavioural therapists working 30 hours per week for 5 years to treat only half of the 3 million OCD sufferers with five 1-hour sessions [2]. Many patients are forced to travel considerable distances and incur much cost to participate in treatment. Behavioural treatment for OCD is difficult in itself, and the added stress of being uprooted and away from families makes it even more so. The overall value of a treatment is a combination of its effectiveness and its ability to be disseminated to the masses. Clearly, ERP's overall impact will be dependent on our ability to bring behavioural treatment to the sufferers (e.g. by adequately training large numbers of clinicians in these techniques) and/or by bringing the sufferers to the behaviour therapists (e.g. via telemedicine and the Internet).

Several possibilities exist to explain this lack of trained behavioural therapists. Few graduate training programs provide training in behavioural techniques. This may be due to the lack of clinicians with enough expertise in this area to provide this training to others, or due to a lack of demand for this type of training. In addition, it appears that few students are interested in becoming specialists. Many clinicians feel that by specializing they will not be able to make a living. They have a "the bigger the net you cast the more fish you will catch" mentality to private practice. We have not found this to be the case. Also, clinicians have discussed with us their concerns that OCD patients are difficult to deal with, and difficult to treat. This is of course not true, assuming you are treating them with the proper techniques. We have found that most OCD patients are extremely motivated, and grateful for the help they receive. Philosophical differences may also play a role. Some clinicians feel that behavioural therapy is only treating the surface symptoms of the underlying problem, or resist the idea that treatment of a DSM-IV defined disorder by targeting current behaviours is in and of itself an appropriate treatment goal.

Given the scarcity of trained behaviour therapists, the questions become (as Foa and Franklin point out) "Can the skills required to do successful ERP be

[1] *Dean Foundation, 2711 Allen Blvd., Middleton, WI 53562, USA*

transported to community-based therapists with no experience with ERP?", and "How successful will it be compared to ERP conducted at centres of expertise, which have typically participated in the clinical trials upon which the efficacy data is based?". Taken from another perspective is the question of whether the skills necessary to do successful ERP can be successfully transported *directly to the patients* themselves. As Foa and Franklin point out, the research literature is mixed on whether therapist-aided exposure is more efficacious than self-exposure. However, both these paradigms involve therapist involvement. There are no published studies that we are aware of examining the efficacy of a patient self-help for OCD that is completely independent of therapist involvement.

A computer-administered self-help behaviour therapy program for OCD has recently been studied that is independent of therapist contact. The system, called BT STEPS™, contains the essential features of effective behaviour therapy for OCD: identifying triggers; designing a hierarchy of exposure goals; monitoring progress and feedback; and patient education. The system uses both a manual and a series of computer interactions that are accessed over the telephone using interactive voice response (IVR). The system helps the patient set treatment goals, and monitors and guides treatment. A series of studies found significant improvement in patients who use the system and complete the ERP exercises [3–5]. Interestingly, in one large ($n = 218$) multicenter study, clinician-administered ERP did slightly (but significantly) better than BT STEPS™ (both did better than relaxation control), but when examining patients who completed at least one ERP session, they did equally well. This support the idea that clinicians may be better in motivating patients to do ERP, but once they do, self-exposure is equally effective as therapist-guided exposure. We agree with Foa and Franklin's comments that more research is needed in the area of how to motivate patients to participate in ERP.

Finally, we know that ERP reduces OCD symptoms, but do these reductions translate into improvements in overall quality of life for these patients? A considerable number report a "now what" syndrome after completing an ERP program. They no longer wash their hands for hours each day, but report not knowing what to do with all of the time they now have. They may not have had a friend or a job in 10 years, and have no ideas as to how to begin reintegrating into the community. Additional therapies may need to be prescribed (e.g. vocational rehabilitation, social or dating skills training) to help these individuals be truly happy and healthy in the long run. We are currently collaborating with researchers investigating this issue.

REFERENCES

1. Meyer V. (1966) Modification of expectations in cases with obsessional rituals. *Behav. Res. Ther.*, **4**: 273–280.
2. Greist J.H. (1989) Computer-administered behavior therapies. *Int. Rev. Psychiatry*, **1**: 267–294.
3. Greist J.H., Marks I.M., Baer L., Parkin R., Manzo P., Mantle J.M., Wenzel K.W., Spierings C.J., Kobak K.A., Dottl S.L. *et al* (1998) Self-treatment for obsessive compulsive disorder using a manual and a computerized telephone interview: a US–UK study. *MD Comput.*, **15**: 149–157.
4. Bachofen M., Nakagawa A., Marks I.M., Park J.-M., Greist J.H., Baer L., Wenzel K.W., Parkin J.R., Dottl S.L. (1999) Home self-assessment and self-treatment of obsessive-compulsive disorder using a manual and a computer-conducted telephone interview: replication of a UK–US study. *J. Clin. Psychiatry*, **60**: 545–549.
5. Greist J.H., Marks I.M., Baer L., Parkin J.R., Manzo P.A., Mantle J.M., Kobak K.A. (1999) Computer-assisted behavior therapy for OCD. Presented at the APA Annual Meeting, Washington, DC, May 15–20.

3.8
Cognitive-Behavioural Therapy and Integrated Approaches in the Treatment of Obsessive-Compulsive Disorder

Fritz Hohagen[1]

For decades, obsessive-compulsive disorder (OCD) has been considered a treatment-refractory mental condition. The review by Foa and Franklin demonstrates the progress made in the psychological treatment of this disorder during the last 30 years. The authors postulate, based on their literature review and their own studies, that exposure with ritual prevention (EX/RP) is the key element in the treatment of OCD. Although in recent years cognitive approaches have been proposed, especially for obsessional ruminations (see [1] for an overview), many of these approaches typically included elements of EX/RP. The cognitive model of OCD was developed based on the general model as applied to anxiety disorders. Proceeding from the work of Rachman and Hodgson [2], Salkovskis and co-workers distinguished between anxiety-producing thoughts and neutralizing thoughts. Besides cognitive techniques, they proposed exposure techniques, such as thought evocation or listening to a "loop tape" of the anxiety-provoking thoughts in the patient's own voice, followed by response prevention (i.e. no overt or covert neutralizing or avoidance behaviour).

[1] *Department of Psychiatry and Psychotherapy, Medical University of Lübeck, Ratzeburger Allee 160, D-23538 Lübeck, Germany*

Schwartz [3] has proposed a cognitive-biobehavioural self-treatment for OCD that integrates the results of neuroimaging research into the cognitive approach, based on the literature on the behavioural neurobiology of the basal ganglia. Again, in addition to the cognitive approach, patients are taught to increase their awareness of avoidant behaviours and to use treatment techniques to perform previously avoided behaviours. Thus, the analysis of the literature suggests that, even in cognitive approaches to the treatment of OCD, EX/RP seems to be the most important element. Foa and Franklin have already pointed out how difficult it is to distinguish between the two. However, Cottraux and co-workers [4] recently compared cognitive therapy with intensive behavioural therapy in a multi-centre study of 64 outpatients. Group 1 received 20 1-hour sessions of cognitive therapy over 16 weeks; group 2 received a 4-week intensive treatment with two 2-hour sessions per week followed by a 12-week maintenance phase with booster sessions. The behavioural therapy program included imaginal and *in vivo* exposure with response prevention during the sessions, and homework. Preliminary data indicate that there were no significant differences between the two treatment groups. This study suggests that cognitive therapy may be as effective as exposure therapy, but further research is needed to resolve this question.

It is generally recognized that at least 25% of OCD patients refuse to comply with EX/RP [5]; about 12% drop out of treatment, while 20–30% do not respond. Thus, approximately half of patients do not benefit from this kind of treatment [6]. The search for ways of treating these patients more effectively has sparked an increasing interest in multimodal therapy programs. Multimodal behavioural therapy analyses and treats early social deficits, reduced tolerance for intensive emotions, and reduced emotional awareness, as well as deficits in problem-solving, self-initiated alternative behaviours, and interpersonal problems. It also employs symptom-directed interventions, i.e. cognitive techniques and EX/RP [7]. Multimodal behavioural therapy has been shown to be effective, with very low drop-out rates in severely ill inpatients [8] and outpatients [7]. Furthermore, its long-term efficacy has been demonstrated in follow-up studies of unselected patients [7]. Although it has not yet been studied whether multi-modal behavioural therapy is superior to exposure therapy alone, this approach may be useful for OCD patients who drop out of, or refuse to undergo, exposure therapy alone, or who do not respond to conventional EX/RP.

A further issue is the question of whether the combination of EX/RP with the administration of serotonin reuptake inhibitors (SRIs) is superior to behavioural therapy (BT) alone. Few studies have investigated therapy combining clomipramine plus exposure *in vivo* against clomipramine and exposure applied singly [9]. When added to exposure therapy, clomipramine showed a transient significant effect as compared to placebo. Cottraux *et al* [10, 11] reported a transient effect of fluvoxamine plus exposure therapy on rituals and depression, which had disappeared at the follow-up 18 months later. A recent placebo-controlled study on the combination of BT with fluvoxamine, as opposed to BT and placebo [8], showed that obsessions in the group that had received fluvoxamine and BT were significantly more reduced than in the group given placebo and BT. Furthermore, the treatment outcome was significantly better for severely depressed patients with OCD who received BT plus fluvoxamine than for those who received BT plus placebo. The study results suggest that the differential analysis of the clinical syndrome of OCD may be helpful in selecting the appropriate treatment strategies. When compulsions dominate the clinical picture, BT alone seems to suffice for the effective treatment of patients. If the patients suffer predominantly from obsessions or from secondary depression, the administration of an SRI seems to enhance the treatment outcome of OCD significantly and should be added to EX/RP therapy. To summarize, the combination of BT and SRIs seems to be superior to BT alone in the acute treatment phase, while the effect of the combined approach in the long-term treatment of OCD has not yet been established.

Another open question is whether the combination of BT and SRIs can prevent the recurrence of obsessive-compulsive symptoms after withdrawal of the medication. Up to now, no controlled studies have been conducted. Our own open 2-year follow-up study of 79 patients has demonstrated that no relapse occurred after SRI withdrawal when patients had been treated with a combination of BT and SRIs. The most likely interpretation of this finding is that having learned an active coping strategy against the obsessive-compulsive urges prevents the recurrence of obsessive-compulsive symptoms after drug discontinuation. At present, a placebo-controlled multicentre study in progress is examining this topic.

Further research should focus upon the treatment of non-responders, the neurobiologic changes during BT, the definition of an adequate treatment setting, the potential merits of combining BT and psychopharmacological treatment, and the recognition of when treatment with SRI, BT or both is warranted.

REFERENCES

1. Salkovskis P.M., Forrester E., Richards C. (1998) Cognitive-behavioural approach to understanding obsessional thinking. *Br. J. Psychiatry*, **173**: 53–63.
2. Rachman S.J., Hodgson R.J. (1980) *Obsessions and Compulsions*, Prentice Hall, Englewood Cliffs.
3. Schwartz J.M. (1998) Neuroanatomical aspects of cognitive-behavioural therapy response in obsessive-compulsive disorder. An evolving perspective on brain and behaviour. *Br. J. Psychiatry*, **173**: 38–44.

4. Cottraux J., Note I., Dartigues J.F. Note B., Sauteraud A., Mollard E., Duboca B., Bourgeois M. (1998) A multicenter controlled trial of cognitive therapy vs. intensive behavior therapy. Presented at the Third International Obsessive-Compulsive Disorder Conference, Madeira, September 11–12.
5. Greist J.H. (1990) Treatment of obsessive compulsive disorder: psychotherapies, drugs, and other somatic treatment. *J. Clin. Psychiatry*, **51**: 44–50.
6. Keijsers G., Hoogduin C., Shaap C. (1994) Predictors of treatment outcome in the behavioural treatment of obsessive-compulsive disorder. *Br. J. Psychiatry*, **165**: 781–786.
7. Hand I. (1998) Out-patient, multi-modal behaviour therapy for obsessive-compulsive disorder. *Br. J. Psychiatry*, **173**: 45–52.
8. Hohagen F., Winkelmann G., Raschle-Räuchle H., Hand I., König A., Münchau N., Hiss H., Geiger-Kabisch C., Käppler C., Schramm P. *et al* (1998) Combination of behaviour therapy with fluvoxamine in comparison with behaviour therapy and placebo. Result of a multicentre study. *Br. J. Psychiatry*, **173**: 71–78.
9. Marks I., Lelliott P., Basoglu M., Noshirvani H., Monteiro W., Cohen D., Kasvikis Y. (1988) Clomipramine, self-exposure and therapist-aided exposure for obsessive-compulsive rituals. *Br. J. Psychiatry*, **152**: 522–534.
10. Cottraux J., Mollard E., Bouvard M., Marks I., Sluys M., Nury A.M., Douge R., Cialdella P. (1990) A controlled study of fluvoxamine and exposure in obsessive compulsive disorder. *Int. Clin. Psychopharmacol.*, **5**: 17–30.
11. Cottraux J., Mollard E., Bouvard M., Marks I. (1993) Exposure therapy, fluvoxamine, or combination treatment in obsessive-compulsive disorder: one year follow-up. *Psychiatry Res.*, **49**: 63–75.

3.9
Mindful Awareness: the Key to Successful Self-directed Treatment Strategies

Jeffrey M. Schwartz[1]

Psychological treatments of obsessive-compulsive disorder (OCD) have generated significant interest in the mental health literature, both because of their proven clinical efficacy and because of their demonstrated ability to systematically alter cerebral physiology (see [1, 2] for review). The core procedures for successful psychological treatment outcome, as Foa and Franklin cogently point out, are "exposure to feared stimuli and simultaneous prevention of rituals". Those committed to enhancing treatment delivery to the millions of OCD sufferers without current access to these highly effective treatment approaches have increasingly come to realize that in many cases (and particularly those in which symptom intensity is less than severe) the basic principles of exposure and ritual prevention (EX/RP)

[1] *Department of Psychiatry, UCLA School of Medicine, 760 Westwood Plaza Los Angeles, CA 90024–1759, USA*

therapy can be realistically applied in new and creative ways that do not require intensive or prolonged contact with experts in the use of these procedures.

As Foa and Franklin wisely state, "motivation and compliance with treatment procedures are important mediators of EX/RP success". This commonsensical yet entirely non-trivial assertion must remain a cardinal working principle in the forefront of every practicing clinician's approach to treatment. Perhaps the single most important means of achieving such motivated compliance is by encouraging the person actually *doing* the treatment to become, to the greatest extent possible, an active participant in the treatment process. In an era in which it seems to have become an all too common occurrence for mental health professionals (of both the pharmacological and psychosocial bent) to at least tacitly believe that *they* are the ones actually doing the treatment, the risks inherent in allowing the patient to implicitly assume the role of mere recipient of treatment, passively waiting for bothersome symptoms to simply "go away", cannot be simply ignored or gainsaid. This is especially true insofar as the proportion of even successful treatments for OCD that do not leave a significant residuum of symptoms still to be coped with is vanishingly small. Training in the development of self-directed treatment skills must become a critical aspect of the treatment principles for OCD, and indeed of all mental health afflictions.

It has been my experience that training in and the use of a type of mental activity often referred to as "mindfulness" or "mindful awareness" significantly enhances patients' active engagement in ongoing treatment. Mindfulness thus provides an extremely helpful adjunct to the use of EX/RP, as well as a wide variety of other treatment modalities (e.g. family-based, pharmacological, etc.). In general terms, the most noteworthy aspect of the application of mindfulness or mindful awareness comes with the ability it affords those utilizing it to observe their sensations and thoughts with the calm clarity of an external witness. While the use of mindfulness has seen its most rigorous development within the Asian cultures most deeply influenced by traditional practices of Buddhist meditation, there has been a growing realization in the West that practices of this sort can be readily applied in modified form to the treatment of a variety of medical and psychological disorders. For example, John Teasdale of Cambridge University has recently described the use of a cognitively-oriented approach to depression relapse prevention termed "mindfulness-based cognitive therapy" (MBCT) [3].

The German monk Nyanaponika Thera, a major figure of twentieth century Buddhist scholarship, coined the term "bare attention" in order to precisely explain to Westerners the type of mental activity required for the attainment of mindful awareness. "Bare attention is the clear and single-minded awareness of what actually happens *to* us and *in* us, at the successive moments of perception. It is called "bare" because it attends just to the bare facts of a perception as presented either through the five physical senses or through the mind... without reacting to them" [4]. As a practical matter, shifting one's perspective in this way has proven to be of substantial benefit in empowering OCD suffers to practice EX/RP-based techniques within both therapist-assisted and self-directed treatment paradigms [1, 2]. Further, work in progress at the University of California at Los Angeles (UCLA), done in collaboration with Eda Gorbis of our OCD Research Group, has demonstrated that training in these mindfulness-based techniques can be readily accomplished in a group therapy setting and practiced effectively between group sessions, either in conjunction with additional individual therapy or in a self-directed manner, depending on coexisting degrees of symptom severity, patient insight, familial support, and other related variables.

Although it requires substantial and quite directed effort to practice mindfulness in the presence of significant anxiety and fear, we have found that the systematic use of what we term "the Four Steps" can significantly enhance the ability of OCD patients to regularly practice mindfulness-based techniques [5]. In very brief overview, the working principle of the Four Steps (Relabel, Reattribute, Refocus, Revalue) is to help the person with OCD come to view the condition's intrusive thoughts and sensations as symptoms of an annoying medical disorder, and to understand that this disorder can be effectively treated by learning to mindfully replace ingrained ritualistic responses to these symptoms with new and adaptive ones. This kind of actively initiated cognitive frame shift can be readily applied in conjunction with a variety of other treatment modalities, both psychological and pharmacological. The critical point is to encourage patients, as much as possible, to realize that the conscious perspective they adopt while coping with their ongoing symptoms (and indeed, with all of their experiences) plays a critical role in the outcome of the treatment in which they are engaged. That this requires a reasonable degree of insight and adaptive function at the outset of treatment is, of course, a given. In cases of profound severity, the application of mindfulness-based techniques may well have to await the effective onset of other treatment modalities. But the principle that self-directed treatment strategies should be a goal to strive for is one that must become a key aspect of all therapeutic armamentaria in the mental health field.

REFERENCES

1. Schwartz J.M. (1998) Neuroanatomical aspects of cognitive-behavioural therapy response in obsessive-compulsive disorder: an evolving perspective on brain and behavior. *Br. J. Psychiatry*, **173** (suppl. 35): 39–45.

2. Schwartz J.M. (1999) A role for volition and attention in the generation of new brain circuitry: toward a neurobiology of mental force. In *The Volitional Brain: Towards a Neuroscience of Free Will* (Eds B. Libet, A. Freeman, K. Sutherland), pp. 115–142, Imprint Academic, Thorverton.
3. Teasdale J.D. (1999) Emotional processing, three modes of mind and the prevention of relapse in depression. *Behav. Res. Ther.*, **37**: S53–S77.
4. Nyanaponika Thera (1962) *The Heart of Buddhist Meditation*, Weiser, York Beach.
5. Schwartz J.M., Beyette B. (1997) *Brain Lock: Free Yourself from Obsessive-Compulsive Behavior*. Harper Collins, New York.

3.10
The Role of Cognitive Therapy in the Treatment of Obsessive-Compulsive Disorder

Lynne M. Drummond[1]

Over the past 20 years, the prognosis of patients with obsessive-compulsive disorder (OCD) has been revolutionized by the development of behavioural psychotherapy and the introduction of serotonin reuptake inhibitors. Despite the relatively clear evidence regarding psychological treatments of OCD, many clinicians are still confused about the best treatment to offer. Foa and Franklin's review should thus be recommended to anyone who treats patients suffering from OCD.

In terms of psychological treatments, the treatment of choice for OCD sufferers is exposure combined with self-imposed response prevention. This assertion is based on many trials conducted over the years. However, over recent years more therapists have been trained in the techniques of cognitive therapy and there has been a tendency to use them increasingly in OCD.

Cognitive therapy refers to a number of techniques which are designed to alter an individual's faulty thinking patterns. Beck's cognitive therapy aims to correct a patient's negative automatic thoughts and errors of thinking by teaching the patient to challenge the truth or usefulness of these beliefs and thoughts [1]. Rational emotive therapy aims to identify irrational beliefs and ideas and to challenge them [2, 3]. Self-instruction training aims to alter the patient's internal dialogue by a number of positive statements which are rehearsed by the patient and repeated at times of stress [4].

Despite the fact that obsessions and rituals of patients with OCD are primarily cognitively mediated, an early study into the efficacy of cognitive

[1] *Department of Mental Health Sciences, St. George's Hospital Medical School, Cranmer Terrace, London SW17 ORE, UK*

therapy was not encouraging [5]. This study investigated whether modifying cognitions using self-instructional training would enhance the efficacy of exposure for patients with OCD. No enhancement was found. However, other workers questioned whether self-instructional training was the most suitable form of cognitive therapy for OCD patients [6].

Emmelkamp *et al* investigated the use of rational emotive therapy in OCD patients by comparing it with exposure and response prevention [7]. Cognitive therapy was found to be as effective as the exposure treatment. However, the patients used for this study were non-chronic, young and well-educated. For this reason, the study was replicated using more typical outpatient OCD patients.

In a later study, Emmelkamp and Beens [8] examined 21 patients with OCD who were referred to the psychology department and were randomly allocated to receive either cognitive therapy or self-exposure instructions. Following six treatment sessions, the patients received no treatment for a further 4 weeks and were then treated with either a further six sessions of exposure or six sessions of a combination of cognitive therapy and exposure. The results showed that cognitive therapy and exposure were equally effective in reducing obsessive-compulsive, anxiety and depressive symptoms. There was no advantage found in combining cognitive therapy with exposure.

These results, however, may not have wide applicability in clinical practice. This study used rational emotive therapy rather than the more common form of cognitive therapy developed by Beck. The therapists involved in the study all worked at a highly specialized unit treating patients with OCD. It cannot, therefore, be concluded that similar results would be obtained at any psychiatric unit.

Many clinicians with extensive experience in treating patients with OCD are concerned by the indiscriminate usage of cognitive therapy with these patients. Too frequently inappropriate usage and type of cognitive therapy leads to patients substituting cognitive rituals for the pre-existing overt rituals.

The studies demonstrate that exposure treatment and rational emotive therapy produce similar results in specialized clinics. Exposure treatment is easily learned by a therapist and requires minimal additional training. Rational emotive therapy requires more specialized training. It would therefore appear more cost-efficient for most psychiatric units to continue to use exposure and self-imposed response prevention for the majority of their OCD patients.

In summary, it appears that cognitive therapy in the form of rational emotive therapy may have a role in the management and treatment of patients with OCD. The specific characteristics of the patients who can most benefit from this approach rather than exposure methods has yet to be identified. A high strength of belief in the validity of the obsessional thoughts may well prove to be one factor [9–11].

REFERENCES

1. Beck A.T., Emery G. (1985) *Anxiety Disorders and Phobias: a Cognitive Perspective*, Basic Books, New York.
2. Ellis A. (1962) *Reason and Emotion in Psychotherapy*, Lyle-Stuart, New York.
3. McFall M.E., Wollersheim J.P. (1979) Obsessive-compulsive neurosis: a cognitive-behavioural formulation and approach to treatment. *Cogn. Ther. Res.*, **3**: 333–348.
4. Meichenbaum D. (1977) *Cognitive-Behavior Modification: an Integrative Approach*, Plenum, New York.
5. Emmelkamp P.M.G., van der Helm M., van Zanten B.L., Plochg I. (1980) Treatment of obsessive-compulsive patients: the contribution of self-instructional training to the effectiveness of exposure. *Behav. Res. Ther.*, **18**: 61–66.
6. Kendell P.C. (1983) Methodology and cognitive-behavioural assessment. *Behav. Psychother.*, **11**: 285–301.
7. Emmelkamp P.M.G., Visser S., Hoekstra R.J. (1988) Cognitive therapy vs. exposure *in vivo* in the treatment of obsessive-compulsives. *Cogn. Ther. Res.*, **12**: 103–114.
8. Emmelkamp P.M.G., Beens H. (1991) Cognitive therapy with obsessive-compulsive disorder: a comparative evaluation. *Behav. Res. Ther.*, **29**: 293–300.
9. Salkovskis P.M., Warwick H.M.C. (1985) Cognitive therapy of obsessive-compulsive disorder: treating treatment failures. *Behav. Psychother.*, **13**: 243–255.
10. Drummond L.M. (1993) The treatment of severe, chronic, resistant obsessive-compulsive disorder: an evaluation of an inpatient programme using behavioural psychotherapy in combination with other treatments. *Br. J. Psychiatry*, **163**: 223–229.
11. Drummond L.M. (1993) The management of obsessive-compulsive disorders. *Curr. Opin. Psychiatry*, **6**: 201–204.

3.11
Psychodynamic Treatment of Obsessive-Compulsive Conditions

David Shapiro[1]

Foa and Franklin's review considers only psychological treatments of a behavioural and cognitive-behavioural sort, in particular exposure and ritual prevention treatments. This limitation is easily understandable,

[1] *Graduate Faculty of Political and Social Science, Clinical Psychology Program, 65 Fifth Avenue, New York, NY 10003, USA*

since it is only on treatments of this kind that systematic research appears to have been done. Nevertheless, psychodynamic treatment, particularly psychoanalytic treatment, of obsessive-compulsive conditions has a long history, beginning with Freud. Indeed, in 1894–95 Freud identified obsessional neurosis as an independent disorder [1], and since that time it has occupied a major place in psychoanalytic literature and clinical practice.

It is true, as Foa and Franklin remark, that obsessive-compulsive conditions were considered for many years particularly refractory to treatment; this was certainly the general opinion among psychoanalysts and psychodynamic therapists in general. Obsessive patients, for example, were thought to be especially prone to fruitless and repetitious intellectual rumination about their condition and comparatively inaccessible to genuinely affecting intervention. It is now clear, however, that the particular difficulty of helping these individuals with psychodynamic therapy does not reflect their intrinsic incapacity for change so much as it does certain inadequacies of the particular sort of psychodynamic therapy that was attempted.

Psychodynamic therapy, especially in its early days and probably to a certain extent still, relied for its effectiveness on interpretations concerning the presumed origins of symptoms in early personal history. These interpretations lent themselves precisely to the sort of intellectual contemplation characteristic of many obsessive individuals and at least in these instances produced little or no therapeutic result, indeed, probably little genuine conviction. In more recent years, however, psychodynamic therapy has undergone important developments; historical interpretations of the traditional sort are no longer relied on as the exclusive therapeutic agent; understanding of the patient in the "here and now" and in the therapeutic relationship itself is emphasized. The occupation with ineffective historical speculation is therefore much diminished in contemporary psychodynamic therapy.

There is, in addition, a particular current in psychodynamic theory and therapy that is critical for the treatment of obsessive-compulsive conditions, namely the development of a characterological viewpoint. A great deal of clinical evidence indicates that obsessive-compulsive symptoms are special expressions of a certain sort of neurotic character or personality [2]. Starting in the late 1920s and early 1930s, especially with the introduction of character analysis by Wilhelm Reich [3], the "intellectualization" and general rigidity of obsessive individuals have been recognized as central to the dynamics of their character, as well as to their symptoms. These characteristics have thus been transformed from an obstacle to treatment, as they had seemed, to an essential focus of treatment. With that recognition and the further development of characterological psychodynamic treatment in more recent years [4, 5], the reasons for considering obsessive-compulsive conditions particularly intractable have disappeared and successful treatment has been reported [4, 5].

Whether all symptomatic obsessive-compulsive conditions are actually reflections of one or another variety of obsessive-compulsive character is, to be sure, an arguable matter. There certainly are those who believe that these symptoms are directly neurophysiological and therefore best, or only effectively, treated medically. In a matter of this sort, of course, no one can say that cases of adult obsessive-compulsive symptoms completely outside of obsessive-compulsive character do not exist. I can say only that in many years of clinical practice I have never seen such a case and, as a result, I suspect that the important features of this kind of personality are not always recognized and identified for what they are.

REFERENCES

1. Freud S. (1894/1958) *The Neuro-Psychoses of Defence*, standard edn III, Hogarth Press, London.
2. Shapiro D. (1965) *Neurotic Styles*, Basic Books, New York.
3. Reich W. (1949) *Character Analysis*, Orgone Institute Press, New York.
4. Fierman L. (Ed.) (1965) *Effective Psychotherapy: the Contribution of Hellmuth Kaiser*, Free Press, New York.
5. Shapiro D. (1989) *Psychotherapy of Neurotic Character*, Basic Books, New York.

CHAPTER

4

Child and Adolescent Obsessive-Compulsive Disorder: A Review

Martine F. Flament and David Cohen

CNRS UMR 7593, Pavillon Clérambault, Hôpital La Salpêtrière, 47 boulevard de l'Hôpital, 75013 Paris, France

INTRODUCTION

Both the adult and the child psychiatric literature contain early descriptions of typical cases of childhood-onset obsessive-compulsive disorder (OCD). In 1838, Esquirol [1] reported the first case of OCD in his famous *Traité des Maladies Mentales*, describing a young woman whose obsessions and compulsions had started before 18 years of age. Forty years later, in 1875, Legrand du Saulle [2] first attempted to isolate, in a monograph called *La Folie du Doute avec Délire du Toucher*, what Janet and Freud would later name "obsessional neurosis" [3]. Legrand du Saulle highlighted that the disorder often develops during the puberty years and may remain hidden for years. At the beginning of the twentieth century, Janet [4] reported on a 5-year old with classical obsessive-compulsive (OC) symptoms, and Freud [5] described, in his adult patients, obsessional behaviours dating back from childhood, while speculating on the strong constitutional influence in the choice of these symptoms. Kanner [6], in 1957, noted the resemblance—and sometimes the association—between compulsive movements and tics, and Despert [7] described, in 1955, the first large series of OC children ($n = 68$), insisting on the preponderance of males and the children's perception of the abnormality and undesirability of their behaviours.

However, it was still believed until recently that OCD was rare in young people. In children, most ritualistic and compulsive-like activity was considered to be part of the normal developmental behavioural repertoire. The first systematic evidence of true OC symptoms occurring at an early age came from retrospective studies with adult OCD patients, suggesting that 30–50% of them had onset of their symptoms during childhood or

Obsessive-Compulsive Disorder. Edited by Mario Maj, Norman Sartorius, Ahmed Okasha and Joseph Zohar.

adolescence [8, 9]. Then epidemiological data showed that OCD is far more prevalent among adolescents than previously thought. Over the last decade, a number of systematic studies conducted on children and adolescents with OCD, both in clinical settings and in the community, have greatly increased our knowledge of the disorder in its early stage. They have shown that, in contrast to other forms of psychopathology, the specific features of OCD are essentially identical in children, adolescents and adults. With a tremendous growth of interest and research on childhood-onset OCD, significant advances have occurred regarding epidemiology, phenomenology, genetics, neurophysiology, pathogenesis and treatment of the disorder.

PREVALENCE

Epidemiological studies on OCD using strict diagnostic criteria and structured clinical interviews have been completed among adolescents from several parts of the world. The first and largest study was conducted in a US population of 5596 high school students [10]. Using a two-stage procedure whereby students with questionnaire scores suggestive of OC symptomatology and controls were blindly reinterviewed by clinicians, the current prevalence of OCD in adolescence (diagnosed by DSM-III criteria) was estimated to be $1 \pm 0.5\%$, and its lifetime prevalence to be $1.9 \pm 0.7\%$. There was a lifetime comorbidity rate of 75% for other psychiatric disorders, including major depression, dysthymia, bulimia nervosa, overanxious disorder, and phobias. Nevertheless, only 20% of the OCD cases identified had ever been under professional care. The study demonstrated that OCD in adolescence was clearly underdiagnosed and undertreated. In a later study [11], examining 562 consecutive inductees into the Israeli Army aged 16 or 17 years, the point prevalence of OCD (using DSM-III-R criteria) was $3.6 \pm 0.7\%$. Of note was the high proportion of subjects with obsessions only (50%), potentially less disruptive of everyday functioning. If the prevalence of OCD was estimated excluding those individuals with only obsessions, the point prevalence dropped to 1.8%. Among the OCD individuals, there was a significant elevation of tic disorders, including Tourette's Syndrome (TS). Reinherz *et al* [12] interviewed 386 adolescents included in a 14-year longitudinal panel study, that began when these youth entered kindergarten, in a working class community from the north-eastern USA: at a mean age of 17.9 years, 2.1% met DSM-III-R criteria for OCD. In New Zealand, Douglass *et al* [13] examined an unselected birth cohort of 930 males and females, when aged 18 years; they found an overall 1-year prevalence rate of OCD of 4%, decreasing to 1.2% when excluding subjects with obsessions only. Additionally, one study comparing various ethnic groups in the USA did not find any significant difference for the prevalence of child and adolescent OCD [14].

Thus, it appears that OCD might be as frequent in adolescents as it is in adults: in the US Epidemiological Catchment Area (ECA) study, the lifetime prevalence of OCD among adults ranged from 1.9 to 3.3% across five different metropolitan sites [15, 16], and in the Cross National Epidemiological Study, lifetime prevalence rates were consistent among the different countries (except Taiwan), ranging from 1.9% to 2.5% [17].

There has been no community study on the prevalence of OCD during childhood, but estimates of the frequency of OCD in clinical samples of children range from 1.3% to 5% [18, 19]. They suggest that many youngsters with OCD still do not come to clinical attention.

CLINICAL CHARACTERISTICS

OCD is defined by the presence of obsessions and/or compulsions, a definition which applies to both the ICD-10 [20] and the DSM-IV [21]. Obsessions are persistently recurring thoughts, impulses or images that are experienced as intrusive, inappropriate and distressing, and that are not simply excessive worries about realistic problems. Compulsions are repetitive behaviours or mental acts that a person feels driven to perform according to a rigidly applied rule, in order to reduce distress or to prevent some dreaded outcome. Obsessions and compulsions are egodystonic, considered by the subject himself as irrational or unrealistic, and they are at least partly resisted. In children and adolescents, they may be long kept secret, or will only appear at home or in the presence of close family members. They are always a source of psychological distress and interfere with personal and occupational functioning, social life and relationships to others.

Phenomenology of Symptoms

The clinical presentation of OCD during childhood and adolescent years has been documented in various cultures, with clinical series reported from the USA [22], Japan [18], India [23], Israel [24], Denmark [25] and Spain [26]. In a group of 70 young patients examined at the National Institute of Mental Health (NIMH) in the USA [22], obsessions dealt primarily with fear of dirt or germs (40%), danger to self or a loved one (24%), symmetry (17%), or scrupulous religiosity (13%); the major presenting ritual symptoms included, in order of decreasing frequency, washing rituals (85%), repeating (51%), checking (46%), touching (20%), ordering (17%), counting (18%), and hoarding (11%). Toro *et al* [26] described a series of 72 children and adolescents with OCD in Barcelona, for whom the most common compulsions were repeating (74%) and cleaning rituals (56%). According to Khanna and Srinath [23], in India, obsessions were less frequently reported by OC children than by adults, fear of harm being the single theme which occurred most often, while, in a group of 61 OC children in Japan [18], the most common obsession was dirt phobia and the most common compulsions were washing rituals. All these reports argue for the isomorphism between childhood and adult presentations of OCD. For comparison, we can refer to a population of 250 adult OCD patients from a speciality clinic in the USA [17]: the most common obsessions were fear of contamination (45%), pathological doubt (42%), somatic obsessions (36%) and the need for symmetry (31%), whereas the most frequent compulsions consisted of checking (63%), washing (50%), counting (36%), and the need to ask or confess (31%).

Typically, children and adolescents with OCD experience multiple obsessions and compulsions, whose content may change over time [10, 22, 28]. Generally, compulsions are carried out to dispell anxiety and/or in response to an obsession (e.g. to ward off harm to someone). Some of the obsessions and rituals involve an internal sense that "it does not feel right" until the thought or action is completed. Certain children with OCD may be unable to specify the dread events that the compulsive rituals are intended to prevent, beyond a vague premonition of something bad happening. Simple compulsions, such as repetitive touching or symmetrical ordering, may even lack any discernable ideational component, and may be phenomenologically indistinguishable from complex tics [29]. Both tics and simple compulsions may be preceded by premonitory physical sensations, urges, and mental perceptions that persist until the action is completed [30].

In some community-based samples of adolescents with OCD, there are high proportions of individuals with either obsessions or compulsions alone [11, 13]. This is less common in referred cases. Obsessional slowness can be seen in adolescents: careful assessment often reveals multiple mental rituals, and the disorder can be very disabling.

Onset of OCD in children may be acute or gradual. In the NIMH study [31], for 30 out of 79 patients (38%), family members or the subjects themselves believed a specific event had precipitated onset of their OC behaviour. However, the most common events involved stressful family events or fears developing from television shows, that is, usually not a particularly traumatic event, or one not commonly encountered by children. If the initial OC symptoms often reflected the content of the reported event, in no case was the symptom specificity preserved later on.

Diagnosis and Classification

Both the DSM-IV [21] and the ICD-10 [20] define OCD, regardless of age, by obsessions and/or compulsions (criterion A), which are described, at some point during the course of the disorder, as excessive or unreasonable (criterion B), and are severe enough to cause marked distress or to interfere significantly with the person's normal routine, or usual social activities or relationships (criterion C). The specific content of the obsessions or compulsions cannot be restricted to another Axis I diagnosis, such as preoccupations about food resulting from an eating disorder, or guilty thoughts from a major depressive disorder, or rituals resulting from hallucinations in schizophrenia (criterion D). The DSM-IV adds that the disturbance is not due to the direct physiological effects of a substance or a general medical condition (criterion E). The ICD-10 allows subclassification of forms with predominant obsessions, predominant compulsions, or mixed symptoms.

In the DSM-IV, the only difference in diagnostic criteria between children and adults regards criterion B stating that, at some point during the course of the disorder, the person must recognize that obsessions are not simply excessive worries about real-life problems, and that compulsions are excessive or unreasonable. Although most children and adolescents acknowledge the senselessness of their obsessions and compulsions, the requirement that insight is preserved (criterion B) is waived for children. However, the difference with adult patients is minimal, since persons of all ages who lack insight receive the designation "poor insight type".

Age of Onset

Reports of the mean age at onset of OCD in referred children and adolescents have ranged from 9.0 years [28] to 11.6 years [18]. In the NIMH series [22], the modal age at onset was 7 years, and the mean (±SD) age at onset was 10.1 (±3.5) years, implying an early-onset group and a group with onset in adolescence. Seven subjects had become ill before 7 years of age. Boys tended to have an earlier (prepubertal) onset, usually around age 9, whereas girls were more likely to have a later (pubertal) illness onset, around age 11. Other studies have found either no difference [35] or an earlier onset for girls [18]. In a community-based sample of adolescents, the age at onset of OCD varied from 7 to 18 years, with a mean at 12.8 years [10].

Sex Ratio

In community-based samples of adolescents with OCD, there are approximately equal numbers of males and females [10, 11], whereas in most studies of referred children and adolescents, males outnumber females 2:1 or 3:1 [7, 19, 22, 33, 34]. The relative overrepresentation of boys in clinical samples may reflect a greater severity of the disorder, and an earlier age of onset [22, 33, 34]; in addition, boys are more likely than girls to have a comorbid tic disorder [35]. In contrast, OCD appears to be more common in adult females than in adult males [17], this being probably related to the later onset in women.

Age and Developmental Effects

Some research has focused on the type of symptoms in relation to age, and their change over time. Minichiello *et al* [36] reported that patients who were predominantly cleaners had a later age of onset than those who checked or had mixed symptoms; additionally, cleaning rituals were more prominent among females, whereas primarily obsessional patients tended to be males. Honjo *et al* [18] noted that compulsions were more apt to appear earlier than obsessions. Typically, there seems to be high degree of overlap within patients between symptom groups of obsessions and compulsions [37], and several investigators have failed to find relationships between OC symptom types and age or sex, in adult [9] as well as child series [25, 32].

In the NIMH study [31], the investigators described the individual symptoms of 79 children and adolescents with severe OCD over an average of 7.9 years (range 2–16 years). The vast majority of patients reported having many different symptoms that spanned several symptom categories. Of seven possible divisions of obsessions and eight possible divisions of compulsions, at baseline, the mean number of obsessions was 2.1 (range 0–5) and the mean number of compulsions was 2.5 (range 0–6). At follow-up, the means were 1.7 and 2.3, respectively. Approximately half of subjects displayed both washing and checking compulsions at some time during their illness. As in the Honjo study [18], there was some evidence that compulsions appear before obsessions, particularly for early onset (before age 6) patients. Early symptoms were sometimes unusual (such as blinking and breathing rituals, arm flapping or repetitive movements), but included also classical OC symptoms (such as washing, walking, touching). Besides this finding, no relationship was found between the number or type of symptoms and developmental phases. Across the follow-up study period, no patient maintained the same constellation of symptoms from presentation to follow-up. With many exceptions, the typical progression of symptoms noted for this group was a gradual increase in the number of symptoms followed by a decrease as the patient reached late adolescence and early adulthood.

Differential Diagnosis

Symptoms of OCD in children are clearly distinct from developmentally normal childhood rituals. Normal rituals [38] include bedtime rituals, not stepping on cracks, counting, having lucky and unlucky numbers, and wanting things in their right place. They appear in both sexes, are most intense in 4-year olds, stress rules about daily life, help the child master anxiety, and enhance the socializing process. They seem to vanish by the age of 8 years [39]. In contrast, OC rituals are perceived—even by young children—as unwanted and irrational; they are incapacitating and painful, prompting social isolation and regressive behaviour.

OCD has to be distinguished from other anxiety disorders. In phobias, subjects are preoccupied by their fears only when confronted to the phobogen stimuli; in separation anxiety disorder, fear of harm to parents or loved ones is part of persistent worries and behaviours which are neither criticized nor resisted by the child.

In mental retardation, autism and other pervasive developmental disorders, stereotyped movements and ritualistic behaviours are frequent. However, they convey no particular intentionality and, despite being a source of functional impairment and being disturbing to others, they do not cause distress to the child, who does not try to resist them.

Children and adolescents with OCD can act in bizarre ways and show nearly delusional conviction, which might resemble the erroneous belief systems of schizophrenic patients. In OCD, the absence of thought disorder and hallucinations, and the preservation of reality testing outside the area of obsessional concern, may help the distinction from schizophrenia. However, Geller *et al* [40] reported psychotic features in 30% of a juvenile OCD sample. On the other hand, the psychomotor symptoms of catatonic schizophrenia may mimic OC rituals when patients are not able to express their hallucinatory phenomena [41]. Schizophrenia can also occur with OCD [42], but the concept of delusional OCD [43] has not been extended to the pediatric age group.

Diagnostic Assessment and Rating Instruments

Diagnosis of OCD in children and adolescents must be established after a careful assessment, which should review current and past OC symptoms, as well as possible associated conditions. The assessment should include interview of both child and parents, and usually requires several sessions. A detailed evaluation of the child's medical, developmental and family history is essential [44].

Specific instruments describing the form, the content and the severity of OC symptoms have been developed. The Yale-Brown Obsessive Compulsive Scale (Y-BOCS) is a semi-structured interview which has been widely used for assessing the severity of symptoms in adults with OCD. Considerable data support its reliability, validity and sensitivity to change [45, 46]. The authors modified the Y-BOCS so that it could be used to assess OC symptoms in children and adolescents, aged 6–17 years (CY-BOCS). The major difference with the Y-BOCS is that both the child and parent(s) are interviewed, and all information combined to estimate the score for each item. The reliability and validity of the CY-BOCS have been assessed, with excellent reliability for obsessions and the total score, and acceptable reliability for compulsions [47]. Both the Y-BOCS and the CY-BOCS have been widely used, for clinical and research purposes, to describe symptoms and to measure change with treatment.

The Child Version of the Leyton Obsessional Inventory (LOI-CV) is a useful self-report symptom and severity inventory, for children older than age 10 years [48]. Both a pen-and-paper and a card-sorting format are available. There are 44 items, generating three scores, for symptom, interference and resistance. The LOI-CV has been used in both clinical and community samples, it has population norms and includes OC personality traits.

Comorbidity

It has been consistently observed that childhood OCD is frequently accompanied by other symptoms, which have important implications in regard to clinical assessment, differential diagnosis and treatment planning. This has been observed both in clinic patients and in community cases, indicating that it is not merely an artefact of referral bias. The main limitations of studies investigating the pattern of OCD comorbidity are the use of exclusionary criteria when recruiting patients in specialized clinics, and the limited number of diagnoses systematically assessed in community studies. However, in both referred and community samples, the overall lifetime comorbidity of OCD in children or adolescents has been shown to be as high as 75% [49].

Mood and anxiety disorders are the most common comorbid conditions, with prevalence ranging across studies from 20% to 73% [40, 50] and from 26% to 70% [22, 40], respectively. Among anxiety disorders, overanxious and separation anxiety disorders are the most frequent in children, and panic and generalized anxiety disorders the most frequent in adolescents. Depression and anxiety disorders can pre-date OCD, or can appear secondarily. Anorexia nervosa has been reported in 8% of OCD adolescents, when this eating disorder has been systematically assessed [26]. Conversely, OCD has been found in 3–66% of girls with anorexia nervosa, with onset earlier than or simultaneous to that of the eating disorder [51]. In a community study [10], bulimia nervosa was observed in 20% of adolescent OCD cases.

Of particular importance in juvenile OCD is the high rate of comorbid tic disorders, including TS, which have been reported in 17–40% of referred OCD patients [26, 40] and in 25% of a community-derived sample [11]. In one study, nearly 60% of children and adolescents seeking treatment for OCD and followed over time proved to have a lifetime history of tics, that ranged across subjects from simple, mild, transient tics through TS [35]. Similarly, about 50% of children and adolescents with TS develop OC symptoms or OCD by adulthood [52], and elevated rates of OCD have been found in first-degree relatives of probands with TS, suggesting a genetic relationship [53, 54]. While occurring less frequently in non-referred subjects, a high rate of disruptive behaviour disorders—attention-deficit/hyperactivity disorder (ADHD) and oppositional defiant disorder—has been reported in subjects seen in childhood OCD clinics [40]. As for tic disorders, these comorbid conditions appear in a chronological sequence, with ADHD or TS often identifiable years before the onset of OC symptoms.

In view of the comorbid patterns, some authors have suggested a distinction between "tic-related" and "non-tic-related" OCD [55]. Tic-related OCD appears to have an earlier onset and to occur more frequently in boys than in girls [54]. The need to touch or rub, blinking and staring rituals, worries over symmetry and exactness, a sense of incompleteness, and intrusive aggressive thoughts and images, are significantly more common in tic-related OCD, whereas contamination worries and cleaning compulsions are more frequent in subjects with non-tic-related OCD [55, 56]. The two putative subtypes of OCD seem to differ in their responsiveness to psychopharmacology, subjects with tic-related OCD having a generally less satisfactory response to selective serotonin reuptake inhibitors (SSRIs) alone [57].

Obsessive-Compulsive Spectrum Disorders

On the basis of shared clinical and phenomenological features, age of onset, course of illness, comorbidity, family history, and sometimes responsiveness to treatment, several disorders have been suggested to belong to an OC spectrum. These disorders might prove to share common neurophysiological or biological substrates, and possibly related genetic transmission.

Trichotillomania, defined as persistent hair-pulling to the point of alopecia, has been related to OCD in view of shared neuropsychological deficits and similar treatment response [58]. Trichotillomania can have an early-onset form, appearing as early as the toddler years. However, although the frequency of OCD seems to be increased in first-degree relatives of children and adolescents with trichotillomania [58], it appears that most youngsters with this condition do not have other obsessive or compulsive symptoms [59, 60]. Another repetitive unwanted behaviour of childhood onset, onychophagia (nail biting), has also been associated with OCD, and shown to respond specifically to pharmacological treatment with a serotonergic agent [61].

Body dysmorphic disorder, which is characterized by obsessional preoccupation with an imagined defect in appearence, often accompanied by compulsive behaviours such as excessive mirror-checking and grooming, has been tentatively classified as an OCD spectrum disorder in adults, and may be seen in adolescents [62]. The relationship of this disorder to OCD, however, remains unclear.

Some authors have suggested that the eating disorders, anorexia nervosa and bulimia nervosa, could belong to the OC spectrum, whether they are or not associated with clinical OCD. Symptoms concerning food, weight, body image or exercise frequently share the characteristics of obsessions or compulsions [63]. In addition, eating disorder patients may exhibit the full range of obsessions and compulsions, including pathological doubt, symmetry and contamination worries, repeating, checking and grooming [64, 65].

The inclusion of pervasive developmental disorders in the OC spectrum is more controversial. The stereotyped and repetitive behaviours seen in the autistic syndrome, similarly to the specific circumscribed interests in Asperger syndrome, may be easily described as obsessive-compulsive [66], but seem different in nature. Furthermore, autistic individuals usually lack insight into their mental state. However, autism has been associated with the OC spectrum on the basis of high rates of OCD in first-degree relatives [67, 68], serotonergic abnormalities [69], and potential responsiveness to SSRIs [70]. Recently, the B lymphocyte antigen D8/17, a possible marker for OCD and TS (see below), has been associated with autism [71].

ETIOPATHOGENESIS

Psychogenetic Factors

Psychological theories of OCD have encompassed psychoanalytic theories as well as more general non-psychodynamic etiological approaches, focusing alternatively on volitional, intellectual and/or emotional impairment. Freud's famous patient, the Rat Man, has long been seen as a paradigm of a psychologically determined illness, illustrating the central role of anal sadistic concerns with control, ambivalence, magical thinking and the salience of defences of reaction formation, intellectualization, isolation and undoing [5]. Freud went on to formulate a theory of pregenital organization of the libido, determined by constitutional rather than experimental factors, and crucial to the obsessional neurosis. He also provided fascinating speculations on the similarity between OC phenomena, children's games and religious rites. Anna Freud [72] stated that "obsessional outcomes are promoted by a constitutional increase in the intensity of the anal-sadistic tendencies... probably as the result of inheritance combined with parental handling". However, despite the beautifully described dynamics of obsessional symptoms, most illustrative of unconscious processes, the psychoanalysts have also pointed out the extreme difficulty in treating severe OCD with classical analytic treatment.

Biochemical Factors

Although a variety of biological etiologies have been proposed in OCD since 1860 [73], modern neurobiological theories began with the clinical studies showing that clomipramine (CMI) and other serotonin reuptake inhibitors (SRIs) had a unique efficacy in treating OCD (see below). This inspired a "serotonergic hypothesis" of OCD [74]. In children and adolescents, a few studies have brought evidence of the involvement of the serotonergic system in the pathophysiology of the disorder. In a double-blind, placebo-controlled CMI treatment study involving 29 children and adolescents, clinical improvement of the OC symptoms during CMI administration was strongly correlated to pre-treatment platelet serotonin concentration, and to the decrease of this measure during treatment [75]. In addition, there have been several reports of decreased density of the platelet serotonin transporter in children and adolescents with OCD, but not in those with TS [76, 77]; in one study [77], the baseline binding capacity (B_{max}) of the ligand ^{3}H-paroxetine was positively correlated to the severity of OC symptoms on the Y-BOCS, in responders to pharmacological treatment only. Another study showed an increase in central serotonin turnover, as evidenced by higher concentrations of 5-hydroxyindoleacetic acid (5-HIAA) in the cerebrospinal fluid (CSF) of children and adolescents with OCD compared to children and adolescents with disruptive behaviour disorder [78].

However, the delayed and incomplete action of serotonergic drugs, suggesting multiple effects on other neurotransmitters as well, and numerous biochemical studies of OCD patients and controls have not yet indicated a single biochemical abnormality as a primary etiological mechanism in OCD. Two studies have carefully examined CSF neurochemical changes during CMI treatment of patients with juvenile OCD at short-term [79] and long-term [80] follow-up. Changes were observed for many measures, including neuropeptides (corticotropin-releasing hormone, vasopressin, somatostatin, and oxytocin) and monoamine metabolites (5-HIAA, homovanillic acid, 3-methoxy-4-hydroxyphenylglycol).

Genetic Factors

The familial nature of OCD has been observed since the 1930s [81], and both Freud [5] and Janet [4] thought it likely that constitutional or genetic factors were important in the pathogenesis of the disorder. Twin studies have provided limited evidence for the importance of genetic factors in OCD manifestation [82]. At the present time, however, it is not clear whether these factors are specific for OCD or whether OCD is part of a broader heritable anxiety spectrum [83]. Several family studies have shown that OCD is much more common among relatives of individuals with OCD than would be expected from estimated occurrence rates for the general population [84]. Lenane *et al* [85] interviewed 145 first-degree relatives of 46 children and adolescents with severe primary OCD at the NIMH. They found that 25% of the fathers and 9% of the mothers had OCD, and that the age-corrected risk for OCD and subthreshold OCD combined for all first-degree relatives was 35%. Pauls *et al* [54] reported that the prevalence rates of OCD and tic disorders were significantly greater among the first-degree relatives of 100 probands with OCD (10.3% and 4.6%, respectively) than among relatives of psychiatrically unaffected subjects (1.9% and 1.0%). Interestingly, when comparing the rates among relatives of early (before 18 years) onset (n = 82) vs. late onset (n = 18) probands, the authors found a two-fold increased risk for OCD, and a four-fold increased risk for subthreshold OCD, in relatives of probands with early onset [54].

It has been suggested that at least some forms of OCD could be genetically related to TS. The pattern of vertical transmission among family members in TS has led to specific genetic hypotheses favouring models of autosomal dominant transmission [86]. In OCD, several studies have examined possible candidate genes related to the putative involvement of the serotonin and the dopamine systems in the physiopathology of the disorder (for review, see [83]). Given that no robust result has been obtained thus far, it is possible that some of these genes might be important in effective treatment, but that does not necessarily imply that those same genes would be involved in the genetic etiology of OCD.

Frontal–Subcortical Circuit Dysfunction

It has been known for a long time that OC symptoms could be associated with neurological disorders of motor control, including TS, Huntington's disease, Parkinson's disease, and traumatic or infectious lesions of the basal ganglia [73]. An increased incidence of motor tics, as well as choreiform movements, has been observed in children and adolescents with OCD, and a significant proportion of children and adults with the disorder show impairment of visuo-motor integration, visual memory, and executive functioning [50, 87, 88]. Since Baxter *et al's* [89] seminal study of OCD with positron emission tomography (PET), neuroimaging techniques have been extensively used in OCD research. Despite some discrepant findings across studies, there is now definite evidence that dysfunction within particular neural pathways is generally associated with OCD.

Seven among 12 studies on brain morphology of OCD patients report findings suggesting the involvement of the caudate nucleus and/or the frontal lobes in some patients [90]. One computerized tomography (CT) study found significantly smaller caudate volumes in young adult males with childhood onset OCD compared to controls [91], and a recent magnetic resonance (MRI) morphologic study showed that treatment-naïve paediatric OCD patients had significantly larger anterior cingulate volumes than did controls [92].

Recent neuroimaging advances have allowed study of brain functioning in young adults with childhood onset OCD and controls. Studies using single photon emission computed tomography (SPECT), PET and functional MRI have tended to demonstrate metabolic abnormalities in the circuits involving the orbito-frontal/cingulate cortex and the basal ganglia—most particularly the caudate nuclei—in OCD patients (for review, see [90]). Studies performed at rest and during symptom provocation demonstrated selective increases in regional blood flow, which correlated with OC symptoms intensity, in the caudate and the orbitofrontal cortex [93]. Furthermore, five among seven studies comparing brain functioning in OCD patients before and after successful pharmacological or psychological treatment, demonstrated reduction of the hypermetabolism of the frontal lobes following treatment [90]. One of these studies was conducted pre- and post-pharmacological treatment in childhood-onset OCD patients at the NIMH [94, 95]

However, it is still unclear whether the dysfunctions observed in the various neuroimaging studies, which remain discrepant across studies, are directly related to the pathophysiology of OCD, or represent non-specific manifestations of the anxious resistance of the patients to their obsessional symptoms.

Autoimmune Factors

A recent finding of potentially wide significance is the strong association demonstrated between acute onset OCD and Sydenham's chorea (SC), and it has been suggested that SC may serve as a model of pathogenesis for certain forms of OCD [96]. SC is a childhood movement disorder associated with rheumatic fever (RF), which is thought to be a result of an antineuronal antibody-mediated response to group A β-haemolytic streptococcus (GABHS), directed at portions of the basal ganglia, in genetically vulnerable individuals.

A first retrospective comparison of obsessionality in 23 SC patients and 24 RF patients without chorea showed significantly increased OC symptoms (with three patients meeting diagnostic criteria for OCD) among the choreic patients [97]. In a second study, 11 children with SC of recent onset were examined by Swedo *et al* [98]: antibodies directed against human caudate tissue were present in the serum of 10 children, and nine of the 11 children experienced an acute onset of OC symptoms, which started shortly before the onset of the movement disorder, peaked as the chorea did, and waned over time, completely disappearing with cessation of the choreic movements. In Brazil, a recent investigation of children and adolescents who had RF with SC ($n = 30$) or without chorea ($n = 20$) found OC symptoms in 70% of subjects with SC, and diagnosable OCD in 16.7%, while OC symptoms were absent in all patients without chorea [99].

Even in the absence of the neurological symptoms of SC, post-streptococcal cases of childhood onset OCD, tics and/or other neuropsychiatric symptoms have been described under the acronym of pediatric autoimmune neuropsychiatric disorders associated with streptococcal infections (PANDAS) [100, 101]. Swedo *et al* [101] define this novel group of patients by five diagnostic criteria: presence of OCD and/or tic disorder, prepubertal onset, episodic course of symptom severity, abrupt onset or dramatic exacerbations of symptoms associated with GABHS infections (as evidenced by positive throat culture and/or elevated anti-GABHS titres), and association with neurological abnormalities (motor hyperactivity and adventitious movements, such as choreiform movements or tics).

Therapeutically, this finding of a probable autoimmune-caused OCD raises the clinical possibility that immunosuppressant and even antibiotic treatments will be effective in treating or preventing some cases of OCD. However, the first double-blind attempt to demonstrate the efficacy of penicillin prophylaxis in preventing tic or OCD symptom exacerbation was negative because of failure to achieve an acceptable level of streptococcal prophylaxis [102].

An antigen labelled D8/17, on the surface of peripheral blood mononuclear cells, has been shown to be a marker for the genetic tendency to generate abnormal antibodies to GABHS. Two independent groups of researchers [103, 104] have found a greater expression of the D8/17 antigen in the B-lymphocytes of patients with childhood-onset OCD or TS compared with healthy controls, indicating that the presence of the D8/17 antigen may serve as a marker of susceptibility for OCD [93].

TREATMENT

The treatment of OCD has changed dramatically over the past 15 years, with two modalities being systematically assessed and empirically shown to ameliorate the core symptoms of the disorder in children and adolescents: pharmacological treatment with agents that are potent SRIs, and specific cognitive-behavioural treatment (CBT).

Psychopharmacological Treatment

Several randomized, controlled clinical trials have been conducted in children and adolescents with OCD, demonstrating, as many more similar studies with adult patients, the selective and unique efficacy of SRIs (CMI, fluoxetine, sertraline) in the short-term treatment of the disorder; a few open studies have given preliminary positive results for other SSRIs (fluvoxamine, citalopram, paroxetine). The design and main results of these studies are summarized in Table 4.1.

CMI was the first known antiobsessional agent. Its efficacy for children and adolescents with OCD has been demonstrated in three controlled studies. The first, by Flament *et al* [33] at the NIMH, was a cross-over study in which CMI was significantly superior to placebo, after 5 weeks of treatment, for improvement of both observed and self-reported obsessions and compulsions; this was independent of the presence of depressive symptoms at baseline. A subsequent cross-over study by Leonard *et al* [105], also at the NIMH, demonstrated the specificity of the antiobsessional effect of CMI, which was clearly superior to desipramine (DMI) in reducing OC symptoms; 64% of patients who received CMI as their first active treatment showed at least some sign of relapse during subsequent DMI treatment. De Veaugh-Geiss *et al* [106] reported on 60 children and adolescents with OCD included in a multicentre parallel group trial of CMI vs. placebo. At the end of 8 weeks, 53% of patients receiving active drug rated themselves as very much improved or much improved, vs. 8% receiving placebo. In a 1-year open-label maintenance treatment for 47 patients, CMI continued to be effective and well tolerated. The secondary effects of CMI include dry mouth, somnolence, dizziness, tremor, headache,

TABLE 4.1 Short-term pharmacological treatment studies of obsessive-compulsive disorder (OCD) in children and adolescents

Study	n (age) Duration of treatment	Drug (daily dose) Study design	Improvement from baseline on active drug across OC symptom measures (%)
Flament *et al* [33]	19 (6–18 years) 5 weeks	Clomipramine (mean: 141 mg) Crossover vs. placebo	22–44
Leonard *et al* [105]	47 (7–19 years) 5 weeks	Clomipramine (mean: 150 mg) Crossover vs. desipramine	19–29
DeVeaugh-Geiss *et al* [106]	60 (10–17 years) 8 weeks	Clomipramine (75–200 mg) Parallel vs. placebo	34–37
Riddle *et al* [108]	14 (8–15 years) 8 weeks	Fluoxetine (20 mg) Crossover vs. placebo	33–44
Apter *et al* [109]	14 (13–18 years) 8 weeks	Fluvoxamine (100–300 mg) Open study	28
Thomsen [112]	23 (9–18 years) 10 weeks	Citalopram (mean: 37 mg) Open study	20–29
March *et al* [110]	187 (6–17 years) 12 weeks	Sertraline (mean: 167 mg) Parallel vs. placebo	21–28
Rosenberg *et al* [113]	20 (8–17 years) 12 weeks	Paroxetine (mean: 41 mg) Open study	28

constipation, stomach discomfort, sweating and insomnia. CMI can cause tachycardia and axis changes with prolongation of the QT interval on electrocardiogram (ECG) [107]; baseline and periodic ECG monitoring is recommended [44].

Fluoxetine was investigated by Riddle *et al* [108] in a 8-week, placebo-controlled, cross-over study involving 14 children and adolescents with OCD. The degree of symptomatic improvement on fluoxetine was comparable with that observed in similar trials of CMI. In a 8-week open-label trial by Apter *et al* [109], fluvoxamine, given to adolescent inpatients treated for OCD or major depressive disorder, also induced a significant decrease in the severity of OC symptoms. The largest controlled study completed to date is a multicentre, 12-week placebo-controlled trial of sertraline including 187 children and adolescents with OCD, in which significant differences between the drug and placebo emerged at week 3 and persisted for the duration of the study [110]. For sertraline, it has been shown that pharmacokinetic parameters are similar in children, adolescent and adult patients [111]. In an open trial with citalopram, 75% of patients showed marked or moderate improvement after 10 weeks, and only minor and transient adverse effects were noted [112]. Similarly, in a 12-week open trial by Rosenberg *et al* [113], paroxetine appeared to be safe and effective on OC symptoms. Although less frequent and disturbing than the secondary effects of CMI, the most commonly described secondary effects of SSRIs include nausea, headache, tremor, gastrointestinal complaints, drowsiness, akathisia, insomnia, sexual problems, disinhibition, agitation or even hypomania, and the worsening of tics in case of comorbidity [44, 63].

The selective efficacy of SRIs is also supported by Leonard *et al*'s [114] DMI substitution study during long-term CMI maintenance treatment of a group of 26 children and adolescents with severe primary OCD. Eight (89%) of nine of the substituted subjects and only two of 11 of the non-substituted subjects relapsed during the 2-month comparison period. All eight patients who relapsed with DMI regained their clinical response within 1 month of CMI reinstallment.

For children and adolescents with OCD and comorbid tic disorder, SRIs alone might have little antiobsessional effect [115], and there are reports suggesting that SSRIs, especially at higher doses, may exacerbate or even induce tics in some patients [108, 116, 117]. In adults with OCD, McDougle *et al* [58] reported that a personal or family history of chronic tic disorder was associated with a positive response to haloperidol augmentation of fluvoxamine treatment; these authors recommend the addition of dopamine antagonists to the treatment regimen of SSRI-resistant OCD patients with a comorbid chronic tic disorder and, possibly, for those with concurrent psychotic spectrum disorders. Preliminary reports in children tend to support this approach [118].

Cognitive-Behavioural Treatment (CBT)

Several case reports [119] and four open studies [120–123] (Table 4.2) have shown the beneficial effects of CBT, alone or in addition to pharmacotherapy, for children and adolescents with OCD. Treatment generally involves a three-stage approach, consisting of information gathering, therapist-assisted graded exposure with response prevention, and homework assignments (for detail, see [119]). Anxiety management training plays an adjunctive role. For children with predominantly internalizing symptoms, treatment also includes relaxation and cognitive training. Family needs to be involved, to varying extents according to individual situations. CBT is usually implemented initially with 13–20 weekly individual or family sessions, and homework assignments. Partial responders or non-responders may require more frequent visits and out-of-office therapist-assisted training.

Bolton *et al* [120] reported the outcome of CBT (generally combined with other treatment approaches) in a series of 15 adolescents: in most cases, symptoms were relieved entirely (47%) or reduced to a mildly incapacitating level (40%). March *et al* [124] presented an open trial of CBT for 15 children and adolescents with OCD, most of whom were also receiving medication. Nine patients experienced at least a 50% reduction in symptoms at post-treatment, and six were asymptomatic. No patients relapsed at follow-up intervals as long as 18 months. Booster behavioural treatment allowed medication discontinuation in six patients. Franklin *et al* [122] found similar results in an open trial of CBT for 14 children and adolescents with OCD: eight patients had concurrent treatment with an SSRI, 12 experienced at least a 50% reduction in symptoms at post-treatment, and the vast majority remained improved at 9-month follow-up.

De Haan *et al* [123] compared CBT ($n = 12$) and CMI ($n = 10$) in a randomized trial for children and adolescents with OCD. CBT produced stronger therapeutic changes than CMI after 12 weeks. Five of the nine initial non-responders showed significant changes after combining both treatment regimens for a further 12 weeks.

Other Treatment Approaches

Although some uncontrolled case studies have found psychodynamic psychotherapy useful in treating juvenile OCD [124, 125], the effectiveness of psychotherapy alone—apart from cognitive interventions—on obsessive and compulsive symptoms remains to be systematically explored. Nevertheless, traditional psychotherapeutic approaches may be useful to help OCD children or adolescents to address the intrapsychic conflicts that affect or result from their illness.

TABLE 4.2 Cognitive-behavioural treatment (CBT) studies of obsessive-compulsive disorder (OCD) in children and adolescents

Study	*n* (age) Duration of treatment	Study design	Short-term improvement	Long-term improvement
Bolton *et al* [120]	15 (12–18 years) 1–48 months	Open trial CBT ± drug or other treatment	7 Asymptomatic, 6 much improved	*9 Months to 4 years:* 11/14 improved
March *et al* [121]	15 (8–18 years) 22 weeks	Open trial CBT ± drug or other treatment	6 Asymptomatic, 3 much improved	*18 Months:* 9/15 improved
Franklin *et al* [122]	14 (10–17 years) 1–4 months	Open trial CBT ± drug or other treatment	12 Responders (> 50% decrease in OC symptoms)	*9 Months:* 10/12 improved
De Haan *et al* [123]	22 (8–18 years) 12 weeks	Randomized trial CBT ($n = 12$) vs. clomipramine ($n = 10$)	8/12 Responders on CBT > 5/10 responders on clomipramine (> 30% decrease in OC symptoms)	Not reported

Family psychopathology is neither necessary nor sufficient for the onset of OCD [126]. Nonetheless, families affect and are affected by the disorder. Some become extensively involved in participating in the child's rituals or reassuring obsessional worries; other become mired in grueling, angry struggles and arguments with their symptomatic child. Work with families on how to manage the child's symptoms, cope with the stress and family disruption that often accompanies OCD, and participate effectively in behavioural or pharmacological treatment is essential [127]. It is important to note that most cognitive-behavioural approaches to paediatric OCD include the involvement of a parent in some therapeutic sessions. Family support groups and patients advocacy groups, now available in many countries, can also provide valuable help and support.

In case of severe OCD, there is some empirical evidence that milieu therapy in an inpatient setting may be a useful resource [120, 124].

Treatment Guidelines

According to expert consensus guidelines [44, 128], the need for pharmacotherapy in children and adolescents with OCD depends on the severity of the illness. CBT alone is favoured as the initial treatment of choice in milder cases without significant comorbidity, whereas severe OCD, presence of comorbid depression, anxiety or disruptive behaviour, and insufficient cognitive or emotional ability to cooperate in CBT, are indications for SRI treatment. The choice of CBT as the initial treatment has the advantage of apparent durability of benefits and of avoiding the potential side effects of pharmacotherapy. The combination treatment might be more efficient than either alone, and CBT may reduce relapse rate in patients withdrawn from medication.

In the absence of direct comparison or meta-analytic studies assessing the efficacy of SRIs/SSRIs in children and adolescents, it is not known whether one SRI/SSRI is more effective than another for treating childhood OCD. In practice, the choice of the agent may depend on the side effect profile and the potential for drug interaction. CMI has the most anticholinergic side effect profile, requires ECG monitoring, and is the most toxic in overdose. An adequate therapeutic trial of CMI generally consists of a dosage of up to 3 mg/kg/day for 3 months. Dosage should not exceed 5 mg/kg/day or 250 mg/day, because of the risks of toxicity, including seizures and ECG changes. In contrast, SSRIs do not require ECG monitoring, are less toxic in overdose, but may be associated with more minor complaints. Thus, a SSRI may be used in first-line treatment of childhood OCD, when medication is necessary. A trial of adequate dosage and duration (10–12 weeks) is necessary to determine whether a child is responder to a given SSRI.

Relatively high doses of SSRIs have been used in published studies (see Table 4.1), while lower doses seem to be active. Systematic dose–response data are not available for children, but side effects generally appear dose-dependent. Therefore, SSRIs are to be started at low doses (fluoxetine, paroxetine, citalopram, 20 mg/day; fluvoxamine, sertraline, 50 mg/day) and progressively increased in case of inefficacy.

Despite differences in potency and selectivity, it is not known which SRI/SSRI will be more effective for treating which type of patients, and failure to respond to one compound does not necessarily predict failure to respond to another. Thus, if there is no clinical response after 10–12 weeks of a first trial with an SSRI, switching to another or to CMI is reasonable. For patients who only have a partial therapeutic response after several successive trials, augmentation strategies may be useful, in particular addition of a low dose of a neuroleptic in children with OCD and comorbid tic disorder or schizotypal personality disorder.

The optimal duration of SSRI/CMI maintenance treatment is unclear, since relapses are frequent when discontinuing medication. Antiobsessional medication should be maintained for at least 12–18 months after a satisfactory response has been obtained. Once the decision is made to attempt reduction or discontinuation, the tapering should be gradual.

In view of recent findings on the possible role of autoimmune factors in OCD, a child with acute onset or exacerbation of OC and/or tic symptoms requires careful consideration of medical illnesses, including upper respiratory tract infections, during the preceding months. A throat culture and an antistreptolysin O or antistreptococcal DNAase B titre may be considered to assist in diagnosing a GABHS infection [44].

SHORT-TERM AND LONG-TERM OUTCOME

Several retrospective or prospective follow-up studies of subjects treated for OCD during childhood or adolescence have looked at the outcome of the disorder into early adulthood (for review, see [129]).

Retrospective Follow-up Studies

Among the retrospective follow-up studies of paediatric OCD, summarized in Table 4.3, we will cite Hollingsworth *et al* [130], who identified 17 cases of severe OC neurosis from a chart review of all children admitted as in- or outpatients at the University of California Neuropsychiatric Institute in Los Angeles for a 16-year period. All OC children had been treated with intensive psychotherapy (for an average of 17.7 months), and one of them also

Table 4.3 Retrospective follow-up studies of children and adolescents with obsessive-compulsive disorder (OCD)

Study (Place)	Sample size (Diagnostic criteria)	Mean age (range) Mean F/U period (range) (years)	Initial treatment	Outcome
Hollingsworth *et al* [130] (Los Angeles, USA)	10/17 (13M, 4F) (Judd's criteria)	Age at F/U: 19.9 (12–30) F/U period: 6.5 (1.5–14)	Intensive psychotherapy	3 (30%) recovered, 7 (70%) some degree of OC symptoms
Allsop & Verduyn [138] (Oxford, UK)	20/26 (14 M, 12 F) (ICD-9 + Judd's criteria)	Age at admission: 15.3 (12.5–18.4) Age at F/U: 25.1 (20.1–28.5)	Behavioural response prevention + family work	10 (50%) recovered, 6 (30%) persistent OCD, 2 (10%) schizophrenia, 2 (10%) depressive disorder
Thomsen & Mikkelsen [132] (Denmark)	47 (28 M, 19 F)/55 + 49 control patients (DSM-III)	Age at admission: 11.8 for boys, 12.4 for girls Age at F/U: 27.4 (18–36) F/U period: 15.6 (6–22)	Diverse (SRIs, psychotherapy, family therapy)	13 (28%) recovered, 12 (25%) subclinical OCD, 10 (21%) phasic OCD, 12 (25%) chronic OCD

M, male; F, female; F/U, follow-up; SRIs, serotonin reuptake inhibitors.

received behavioural therapy. The authors interviewed 10 of these cases, 1.5–14 years after their first admission. Only three of the ten (30%) denied any obsessive thoughts or compulsions, while seven (70%) reported that the OC behaviour still continued to some degree but was less than pre-treatment level. One had decompensated during adolescence in an acute schizophrenic reaction, which had resolved without recurrence. On follow-up, all 10 subjects reported problems with social life and peer relationships; none was married.

Another study by Thomsen and Mikkelsen [131, 132] in Denmark examined clinical course of childhood OCD in 47 subjects re-evaluated 6–22 years after initial referral, in comparison with a control group of age- and sex-matched control patients admitted for other non-psychotic disorders during the same period. At follow-up, 47% of the OCD probands (vs. 0% of the controls) still had OCD, and 68% (vs. 61% of the controls) had at least one personality disorder; among the OCD probands, the most common personality disorder was the avoidant (23% vs. 8% of the controls), whereas obsessive-compulsive personality disorder (OCPD) was not found more often than among controls (17% vs. 10%). However, in the OCD group, seven of the eight subjects with OCPD had continued OCD at follow-up. Generally, most personality disorders were found in the group of patients with chronic OCD at follow-up.

Prospective Follow-up Studies

The prospective follow-up studies of children and adolescents with OCD are summarized in Table 4.4. An early study by Warren [133] described 15 adolescents admitted to the Maudsley Hospital in London with OC states, and re-examined when aged 19–24 years. No treatment was specified, except for one patient who had been leucotomized. At follow-up, only two subjects were considered completely recovered, four had a tendency to mild OC symptoms under stress, four were somewhat handicapped by obsessional symptoms, and the remaining five still had severe symptomatology, one being hospitalized.

Two prospective longitudinal studies of children and adolescents with OCD have been successively conducted at the NIMH Child Psychiatry Branch. In the first one [50], subjects were 27 patients admitted between 1977 and 1983 for a 5-week treatment trial with CMI and matched for sex, age and IQ with normal controls from the local community. Following the initial drug trial, only seven patients were maintained on CMI (not available in the USA at the time), between a few months and 3 years. Others received non-specific medication (other tricyclic antidepressants, neuroleptics, anxiolytics) or psychological treatment (supportive psychotherapy, family or

TABLE 4.4 Prospective follow-up studies of children and adolescents with obsessive-compulsive disorder (OCD)

Study (Place)	Sample size (Diagnostic criteria)	Mean age (range) in years	Interim treatment	Outcome
Warren [133] (Maudsley, London, UK)	15 (No specific criteria)	Admission: (12–17) F/U: (19–24)	No treatment specified (except 1 leucotomized)	2 (13%) recovered, 4 (27%) mild OC symptoms under stress, 4 (27%) handicapping OC symptoms, 5 (33%) severe OC symptoms
Flament *et al* [50] (NIMH, USA)	25 (16M, 4F)/27 (DSM-III) + 23/29 normal controls	Admission: 14.4 (10–18) F/U: 18.8 (13–24)	Intermittent and non-specific medication or psychotherapy	7 (28%) recovered, 17 (60%) OCD, 1 (4%) psychosis
Leonard *et al* [134] (NIMH, USA)	54/54 (36M, 18F) (DSM-III)	Admission: 14 (7–19) F/U: 17.4 (10–24)	96% SRIs, 46% behavioural therapy	6 (11%) recovered (3 on medication), 15 (28%) OC features, 10 (18%) subclinical OCD, 23 (43%) OCD
Thomsen & Mikkelsen [135] (Denmark)	23 (17M, 6F)/26 (DSM-III-R) + 24 control patients	Admission: 14.1 (9–17) F/U: 16.6 (12–22)	57% SRIs, behavioural therapy (rate not specified)	6 (26%) recovered, 9 (39%) subclinical OCD, 8 (35%) clinical OCD
Bolton *et al* [136] (Maudsley, London, UK)	14/15 (8M, 7F) (DSM-III-R)	Admission: 14.1 (12–18) F/U: 27 (23–31)	50% SRIs and/or behavioural therapy	8 (57%) recovered, 6 (43%) OCD (2 unremitting, 4 with relapse)

M, male; F, female; F/U, follow-up; SRIs, serotonin reuptake inhibitors.

group therapy); these treatments had often been only briefly or irregularly administered. At follow-up, more patients (74%) than controls (57%) were still living with their families, more controls (86%) than patients (59%) were still at school. Seventeen patients (68%) still met criteria for OCD, and comorbidity was common, as 13 (52%) of the group had another Axis I psychiatric disorder, most commonly an anxiety and/or depressive disorder.

The second study, by Leonard *et al* [134], concerned children and adolescents who participated in the NIMH CMI treatment studies between 1984 and 1988. The objective of this later study was to assess the outcome of patients who had access to continued psychopharmacological treatment, to determine whether there had been any long-term gains and if there were any predictors of outcome. After discharge from the NIMH, 96% of the patients received additional pharmacological treatment with CMI or another SRI, 33% behavioural therapy, 54% individual psychotherapy and 20% family therapy. At the time of follow-up, 70% were still taking psychoactive medication. During the follow-up period, several interim contacts with most of the subjects showed that many patients met DSM-III-R criteria for OCD at some times but not at others, illustrating the waxing and waning pattern of the disorder. All subjects were assessed 2–7 years after first referral. Only six (11%) were free of any obsession or compulsion. Of those six, three were still under medication; therefore, only three (6% of the sample) could be considered in true remission. Although OC symptoms continued for most subjects, the group as a whole was significantly improved from endpoint of initial CMI treatment on measures of OCD, anxiety, depression and global functioning, indicating significant gains over those of short-term treatment; only 10 subjects (19%) were rated as unchanged or worse. Three patients had developed a psychotic disorder subsequent to baseline evaluation, but this had resolved in two (one only had a brief reactive psychosis while receiving medication).

In a second Danish study [135], 23 of 26 children and adolescents with OCD were prospectively evaluated every 6 months for OC symptomatology. After discharge from initial treatment, all children had individual or family sessions with behavioural therapy, and 13 received medication (CMI or citalopram) for a period of 0.5–2 years. At follow-up, 1.5–5 years after referral, eight subjects (35%) retained an OCD diagnosis, including three who were still receiving medication (with OC symptoms on a much less severe level than at baseline); nine subjects (39%) had subclinical OCD, mostly with the same form and content as the clinical OCD presented at baseline, although they were neither distressed nor functionally or socially affected by these subclinical symptoms; the remaining six (26%) had no OCD. Interim evaluations supported the theories of OCD as an illness of fluctuating severity.

Bolton *et al* [136] reported on 14/15 young adults treated for OCD during adolescence [120], mainly by behavioural and family task-setting therapy; five subjects had also received CMI. Among 13 of the 15 patients who had responded positively to treatment in adolescence, seven had stayed well and were treatment-free at follow-up, one had rapidly settled into a chronic course, and four had relapsed between 3 and 6 years after initial treatment (the last one was lost to follow-up). As to the two patients with no response to protracted treatment in adolescence, one case (with obsessional slowness) remained chronic, while the other responded well to further behavioural therapy a year later.

Apart from these, we will cite a 2-year prospective follow-up of OCD cases identified in a community study [10, 137]. The follow-up study showed the relative stability of the diagnosis of OCD in a natural setting, with variations in symptom severity. Contrary to the authors' expectations, subjects initially diagnosed with subclinical OCD did not progress into true cases of OCD, reinforcing the importance of using a high diagnostic threshold of severity.

Risk and Prognostic Factors

Several studies, both on the natural course of OCD and on clinical response to treatment interventions, have attempted to identify demographic or clinical features that may influence outcome or course of illness in OCD, with mainly negative or inconsistent results (for review, see [129]).

In Thomsen and Mikkelsen's retrospective follow-up study [132], a number of baseline variables were examined, using multivariate analysis, as possible predictors of OCD outcome. None seemed to predict outcome, except OCD severity in childhood, as measured by the number of hours spent on symptoms. More women than men had an episodic course, and more males than females belonged to the poorest outcome group. However, just as many females as males had OCD at follow-up.

Except for one short-term pharmacological study, in which male subjects responded significantly better than did female subjects [33], in the other studies, initial treatment response could not be predicted by sex, age of onset, duration or severity of illness, or type of symptoms [105, 106].

As for long-term course, a stepwise regression analysis was performed in Leonard *et al*'s [134] study, with representative baseline and week 5 variables: a worse OCD outcome at follow-up was predicted, in a stepwise multiple regression, by a more severe OCD symptom score after 5 weeks of CMI therapy (31% of the variance), the presence of parental Axis I psychiatric diagnosis (16%), and a lifetime history of tics at baseline (15%). In Bolton *et al*'s [136] study, good treatment outcome in adolescence predicted medium-term prognosis (between 1 and 4 years) fairly well, but it failed to predict long-term prognosis (between 9 and 14 years), reflecting the fact that some patients relapsed into a chronic course even after several years of remission following treatment.

SUMMARY

Consistent Evidence

Childhood OCD may represent the disorder in child psychiatry whose clinical picture most closely resembles its adult counterpart. Despite a relative diversity, the symptom "pool" is remarkably finite and very similar to that seen in older individuals. Prevalence, comorbidity and response to pharmacological and behavioural treatment, also appear continuous across the life span.

Children and adolescents with OCD usually suffer from a range of symptoms simultaneously, that may change over time. Most subjects have both obsessions and compulsions, and apparently there are no age-related patterns in the prevalence of specific types of symptoms. For reasons still unknown, the onset of OCD generally occurs earlier in males than in females.

All follow-up studies clearly demonstrate the continuity of the diagnosis of OCD from childhood to adulthood: when subjects are still symptomatic at follow-up, the main diagnosis is almost invariably OCD, although comorbid disorders, especially mood and/or anxiety disorders, are frequent. Evolution towards psychosis is exceptional. Spontaneous course is most often marked by a waxing and waning severity of the disorder, whereas remissions under treatment may be followed by relapses, even after long periods of time.

One might infer from the results of short-term and longer longitudinal studies that two types of treatment intervention can markedly improve prognosis of childhood onset OCD, and significantly reduce impairment from the condition. There is now clear evidence that pharmacological treatment with drugs that are potent serotonin reuptake inhibitors (CMI and SSRIs)—at doses comparable to those used for adults—induces a clinically substantial reduction of OC symptoms for most children and adolescents with the disorder. However, improvement is often incomplete, few patients become asymptomatic, and long-term maintenance treatment may be required. CBT, based on graded exposure with response prevention, might have more durable benefits, and is considered as the first-line treatment in mild non-comorbid OCD. Because OCD frequently occurs in the context of other psychopathology and adaptative difficulties, additional individual and family psychotherapeutic, and educational interventions are often necessary.

Incomplete Evidence

Although invaluable benefits can now be obtained from available pharmacological and behavioural treatments, complete remission remains uncertain, and long-term management is still required for many cases of paediatric onset OCD.

Ongoing studies are examining whether there would be distinct subtypes of OCD that could differ in clinical phenomenology, neurobiological concomitants, and responsiveness to psychological or pharmacological interventions. For example, children and adolescents with OCD vary in age of onset (prepubertal vs. pubertal), mode of onset (insidious vs. abrupt), personal comorbidity, family history, course of illness, associated neurological or biological abnormalities (e.g. tic disorders, post-infectious conditions). These characteristics could help delineate specific subtypes of OCD, associated with distinct patterns of etiology, response to treatment and long-term outcome. The distinction between tic-related and non-tic-related OCD might prove to be particularly relevant in these respects.

Data from the last 10 years of neuroimaging studies suggest that OCD is associated with dysfunction in particular neural pathways. Results from neuroanatomical and neurophysiological studies are still partial and sometimes contradictory, although the involvement of the basal ganglia and the orbitofrontal cortex is strongly suspected. However, it is still unclear whether the functional abnormalities observed in these studies are specific to the pathophysiology of OCD, or reflect the anxious resistance of the OC patients to their symptoms.

Similarly, despite accumulating evidence for a serotonin hypothesis in the etiopathogenesis or treatment of OCD, it is not yet clear whether the biochemical changes observed before or after treatment reflect primary or adaptative mechanisms. More research is needed on other neurotransmitter systems as well, since numerous biochemical studies of OCD patients and controls have not yet indicated a single biochemical abnormality as a primary etiological mechanism in the disorder.

Areas Still Open to Research

One of the main problems we are still facing with childhood onset OCD is the difficulty in predicting the long-term outcome of the disorder.

According to both course and treatment literature, surprisingly few demographic and clinical features seem apt to predict long-term course.

Partial or complete treatment resistance remains a major area of concern, and urgently needs further research, as resistant juvenile OCD patients usually exhibit severe forms of the illness. New pharmacological treatment strategies should be systematically investigated, including augmentation or association treatment regimens, but also the search for novel compounds with new pharmacological profiles. Besides classical behavioural interventions, psychological treatments should also encompass more comprehensive cognitive techniques, to be empirically explored.

The major area of research for the coming years remains etiology or, more likely, etiologies of OCD. Although the family aggregation of the disorder has been long recognized, the search for genes responsible for the expression of OCD, or for susceptibility to the disorder, remains an open task. It might help to examine in more detail the interaction between genotype and environment. The association between some forms of neurological damage and OC symptoms has also been known for a long time, but modern neuroimaging tools should allow to study regional brain functioning of OCD individuals in different states and at different stages of their illness. Although probably a numerical minority, the identification of autoimmune cases of OCD certainly represents a major breakthrough in the understanding of a disorder long considered as a purely psychologically determined illness. It might serve as a medical model of OCD, and help identify the neuroanatomical, neurophysiological or biochemical mechanisms involved in the onset or maintenance of the disorder.

In conclusion, OCD is a frequent and probably heterogeneous disorder, which should be recognized in its early stage, that is, often during childhood or adolescence years. Although current available treatments are not generally curative, most children and adolescents given a correct diagnosis and an individually targeted treatment, may be substantially helped to resume a normal developmental trajectory. More research is needed into basic neurobiological mechanisms to improve understanding and long-term outcome of the disorder.

REFERENCES

1. Esquirol J.E.D. (1838) *Traité des Maladies Mentales*, Baillère, Paris.
2. Legrand du Saulle H. (1875) *La Folie du Doute avec Délire du Toucher*, Delahaye, Paris.
3. Haustgen T. (1998) Les obsessions avant la psychanalyse. *Synapse*, **150**: 51–54.
4. Janet P. (1903) *Les obsessions et la psychasthénie*, Alcan, Paris.
5. Freud S. (1909) Bemerkungen über einen Fall von Zwangsneurose. *Jahrbuch für Psychoanalytische und Psychopathologische Forschungen*, **1**: 357–421.

6. Kanner L. (1957) *Child Psychiatry*, Thomas, Springfield.
7. Despert L. (1955) Differential diagnosis between obsessive-compulsive neurosis and schizophrenia in children. In *Psychopathology of Childhood* (Eds P.H. Hoch, J. Zubin), pp. 240–253, Grune and Stratton, New York.
8. Black A. (1974) The natural history of obsessional neurosis. In *Obsessional States* (Ed. H.R. Beech), pp. 19–54, Methuen, London.
9. Rasmussen S.A., Eisen J.L. (1990) Epidemiology of obsessive compulsive disorder. *J. Clin. Psychiatry*, **51** (suppl. 2): 10–13.
10. Flament M.F., Whitaker A., Rapoport J.L., Davies M., Berg C.Z., Kalikow K., Sceery W., Schaffer D. (1988) Obsessive compulsive disorder in adolescence: an epidemiological study. *J. Am. Acad. Child Adolesc. Psychiatry*, **27**: 764–771.
11. Zohar A.H., Ratzosin G., Pauls D.L., Apter A., Bleich A., Kron S., Rappaport M., Weizman A., Cohen D.J. (1992) An epidemiological study of obsessive-compulsive disorder and related disorders in Israeli adolescents. *J. Am. Acad. Child Adolesc. Psychiatry*, **31**: 1057–1061.
12. Reinherz H.Z., Giaconia R.M., Lefkowitz E.S., Pakiz B., Frost A.K. (1993) Prevalence of psychiatric disorders in a community population of older adolescents. *J. Am. Acad. Child Adolesc. Psychiatry*, **32**: 369–377.
13. Douglass H.M., Moffitt T.E., Dar R., McGee R., Silva P. (1995) Obsessive-compulsive disorder in a birth cohort of 18-year-olds: prevalence and predictors. *J. Am. Acad. Child Adolesc. Psychiatry*, **34**: 1424–1431.
14. Costello E., Angold A., Burns B., Erkanli A., Stangl D., Tweed D. (1996) The Great Smoky Mountains study group. *Arch. Gen. Psychiatry*, **53**: 1129–1136.
15. Robins L.N., Helzer J.E., Weissman M.M., Orvaschel H., Gruenberg E., Burke J.D., Regier D.A. (1984) Lifetime prevalence of specific disorders in three sites. *Arch. Gen. Psychiatry*, **41**: 949–958.
16. Karno M., Golding J.M., Sorenson S.B., Burnam M.A. (1988) The epidemiology of obsessive-compulsive disorder in five US communities. *Arch. Gen. Psychiatry*, **45**: 1094–1099.
17. Weissman M.M., Bland R.C., Canino G.L., Greenwald S., Hwu H.G., Lee C.K., Newman S.C., Oakley-Browne M.A., Rubio-Stipec M., Wickramaratne P.J. *et al.* (1994) The Cross National Epidemiology of obsessive-compulsive disorder. *J. Clin. Psychiatry*, **55**: 5–10.
18. Honjo S., Hirano C., Murase S., Kaneko T., Sugiyama T., Othaka K., Ayoma T., Takei T., Inoko K., Wakabayashi S. (1989) Obsessive-compulsive symptoms in childhood and adolescence. *Acta Psychiatr. Scand.*, **80**: 83–91.
19. Thomsen P.H., Mikkelsen H.U. (1991) Children and adolescents with obsessive-compulsive disorder. The demographic and diagnostic characteristics of 61 Danish patients. *Acta Psychiatr. Scand.*, **83**: 262–266.
20. World Health Organization (1992) *The ICD-10 Classification of Mental and Behavioural Disorders. Clinical Descriptions and Diagnostic Guidelines*, World Health Organization, Geneva.
21. American Psychiatric Association (1994) *Diagnostic and Statistical Manual of Mental Disorders*, 4th edn, American Psychiatric Association, Washington, DC.
22. Swedo S.E., Rapoport J.L., Leonard H., Lenane M., Cheslow D. (1989) Obsessive-compulsive disorder in children and adolescents. Clinical phenomenology of 70 consecutive cases. *Arch. Gen. Psychiatry*, **46**: 335–340.
23. Khanna S., Srinath S. (1989) Childhood obsessive compulsive disorder. I. Psychopathology. *Psychopathology*, **32**: 47–54.
24. Apter A., Tyano S. (1988) Obsessive compulsive disorders in adolescence. *J. Adolesc.*, **11**: 183–194.

25. Thomsen P.H. (1991) Obsessive-compulsive symptoms in children and adolescents. A phenomenological analysis of 61 Danish cases. *Psychopathology*, **24**: 12–18.
26. Toro J., Cervera M., Osjeo E., Salamero M. (1992) Obsessive-compulsive disorder in childhood and adolescence: a clinical study. *J. Child Psychol. Psychiatry*, **33**: 1025–1037.
27. Rasmussen S.A., Eisen J.L. (1992) The epidemiology and differential diagnosis of obsessive compulsive disorder. *J. Clin. Psychiatry*, **53** (suppl. 4): 4–10.
28. Riddle M.A., Scahill L., King R., Hardin M.T., Towbin K.E., Ort S.I., Leckman J.F., Cohen D.J. (1990) Obsessive compulsive disorder in children and adolescents: phenomenology and family history. *J. Am. Acad. Child Adolesc. Psychiatry*, **29**: 766–772.
29. Cohen D., Leckman J. (1994) Developmental psychopathology and neurobiology of Tourette's syndrome. *J. Am. Acad. Child Adolesc. Psychiatry*, **33**: 2–15.
30. Leckman J., Walker W., Goodman W., Pauls D., Cohen D. (1994) Just right perceptions associated with compulsive behaviors in Tourette's syndrome. *Am. J. Psychiatry*, **151**: 675–680.
31. Rettew D.C., Swedo S.E., Leonard H.L., Lenane M., Rapoport J.L. (1992) Obsessions and compulsions across time in 79 children and adolescents with obsessive-compulsive disorder. *J. Am. Acad. Child Adolesc. Psychiatry*, **31**: 1050–1056.
32. Hanna G.L. (1995) Demographic and clinical features of obsessive-compulsive disorder in children and adolescents. *J. Am. Acad. Child Adolesc. Psychiatry*, **34**: 19–27.
33. Flament M.F., Rapoport J.L., Berg C.J., Sceery W., Kilts C., Mellström B., Linnoila M. (1985) Clomipramine treatment of childhood obsessive-compulsive disorder. A double-blind controlled study. *Arch. Gen. Psychiatry*, **42**: 977–983.
34. Last C.G., Strauss C.C. (1989) Obsessive-compulsive disorder in childhood. *J. Anxiety Disord.*, **3**: 295–302.
35. Leonard H.L., Lenane M.C., Swedo S.E., Rettew D.C., Gershon E.S., Rapoport J.L. (1992) Tics and Tourette's disorder. A 2- to 7-year follow-up study of 54 obsessive-compulsive children. *Am. J. Psychiatry*, **149**: 1244–1251.
36. Minichiello W.E., Baer L., Jenike M.A., Holland A. (1990) Age of onset of major subtypes of obsessive-compulsive disorder. *J. Anxiety Disord.*, **4**: 147–150.
37. Hafner R.J., Miller R.J. (1990) Obsessive-compulsive disorder: an exploration of some unresolved clinical issues. *Austr. N.Z.J. Psychiatry*, **24**: 480–485.
38. Leonard H.L., Goldberger E.L., Rapoport J.L., Cheslow D.L., Swedo S.E. (1990) Childhood rituals: normal development or obsessive-compulsive symptoms? *J. Am. Acad. Child Adolesc. Psychiatry*, **29**: 17–23.
39. Evans D.W., Leckman J.F., Carter A., Reznick J.S., Henshaw D., King R.A., Pauls D. (1997) Ritual, habits, and perfectionism: the prevalence and development of compulsive like behavior in normal young children. *Child Develop.*, **68**: 58–68.
40. Geller D.A., Biederman J., Griffin S., Jones J., Lefkowitz T.D. (1996) Comorbidity of obsessive-compulsive disorder with disruptive behavior disorders. *J. Am. Acad. Child Adolesc. Psychiatry*, **35**: 1637–1646.
41. Cohen D., Flament M., Dubos P.F., Basquin M. (1999) The catatonic syndrome in young people. *J. Am. Acad. Child Adolesc. Psychiatry*, **38**: 1040–1046.
42. Fenton W., Mc Glashan TH. (1986) The prognostic significance of obsessive-compulsive symptoms in schizophrenia. *Am. J. Psychiatry*, **143**: 437–441.
43. Eisen J., Rasmussen S. (1993) Obsessive compulsive disorder with psychotic features. *J. Clin. Psychiatry*, **54**: 373–379.

44. American Academy of Child and Adolescent Psychiatry (1998) Practice parameters for the assessment and treatment of children and adolescents with obsessive-compulsive disorder. *J. Am. Acad. Child Adolesc. Psychiatry*, **37** (suppl. 10): 27S–45S.
45. Goodman W.K., Price L.H., Rasmussen S.A., Mazure C., Rleischmann R.L., Hill C.L., Heninger G.R., Charney D.S. (1989) The Yale–Brown Obsessive Compulsive Scale: I. Development, use and reliability. *Arch. Gen. Psychiatry*, **46**: 1006–1011.
46. Goodman W.K., Price L.H., Rasmussen S.A., Mazure C., Delgado P., Heninger G.R., Charney D.S. (1989) The Yale–Brown Obsessive Compulsive Scale: II. Validity. *Arch. Gen. Psychiatry*, **46**: 1012–1016.
47. Scahill L., Riddle M.A., McSwiggan-Hardin M.T., Ort S.I., King R.A., Goodman W.K., Cicchetti D., Leckman J. (1997) The Children's Yale–Brown Obsessive-Compulsive Scale: preliminary report of reliability and validity. *J. Am. Acad. Child Adolesc. Psychiatry*, **36**: 844–853.
48. Berg C.Z., Whitaker A., Davies M., Flament M.F., Rapoport J.L. (1988) The survey form of the Leyton Obsessional Inventory-child version: norms from an epidemiological study. *J. Am. Acad. Child Adolesc. Psychiatry*, **27**: 759–763.
49. Flament M., Chabane N. (2000) Obsessive-compulsive disorder and tics in childhood and adolescence. In *The New Oxford Textbook of Psychiatry* (Eds M. Gelder, J.J. Lopez-Ibor, N.C. Andreasen), Oxford University Press, Oxford, in press.
50. Flament M.F., Koby E., Rapoport J.L., Berg C.J., Zahn T., Cox C., Denckla M., Lenane M. (1990) Childhood obsessive-compulsive disorder: a prospective follow-up study. *J. Child Psychol. Psychiatry*, **31**: 363–380.
51. Godart N., Flament M.F., Jeammet P., Lecrubier Y. (2000) Eating disorders and anxiety disorders: comorbidity and chronology of appearance. *Eur. Psychiatry*, in press.
52. Leckman J.F. (1993) Tourette's syndrome. In *Obsessive-Compulsive Related Disorders* (Ed. E. Hollander), pp. 113–138, American Psychiatric Press, Washington, DC.
53. Pauls D.L., Raymond C.L., Leckman J.F., Stevenson J.M. (1991) A family study of Tourette's syndrome. *Am. J. Human Genet.*, **48**: 154–163.
54. Pauls D., Alsobrook J., Goodman W., Rasmussen S., Leckman J. (1995) A family study of obsessive-compulsive disorder. *Am. J. Psychiatry*, **152**: 76–84.
55. Leckman J.F., McDougle C.J., Pauls D., Peterson B.S., Grice D.E., King R.A., Scahill L., Price L.M., Rasmussen S.A. (2000) Tic-related versus non-tic-related obsessive-compulsive disorder. In *Obsessive-Compulsive Disorders: Contemporary Issues in Treatment* (Eds W.K. Goodman, M.V. Rudorfer, J.D. Mazur, Erlbaum, New York.
56. Holzer J., Goodman W., McDougle C.J., Boyarsky B., Leckman J.F., Price L. (1994) Differential symptoms in obsessive-compulsive disorder with and without a chronic tic disorder. *Br. J. Psychiatry*, **164**: 469–473.
57. McDougle C.J., Goodman W.K., Leckman J.F., Lee N.C., Heninger G.R., Price L.H. (1994) Haloperidol addition in fluvoxamine refractory obsessive-compulsive disorder: a double-blind, placebo-controlled study in patients with and without tics. *Arch. Gen. Psychiatry*, **51**: 302–308.
58. Swedo S.E. (1993) Trichotillomania. *Child Adolesc. Psychiatr. Clin. N. Am.*, **2**: 685–694.
59. Lenane M., Swedo S., Rapoport J., Leonard H., Sceery W., Guroff J. (1992) Rates of obsessive compulsive disorder in first degree relatives of

patients with trichotillomania: a research note. *J. Child Psychol. Psychiatry*, **33**: 925–933.
60. Hanna G.L. (1997) Trichotillomania and related disorders in children and adolescents. *Child Psychiatry Hum. Develop.*, **27**: 255–268.
61. Leonard H., Lenane M., Swedo S., Rettew D., Rapoport J. (1991) A double-blind comparison of clomipramine and desipramine treatment of severe onychophagia (nail biting). *Arch. Gen. Psychiatry*, **48**: 821–827.
62. Phillips K., Atala K., Albertini R. (1995) Body dysmorphic disorder in adolescents. *J. Am. Acad. Child Adolesc. Psychiatry*, **34**: 1216–1220.
63. Thompsen P.H. (1998) Obsessive-compulsive disorder in children and adolescents. Clinical guidelines. *Eur. Child Adolesc. Psychiatry*, **7**: 1–11.
64. Thiel A., Broocks A., Ohlmeir M., Jacoby G.E., Schuble G. (1995) Obsessive-compulsive disorder among patients with anorexia nervosa and bulimia nervosa. *Am. J. Psychiatry*, **152**: 72–75.
65. Flament M., Cohen D. (1999) Comorbidity and spectrum disorders in childhood-onset obsessive-compulsive disorder. *Eur. Neuropsychopharmacol.*, **9** (suppl. 5): S186.
66. Cohen D., Volkmar F. (1997) *Handbook of Autism and Pervasive Developmental Disorders*, Wiley, New York.
67. Bailey (1996) Obsessive and compulsive behaviors and risk factors in high-functioning pervasive developmental disorder. PhD Thesis, Yale University, New Haven.
68. Bolton P.F., Pickles A., Murphy M., Rutter M. (1998) Autism, affective and other psychiatric disorders: patterns of familial aggregation. *Psychol. Med.*, **28**: 385–395.
69. Trottier G., Srivastava L., Walker C.D. (1999) Etiology of infantile autism: a review of recent advances in genetic and neurobiological research. *J. Psychiatry Neurosci.*, **24**: 103–115.
70. McDougle C.L., Naylor S.T., Cohen D.J., Volkmar F.R., Heninger G.R., Price L.H. (1996) A double-blind, placebo-controled study of fluvoxamine in adults with autistic disorder. *Arch. Gen. Psychiatry*, **53**: 1001–1008.
71. Hollander E., Del Giudice-Asch G., Simon L., Schmeidler J., Cartwright C., DeCaria C.M., Kwon J., Cunningham-Rundles C., Chapman F. (1999) B lymphocyte antigen D8/17 and repetitive behaviors in autism. *Am. J. Psychiatry*, **156**: 317–320.
72. Freud A. (1966) Obsessional neurosis: a summary of psychoanalytic views. *Int. J. Psychoanal.*, **47**: 116–122.
73. Rapoport J.L. (1989) The neurobiology of obsessive compulsive disorder. *JAMA*, **260**: 2888–2890.
74. Insel T., Zohar J., Benkelfat C., Murphy D. (1990) Serotonin in obsessions, compulsions, and the control of aggressive impulses. *Ann. N.Y. Acad. Sci.*, **600**: 574–585.
75. Flament M.F., Rapoport J.L., Murphy D.L., Lake C.R., Berg C.J. (1987) Biochemical changes during clomipramine treatment of childhood obsessive compulsive disorder. *Arch. Gen. Psychiatry*, **44**: 219–225.
76. Weizman A., Mandel A., Barber Y., Weitz R., Cohen A., Mester R., Rehavi M. (1992) Decreased platelet imipramine binding in Tourette syndrome children with obsessive-compulsive disorder. *Biol. Psychiatry*, **31**: 705–711.
77. Sallee F.R., Richman H., Beach K., Sethuraman G., Nesbitt L. (1996) Platelet serotonin transporter in children and adolescents with obsessive-compulsive

disorder or Tourette's syndrome. *J. Am. Acad. Child Adolesc. Psychiatry*, **35**: 1647–1656.

78. Zahn T.P., Kruesi M.J.P., Swedo S.E., Leonard H.L., Rapoport J.L. (1992) Autonomic activity in relation to cerebrospinal fluid neurochemistry in obsessive and disruptive children and adolescents. *Psychophysiology*, **33**: 731–739.
79. Swedo S.L., Leonard H.L., Kruesi M.J.P., Rettew D.C., Listwak S.J., Berrettini W., Stipetic M., Hamburger S., Gold P.W., Potter W.Z. *et al* (1992) Cerebrospinal fluid neurochemistry in children and adolescents with obsessive-compulsive disorder. *Arch. Gen. Psychiatry*, **49**: 29–36.
80. Altemus M., Swedo S.L., Leonard H.L., Richter D., Rubinow D.R., Potter W.Z., Rapoport J.L. (1994) Changes in cerebrospinal fluid neurochemistry during treatment of obsessive-compulsive disorder with clomipramine. *Arch. Gen. Psychiatry*, **51**: 794–803.
81. Luxeburger H. (1930) Hereditat und familientypus der Zwangsneurotiker. *Arch. Psychiatr.*, **91**: 590–594.
82. Rasmussen S.A., Tsuang M.T. (1986) Clinical characteristics and family history in DSM-III obsessive-compulsive disorder. *Am. J. Psychiatry*, **143**: 317–322.
83. Pauls D.L., Alsobrook J.P. (1999) The inheritance of obsessive-compulsive disorder. *Child. Adolesc. Psychiatr. Clin. N. Am.*, **8**: 481–496.
84. Rasmussen S.A. (1994) Genetic studies of obsessive compulsive disorder. In *Current Insights in Obsessive-Compulsive Disorder* (Eds E. Hollander, J. Zohar, D. Marazziti, B. Olivier) pp. 105–114, Wiley, New York.
85. Lenane M.C., Swedo S.E., Leonard H., Pauls D., Sceery W., Rapoport J.L. (1990) Psychiatric disorders in first degree relatives of children and adolescents with obsessive compulsive disorder. *J. Am. Acad. Child Adolesc. Psychiatry*, **29**: 407–412.
86. Pauls D., Leckman J.F. (1986) The inheritance of Gilles de la Tourette syndrome and associated behaviors. Evidence for an autosomal dominant transmission. *N. Engl. J. Med.*, **315**: 993–997.
87. Behar D., Rapoport J., Berg C., Denckla M., Mann L., Cox C., Fedio P., Zahn T., Wolfman M. (1984) Computerized tomography and neuropsychological test measure in adolescents with obsessive-compulsive disorder. *Am. J. Psychiatry*, **141**: 363–368.
88. Hollander E., Cohen L., Richards M., Mullen L., DeCaria C., Stern Y. (1997) A pilot study of the neuropsychology of obsessive-compulsive disorder and Parkinson's disease: basal ganglia disorders. *J. Neuropsychiat. Clin. Neurosci.*, **5**: 104–107.
89. Baxter L., Mazziotta J., Guze B., Schwartz J., Selin G. (1987) Local cerebral glucose metabolic rates in obsessive-compulsive disorder. *Arch. Gen. Psychiatry*, **44**: 211–218.
90. Cottraux J., Gérard D. (1998) Neuroimaging and neuroanatomical issues in obsessive-compulsive disorder. In *Obsessive-Compulsive Disorder: Theory, Research, and Treatment* (Eds R.P. Swinson, M.M. Antony, S. Rachman, M.A. Richter), pp. 154–180, Guilford, New York.
91. Luxemberg J., Swedo S., Flament M., Friedland R., Rapoport J., Rapoport S. (1988) Neuroanatomical abnormalities in obsessive-compulsive disorder detected with quantitative X-ray computed tomography. *Am. J. Psychiatry*, **145**: 1089–1093.
92. Rosenberg D.R., Keshavan M.S. (1998) Toward a neurodevelopmental model of obsessive-compulsive disorder. *Biol. Psychiatry*, **43**: 623–640.

93. Rapoport J.L., Fiske A. (1998) The new biology of obsessive compulsive disorder: implications for evolutionary psychology. *Perspect. Biol. Med.*, **41**: 159–175.
94. Swedo S., Shapiro M., Grady C., Cheslow D., Leonard H., Kumar A., Friedland R., Rapoport S., Rapoport J. (1989) Cerebral glucose metabolism in childhood obsessive-compulsive disorder. *Arch. Gen. Psychiatry*, **46**: 518–523.
95. Swedo S., Pietrini P., Leonard H., Shapiro M., Rettew D., Goldberger E., Rapoport S., Rapoport J., Grady C. (1992) Cerebral glucose metabolism in childhood obsessive-compulsive disorder: revisualization during pharmacotherapy. *Arch. Gen. Psychiatry*, **49**: 690–694.
96. Swedo S.E. (1994) Sydenham's chorea: a model for childhood autoimmune neuropsychiatric disorders. *JAMA*, **272**: 1788–1791.
97. Swedo S.E., Rapoport J.L., Cheslow D.L., Leonard H.L., Ayoub E.M., Hosier D.M., Wald E.R. (1989) High prevalence of obsessive-compulsive symptoms in patients with Sydenham's chorea. *Am. J. Psychiatry*, **146**: 246–249.
98. Swedo S.E., Leonard H., Shapiro M.B., Casey B.J., Mannheim G.B., Lenane M., Rettew D.C. (1993) Sydenham's chorea: physical and psychological symptoms of Saint Vitus' dance. *Pediatrics*, **91**: 706–713.
99. Asbahr F.R., Negrao A.B., Gentil V., Zanetta D.M., da Paz J.A., Marques-Dias M.J., Kiss M.H. (1998) Obsessive-compulsive and related symptoms in children and adolescents with rheumatic fever with and without chorea: a prospective 6-month study. *Am. J. Psychiatry*, **155**: 1122–1124.
100. Allen A.J., Leonard H.L., Swedo S.E. (1995) Case study: a new infection triggered, autoimmune subtype of pediatric OCD with chronic tic disorder, not otherwise specified. *J. Am. Acad. Child Adolesc. Psychiatry*, **34**: 307–311.
101. Swedo S., Leonard H.L., Garvey M., Mittleman B., Allen A.J., Perlmutter S.J., Lougee L., Dow S., Zamkoff J., Dubbert B. (1998) Pediatric autoimmune neuropsychiatric disorders associated with streptococcal infections (PANDAS): clinical description of the first 50 cases. *Am. J. Psychiatry*, **155**: 264–271.
102. Garvey M.A., Perlmutter S.J., Allen A.J., Hamburger S., Lougee L., Leonard H.L., Witowski M.E., Dubbert B., Swedo S.E. (1999) A pilot study of penicillin prophylaxis for neuropsychiatric exacerbations triggered by streptococcal infections. *Biol. Psychiatry*, **45**: 1564–1571.
103. Swedo S., Leonard H., Mittleman B., Allen A., Rapoport J., Dow S., Kanter M., Chapman F., Zabriskie J. (1997) Identification of children with pediatric autoimmune neuropsychiatric disorders associated with streptococcal infections by a marker associated with rheumatic fever. *Am. J. Psychiatry*, **154**: 110–112.
104. Murphy T., Goodman W., Fudge M., Williams R., Ayoub E., Dalal M., Lewis M., Zabriskie J. (1997) B lymphocyte antigen D8/17: a peripheral marker for childhood onset obsessive-compulsive disorder and Tourette's syndrome? *Am. J. Psychiatry*, **154**: 402–407.
105. Leonard H.L., Swedo S.E., Rapoport J.L., Koby E.V., Lenane M.C., Cheslow D.L., Hamburger S.D. (1989) Treatment of obsessive-compulsive disorder with clomipramine and desipramine in children and adolescents. *Arch. Gen. Psychiatry*, **46**: 1088–1092.
106. DeVeaugh-Geiss J., Moroz G., Biederman J., Cantwell D., Fontaine R., Greist J.H., Reichler R., Katz R., Landau P. (1992) Clomipramine hydrochloride in childhood and adolescent obsessive-compulsive disorder: a multicenter trial. *J. Am. Acad. Child Adolesc. Psychiatry*, **31**: 45–49.

107. Leonard H., Meyer M., Swedo S., Richter D., Hamburger S., Allen A., Rapoport J., Tucker E. (1995) Electrocardiographic changes during desipramine and clomipramine treatment in children and adolescents. *J. Am. Acad. Child Adolesc. Psychiatry*, **34**: 1460–1468.
108. Riddle M.A., Scahill L., King R.A., Hardin M.T., Anderson G.M., Ort S.I., Smith J.C., Leckman J.F., Cohen D.J. (1992) Double-blind, crossover trial of fluoxetine and placebo in children and adolescents with obsessive-compulsive disorder. *J. Am. Acad. Child Adolesc. Psychiatry*, **31**: 1062–1069.
109. Apter A., Ratzoni G., King R.A., Weizman A., Iancu I., Binder M., Riddle M. (1994) Fluvoxamine open-label treatment of adolescent inpatients with obsessive-compulsive disorder or depression. *J. Am. Acad. Child Adolesc. Psychiatry*, **33**: 342–348.
110. March J.S., Biederman J., Wolkow R., Safferman A., Mardekian J., Cook E.H., Cutler N.R., Dominguez R., Fergusson J., Muller B. *et al* (1998) Sertraline in children and adolescents with obsessive-compulsive disorder: a multicenter randomized controlled trial. *JAMA*, **280**: 1752–1756.
111. Alderman J., Wolkow R., Chung M., Johnston H.F. (1998) Sertraline treatment of children and adolescents with obsessive-compulsive disorder or depression: pharmacokinetics, tolerability, and efficacy. *J. Am. Acad. Child Adolesc. Psychiatry*, **37**: 386–394.
112. Thomsen P.H. (1997) Child and adolescent obsessive-compulsive disorder treated with citalopram: findings from an open trial of 23 cases. *J. Child Adolesc. Psychopharmacol.*, **7**: 157–166.
113. Rosenberg D.R., Stewart C.M. Fitzgerald K.D., Tawile V., Caroll E. (1999) Paroxetine open-label treatment of pediatric outpatients with obsessive-compulsive disorder. *J. Am. Acad. Child Adolesc. Psychiatry*, **38**: 1180–1185.
114. Leonard H.L., Swedo S.E., Lenane M.C., Rettew D.C., Cheslow D.L., Hamburger S.D., Rapoport J.L. (1991) A double-blind desipramine substitution during long-term clomipramine treatment in children and adolescents with obsessive-compulsive disorder. *Arch. Gen. Psychiatry*, **48**: 922–927.
115. Kurlan R., Como P., Deeley C., McDermott M., McDermott M.P. (1993) A pilot controlled study of fluoxetine for obsessive-compulsive symptoms in children with Tourette's syndrome. *Clin. Neuropharmacol.*, **16**: 167–172.
116. Delgado P.L., Goodman W., Price L., Heninger G., Charney D. (1990) Fluvoxamine/pimozide treatment of concurrent Tourette's and obsessive-compulsive disorder. *Br. J. Psychiatry*, **157**: 762–765.
117. Fennig S., Naisberg-Fennig S., Pato M., Weitzman A. (1994) Emergence of symptoms of Tourette's syndrome during fluvoxamine treatment of obsessive compulsive disorder. *Br. J. Psychiatry*, **164**: 839–841.
118. Hawkridge S., Stein D.J., Bouwer C. (1996) Combined pharmacotherapy for TS and OCD. *J. Am. Acad. Child Adolesc. Psychiatry*, **35**: 703–704.
119. March J.S. (1995) Cognitive-behavioral psychotherapy for children and adolescents with OCD: a review and recommendations for treatment. *J. Am. Acad. Child Adolesc. Psychiatry*, **34**: 7–18.
120. Bolton D., Collins S., Steinberg D. (1983) The treatment of obsessive-compulsive disorder in adolescence. A report of fifteen cases. *Br. J. Psychiatry*, **142**: 456–464.
121. March J.S., Mulle K., Herbel B. (1994) Behavioural psychotherapy for children and adolescents with obsessive-compulsive disorder: an open trial of a new protocol-driven treatment package. *J. Am. Acad. Child Adolesc. Psychiatry*, **33**: 333–341.

122. Franklin M.E., Kozak M.J., Cashman L., Coles M., Rheingold A., Foa E.B. (1998) Cognitive-behavioral treatment of pediatric obsessive compulsive disorder: an open clinical trial. *J. Am. Acad. Child Adolesc. Psychiatry*, **37**: 412–419.
123. De Haan E., Hoogduin K.A., Buitelaar J.K., Keijsers G. (1998) Behaviour therapy versus clomipramine for the treatment of obsessive-compulsive disorder in children and adolescents. *J. Am. Acad. Child Adolesc. Psychiatry*, **37**: 1022–1029.
124. Apter A., Bernhout E., Tyano S. (1984) Severe obsessive compulsive disorder in adolescence: a report of eight cases. *J. Adolesc.*, **7**: 349–358.
125. Target M., Fonagy P. (1994) Efficacy of psychoanalysis for children with emotional disorders. *J. Am. Acad. Child Adolesc. Psychiatry*, **33**: 361–371.
126. Lenane M. (1989) Families in obsessive-compulsive disorder. In: *Obsessive-Compulsive Disorder in Children and Adolescents* (Ed. J. Rapoport), pp. 237–249, Psychiatric Press, Washington, DC.
127. Lenane M. (1991) Family therapy for children with obsessive-compulsive disorder. In *Current Treatments of Obsessive-Compulsive Disorder—Clinical Practice* (Eds M. Pato, M. Zohar), pp. 103–113, American Psychiatric Association, Washington, DC.
128. March J., Frances A., Carpenter D., Kahn D. (Eds) (1997) The expert consensus guideline series: treatment of obsessive-compulsive disorder. *J. Clin. Psychiatry*, **58S**: 1–72.
129. Flament M. (1999) Obsessive-compulsive disorders. In *Risks and Outcomes in Developmental Psychopathology* (Eds H.C. Steinhausen, F. Verhulst), pp. 134–150, Oxford University Press, Oxford.
130. Hollingsworth C.E, Tanguay P.E., Grossman L., Pabst P. (1980) Long-term outcome of obsessive-compulsive disorder in childhood. *J. Am. Acad. Child Adolesc. Psychiatry*, **19**: 134–144.
131. Thomsen P. H., Mikkelsen H. U. (1993) Development of personality disorders in children and adolescents with obsessive-compulsive disorder. A 6- to 22-year follow-up study. *Acta Psychiatr. Scand.*, **87**: 456–462.
132. Thomsen P. H., Mikkelsen H. U. (1995) Obsessive-compulsive disorder in children and adolescents: predictors in childhood for long-term phenomenological course. *Acta Psychiatr. Scand.*, **92**: 255–259.
133. Warren W. (1960) Some relationships between the psychiatry of children and adults. *J. Ment. Sci.*, **106**: 815–826.
134. Leonard H.L., Swedo S.E., Lenane M.C., Rettew D., Hamburger S.D., Bartko J.J., Rapoport J.L. (1993) A 2- to 7-year follow-up study of 54 obsessive-compulsive children and adolescents. *Arch. Gen. Psychiatry*, **50**: 429–439.
135. Thomsen P. H., Mikkelsen H. U. (1995) Course of obsessive-compulsive disorder in children and adolescents: a prospective follow-up study of 23 Danish cases. *J. Am. Acad. Child Adolesc. Psychiatry*, **34**: 1432–1440.
136. Bolton D., Luckie M., Steinberg D. (1995) Long-term course of obsessive-compulsive disorder treated in adolescence. *J. Am. Acad. Child Adolesc. Psychiatry*, **34**: 1441–1450.
137. Berg C.Z., Rapoport J.L., Whitaker A., Davies M., Leonard H., Swedo S.E., Braiman S., Lenane M. (1989) Childhood obsessive compulsive disorder: a two-year prospective follow-up study of a community sample. *J. Am. Acad. Child Adolesc. Psychiatry*, **28**: 528–533.
138. Allsopp M., Verduyn C. (1988) A follow-up of adolescents with obsessive-compulsive disorder. *Br. J. Psychiatry*, **154**: 829–834.

Commentaries

4.1 Theoretical and Clinical Implications of the Spectrum of Childhood Obsessionality

Robert A. King[1]

The contemporary resurgence of interest in childhood obsessive-compulsive disorder (OCD) dates from the seminal studies of Flament, Rapoport, Swedo, Leonard, and their colleagues at the National Institute of Mental Health [1]. That work demonstrated that childhood OCD was common; descriptively similar to adult OCD and diagnosable using the same criteria; frequently familial, persistent, and accompanied by considerable comorbidity and neuropsychological abnormalities; and at least partially responsive to serotonergic agents and/or behavioural therapy.

As with other disorders, research in this area has progressed by studying clinical samples of children with forms of OCD clearly diagnosable by DSM criteria. However, in addition to the large number of children seen with classic OCD, there also exists a large penumbra or spectrum of children with prominent or troublesome repetitive behaviours that are less easily classified or treated [2]. How are we to understand this broad spectrum of psychopathology from a theoretical point of view?

Many forms of developmental psychopathology represent a dysregulation of usually adaptive mechanisms or capacities. Neuro-ethological models of OCD suggest that OCD symptoms reflect an inappropriate release or failure to terminate evolutionarily conserved mammalian fixed-action or comparator functions—grooming, checking, arranging, pair-bonding, etc. [1, 3]. According to this view, diverse pathological processes affecting the basal ganglia and related structures, the neurological substrate for these functions, can result in excessive checking, washing or arranging; contamination fears; hoarding; and other OC symptoms.

From a developmental perspective, Freud, Piaget, Gesell and others have noted the ubiquitous repetitive activities and rituals that characterize the daily behaviour of young children. Some of these represent a pleasurable exercise of burgeoning capacities for seriation and categorization;

[1] *Yale Child Study Center, Yale School of Medicine, 230 South Frontage Road, PO Box 207900, New Haven, CT 06520–7900, USA*

others serve to reduce anxiety by reinforcing object constancy at times of separation or uncertainty (e.g. bedtime); still others may ward off or control potentially dangerous impulses. Developmental studies find that obsessive concerns about symmetry or order and compulsive insistence on sameness, with upset if thwarted, are very common in preschoolers, but that when they persist beyond age 4 or 5 years, they tend to be associated with poorer adaptation and increased levels of parental obsessionality [4, 5]. Longitudinal studies of these phenomena are sorely needed. Preliminary findings from prospective studies of children at high family risk for Tourette's syndrome (TS) indicate that extreme levels of pre-schooler compulsivity, such as "stickiness", and concern for sameness, may be harbingers of later tic/OCD spectrum pathology [6].

Epidemiological studies also find that, although about 2–4% of adolescents in community samples meet full DSM criteria for OCD, many additional youngsters have obsessions and compulsions that fail to meet these criteria by virtue of being less distressing, impairing or time consuming [7].

Clinically, one also encounters many children who have perseverative behaviours, constricted or obsessional interests, irritable inflexibility and difficulty in shifting activities, and repetitive behaviours that may have been diagnosed by different clinicians as stereotypies, simple compulsions or complex tics [2]. Such children, who have been described in the literature under various diagnostic rubrics (e.g. atypical pervasive developmental disorder, "compulsively difficulty temperament"), often have a multiplicity of other developmental and social difficulties; typically they do not regard their repetitive behaviours, which are usually more distressing to others, as ego-dystonic. Their lack of self-reflective language often makes their subjective experience of these behaviours difficult to assess.

It remains an important unanswered question to what extent the broad spectrum of obsessions and compulsions found in the general population, as well as the "atypical" forms just described, share genetic risk factors, neurobiological characteristics or therapeutic responsiveness with the more classical forms of OCD.

TS provides a model for one heuristically important subtype of childhood onset OCD [8]. Factor analytic studies find that obsessions and compulsions regarding symmetry, arranging, checking, and hoarding are more common in subjects with histories of tic disorder, while contamination fears may occur with equal frequencies in subjects with non-tic related OCD. As is the case with many children with OCD, the compulsions associated with TS often have no accompanying obsessions and are experienced as occurring in response to a quasi-somatic urge or "just-right" sensation, rather than as an attempt to reduce anxiety or prevent some feared outcome. Not only are tic-related OCD symptoms less responsive to selective serotonin reuptake inhibitors (SSRIs); the lack of an anxious, obsessional trigger makes traditional exposure/response prevention approaches difficult to implement and may require habit-reversal techniques instead.

Comorbidity is the rule rather than the exception in childhood disorders, including OCD, and suggests that we do not yet have a nosology that reflects the underlying structure of psychopathology. Even in children with clear-cut OCD, associated symptoms of depression, anxiety, impulsiveness and agitation may be as disabling as the obsessions and compulsions *per se* and necessitate a multifaceted approach to assessment and treatment [2]. Studies of other basal ganglia disorders, including TS and Sydenham's chorea, suggest that the often extensive psychopathology accompanying childhood OCD may have a neurobiological basis. Indeed, Kurlan and colleagues [9] have posited the notion of a spectrum of developmental basal ganglia disorders.

A final set of challenges concern childhood OCD's chronicity. A 47-year follow-up of individuals with OCD found that, at least for men, onset under 20 years was ominous; at follow-up, only 28% of such men were recovered and 44% were unchanged or deteriorated [10]. In our current epoch, although the SSRIs provide significant relief for many children, subjects' mean post-treatment symptom scores at the end of most clinical drug trials are still severe enough to meet the initial inclusion criteria.

Further progress in delineating the different subtypes and spectrum of childhood-onset OCD and their underlying causes promise to lead to more effective means of intervention.

REFERENCES

1. Rapoport J. (Ed.) (1989) *Obsessive-Compulsive Disorder in Children and Adolescents*, American Psychiatric Press, Washington, DC.
2. King R.A., Scahill L. (1999) The assessment and coordination of treatment of children and adolescents with OCD. *Child Adolesc. Psychiatr. Clin. N. Am.*, **8**: 577–597.
3. Leckman J.F., Mayes L.C. (1999) Preoccupations and behaviors associated with romantic and parental love: perspectives on the origin of obsessive-compulsive disorder. *Child Adolesc Psychiatr. Clin. N. Am.*, **8**: 635–665.
4. Evans D.W., Leckman J.F., Carter A., Reznick J.S., Henshaw D., King R.A., Pauls D. (1997) Ritual, habit, and perfectionism: the prevalence and development of compulsive-like behavior in normal young children. *Child Develop.*, **68**: 58–68.
5. Evans D., unpublished data.
6. Pauls D., Carter A., unpublished data.
7. Apter A., Fallon T.J., King R.A., Ratzoni G., Zohar A. H., Binder M., Weizman A., Leckman J.F., Pauls D.L., Kron S., *et al* (1996) Obsessive-compulsive characteristics: from symptoms to syndrome. *J. Am. Acad. Child Adolesc. Psychiatry*, **35**: 907–912.

8. Leckman J.F., Cohen D.J. (Eds) (1999) *Tourette's Syndrome—Tics, Obsessions, Compulsions: Developmental Psychopathology and Clinical Care*, Wiley, New York.
9. Palumbo D., Maughan A., Kurlan R. (1997) Hypothesis III. Tourette syndrome is only one of several causes of a developmental basal ganglia syndrome. *Arch. Neurol.*, **54**: 475–83.
10. Skoog G., Skoog I. (1999) A 40-year follow-up of patients with obsessive-compulsive disorder. *Arch. Gen. Psychiatry*, **56**: 121–127.

4.2
Developmental Perspectives in Pediatric Onset Obsessive-Compulsive Disorder

Daniel A. Geller[1]

Despite the similar phenotypic presentation of obsessive-compulsive disorder (OCD) in subjects at all ages, the assumption that childhood onset disorder is identical to adult onset OCD may be challenged by a review of the extant literature. Such a review indicates that onset of OCD in childhood is characterized by male predominance, increased familial loading, limited insight and higher rates of comorbid tic, disruptive behaviour and specific and pervasive developmental disorders than described in adult samples. In fact, the similarity in phenotypic presentation could obscure important developmental differences in OCD. Systematic comparison of OCD symptomatology in children and adults has not been reported to date. Such an effort is complicated by the waxing and waning nature of the symptoms and the tendency for symptom clusters to change or emerge over time.

Using the Children's Yale–Brown Obsessive Compulsive Scale (CY-BOCS), we have compared the rates of individual symptoms in children, adolescents and adults, using our pediatric OCD data and published reports of adult OCD. We found that children and adolescents had significantly higher rates of aggressive and catastrophic obsessions (fears of death or harm to self or loved ones) compared with adults, and that these represented the most common obsessions in the juvenile age group. In addition, the rate of sexual obsessions increased significantly from childhood to adolescence to levels similar to those reported in adults. Religious obsessions were found more frequently in adolescents than either children or adults. Hoarding compulsions were found significantly more often in the child subjects, compared with adolescents or adults. These findings reflect the developmental concerns and conflicts unique to each age group.

[1] *McLean Hospital, Pediatric Psychopharmacology Clinic, 115 Mill Street, Belmont, MA 02478, USA*

In their comprehensive review, Flament and Cohen note that the prevalence of OCD in children and adolescents is the same as that reported in adults. This is an important point [1]. If true, then it suggests a variable outcome in the pediatric-onset cases, because if all pediatric cases had chronic illness persisting into adulthood, we would expect an increasing cumulative prevalence with age as new cases are added to the population. Since this is not observed, it suggests a variable outcome, with some children and adolescents becoming subclinical over time, so that cases are both added and lost to the OCD population.

In a review of 11 pediatric OCD clinical studies, we [2] found a mean age at onset of 10 years, although the mean age at presentation in these same studies was over 12 years, indicating a lag of more than 2 years between onset (defined by clinical impairment) and presentation. This is quite different from reports of adult samples, including the Epidemiological Catchment Area (ECA) study [3], which finds a mean age at onset of 21 years. Thus, OCD appears to be a disorder with bimodal peaks of incidence. Differences in gender prevalence between children and adults with OCD could reflect a greater severity of the disorder and an earlier age of onset in boys, as suggested by Flament and Cohen in their excellent review, or it could mean that the early-onset patients represent an etiologically distinct group. In our pediatric cohort, severity measures, using both CY-BOCS and Clinical Global Impression (CGI) scores, are similar in boys and girls who had a similar age at onset.

One of the important differences between child and adult OCD is the pattern of comorbidity. Flament *et al* report lifetime comorbidity rates of 75% for other psychiatric disorders, including major depression, dysthymia, bulimia nervosa, overanxious disorder and phobias [1]. It should be noted that this was an epidemiological and not a clinically referred sample. The rates of comorbid disorders may be even higher in clinically referred samples of children and adolescents with OCD. In addition, many of the early clinical samples of OCD patients used numerous exclusion criteria in order to obtain more homogenous samples, sometimes for the purpose of conducting drug treatment trials. For example, the exclusion of Tourette's syndrome (TS) subjects in the National Institute of Mental Health (NIMH) study [4] would be expected to lead to underestimates of the true rate of both comorbid TS and attention-deficit/hyperactivity disorder (ADHD) compared to naturalistic samples. In fact, tic disorders, ADHD and anxiety disorders are over-represented in childhood OCD cases compared to adults. These distinct patterns of comorbid disorders in pediatric OCD subjects have implications for pharmacologic treatment of the OCD youngster, since the treatments for OCD (serotonergics), tics (alpha agonists, dopamine antagonists and secondary amine tricyclics) and ADHD (dopaminergics) diverge markedly. OCD that is comorbid with TS may require novel pharmacological approaches, such as multiple targeted pharmacotherapy for each set of symptoms. For example, the addition of alpha-2 agonists, such as clonidine or guanfacine, to a selective serotonin reuptake inhibitor (SSRI) may be useful in reducing tic severity and impulsivity. The McDougle study [5] of neuroleptic augmentation in OCD with tics is an important one to replicate in children, since predictors of treatment response, with a focus on comorbid disorders, are much needed. Although SSRIs are selective serotonergic agents, they may have subtle dopaminergic (sertraline) or noradrenergic (fluoxetine) effects that could affect tic frequency or severity. Clomipramine has unique properties in that it is metabolized to chlordesmethylimipramine, a compound closely related to desipramine. This agent has been reported to be effective in the treatment of tic disorders as well as ADHD. Thus, the use of clomipramine, either alone or as augmentation of the SSRIs, has theoretical advantage for the comorbid OCD child or adolescent. Although a common clinical practice, controlled trials of this common combination are urgently needed. Stimulants may also have a role in treatment of comorbid OCD youth when ADHD is present. Despite theoretical concerns that anxiety or obsessions could be increased, their effect on symptoms of OCD in children have not been systematically studied. Finally, the impact of ADHD or other disruptive behaviour, such as oppositional defiant disorder, on the ability of young OCD patients to successfully engage in cognitive-behavioural therapy must be considered.

Behavioural disinhibition is a relatively common (25%) [6] and occasionally serious problem in pediatric subjects. It appears to be much more common in children than adults and may preclude use of the SSRIs entirely without concomitant addition of mood stabilizers or atypical neuroleptics. In our experience, it is a dose-related phenomenon and may have a late onset (after 4 weeks), often parallel to the clinical improvement in OCD symptoms. It appears that serotonergic drugs, in addition to reducing OCD symptoms, reduce behavioural inhibition in a number of domains, which may in turn cause difficulties for the treated child.

Pharmacokinetic studies in children and adolescents have been undertaken for sertraline and fluoxetine and suggest that the metabolic profiles of youthful subjects are somewhat more active. However, there is little impact on dosing schedules in pediatric subjects.

In summary, OCD in children and adolescents presents a distinct clinical picture with implications for etiology, genetics, treatment and perhaps outcome. OCD studies with a developmental perspective are urgently needed.

REFERENCES

1. Flament M., Whitaker A., Rapoport J., Davies M., Berg C., Kalikow K., Sceery W., Shaffer D. (1988) Obsessive compulsive disorder in adolescence: an epidemiological study. *J. Am. Acad. Child Adolesc. Psychiatry*, **27**: 764–771.

2. Geller D.A., Biederman J., Jones J., Shapiro J. (1998) Obsessive-compulsive disorder in children and adolescents: a review. *Harvard Rev. Psychiatry*, **5**: 260–273.
3. Karno M., Golding J., Sorenson S., Burnam A. (1998) The epidemiology of obsessive-compulsive disorder in five US communities. *Arch. Gen. Psychiatry*, **45**: 1094–1099.
4. Rapoport J. (Ed.) (1989) *Obsessive-Compulsive Disorder in Children and Adolescents*, American Psychiatric Press, Washington, DC.
5. McDougle C., Goodman W., Leckman J., Lee N., Heninger G., Price L. (1994) Haloperidol addiction in fluvoxamine-refractory obsessive compulsive disorder: a double-blind, placebo-controlled study in patients with and without tics. *Arch. Gen. Psychiatry*, **51**: 302–308.
6. Geller D., Biederman J., Reed E., Spencer T., Wilens T. (1995) Similarities in response to fluoxetine in the treatment of children and adolescents with obsessive-compulsive disorder. *J. Am. Acad. Child Adolesc. Psychiatry*, **34**: 36–44.

4.3
A Concept of Disorder in Some Disorder

Derek Bolton[1]

Flament and Cohen's review brings out that obsessive-compulsive disorder (OCD) in childhood and adolescence is a relatively common disorder, that it presents in quite similar ways throughout the age range, that it shows high levels of comorbidity with a variety of other disorders, and that it responds well to at least two forms of treatment, pharmacotherapy using selective serotonin reuptake inhibitors (SSRIs) and cognitive behavioural therapy. Much less is understood, however, about the etiology of the disorder, or indeed about what kind of disorder it is. The disorder is highly selective in its response to psychotropic medication, suggesting a relatively circumscribed underlying neurochemistry involving the serotonergic system. However, the normal role of this system in regulating affect and behaviour, such as aggression and anxiety, remains speculative, as does the question whether statistical abnormalities in the system in OCD merely reflect the unusual affect and behaviour characteristics of the disorder, or whether they represent its primary cause. A similar point applies to functional imaging studies, also reviewed by Flament and Cohen. Orbito-frontal/basal ganglia circuitry seems to be involved in OCD, but so far these findings do neither more nor less than locate the neural structures which serve obsessive-compulsive symptomatology; they are so far neutral as to etiology.

[1] *Institute of Psychiatry, De Crespigny Park, London SE5 8AF, UK*

An example of an etiological question is this: are compulsions functional behaviours performed because they reduce anxiety generated by obsessions? A positive answer to this question about the etiology of compulsions is still to be found in the DSM-IV and ICD-10 diagnostic criteria. It is compatible with the typical phenomenology in adults, and to some extent with that in children, although, as Flament and Cohen remark, some children with OCD may be able to specify only a vague reason for their compulsions, and some compulsions apparently lack an ideational component.

The view that compulsions have an anxiety-relieving function is built into psychological formulations of OCD, from Freud's, to conditioning models, to contemporary cognitive models. But of course it is questionable, and is rejected in models such as Rapoport's [1], which regards compulsive behaviours as primary, as triggered by some kind of neurological deficit, either structural or functional (biochemical) or both, and obsessions as being either mental versions of compulsive behaviours, or *post hoc* rationalizations of—confabulations about—compulsive behaviours. Neither psychopharmacological nor functional imaging data can readily distinguish between these two fundamentally different views of the etiology of compulsions. The question is of course fundamental, and indeed has implications for how the disorder should be classified. Rapoport's etiological model of OCD makes no essential reference to anxiety, and to this extent it has no obvious way of explaining why anxiolytic psychological methods, whether behavioural or cognitive, should have an effect on the disorder. On the other hand, psychological models apparently have no hope of anything other than a *post hoc* explanation of association between OCD and neuropsychiatric disorders such as tics or pediatric autoimmune neuropsychiatric disorders associated with streptococal infections (PANDAS), as reviewed by Flament and Cohen.

Interestingly, the current uncertainty about the nature of OCD has a long history. What faced the early psychopathologists was a syndrome, or collection of related syndromes, that comprised many aspects. It evidently involves cognition, with thoughts or doubts at or beyond the border of sanity; it frequently involves the emotions, particularly fear and melancholia; it typically involves an apparent impairment of the power of the will, and the behavioural aspects of the disorder are in some cases akin to complex tics, or even to motor movements induced by brain seizure. Hence during the nineteenth century what we now know as OCD was variously conceived as a disorder of intellect, volition or emotions, and classified variously along with psychoses, neurologically-based motor disorders and anxiety disorders [2]. The clear conception of OCD as an anxiety disorder, and in particular the functional relationship between anxiolytic compulsions and anxiogenic obsessions, was consolidated by psychoanalytic theory, reinforced by behavioural theorizing, and embraced by the major nosological systems. But in retrospect this certainty was probably a quiet interlude, and we have returned to a period of uncertainty and speculation. Hence the strong and increasing interest in the concept of "OCD spectrum disorders" and "subtypes" of OCD, which respectively broaden and narrow the conventional nosological classification. There are many such attempts current, all to a considerable degree speculative. Flament and Cohen refer to some major ones in their review. Of particular relevance to child and adolescent OCD is the possibility of a neurodevelopmental subtype of OCD, though validity and utility are so far unconfirmed [3–6].

REFERENCES

1. Rapoport J.L. (1990) Obsessive compulsive disorder and basal ganglia dysfunction. *Psychol. Med.*, **20**: 465–469.
2. Berrios G. E. (1995) Obsessive-compulsive disorder. In *A History of Clinical Psychiatry: the Origin and History of Psychiatric Disorders* (Eds G. E. Berrios, R. Porter), pp. 573–592, Athlone, London.
3. Blanes T., McGuire P. (1997) Heterogeneity within obsessive-compulsive disorder: evidence for primary and neurodevelopmental subtypes. In *Neurodevelopmental Models of Psychopathology* (Eds M.S. Keshavan, R. Murray), pp. 206–213, Cambridge University Press, Cambridge.
4. Bolton D. (1996) Annotation: developmental issues in obsessive compulsive disorder. *J. Child Psychol. Psychiatry*, **37**: 131–137.
5. Geller D., Biederman J., Jones J., Park K., Schwartz S., Shapiro S., Coffey B. (1998) Is juvenile obsessive-compulsive disorder a developmental subtype of the disorder? A review of the pediatric literature. *J. Am. Acad. Child Adolesc. Psychiatry*, **37**: 420–427.
6. Rosenberg D.R., Keshavan M.S. (1998) Towards a neurodevelopmental model of obsessive-compulsive disorder. *Biol. Psychiatry*, **43**: 623–640.

4.4
Obsessive-Compulsive Disorder: A Model for Closing the "Gap" between Adult and Pediatric Psychiatry

Joseph DeVeaugh-Geiss[1]

Flament and Cohen provide a detailed review of the literature on obsessive-compulsive disorder (OCD) in children and adolescents. They emphasize that OCD was considered, until very recently, rare among this population.

[1] *Glaxo Wellcome Inc., Five Moore Drive, PO Box 13398, Research Triangle Park, NC 27709, USA*

This must be viewed in the context that this disorder, regardless of age, was viewed as rare until recently. It is only in the last 20–25 years that OCD has come into prominence, in terms of prevalence as well as treatment. Nevertheless, Flament and Cohen accurately reflect the delay in our recognizing the significance of OCD in children and adolescents. This is a phenomenon that appears to apply to the diagnosis and treatment of psychiatric disorders in children and adolescents generally; i.e., there is a delay (or "gap") between advances in adult psychiatry and their application to the child and adolescent population.

The recognition of OCD as a common, treatable disorder is partly attributable to good epidemiologic studies conducted in the last quarter of the last century, and also is a result of the development of behavioural and pharmacologic treatments for the disorder. It is important to recognize that the first epidemiologic study of OCD in adolescents was published only in 1988. Thus, it is easy to understand the persistence of the incorrect notion that OCD is rare in this population. There is now a substantial body of evidence supporting a high prevalence of OCD in the adolescent population. Retrospective studies show onset of OCD for many patients in childhood or adolescence and longitudinal studies show persistence of symptoms over an extended period of time. Thus, as with many chronic psychiatric disorders, OCD may appear early in life and persist through adulthood. The phenomenology of OCD in children, adolescents and adults is strikingly similar, and perhaps this similarity facilitated the recognition of the disorder in children and adolescents, and encouraged clinical studies in this population.

In addition to clinical phenomenology, Flament and Cohen's review provides a comprehensive and valuable review of theories and evidence regarding etiology and pathogenesis. There is considerable evidence implicating a serotonergic mechanism. Certainly, the pharmacologic treatment of OCD relies primarily on drugs that affect serotonin. The authors review biochemical evidence as well as familial and genetic evidence, all pointing to a biologic basis for OCD. Neuroimaging studies point to dysfunction in frontal, subcortical circuits as well as basal ganglia. There is also intriguing, recent evidence suggesting an autoimmune-related form of OCD.

In the past 15 years, both behavioural and pharmacologic therapies have emerged for the treatment of OCD. Cognitive behavioural therapy has been evaluated in controlled trials for adults and in case studies and open trials for children and adolescents. Pharmacologic therapy has advanced dramatically following early observations of the effectiveness of clomipramine (CMI), a serotonergic tricyclic antidepressant. Consistent demonstration of efficacy in controlled clinical trials with CMI led Ciba-Geigy to undertake a full development program for the drug in the treatment of OCD. This program included a multicenter controlled clinical trial in children and adolescents and, to my knowledge, represents the first time that a psychopharmacologic agent was developed simultaneously for the adult and pediatric population. Other treatments for OCD (selective serotonin reuptake inhibitors) have also been studied in the pediatric population, providing evidence for safety, efficacy and guidelines for use in this age group. Unfortunately, this is not the norm and most pharmacologic treatments that are used in children and adolescents have been adequately studied only in adults [1].

This traditional approach—developing and marketing of new drugs mainly for adults—leaves the child and adolescent population as "pharmaceutical orphans". Those who treat children must extrapolate dosing and other information from adult studies. Furthermore, it fosters long delays between advances in adult psychopharmacology and their application in younger patients.

Why was OCD different? I suggest this is primarily because of the work of child and adolescent psychiatrists, such as Professors Flament and Cohen and the many contributors to the field whose work is reviewed in their review. The scope and level of sophistication of knowledge made available concerning this disorder in children and adolescents provided the rationale and justification for the pharmaceutical industry to approach OCD in a less traditional fashion. Secondarily, there needed to be advocates for this population within the industry. More recently, the US Food and Drug Administration has provided incentives for companies willing to conduct studies in the pediatric population and similar efforts are ongoing in Europe. These regulatory efforts should be helpful. It is also important that the investigation of other psychiatric disorders be as thorough and inclusive with regard to the child and adolescent population, as has been done with OCD.

In this way, we can expect fewer "pharmaceutical orphans" in the future, and should be able to close the "gap" between advances in adult and pediatric psychopharmacology.

REFERENCE

1. Conroy S., Choonara I., Impicciatore P., Mohn A., Arnell H., Rane A., Knoeppel C., Seyberth H., Pandolfini C., Raffaelli M.P. *et al* (2000) Survey of unlicensed and off label drug use in paediatric wards in European countries. *Br. Med. J.*, **320**: 79–82.

4.5 The Spectrum of Obsessive-Compulsive Symptoms in Children and Adolescents

Per Hove Thomsen[1]

Obsessive-compulsive disorder (OCD), defined as the presence of severe intrusive obsessions and unwelcome and annoying compulsions, is far from that rare disorder in children and adolescents it was thought to be about 20 years ago. Epidemiological data from throughout the world document that OCD in both boys and girls is frequent [1, 2], and that it affects these children's lives severely. The focus upon and the research in OCD (children and adults), in regard to both etiological factors/pathogenesis and treatment, has been immense, giving us new knowledge, not only on obsessions and compulsions, but also on a spectrum of related disorders and, furthermore, information on the normal development of ritualistic behaviour seen in most normal children [3].

Flament and Cohen describe the differential diagnosis between OCD and psychotic disorders such as schizophrenia, and pervasive developmental disorders such as Asperger's syndrome. The differentiation between ego-dystonic obsessions and compulsions and the ritualistic behaviour seen in schizophrenia as well as in Asperger's syndrome raises the question of the usability of the concept of ego-dystonicity/syntonicity in all children with OCD. In fact, the cognitive development of some children with OCD prevents them from taking the mental perspective necessary in order to describe obsessions as being unwelcome, with origin from their own thoughts, and with a feeling of them being excessive and not rational. Further research in the connection and relation between obsessive-compulsive-like symptoms in schizophrenia and pervasive developmental disorders and OCD is still needed.

Flament and Cohen describe the intriguing finding of a high rate of OCD in first-degree relatives of autistic individuals and the fact that serotonergic abnormalities and potential responsiveness to specific serotonin reuptake inhibitors relate autism to the OCD spectrum disorders. Further research in OCD spectrum disorders, and their mutual similarities and differences, may lead to a better understanding of potential common pathways for these disorders, and to a better treatment approach.

The documentation of treatment efficacy, as regards both medical treatment and cognitive-behavioural treatment (CBT), is reviewed by Flament and Cohen. However, we still need data on treatment prediction. We must admit that we as clinicians are still ignorant as to what specific factors seem to make a significant difference in treatment response,

[1] *Children's Psychiatric Hospital, Harald Selmersvej 66, DK-8240 Risskov, Denmark*

and to what factors seem to influence the course and prognosis of the disorder. In our search for treatment prediction, we might be able to identify different subtypes of OCD, some of which are related to tic disorders and Tourette's syndrome or different kinds of neurological disorders, others to the spectrum of anxiety and panic disorders, and a third, perhaps, to disorders of empathy (such as schizophrenia, Asperger's syndrome and pervasive developmental disorder). As regards treatment approaches, we still need documentation on the efficacy of CBT in children with OCD, in both the short and long term. Studies including combinations of different kinds of treatments, such as CBT with or without drugs, are also much needed.

REFERENCES

1. Flament M., Whitaker A., Rapoport J.L., Davies M., Berg C.Z., Kalikow K. Sceery W., Schaffer D. (1988) Obsessive compulsive disorder in adolescence: an epidemiological study. *J. Am. Acad. Child Adolesc. Psychiatry*, **27**: 764–771.
2. Zohar A.H., Ratzosin G., Pauls D.L., Apter A., Bleich A., Kron S., Rappaport M., Weizman A., Cohen D.J. (1992) An epidemiological study of obsessive-compulsive disorder and related disorders in Israeli adolescents. *J. Am. Acad. Child Adolesc. Psychiatry*, **31**: 1057–1061.
3. Yaryura-Tobias J.A., Neziroglu F. (1997) *Obsessive-Compulsive Disorder Spectrum. Pathogenesis, Diagnosis, and Treatment*, American Psychiatric Press, Washington, DC.

4.6
Obsessive-Compulsive Disorder in Children and Adolescents: Narrowing the Gap between Knowledge and Clinical Practice

Jovan G. Simeon[1]

The review by Flament and Cohen on pediatric obsessive-compulsive disorder (OCD) is a comprehensive and up-to-date review of rather remarkable advances in a complex disorder affecting many individuals from childhood into adulthood. OCD in children and adolescents is often very disabling, interfering with all aspects of life—individual, family, social and academic. The prevalence of the disorder is underestimated, and in many adolescents the diagnosis is made years after the onset of symptoms. Current evidence for a biological substrate (genetic and autoimmune factors, frontal–subcortical

[1] *Royal Ottawa Hospital, 1145 Carling Avenue, Ottawa, Ontario, Canada K1Z 7K4*

and serotonergic dysfunctions) has greatly facilitated our understanding of OCD and its management, as well as invalidated psychoanalytic concepts of etiology and therapy.

In clinical practice, many children and adolescents are referred for a variety of complaints which are not typical of OCD, while in fact they suffer from OCD. Thus, as recommended by the American Academy of Child and Adolescent Psychiatry [1], a comprehensive diagnostic assessment and the use of relevant rating scales are essential to properly manage OCD and any comorbid disorders. The use of rating scales facilitates the assessment of the type and severity of symptoms and their response to therapy.

The significance of findings related to OCD "subtypes" and OC "spectrum" disorders is unclear [2]. Similar theoretical and practical problems relate to the concept of "comorbid" disorders: comorbidity implies that the boundaries of coexisting disorders are clear; comorbid disorders can coexist independently, represent different manifestations of the same disorder, or be causally related. Further multidisciplinary research in the genetic, neuroimaging, biochemical and immunological aspects of these disorders may clarify their causal relationship and biological substrates.

Specific cognitive-behavioural techniques (CBT) and pharmacotherapies have dramatically improved the management and outcome of OCD in children, adolescents and adults alike. Successful psychological therapy of OCD appears to have resulted in a decrease of hypermetabolism of the frontal lobes, thus providing a scientific base for effective psychotherapy of a biological disorder. While CBT offers significant advantages over pharmacotherapy, the scarcity of trained therapists, and the inability of children and reluctance of adolescents to comply with the demands of CBT appears to result in a preponderant use of medications in pediatric OCD. The treatment of cases suffering from both OCD and Tourette's syndrome is often a challenge, necessitating combined pharmacotherapy. In certain clinical centers and possibly countries, Tourette's syndrome appears over-diagnosed, while in others under-diagnosed. Treatment-resistant OCD may also benefit from combined pharmacotherapy [3]. As most OCD patients also suffer from comorbid conditions, these are usually treated with drug combinations. Clinical evaluations of therapeutic and adverse effects of combined pharmacotherapy ought to be a priority. To deal most effectively with OCD cases and their families, a team approach is important, in order to develop a community program for the early identification and referral of OCD cases, their assessment, and especially therapy of any comorbid and family pathology. Family pathology may either precede an individual's OCD or result from it.

General awareness of the nature of OCD in the light of recent discoveries has greatly been promoted by books such as that by Rapoport [4]. A recent monograph on OCD in children and adolescents illustrates the importance of multidisciplinary research in this area, the achievements obtained in the past 25 years, and the many theoretical and practical problems which need to be resolved [5]. The study of outcome predictors appears quite important. Outcome comparisons of medicated vs. unmedicated OCD patients may be biased, as usually more chronic or severe cases are treated with psychotropic drugs. The review by Flament and Cohen should stimulate further collaborative research and especially narrow the gap between the available knowledge related to OCD and clinical practice. It is also hoped it may help the development of a consensus on diagnosis and therapy of pediatric OCD at an international level.

REFERENCES

1. American Academy of Child and Adolescent Psychiatry (1998) Practice parameters for the assessment and treatment of children and adolescents with obsessive-compulsive disorder. *J. Am. Acad. Child Adolesc. Psychiatry*, **37**: 27S–45S.
2. Riddle M. (1998) Obsessive-compulsive disorder in children and adolescents. *Br. J. Psychiatry*, **173**: 91–96.
3. Simeon J.G., Thatte S., Wiggins D. (1990) Treatment of adolescent obsessive-compulsive disorder with a clomipramine–fluoxetine combination. *Psychopharmacol. Bull.*, **26**: 285–290.
4. Rapoport J.L. (1989) *The Boy Who Couldn't Stop Washing*, Dutton, New York.
5. King R.A., Scahill L. (Eds) (1999) *Child and Adolescent Psychiatric Clinics of North America. Obsessive-Compulsive Disorder*, Saunders, Philadelphia.

4.7
Obsessive-Compulsive Disorder in Children and Adolescents: Data from a Developing Country

Carlos E. Berganza[1]

Obsessions and compulsions have attracted the attention of researchers and clinicians since the early inceptions of adult as well as of child psychiatry and, as they consolidate into one of the most conspicuous disorders affecting human behaviour, feelings and cognitions, are probably strong representatives of the paradigmatic developments in psychiatry at all times.

[1] *Clinica de Psiquiatria Infantil, Avenida La Reforma 13–70, Zona 9, Guatemala 00109, Guatemala*

From a strong psychoanalytic conceptualization in the early stages of etiological understanding, to a more biologically-oriented one dominating the current Zeitgeist, child psychiatry has dealt with the obsessive-compulsive disorders(OCD) not only as a clinical condition of significant impact upon the general functioning of the patient, but also as a model of the mental disorders, due to the genetic, biochemical, cognitive, psychodynamic and systemic concomitants implicit in their phenomenology.

Flament and Cohen present a comprehensive review of OCD in children and adolescents, examining the extant literature, and summarizing the most solid evidence in issues concerning prevalence, comorbidity, phenomenology, etiology and treatment, among others. Conspicuously, the literature these authors summarize comes predominantly from north-western centers of research, with the exception of few papers including data from Japan, Taiwan, New Zealand, India and Brazil. Thus, although we may conclude that the prevalence of these disorders seems quite similar in different parts of the world, how culture may affect phenomenology, especially in developing areas or in more "unsophisticated" cultures, still remains an issue to be resolved. This is of special importance for clinicians dealing with these types of patients in developing countries, not only in terms of case detection, but also in terms of treatment selection and assessment of treatment effectiveness. Also, as developed countries embrace mounting immigration of people from other cultures, and as these groups assert their cultural identities, local clinicians need to understand the phenomenological differences that characterize these disorders for purposes of diagnosis and management.

Concerning the prevalence of obsessive-compulsive symptoms, it may be of interest to the reader to know that we have conducted a survey in over 2000 parents of children and adolescents from three samples: (a) 100 outpatients of a child psychiatry clinic; (b) 200 outpatients of a pediatric clinic; and (c) 1849 students from eight schools in Guatemala City. The purpose of the study was to establish the prevalence of different psychiatric disorders, the levels of psychosocial dysfunction, and the risk factors in those children and adolesents. For that purpose, we developed three questionnaires, one of which was an inventory of psychiatric disorders based on ICD-10 diagnostic criteria.

The item designed to detect obsessive-compulsive symptoms, part of a 30-item questionnaire, read as follows: "He/she is perfectionist, has repetitive ideas that he/she can not shut off from his/her mind; or he/she shows behaviours that are repetitive, without apparent sense (washing hands excessively, counting steps, walking along square lines, checking something too many times)". The parents were asked to rate all items in a scale from 0 to 3, where 0 = nothing, or almost nothing, never or almost never; 1 = a little, sometimes; 2 = some, frequently; 3 = a lot, always or almost always.

Based on the results of the school sample, and taking as positive only those cases where parents scored their children with either 2 or 3 (which we considered moderate and severe, respectively), we were able to detect 40 cases out of the 1849 students surveyed (age range 1–18 years), for a point prevalence of 2.2% for the school population in Guatemala City. Prevalence was 2.1% (20/949) for females, and 2.2% (20/900) for males.

Obsessive-compulsive symptoms were clearly associated with high levels of psychosocial dysfunction, as shown by significantly higher scores on the Child's Health Scale (CHS, [1]), a 12-item questionnaire measuring levels of dysfunction in children and adolescents. The 40 subjects with OCD presented a mean total score on the CHS of 7 (SD = 6.7), whereas the subjects without OCD had a mean total score on the CHS of only 2.28 (SD = 3.1). This difference reached statistical significance. It must be remembered that the higher the score on the CHS, the higher the level of psychosocial dysfunction; in addition, a total score of 5 effectively discriminates between a psychiatric sample of children and adolescents and one of normal controls. Thus, children with OCD in the school population not receiving treatment were presenting significant difficulties in their everyday functioning.

Concerning comorbidity, we found, as in studies from other areas, high levels of comorbid disorders in these subjects. Moderate to severe depression was present in 5/40 ($p < 0.0001$); anxiety in 11/40 ($p < 0.0001$); tics in 1/40 ($p = 0.0004$); attention deficit in 15/40 ($p < 0.0001$); eating disorders in 4/40 ($p = 0.037$) and oppositional defiance in 17/40 ($p < 0.0001$).

Although no systematic studies of the phenomenology of these disorders have been carried out in our center, our clinical experience indicates that a high number of our patients with eating disorders present conversely with a number of obsessive and compulsive symptoms, other than the ones concerning weight and body image. We think that this is important, because the DSM-IV, contrary to the research diagnostic criteria of ICD-10, makes it explicit that "if another Axis I disorder is present, the content of the obsessions or compulsions is not restricted to it (e.g. preoccupation with food in the presence of an eating disorder...)". We see it common that when the clinician finds such preoccupation with matters of food and weight in the presence of an eating disorder, he is discouraged to continue searching for other types of obsessions and compulsions, overlooking a strong obsessive-compulsive symptomatology.

In summary, although issues of etiology dominate the interest of researchers of OCD, we believe it is also important to advance in the understanding of how culture influences the symptomatic expression of these disorders, in order to increase the diagnostic sensitivity of clinicians across different areas of the world.

REFERENCE

1. Berganza C.E., Cazali L., Gaitán I., Mezzich J. (1996) Validez de criterio de la Escala de Salud del Niño [Criterion validity of the Child Health Scale]. *Revista Latinoamericana de Psicología*, **28**: 317–339.

CHAPTER

5

Obsessive-Compulsive Spectrum Disorders: A Review

Eric Hollander and Jennifer Rosen

Department of Psychiatry, Mount Sinai School of Medicine, Box 1230, One Gustave L. Levy Place, New York, NY 10029-6574, USA

INTRODUCTION

Obsessive-compulsive disorder (OCD) is characterized by obsessions (recurrent, intrusive and disturbing ideas, thoughts, impulses or images) as well as compulsions (repetitive behaviours performed according to certain rules or in a stereotyped fashion, designed to reduce discomfort) [1]. As our current understanding of OCD has grown, we have identified other disorders that may share features of OCD. Among these shared features are symptom profile, neurobiology, etiology and treatment response [2–5]. Recognizing these features that span across several disorders has led to the idea of an obsessive-compulsive spectrum of disorders (OCSD). Many of these disorders are quite devastating to afflicted individuals, their families and society as a whole. We will discuss clinical approaches used to view the OCSDs and symptom overlap between the disorders. In particular, we will focus on the impulse control disorders, somatoform disorders, and neurological disorders with repetitive behaviours. Studies on the effectiveness of serotonin reuptake inhibitors (SRIs) in treating these disorders will be presented.

COMPULSIVITY AND IMPULSIVITY

Dimensional Models

OCSDs may be visualized on a compulsive-impulsive dimension, with an exaggerated sense of harm at the compulsive end and an underestimate of

Obsessive-Compulsive Disorder. Edited by Mario Maj, Norman Sartorius, Ahmed Okasha and Joseph Zohar.

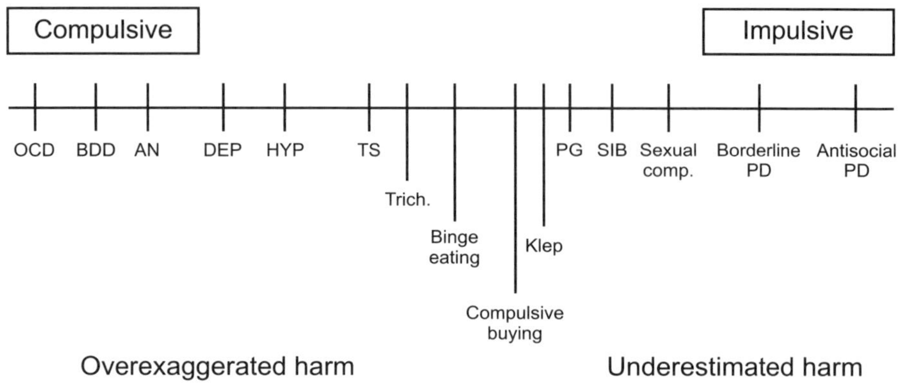

FIGURE 5.1 Obsessive-compulsive spectrum disorders visualized on a compulsive-impulsive dimension. OCD, Obsessive-compulsive disorder; BDD, body dysmorphic disorder; AN, anorexia nervosa; DEP, depersonalization disorder; HYP, hypochondriasis; TS, Tourette's syndrome; Trich., trichotillomania; Klep, kleptomania; PG, pathological gambling; SIB, self-injurious behaviour; Sexual comp., sexual compulsions; PD, personality disorder

Source: adapted from Hollander and Wong [6], by permission

harm at the impulsive end (Figure 5.1). Disorders characterized by substantial impulsivity include disorders of impulse control, paraphilias and sexual addictions. Disorders of compulsivity include OCD, body dysmorphic disorder, hypochondriasis, depersonalization disorder, and anorexia nervosa. The driving force behind the behaviours may also distinguish compulsivity and impulsivity. Compulsivity is driven by an attempt to alleviate anxiety or discomfort, while impulsivity is driven by the desire to obtain pleasure, arousal and gratification. Both share the inability to inhibit or delay the repetitive behaviours [6]. Impulsive and compulsive features may be present at the same time or at different times during the same illness [7].

Symptom Clusters

The OCSDs can be conceptualized as consisting of distinct symptom clusters. One of the clusters includes disorders of impulse control (i.e. intermittent explosive disorder, pyromania, kleptomania, pathological gambling (PG), trichotillomania, paraphilias, sexual impulsions and sexual addictions, and impulsive aggression personality disorders (i.e. borderline, antisocial, histrionic, narcissistic personality disorders). The second OC spectrum cluster is characterized by an exaggerated preoccupation with appearance, weight or bodily sensations, as in body dysmorphic disorder (BDD), eating disorders, hypochondriasis and depersonalization disorder [2, 3, 8]. The third spectrum cluster includes neurological disorders with repetitive behaviours, such as autism and Asperger's disorder, Tourette's syndrome and Sydenham's chorea [5]. Affected individuals are not restricted to one disorder and comorbidity among the spectrum disorders is common.

Response to Treatment

OCD and OCSDs display a preferential response to SRIs and behavioural therapy. Norephinephrine reuptake inhibitors, on the other hand, have not been effective.

Goodman *et al* [9] conducted an 8-week, double-blind OCD treatment study with fluvoxamine (an SRI) vs. desipramine (a norepinephrine reuptake inhibitor). Of the patients on fluvoxamine, 11 of 21 responded to treatment; of those on desipramine, two of 19 responded. In another 5-week, double-blind study by Thoren *et al* [10], clomipramine (an SRI) was superior to nortriptyline and placebo, although the difference was not obvious until the 5th week of treatment. In both studies, however, the period of treatment should have been longer. Some studies show response rates to increase up to 80–90% with augmentation therapy, including serotonergic (buspirone, fenfluramine), dopaminergic (haloperidol, pimozide) or GABA-ergic (clonazepam) agents [4]. Poor treatment response may be due to treatment resistance or comorbidity of OCSDs.

The OCSDs are less well characterized than OCD. Treatment for the OCSDs has been determined predominantly by open clinical trials. Like OCD, the OCSDs, including BDD [11], hypochondriasis [12], depersonalization disorder [13], anorexia nervosa [14], PG [15], sexual compulsions and paraphilias [16], self-injurious behaviour [17] and borderline personality disorder (BPD) [18], display a preferential response to SRIs.

The compulsive and impulsive disorders have a differential response to SRIs, with respect to dosage, response lag time, and maintenance of symptom response [4]. This difference may reflect a difference in baseline serotonin function. The compulsive disorders have a long lag period before they respond to the SRIs. However, after the initial response, the response is maintained for the duration of treatment, assuming the patient is given an adequate trial with high enough doses. Impulsive disorders have a quicker response to SRIs, but their response can decrease over time with continued treatment. Therefore, treatment augmentation may be important once the patient is initially stabilized [4].

Behavioural therapy is helpful in OCD and OCSDs. Two important aspects of behavioural therapy are repeated exposures (which are anxiety-provoking) and response prevention (to stop the rituals) [2, 3]. For some treatment-refractory patients, neurosurgery may be therapeutic. Neurosurgical procedures which interrupt pathways connecting frontal and limbic systems include cingulotomy and anterior capsulotomy, and "gamma knife" procedures, which are less invasive [2, 3].

Neurobiological Models

We have hypothesized that the compulsive disorders may be characterized by increased frontal lobe activity and increased sensitivity of specific serotonin receptor subsystems. In contrast, decreased frontal lobe activity and decreased presynaptic serotonergic function may underlie the impulsive disorders [6].

Important areas involved in the neurocircuitry of OCD are orbital–frontal cortex, basal ganglia, and limbic structures. OCD positron emission tomography (PET) scans have shown hyperfrontality and increased caudate metabolism [19]. Treatment with SRIs and behavioral therapy have resulted in decreased hypermetabolism of the caudate nucleus [20]. Neurosurgical treatments may be used to interrupt the pathways from orbital–frontal to deeper limbic structures. In patients that experienced increased OCD symptoms following m-chlorophenylpiperazine (m-CPP) challenges, increased cortical blood flow (particularly to frontal areas) occurred [21].

Serotonergic pathways play a large role in compulsive and impulsive disorders. During acute challenge with the partial 5-HT_{2C} agonist m-CPP in compulsive patients, about 50% of individuals with OCD experienced a worsening of their OC symptoms [22]. They also experienced a blunted prolactin response. The reduced prolactin response in OCD was associated with a greater behavioural response to m-CPP. Zohar *et al* [23] reported similar behavioural findings.

Hollander *et al* [24] conducted m-CPP challenges in 12 very impulsive BPD patients and 15 healthy controls. The administration of m-CPP resulted in marked emotional responses in most of the patients. Seven of the BPD patients reported feelings of spaciness, depersonalization and derealization. Three individuals reported a "high" feeling, similar to that produced by LSD. Peak m-CPP blood levels correlated with heightened impulsivity but not obsessions, which may suggest a possible role of the serotonergic system in the disinhibition in BPD [24].

Patients with other compulsive disorders (OCD, Tourette's syndrome and anorexia nervosa) had blunted prolactin responses to m-CPP challenges, whereas impulsive patients (BPD, PG and trichotillomania), had regular or much greater m-CPP neuroendocrine responses [24]. Platelet monoamine oxidase (MAO) activity, a peripheral indicator of serotonin function, was also lower in impulsive disorders (i.e. PG) [25].

Compulsive and impulsive disorders seem to have a different dysregulation in serotonin pathways, which may explain differential response to SRI treatment (longer therapeutic lag and higher dose required in compulsive disorders).

IMPULSE-CONTROL DISORDERS

Disorders of impulse control are characterized by impulsivity or aggression and lack of control (disinhibition). Affected individuals derive pleasure, arousal and gratification from their impulsive behaviour. Males and females can both express impulsivity, but they do so in different ways. Males are more likely to gamble, explode, set fires and act out sexually. Females are more likely to pull out their hair, injure themselves and shop compulsively [7]. It is unclear whether these phenotypic differences in the expression of impulsivity are due to genetic factors, differences in serotonin turnover, hormonal differences such as testosterone levels, or social/environmental pressures that vary between the sexes.

Low platelet MAO activity has been associated with sensation seeking, impulsivity, violence and borderline personality disorder [26]. On the other hand, high platelet MAO activity may be related to compulsivity, OCD and anxiety. Carrasco *et al* looked at the role of temperament in the OCD spectrum in a series of studies [26]. In one study, MAO activity was evaluated in non-pathological, sensation-seeking, impulsive individuals (including bullfighters and Spanish police explosives experts), and in impulsive, pathological subjects, such as pathological gamblers. Temperament was measured with Cloninger's Tridimensional Personality Questionnaire (TPQ), the Eysenck Personality Questionnaire (EPQ) and the Zuckerman's Sensation Seeking Scale. The sensation seekers and bullfighters had significantly lower platelet MAO activity as compared to controls. The explosives experts did not have lower MAO activity than controls, which is expected, as they were not sensation seekers or impulsive. Platelet MAO activity and sensation seeking had a significant inverse correlation [27]. Results showed 15 pathological gamblers to have a significantly lower MAO activity as compared to 25 normal controls. There was a negative correlation between MAO activity and sensation-seeking scores in controls and a positive correlation between MAO activity and sensation-seeking in the gamblers. Of note, families with low-MAO probands have been shown to have a much greater rate of suicidality compared to families with high-MAO probands [27].

Pathological Gambling (PG)

PG is classified as a disorder of impulse control in DSM-IV [1]. These patients, however, often feel that they have a compulsion to gamble. We have also studied PG as a more homogenous form of addiction in general, and thus it is sometimes viewed as an addictive disorder [28]. Pathological gambling is characterized by the inability to resist the urges to gamble, which disrupts many aspects of personal, family and vocational functioning. Their gambling may ultimately lead to bankruptcy, divorce and legal problems resulting from money embezzlement to continue to gamble. During stressful times, the gambling frequency increases. During a gambling episode, the individual feels gratification, release or pleasure. Also, dissociative or trance-like states may occur in the pathological gambler during gambling episodes [7]. These feelings persuade the individual to gamble more, in effect, exacerbating the situation.

PG is rapidly becoming a major public health problem. As access to legalized gambling has increased via greater numbers of casinos, state-run lotteries and various forms of gambling via the Internet, more potential pathological gamblers are exposed to gambling activities. Studies have shown that 68% of the population participated in recreational gambling to some extent [29], but up to 3% of the US population become pathological gamblers [4]. Pathological gambling occurs in high school at a frequency of 2–4% [30], but reaches 14.4% of 18–21-year olds [31]. Several comorbid psychiatric disorders are associated with pathological gambling, including attention-deficit/hyperactivity disorder (ADHD) [32], bipolar spectrum disorders, and substance abuse [7]. There is a high frequency of suicidal attempts in PG, due in part to impulsivity, depression, substance abuse and legal, marital and financial problems [28, 29].

Genetics

Several genes, including those coding for the D1, D2, D3 and D4 dopamine receptors, have been implicated in PG [33]. These genes may have an additive effect, indicating polygenic inheritance of susceptibility to PG. Abnormal dopamine reward pathways seem to be involved in PG and other addictive behaviours [33–35]. A reward deficiency syndrome [36] has been associated with genetic abnormalities of the dopamine reward pathways, which increase the risk for addictive and impulsive disorders, including PG [33]. Thus, PG may be conceptualized on a spectrum with disorders in which impulsive, compulsive and addictive behaviours are interrelated pathophysiologically and present common genetic contributions [33]. These risk factors may lead to the development of PG, substance abuse, sexual addictions, ADHD or Tourette's syndrome. Both environmental and genetic factors may play a role in pathological gambling.

Serotonergic defects have also been associated with many impulsive and compulsive disorders [33, 37, 38]. Two polymorphic alleles have been identified for tryptophan 2,3-dioxygenase gene (TD02), which is involved in serotonin metabolism [39]. Comings [33] has shown that a significantly larger percentage of individuals with impulsive addictive disorders, ADHD, Tourette's syndrome and drug addiction possessed one of the two alleles as compared to normal controls. Although the study did not show a significant increase in the frequency of these two alleles in pathological gamblers, the gene may be one of several that are polygenically related to pathological gambling.

Neurobiology

PG may be associated with decreased activity of the frontal lobes [32], as is also seen in patients with ADHD and impulsivity. Noradrenergic dysfunction is also likely to be involved in PG [40]. Cerebrospinal fluid plasma 3-methoxy-4-hydroxyphenylglycol (MHPG), a measure of central noradrenergic function, is increased in pathological gamblers compared to normal controls [41]. Activation of the noradrenergic system may be involved in the expression of high levels of arousal and extraversion seen in PG [40]. Also, low platelet MAO activity has been linked to tendencies toward impulsivity and monotony avoidance [42], risk-taking and sensation-seeking behaviour [43–45], and suicidality [46, 47]. Lower MAO activity is also observed in pathological gamblers compared to normal controls [25, 48], which is noteworthy given the high levels of risk taking and impulsivity seen in PG patients.

In a study by our group, pathological gamblers ($n = 10$) and controls ($n = 10$) received a m-CPP challenge [31]. Following a single oral dose of m-CPP (0.5 mg/kg), pathological gamblers had an increased "high" response, independent of placebo response, compared to controls. The "high" they experienced was phenomenologically similar to the "high" they felt after an early big gambling win which seemed to initiate the gambling cycle. In similar studies, m-CPP administration caused a euphoric "high" response in impulsive antisocial [49], borderline [24], trichotillomanic [50] and alcoholic [51] patients.

Treatment

Treatment for PG is available in the form of self-help groups such as Gamblers Anonymous. However, there is a high drop-out rate and, after a 1-year follow-up, up to 92% of patients relapse in gambling [52, 53]. Behavioural or psychodynamic therapies and inpatient and rehabilitation programs are helpful for some PG patients. After a 1-year follow-up, studies of inpatient rehabilitation programs have shown a 55% rate of complete abstinence [54]. Pharmacotherapy with lithium has also been used, particularly for PG patients with comorbid bipolar spectrum disorders [4]. The efficacy of SRIs in treatment of PG has also been studied. Because of a lack of instruments to assess the severity and change in PG behaviour, the Yale–Brown Obsessive Compulsive Scale (Y-BOCS) [55–56] has been modified for PG (PG-YBOCS).

The reliability and validity of the PG-YBOCS was evaluated in a single-blind, placebo-controlled study of PG treatment with fluvoxamine [57]. Intraclass correlation between pairs of ratings was used to determine inter-rater reliability ($r = 0.992$ total PG-YBOCS score). Cronbach's alpha coefficient (alpha $= 0.825$) indicated high internal consistency. Good convergent validity was determined by high Pearson correlation between the PG-YBOCS and the PG-Clinical Global Impression (CGI) ($r = 0.908$, $p = 0.000$, $n = 10$) and the South Oaks Gambling Screen (SOBS) ($r = 0.86$, $p = 0.003$, $n = 10$). Pearson correlation between PG-YBOCS and Hamilton Rating Scale for Depression (HAM-D) ($r = 0.22, p = 0.38, n = 10$) measured divergent validity. There was a significant Pearson correlation between change in total PG-YBOCS score (treatment endpoint vs. baseline) and CGI change score ($r = 0.778, p = 0.007$) as well as PG Self-Report number of gambling episodes/week ($r = 0.801, p = 0.009$). No significant correlation was found between change in PG-YBOCS and change in HAM-D ($r = 0.242, p = 0.5$). According to this pilot study, PG-YBOCS is a reliable and valid measure of severity of PG behaviour and change.

The efficacy of the selective serotonin reuptake inhibitor (SSRI) fluvoxamine was assessed in 16 pathological gamblers in a 16-week, single-blind cross-over trial with two 8-week phases (Figure 5.2). As measured by the PG-CGI, 70% were fluvoxamine responders at the endpoint (very much or much improved scale scores). There was a greater than 25% decrease in the PG-YBOCS gambling behaviour score [58]. These patients reported decreased thoughts and urges to gamble, greater control over resisting the urges and complete abstinence. The 30% of patients who did not respond had comorbid cyclothymia, which was perhaps exacerbated by the SSRI, resulting in increased impulsivity and a relapse [58].

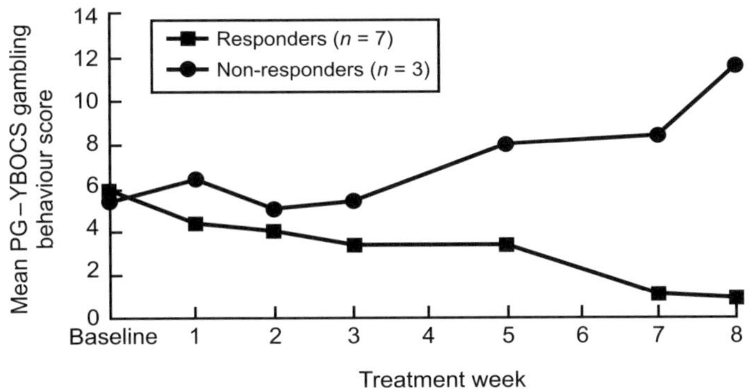

FIGURE 5.2 Efficacy of Fluvoxamine in Pathological Gambling. PG–YBOCS, Pathological Gambling–Yale-Brown Obsessive Compulsive Scale

Source: Created from data in Hollander *et al* [58]

Sexual Addictions and Paraphilias

Paraphilias are defined in DSM-IV as sexual fantasies with non-typical arousal patterns that cause distress and interfere with the ability to be intimate sexually [1]. They include exhibitionism, voyeurism and sexual masochism. Sexual addictions or impulsions are normative arousal behaviours carried out at a frequency or intensity that creates a problem in sexual intimacy [59]. The behaviours are pleasure producing and include compulsive masturbation and reactive promiscuous sexual behaviour. Individuals with true sexual obsessions experience intrusive images that the individual considers morally repugnant.

Treatment

Our group measured the response of 13 patients with paraphilias, non-paraphilic sexual addictions and sexual obsessions to SRIs, including fluvoxamine, clomipramine and fluoxetine [16]. The results suggested that paraphilias, sexual addictions and sexual obsessions may have somewhat different responses to SRIs. Patients with sexual obsessions had the greatest response to SRI treatment, those with paraphilias had a moderate response, while those with non-paraphilic sexual addictions had a worsening of symptoms on high doses of SSRIs, but a positive response at low doses [16].

The SSRI sertraline was studied in an open-label trial of 13 men with paraphilias and 11 men with paraphilia-related disorders [60] (Figure 5.3).

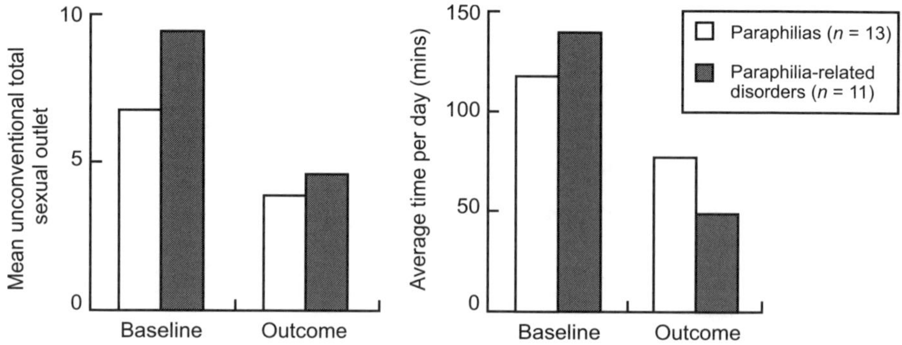

FIGURE 5.3 Efficacy of sertraline in paraphilias and paraphilia-related disorders
Source: Created from data in Kafka [60]

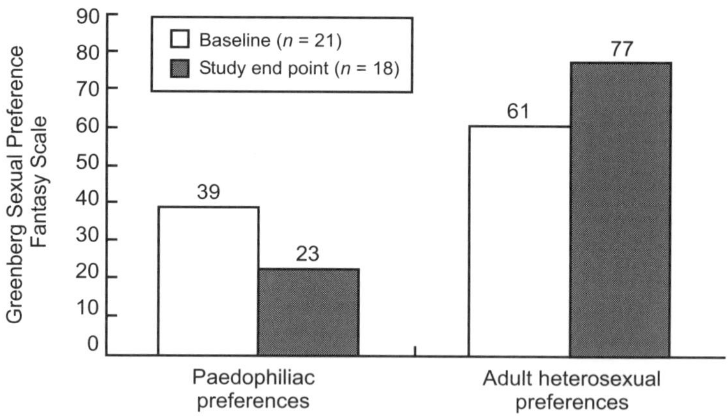

FIGURE 5.4 Efficacy of sertraline in paedophilia
Source: Created from data in Bradford *et al* [61]

Patients were treated with a mean dose of 99 mg/day for 4–64 weeks. The total sexual outlet (TSO) and average time per day (ATD) spent in unconventional sexual behaviour were decreased at outcome in both groups studied. About 50% of the men who completed 4 or more weeks of sertraline treatment felt that the treatment produced clinically significant changes for them [60].

The therapeutic effect of sertraline in 21 patients with paedophilia, a subset of paraphilias, was studied in a 12-week, open-label study, at doses of 50–200 mg/day [61] (Figure 5.4). A statistically significant improvement in paedophiliac preferences was seen on the Greenberg Sexual Preference

Fantasy Scale. The increase in adult heterosexual preferences is notable and indicates that the change in paedophiliac preferences was not just due to sexual side effects.

SOMATOFORM AND EATING DISORDERS CLUSTER

Disorders of this cluster are characterized by obsessions and compulsions involving the body. Compulsions are carried out with the intention of alleviating the anxiety caused by one's preoccupations. Disorders of this cluster include BDD, hypochondriasis and eating disorders. Treatment resistance is due in part to the unyielding beliefs held by affected individuals. Individuals with eating disorders have relentless obsessions and compulsions dealing with body image and eating. Anorexia, for example, is characterized by a relentless pursuit of being thin and an obsessive fear of being fat. In hypochondriasis, the obsessions and preoccupations deal with the presence of physical illness with no clinical evidence to confirm the belief [12, 62].

Body Dysmorphic Disorder (BDD)

BDD is included in the DSM-IV [1] as a somatoform disorder characterized by a gross preoccupation with one or more imagined defects in appearance (excluding body weight). The obsessive preoccupations of patients with BDD are focused on one or more body parts. Frequently targeted body parts include the head (nose, eyes, hair, skin, mouth or jaw), body size or symmetry, sexual parts (penis, testes, breasts, buttocks) or gender identity [63]. In BDD, women can think they are too large and men can believe they are too small. The perceived defects and associated obsessions may even appear on another individual in a variant called "BDD by proxy". In order to allieve their anxiety, patients may partake in compulsive ritualistic behaviours, such as mirror-checking and excessive grooming and dressing actions. These compulsive behaviours, however, usually do not relieve their anxiety. The individuals often fear they will be rejected by others or embarrassed in a social situation. The disorder causes marked psychological distress and is highly debilitating in social and occupational functioning [64].

BDD patients often visit physicians and cosmetic surgeons. Repeat visits are common and the patients often feel unsatisfied with the results, believing their condition to be unchanged or exacerbated, or they become concerned with a different part of their body [64]. The extent to which BDD patients seek cosmetic surgery may be larger than realized and it is questionable if they should be allowed surgery. Almost 50% of BDD patients truly believe their defect really exists [65]. The individuals may actually have visual illusions which increase their belief in the defect. This is interesting in that symptoms are egosyntonic only in about 5% of OCD patients [66].

Epidemiology and Comorbidity

BDD may be common among males and females to almost the same extent [67], or slightly more frequent in males [68]. The symptoms often present in late adolescence to early 20s. Whereas the prevalence of OCD is 1.2–3.3% of the population [65], that of BDD is only 0.1–1% [4]. Comorbidity with OCD may be up to 38% [4]. Other disorders also frequently accompany BDD, including depression, social phobia and impulse control disorders [4, 64]. Phillips *et al* [64] found that the lifetime prevalence in BDD patients was 83% for depression, 35% for social phobia and 29% for OCD. Most of the time the BDD preceded major depression by about one year. Family histories of BDD patients often present with mood disorders and substance abuse [69].

Etiology

Psychological and environmental factors may play a role in the etiology of BDD. Since there is a high rate of comorbidity between BDD and OCD, it is possible that similar neurobiological factors are also involved.

The head, hands, feet and sexual organs (frequent areas of BDD foci) cover a large area of the somatosensory and motor strips in brain which are involved with self-esteem and social functioning [21, 63]. Preferential response to SSRI treatment also indicates that serotonin is involved in BDD [64, 70].

Treatment

Pharmacotherapy. Both delusional and non-delusional BDD patients seem to respond preferentially to SRI treatment. On the other hand, standard neuroleptics, benzodiazepines, tricyclics (TCAs) with the exception of clomipramine, and anticonvulsants seem to be less effective.

Phillips *et al* [64] followed 374 courses of treatment of 130 BDD patients with SSRIs (fluvoxamine, fluoxetine, paroxetine, sertraline), clomipramine, monoamine oxidase inhibitors (MAOIs) and conventional TCAs. There was a 54% significant improvement in 113 treatments with SSRIs or clomipramine (mean CGI improvement score was 1.8 and there was 49% improvement on the modified Y-BOCS). There was a 30% significant improvement in 23 treatments with MAOIs, and 15% significant improvement in 56 treatments with TCAs.

Hollander *et al* [71] conducted an open-label trial in 21 BDD patients with fluvoxamine (mean 260 mg/day) and standard TCAs. Body preoccupation was "much" or "very much" improved after fluvoxamine treatment. Following treatment, CGI improvement score was 1.8. Following TCA treatment (non-serotonin reuptake properties; mean dose 178 mg/day), CGI mean score was 3.9, indicating no change.

Adequate doses for treating BDD are greater than those for treating depression [64]. Note above, the mean dose for the BDD patients using fluvoxamine was 260 mg/day as compared to the normal dose of 100 mg/day for depressed patients. Without continued treatment, there is a high rate of relapse. It takes 8–12 or more weeks for treatment response [64]. Hence, long-term treatment is often necessary.

We recently reported that the SRI clomipramine was significantly more effective than the norepinephrine reuptake inhibitor desipramine in the treatment of BDD, suggesting a selective efficacy of SRIs in BDD, as is also seen in OCD [72].

Other forms of treatment. There have been mixed results in studies of psychotherapy, including behavioural therapy and insight-oriented psychotherapy. Some success has been seen with systematic desensitization, exposure therapy and self-confrontation [73–76]. Electroconvulsive therapy has not been helpful in treatment of BDD. It can be beneficial to encourage the BDD patients to abstain from carrying out their repetitive compulsions. The patients should also be encouraged to confront routine situations that they tend to avoid.

NEUROLOGICAL DISORDERS

The cluster of neurological disorders include Sydenham's chorea, autism, Asperger's disorder and Tourette's syndrome. The stereotypic movements involved in these disorders originate from the basal ganglia. As in OCD, these individuals display both obsessive and compulsive behaviour. However, behaviours differ from those expressed in individuals with OCD. Autistic individuals present more frequent repetitive behaviours and interests, ordering, hoarding and stereotypic movements, and a less frequent focus on aggression, counting, sexual and religious issues, symmetry and somatic obsessions [77]. Individuals with tic disorders express more touching, tapping, rubbing, blinking and staring rituals, and fewer cleaning rituals [78]. In Tourette's disorder, sensory experiences often present prior to voluntary repetitive behaviours. In OCD, cognitions and autonomic precede voluntary repetitive behaviours [79].

Autism

Autism is a pervasive developmental disorder characterized by three core components: social deficits, speech and communication impairment, repetitive behaviours and restricted interests. Other symptoms include affective lability, impulsivity and aggressivity, self-injurious behaviour and hyperactivity.

Clinical Features and Epidemiology

Lifetime prevalence estimates of the full syndrome of classical autistic disorder are 2–5 per 10 000. Symptoms typically present by the age of 3 and often begin in infancy. As changes in brain growth occur, autistic symptoms tend to change. The etiology of autism is still unknown, and there is no known cure. Clinical symptomatology and treatment response are both heterogeneous. The differential diagnosis of autism includes Asperger's disorder, in which only the social deficits and compulsive components are seen.

Serotonin Involvement

The anterior cingulate, with abundant serotonin receptors, may be involved in social, cognitive and affective functions in autism. There may be a correlation between increased activity of the anterior cingulate and compulsiveness [80].

Neurobiological studies in autism have focused on serotonin [81], implicated in the regulation of many functions relevant to disorder, such as learning, memory, repetitive behaviours, sensory and motor processes [83].

Studies in whole blood and plasma suggest an elevation of serotonin in some autistic individuals [83, 84]. However, other studies have not shown serotonin levels to correlate with specific clinical features [81]. In autistic individuals with affected relatives, blood serotonin levels were significantly higher than in those without affected relatives [85, 86]. In addition, relatives of autistic probands with high serotonin levels were found to be rated high on scales for depression, anxiety and OCD [80]. Thus, blood serotonin levels may be familial and possibly associated with genetic liability to specific subtypes of autism.

Preliminary studies of the serotonergic system in autism indicate that acute depletion of the serotonin precursor, tryptophan, may worsen several behavioural symptoms of autistic disorder [87]. McBridge *et al* [88] demonstrated a blunted prolactin response to fenfluramine, a serotonin releaser, in autistic adults. We have recently reported that increased 5–HT_{1D} receptor sensitivity, as measured by increased growth hormone response to sumatriptan, significantly correlates with the severity of repetitive behaviours in autistic patients, as measured by Y-BOCS severity [89]. Autoimmune factors may also be associated with the 5–HT_{1A} receptors in the blood of a subgroup of autistic patients [90]. We recently reported that increased expression of the B cell autoimmune marker D8/17 significantly correlates with increased repetitive behaviour in autism, measured by Y-BOCS [91].

Treatment

Currently no medication treatments have established indications for autism [92], although medications have been used to treat some core symptoms, concurrent psychiatric disorders, or associated medical conditions such as seizures. SRIs seem to be promising in improving global severity and dimensional deficits in autism, including compulsive/obsessional symptoms, involuntary movements, and some social and language deficits; they are well tolerated in low doses, and do not have the seizure and cardiac risks associated with clomipramine.

A double-blind cross-over study was conducted with clomipramine and placebo [93] in 12 autistic children and adolescents. Twelve others participated in a double-blind study with clomipramine and desipramine. The results showed clomipramine to be significantly better than desipramine in stopping compulsive core symptoms, social deficit and problem behaviours (i.e. self-injury, aggression) ($p < 0.05$). Clomipramine was better in autistic, speech and anger ratings, but desipramine rated better in hyperactivity.

Cook *et al* [94] have carried out studies with fluoxetine in autism and mental retardation. In an open trial with a daily dose of 20–40 mg, there was significant improvement in CGI severity scale scores in 15 of 23 (65.2%) autistic patients and 10 of 16 (62.5%) mentally retarded subjects. Twenty-one of the 23 autistic patients had comorbid mental retardation. However, the study was open-label and not placebo-controlled.

Our group has conducted a 16-week double-blind, placebo-controlled cross-over study with fluoxetine in 11 adults and children with autism and Asperger's disorder. We found fluoxetine to improve the CGI score significantly as compared to placebo [80].

SUMMARY

Consistent Evidence

Consistent research evidence suggests shared features among OCD and the OCSDs, including phenomenology, clinical features, neurobiology, family history and treatment response. Effective treatment with SRIs and various neurobiological studies suggest serotonergic but not noradrenergic dysfunction in OCD and OCSDs.

Compulsive and impulsive disorders have shown differential SRI treatment responses, indicating differential biological mechanisms. Compulsive disorders are characterized by hyperfrontality and increased serotonergic sensitivity; impulsive disorders are marked by hypofrontality and reduced presynaptic serotonergic sensitivity. Platelet MAO activity is reduced in impulsive disorders, but increased in compulsive disorders. Compulsive disorders have a long lag period prior to SRI treatment response, often followed by continued maintenance during treatment; impulsive disorders respond more quickly to SRIs, but continued treatment is often unsuccessful on the long term. OCSDs can have a devastating impact on quality of life, morbidity and mortality.

Incomplete Evidence

While the etiology of OCD and OCSDs seems to be multifactorial, the involvement of environmental, genetic, and possibly immunologic factors needs to be further studied. It is also uncertain whether the basis for phenotypic differences in the presentation of impulsivity between males and females, lies in differences of serotonin turnover, hormonal differences, or differential social/environmental pressures.

Areas Still Open to Research

Further family and genetic studies need to be conducted for a better understanding of subtyping and more specific characterization of the OCSDs. While preliminary studies suggest efficacy of SSRIs in treating BDD, PG, sexual addictions, and autism, further large-scale controlled studies need to be conducted in order to replicate these favourable findings. Further, neurobiological and brain imaging studies can aid in our understanding of differential diagnosis and could help define predictors of treatment response. An OCSD brain bank would be beneficial in conducting neuroanatomical studies with post-mortem brains and an OCSD gene bank would facilitate genetic linkage studies. Additional specific animal models would also be extremely useful in defining the pathophysiology and developing new and more effective treatments.

REFERENCES

1. American Psychiatric Association (1994) *Diagnostic and Statistical Manual of Mental Disorders*, 4th edn, American Psychiatric Association, Washington, DC.
2. Hollander E. (1993) *Obsessive-Compulsive Related Disorders*, American Psychiatric Press, Washington, DC.
3. Hollander E. (1993) Obsessive-compulsive spectrum disorders: an overview. *Psychiatr. Ann.*, **23**: 355–358.
4. Hollander E., Wong C.M. (1995) Body dysmorphic disorder, pathological gambling, and sexual compulsions. *J. Clin. Psychiatry*, **56** (suppl. 4): 7–12.
5. Hollander E., Wong C. (2000) Spectrum boundary and subtyping issues: implications for treatment refractory obsessive-compulsive disorder. In *Obsessive-Compulsive Disorder: Contemporary Issues in Treatment* (Eds. W.K. Goodman, M.V. Rudorfer, J. Maser), Erlbaum, Hillsdale, in press.
6. Hollander E., Wong C. (1995) Obsessive-compulsive spectrum disorders. *J. Clin. Psychiatry*, **56** (suppl. 4): 3–6.
7. Hollander E. (1998) Treatment of obsessive-compulsive spectrum disorders with SSRIs. *Br. J. Psychiatry*, **173** (suppl. 35): 7–12.
8. Theil A., Broocks A., Ohlmeier M. (1995) Obsessive-compulsive disorder among patients with anorexia nervosa and bulimia nervosa. *Am. J. Psychiatry*, **152**: 72–75.
9. Goodman W.K., Delgado P.L., Price L.H. (1990) Specificity of serotonin reuptake inhibitors in the treatment of OCD: comparison of fluvoxamine and desipramine in OCD. *Arch. Gen. Psychiatry*, **47**: 577–585.
10. Thoren O., Asberg M., Bertilsson L., Mellström B., Sjöquist F., Träskman L. (1980) Clomipramine treatment of obsessive-compulsive disorder: II. Biological aspects. *Arch. Gen. Psychiatry*, **37**: 1281–1289.
11. Hollander E., Liebowitz M.R., Winchel R., Klumker A., Klein D.F. (1989) Treatment of body dysmorphic disorder with serotonergic reuptake blockers. *Am. J. Psychiatry*, **146**: 768–770.
12. Fallon B.A., Liebowitz M.R., Salman E., Schneier F.R., Jusino C., Hollander E., Klein D.F. (1993) Fluoxetine for hypochondriacal patients without major depression. *J. Clin. Psychopharmacol.*, **13**: 438–431.
13. Hollander E., Liebowitz M.R., DeCaria C., Fairbanks J., Fallon B., Klein D.F. (1990) Treatment of depersonalization with serotonin reuptake blockers. *J. Clin. Psychopharmacol.*, **10**: 200–203.
14. Gwirtsman H.E., Guze B.H., Yager J., Eainsley B. (1990) Fluoxetine treatment of anorexia nervosa: an open clinical trial. *J. Clin. Psychiatry*, **51**: 378–382.
15. Hollander E., Frenkel M., DeCaria C., Trungold S., Klein D.F. (1992) Treatment of pathological gambling with clomipramine. *Am. J. Psychiatry*, **149**: 710–711.
16. Stein D.J., Hollander E., Anthony D., Schneier F.R., Fallon B.A., Liebowitz M.R., Klein D.F. (1992) Serotonergic medications for sexual obsessions, sexual addictions, and paraphilias. *J. Clin. Psychiatry*, **53**: 267–271.
17. Favazza A.R. (1992) Repetitive self-mutilation. *Psychiatr. Ann.*, **22**: 60–63.

18. Markovitz P. J., Calabrese J.R., Schultz S.C., Meltzer H.Y. (1991) Fluoxetine in the treatment of borderline and schizotypal personality disorders. *Am. J. Psychiatry*, **148**: 1064–1067.
19. Baxter L.R., Phelps M.E., Mazziotta J.C., Guze B.H., Schwartz J.M., Selin C.E. (1987) Local cerebral glucose metabolic rates in obsessive-compulsive disorder: a comparison with rates in unipolar depression and in normal controls. *Arch. Gen. Psychiatry*, **44**: 211–218.
20. Baxter L.R., Schwartz J.M., Bergman K.S., Szuba M.P., Guze B.H., Mazziotta J.C., Alazraki A., Selin C.E., Huan-Kwang F., Munford P., Phelps M.E. (1992) Caudate glucose metabolic rate changes with both drug and behavioral therapies for obsessive-compulsive disorder. *Arch. Gen. Psychiatry*, **49**: 681–689.
21. Hollander E., Prohovnik, I., Stein D. (1995) Increased cerebral blood flow during m-CPP exacerbation of obsessive-compulsive disorder. *J. Neuropsychiat. Clin. Neurosci.*, **7**: 485–490.
22. Hollander E., DeCaria C.M., Niteseu A., Gully R., Suckow R. F., Cooper T.B., Gorman J.M., Klein D.F., Liebowitz M.R. (1992) Serotonergic function in obsessive-compulsive disorder: behavioral and neuroendocrine responses to oral m-chlorophenylpiperazine and fenfluramine in patients and healthy volunteers. *Arch. Gen. Psychiatry*, **49**: 21–28.
23. Zohar J., Muellar E.A., Insel T.R., Zohar-Kadouch R.C., Murphy D.L. (1987) Serotonergic responsivity in obsessive-compulsive disorder: comparison of patients and healthy controls. *Arch. Gen. Psychiatry*, **44**: 946–951.
24. Hollander E., Stein D., DeCaria C.M., Cohen L., Saoud J.B., Skodol A.E., Kellman D., Rosnick L., Oldham J.M. (1994) Serotonergic sensitivity in borderline personality disorder: preliminary findings. *Am. J. Psychiatry*, **151**: 277–280.
25. Carrasco J., Saiz-Ruiz J., Moreno I., Hollander E., Lopez-Ibor J.J. (1994) Low platelet monoamine oxidase activity in pathological gambling. *Acta Psychiatr. Scand.*, **90**: 427–431.
26. Carrasco J. (1998) OCD spectrum: low platelet MAO as a marker of the impulsive pole. Presented at the Third International Obsessive-Compulsive Disorder Conference, Madeira, Portugal, September 11–13.
27. Buchsbaum M.S., Coursey R.D., Murphy D.L. (1976) The biochemical high risk paradigm: behavioral and familial correlates of low platelet monoamine oxidase activity. *Science*, **194**: 339–341.
28. DeCaria CM, Hollander E. (1993) Pathological gambling. In *Obsessive-Compulsive-Related Disorders* (Ed. E. Hollander), pp. 155–178, American Psychiatric Press, Washington, DC.
29. Commission on the Review of the National Policy Toward Gambling (1976) *Gambling in America*, Government Printing Office, Washington, DC.
30. Ladouceur R., Mireault C. (1988) Gambling behaviour among high school students in the Quebec area. *J. Gambling Behaviour*, **4**: 3.
31. DeCaria C., Hollander E., Nora R., Stein D., Simeon D., Cohen L. (1997) Gambling: biological/genetic, treatment, government, and gambling concerns: neurobiology of pathological gambling. Presented at the APA Meeting, San Diego, May 17–22.
32. Carlton O.L., Goldstein L. (1987) Physiological determinants of pathological gambling. In *Handbook of Pathological Gambling* (Ed. T. Galski), pp. 657–663, Thomas, Springfield.
33. Comings D.E. (1998) The molecular genetics of pathological gambling. *CNS Spectrums*, **3**: 20–37.

34. Di Chiara G., Imperato A. (1988) Drugs abused by humans preferentially increase synaptic dopamine concentrations in the mesolimbic system of freely moving rats. *Proc. Natl. Acad. Sci. USA*, **85**: 5274–5278.
35. Wise R.A., Rompre P.P. (1989) Brain dopamine and reward. *Ann. Rev. Psychol.*, **40**: 191–225.
36. Blum K., Cull J.G., Braverman E.R., Comings D.E. (1996) Reward deficiency syndrome. *Am. Sci.*, **84**: 132–145.
37. Banki C.M., Arato M., Papp Z., Kurz M. (1984) Biochemical markers in suicidal patients. Investigations with cerebrospinal fluid amine metabolites and neuroendocrine tests. *J. Affect. Disord.*, **6**: 341–350.
38. Brown G., Ebert M., Goyer P., Jimerson D., Klein W., Bunney W., Goodwin F. (1982) Aggression, suicide, and serotonin: relationships to CSF amine metabolites. *Am. J. Psychiatry*, **139**: 741–746.
39. Comings D.E., Gade R., Muhleman D., Chiu C., Wu S., To M., Spence M., Dietz G., Winn-Deen E., Rosenthal R.J., *et al* (1996) Exon and intron mutations in the human tryptophan 2,3-dioxygenase gene and their potential association with Tourette's syndrome, substance abuse and other psychiatric disorders. *Pharmacogenetics*, **6**: 307–318.
40. DeCaria C.M., Begaz T., Hollander E. (1998) Serotonergic and noradrenergic function in pathological gambling. *CNS Spectrums*, **3**: 38–47.
41. Roy A., Custer R., Lorenz V., Linnoila M. (1988) Depressed pathological gamblers. *Acta Psychiatr. Scand.*, **77**: 163–165.
42. Perris C., Jacobsson L., von Knorring L., Oreland L., Perris H., Ross S. (1980) Enzymes related to biogenic amine metabolism and personality characteristics in depressed patients. *Acta Psychiatr. Scand.*, **61**: 477–484.
43. Murphy K., Belmaker R., Buchsbaum M. (1977) Biogenic amine related enzymes and personality variations in normals. *Psychol. Med.*, **7**: 149–157.
44. von Knorring L., Oreland L., Winblad B. (1984) Personality traits related to monoamine oxidase activity in platelets. *Psychiatry Res.*, **12**: 11–26.
45. Ward P., Catts S., Norman T., Burrows G., McConaghy N. (1987) Low platelet monoamine oxidase and sensation seeking in males: an established relationship? *Acta Psychiatr. Scand.*, **75**: 86–90.
46. Buschsbaum M., Haier R., Murphy D. (1977) Suicide attempts, platelet monoamine oxidase and the average evoked response. *Acta Psychiatr. Scand.*, **56**: 69–79.
47. Gottfries C., von Knorring L., Oreland L. (1980) Platelet monoamine oxidase activity in mental disorders: 2. Affective psychoses and suicidal behavior. *Progr. Neuropsychopharmacol.*, **4**: 185–192.
48. Blanco C., Orensanz-Munoz L., Blanco-Jerez C., Saiz-Ruiz J. (1996) Pathological gambling and platelet MAO activity: a psychobiological study. *Am. J. Psychiatry*, **153**: 119–121.
49. Moss H.B., Yao J.K., Panzak G.L. (1990) Serotonergic responsivity and behavioral dimensions in antisocial personality disorder with substance abuse. *Biol. Psychiatry*, **28**: 325–338.
50. Stein D.J., Hollander E., DeCaria C., Cohen L., Simeon D. (1997) Behavioral response to m-chlorophenyl-piperazine and clonidine in trichotillomania. *J. Serotonin Res.*, **4**: 11–15.
51. Benkelfat C., Murphy D.L., Hill, J.L., George T., Nutt D., Linnoila M. (1991) Ethanol-like properties of the serotonergic partial agonist m-chlorophenylpiperazine in chronic alcoholic patients. *Arch. Gen. Psychiatry*, **48**: 383.
52. Brown R.I.F. (1987) Dropouts and continuers in Gamblers Anonymous: 4. Evaluation and summary. *J. Gambling Behav.*, **3**: 202–210.

53. Stewart R.M., Brown R.I.F. (1988) An outcome study of Gamblers Anonymous. *Br. J. Psychiatry*, **152**: 284–288.
54. Russo A.M., Taber J.I., McCormick R.A., Ramirez L.F. (1984) An outcome study of an inpatient treatment program for pathological gamblers. *Hosp. Comm. Psychiatry*, **35**: 823–827.
55. Goodman W.K., Price L.H., Rasmussen S.A., Mazure C., Fleischmann R., Hill C., Heninger G., Charney D. (1989) The Yale-Brown Obsessive Compulsive Scale. I. Development, use and reliability. *Arch. Gen. Psychiatry*, **46**: 1006–1011.
56. Goodman W., Price L., Rasmussen S.A., Mazure C., Delgado P., Heninger G., Charney D. (1989) The Yale–Brown Obsessive Compulsive Scale: II. Validity. *Arch. Gen. Psychiatry*, **49**: 1012–1016.
57. DeCaria C.M., Hollander E., Begaz T., Schmeidler J., Wong C., Cartwright C., Mosovich S. (1998) Reliability and validity of a pathological gambling modification of the Yale–Brown Obsessive Compulsive Scale (PG–YBOCS): preliminary findings. Presented at the Third International Obsessive-Compulsive Disorder Conference, Madeira, Portugal, September 11–13.
58. Hollander E., DeCaria C., Mari E., Wong C., Mosovich S., Grossman R., Begaz T. (1998) Short-term single-blind fluvoxamine treatment of pathological gambling. *Am. J. Psychiatry*, **155**: 1781–1783.
59. Kafka M.P. (1991) Successful antidepressant treatment of nonparaphilic sexual addictions and paraphilias in men. *J. Clin. Psychiatry*, **52**: 60–65.
60. Kafka M.P. (1994) Sertraline pharmacotherapy for paraphilias and paraphilia related disorders: an open trial. *Ann. Clin. Psychiatry*, **6**: 109–125.
61. Bradford J., Greenberg D., Gojer J., Martindale J., Goldberg M. (1995) Sertraline in the treatment of pedophilia: an open label study. Presented at the APA Meeting, Miami, May 20–25.
62. Ford C.V. (1995) Dimensions of somatization and hypochondriasis. *Neurol. Clin.*, **13**: 241–253.
63. Hollander E., Cohen L.J., Simeon D. (1993) Body dysmorphic disorder. *Psychiatr. Ann.*, **23**: 359–364.
64. Phillips K.A., McElroy S.L., Hudson J.I., Pope H.G. (1995) Body dysmorphic disorder: an obsessive-compulsive spectrum disorder, a form of affective spectrum disorder, or both? *J. Clin. Psychiatry*, **6** (suppl. 4): 41–51.
65. Karno M., Golding J.M., Sorenson S.B., Burnam M.A. (1988) The epidemiology of obsessive-compulsive disorder in five US communities. *Arch. Gen. Psychiatry*, **45**: 1004–1099.
66. Foa E.B., Kozak M.J., Goodman W.K., Hollander E., Jenike M.A., Rasmussen S.A. (1995) DSM-IV field trial: obsessive-compulsive disorder. *Am. J. Psychiatry*, **152**: 90–96.
67. Phillips K.A., McElroy S.L., Keck P.E., Jr. Hudson J.I., Pope H.G. (1994) A comparison of delusional and nondelusional body dysmorphic disorder in 100 cases. *Psychopharmacol. Bull.* **30**: 179–186.
68. Fukuda O. (1977) Statistical analysis of dysmorphophobia in out-patient clinic. *Jpn. J. Plastic Reconstr. Surg.*, **29**: 569–577.
69. McElroy S.L., Phillips K.A., Keck P.E., Hudson J.I., Pope H.G. (1993) Body dysmorphic disorder: does it have a psychotic subtype? *J. Clin. Psychiatry*, **54**: 389–395.
70. Hollander E., Wong C.M. (1995) Developments in the treatment of obsessive-compulsive disorder. *Primary Psychiatry*, **2**: 28–33.
71. Hollander E., Cohen L.J., Simeon D., Rosen J. (1994) Fluvoxamine treatment of body dysmorphic disorder. *J. Clin. Psychopharmacol.*, **14**: 75–77.

72. Hollander E., Allen A., Kwon J., Aronowitz B., Schmeidler J., Wong C., Simeon D. (1999) Clomipramine vs. desipramine crossover trial in body dysmorphic disorder: selective efficacy of a serotonin reuptake inhibitor in imagined ugliness. *Arch. Gen. Psychiatry*, **56**: 1033–1039.
73. Philippopoulos G. (1979) The analysis of a case of dysmorphophobia. *Can. J. Psychiatry*, **24**: 397–401.
74. Vitiello B., de Leon J. (1990) Dysmorphophobia misdiagnosed as obsessive-compulsive disorder. *Psychosomatics*, **31**: 220–222.
75. Marks I., Mishan J. (1988) Dysmorphophobic avoidance with disturbed bodily perception: a pilot study of exposure therapy. *Br. J. Psychiatry*, **152**: 674–678.
76. Neziroglu F., Yaryura-Tobias A.J. (1993) Exposure, response prevention, and cognitive therapy in the treatment of body dysmorphic disorder. *Behav. Ther.*, **24**: 431–438.
77. McDougle C.J., Kresch L.E., Goodman W.K., Naylor S.T., Volkmar F.R., Cohen D.J., Price L.H. (1995) A case-controlled study of repetitive thoughts and behaviors in adults with autistic disorder and obsessive-compulsive disorder. *Am. J. Psychiatry*, **152**: 772–777.
78. Holzer J.C., Goodman W.K., McDougle C.J., Baer L., Boyarsky B.K., Leckman J.F., Price L.H. (1994) Obsessive-compulsive disorder with and without chronic tic disorder: a compilation of symptoms in 70 patients. *Br. J. Psychiatry*, **164**: 469–473.
79. Miguel E.C., Coffey B.I., Baer L., Savage C.R., Rauch S.L., Jenike M.A. (1995) Phenomenology of intentional repetitive behaviors in obsessive-compulsive disorder and Tourette's disorder. *J. Clin. Psychiatry*, **56**: 246–255.
80. Hollander E., Cartwright C., Wong C., DeCaria C., DelGiudice-Asch G., Monte B., Aronowitz B. (1998) A dimensional approach to the autism spectrum. *CNS Spectrums*, **3**: 22–39.
81. Schain R.J., Freedman D.X. (1961) Studies on 5-hydroxyindoleamine metabolism in autistic and other mentally retarded children. *J. Pediatrics*, **58**: 315–320.
82. Ciaranello R.D., Vanderberg S.R., Anders T.F. (1982) Intrinsic and extrinsic determinants of neuronal development: relevance to infantile autism. *J. Autism Dev. Disord.*, **12**: 115–145.
83. Campbell M., Plij M. (1985) Behavioral and cognitive measures used in psychopharmacological studies of infantile autism. *Psychopharmacol. Bull.*, **21**: 1047–1053.
84. Ritvo E.R., Yuwiler A., Geller E., Ornitz E.M., Saeger K., Plotkin S. (1970) Increased blood serotonin and platelets in early infantile autism. *Arch. Gen. Psychiatry*, **23**: 566–572.
85. Kuperman S., Beeghly J.H., Burns T.L., Tsai L.Y. (1985) Serotonin relationships of autistic probands and their first-degree relatives. *J. Am. Acad. Child Adolesc. Psychiatry*, **24**: 186–190.
86. Piven J., Tsai G., Nehme E., Coyle J.T. (1991) Platelet serotonin: a possible marker for familial autism. *J. Autism Dev. Disord.*, **21**: 51–59.
87. McDougle C., Naylor S.T., Goodman W.K., Volkmar F.R., Cohen D.J., Price L.H. (1993) Acute tryptophan depletion in autistic disorder: a controlled case study. *Biol. Psychiatry*, **33**: 547–550.
88. McBride P.A., Anderson G.M., Hertzig M.E., Sweeney J.A., Kream J., Cohen D.J., Mann J.J. (1989) Serotonergic response in male young adults with autistic disorder. *Arch. Gen. Psychiatry*, **46**: 213–221.

89. Hollander E., Novotny S., Allen A., Aronowitz B., Cartwright C., DeCaria C. (1999) The relationship between repetitive behaviors and growth hormone response to sumatriptan challenge in adult autistic disorder. *Neuropsychopharmacology*, in press.
90. Todd R.D., Ciaranello R.D. (1985) Demonstration of inter- and intraspecies differences in serotonin binding sites by antibodies from an autistic child. *Proc. Natl. Acad. Sci. USA*, **82**: 612–616.
91. Hollander E., DelGiudice-Asch G., Simon L., Schmeidler J., Cartwright C., DeCaria C.M., Kwon J., Cunningham-Rundles C., Chapman F., Zabriskie J. (1999) B lymphocyte antigen D8/17 and repetitive behaviors in autism. *Am. J. Psychiatry*, **156**: 317–320.
92. Aman M., Van Bourgondien M.E., Wolford P., Sarphare G. (1995) Psychotropic and anticonvulsant drugs in subjects with autism: prevalence and patterns of use. *J. Am. Acad. Child Adolesc. Psychiatry*, **34**: 1672–1680.
93. Gordon C.T., State R.C., Nelson J.E., Hamburger S.D., Rapoport J.L. (1993) A double-blind comparison of clomipramine, desipramine, and placebo in the treatment of autistic disorder. *Arch. Gen. Psychiatry*, **50**: 441–447.
94. Cook E., Rowlett R., Jaselskis C., Leventhal B. (1992) Fluoxetine treatment of patients with autism and mental retardation. *J. Am. Acad. Child Adolesc. Psychiatry*, **31**: 739–745.

Commentaries

5.1
The Obsessive-Compulsive Spectrum: Promises and Pitfalls

Katharine A. Phillips[1]

The obsessive-compulsive spectrum hypothesis offers both promises and pitfalls. The promises are many. For one, this hypothesis has heuristic and practical clinical utility, as well as some face validity. Some of the putative spectrum disorders, such as body dysmorphic disorder (BDD) and hypochondriasis, are strikingly similar to obsessive-compulsive disorder (OCD) in terms of their prominent obsessions and compulsions. Perhaps these disorders should be classified together in ICD and DSM, as the spectrum model would imply, rather than scattered around the nomenclature. Regarding potential clinical utility, if further studies confirm that spectrum disorders tend to cluster together in patients and their families, this would have implications for patient assessment. The suggestion that serotonin reuptake inhibitors (SRIs) are preferentially effective for these disorders also has implications for patient care, and would support allocation of funds to study the efficacy of SRIs in these disorders. The model also has implications for neurobiological research. For example, candidate gene studies of spectrum disorders might fruitfully focus on serotonin system genes, such as the serotonin transporter gene.

But the obsessive-compulsive spectrum hypothesis also has some potential pitfalls. First, the hypothesis, as articulated by Hollander and Rosen, may be overly broad in terms of the disorders included. Clinicians, for example, are likely to be struck more by the differences than the similarities between a typical patient with OCD vs. one with depersonalization disorder or with borderline or antisocial personality disorder. Indeed, as the authors note, the disorders at the compulsive and impulsive ends of their spectrum have a number of differences. Furthermore, the relationship among the spectrum disorders will likely prove far more complex than is represented by the current unidimensional model, with its single continuum from compulsivity to impulsivity. A related problem is that OCD itself (as well as the spectrum disorders) is probably heterogeneous, comprising a number of entities with at least somewhat distinct etiologies. PANDAS (pediatric

[1] *Butler Hospital, 345 Blackstone Blvd., Providence, RI 02906, USA*

autoimmune neuropsychiatric disorders associated with streptococcal infections), for example, may represent a distinct OCD subtype. Some spectrum disorders may prove more similar to some types of OCD, and others to other types. For example, are Tourette's syndrome and trichotillomania more similar to a putative "incompleteness" subtype of OCD, and BDD and hypochondriasis more similar to a putative "harm avoidance" OCD subtype? This problem does not invalidate the spectrum hypothesis but does complicate it.

An additional problem is that the OCD spectrum concept lacks precision and is poorly operationalized. Although the definition provided by Hollander and Rosen is a useful starting point, it lacks criteria for spectrum membership. To be included in the spectrum, how similar must a disorder be to OCD in each domain, and in how many domains must similarities exist? Another limitation is the paucity of research on many of the spectrum disorders, making it difficult to evaluate the model's validity. Family studies, follow-up studies and treatment studies are limited. Relatively few placebo-controlled treatment studies of spectrum disorders have been published, and there is a paucity of studies comparing SRIs with other medications. In addition, many spectrum disorders (other than Tourette's syndrome) have received little neurobiological investigation, the approach with the greatest potential for solving the spectrum mystery.

BDD (dysmorphophobia) is one of the putative spectrum disorders that may be most closely related to OCD; as such, it provides a window on the spectrum model. BDD is a distressing and impairing disorder that usually begins during early adolescence and is associated with high rates of hospitalization and suicide attempts. It appears relatively common, although is usually unrecognized, in psychiatric, surgical and dermatological populations. The only published epidemiologic study, while relatively small, reported a 1-year prevalence of 0.7%. Although BDD's boundary with OCD has received considerable attention, BDD also shares features with social phobia and depression. Its relationship to gender identity disorder and eating disorders (and the question of whether weight concerns should be included under the BDD rubric) are unclear and of interest [1].

Similarities between BDD and OCD—most notably, the prominent obsessions and compulsions that characterize both disorders—have been noted for more than a century. One study found no significant differences between the disorders in terms of sex ratio, employment status, most course variables, illness severity and most comorbid disorders [2]. Two neuropsychological studies found that BDD patients had executive dysfunction similar to that reported for OCD [3]. BDD's treatment response also appears similar to that of OCD; however, treatment data for BDD are still preliminary, with no placebo-controlled studies yet published.

But BDD and OCD also appear to have some differences. In the previously mentioned BDD – OCD comparison study, BDD patients were less likely to be married and more likely to have had suicidal ideation and attempted suicide as a result of their disorder. BDD subjects also had earlier onset of major depression and higher lifetime rates of major depression and social phobia. Their first-degree relatives had a higher rate of substance use disorders. In another study, BDD subjects had poorer insight and more ideas and delusions of reference than OCD subjects [4]. One way to conceptualize these findings is that BDD is a more depressed, socially phobic and psychotic "relative" of OCD. Clinical observations suggest that BDD's core features include profound shame, embarrassment, low self-esteem and rejection sensitivity—features that seem less characteristic of OCD. Unlike OCD, BDD compulsions (such as mirror checking) seem to often increase rather than decrease anxiety. In addition, preliminary data suggest that quality of life may be poorer in BDD than in OCD (although the disorders have not been directly compared).

Until BDD's and OCD's etiology and pathophysiology are elucidated, the exact nature of their relationship will remain unknown. This is of course true for all of the spectrum disorders. It is likely that some of these disorders' etiological and pathophysiological factors will be shown to overlap, whereas others will prove to be distinct. More research on the spectrum hypothesis is clearly needed and will tell us whether this hypothesis is correct.

REFERENCES

1. Phillips K.A. (1996) *The Broken Mirror: Understanding and Treating Body Dysmorphic Disorder*, Oxford University Press, New York.
2. Phillips K.A., Gunderson C.G., Mallya G., McElroy S.L., Carter W. (1998) A comparison study of body dysmorphic disorder and obsessive compulsive disorder. *J. Clin. Psychiatry*, **59**: 568–575.
3. Hanes K.R. (1998) Neuropsychological performance in body dysmorphic disorder. *J. Int. Neuropsychol. Soc.*, **4**: 167–171.
4. Phillips K.A., McElroy S.L., Keck P.E., Jr, Pope H.G., Jr, Hudson J.I. (1993) Body dysmorphic disorder: 30 cases of imagined ugliness. *Am. J. Psychiatry*, **150**: 302–308.

5.2
Understanding the Obsessive-Compulsive Spectrum: A Four-factor Model of Obsessive-Compulsive Symptoms

David Watson and Kevin Wu[1]

Hollander and Rosen have performed a valuable service by emphasizing the links between obsessive-compulsive disorder (OCD) and a broad array of "obsessive-compulsive spectrum disorders". They classify these spectrum disorders into three broad symptom clusters: (a) disorders of impulse control (e.g. kleptomania, pathological gambling, sexual addictions); (b) syndromes characterized by an exaggerated preoccupation with body appearance or bodily sensations (e.g. body dysmorphic disorder, hypochondriasis); and (c) neurological disorders with repetitive behaviours (e.g. autism, Tourette's syndrome).

It is noteworthy, however, that although Hollander and Rosen fully recognize the heterogeneity of these spectrum disorders, they do not emphasize the symptomatic heterogeneity within OCD itself. Structural analyses clearly establish that OCD is phenotypically heterogeneous; moreover, the data offer little support for the traditional distinction between obsessions and compulsions. Instead, recent analyses have documented the existence of at least four replicable symptom subdimensions within OCD, each of which is characterized by prominent obsessions and compulsions.

Leckman *et al* [1] first identified these symptom dimensions in exploratory factor analyses of two samples of OCD patients. Their analyses revealed four replicable factors: (a) obsessions (including thoughts involving aggressive, sexual, religious and somatic themes) and checking; (b) symmetry and ordering; (c) cleanliness and washing; and (d) hoarding. Summerfeldt *et al* [2] subsequently reported that this four-factor model fitted the data well in a confirmatory factor analysis involving more than 200 OCD patients. We also have replicated this structure in a large non-clinical sample, and have created brief, reliable scales to assess each dimension.

Analyses of these symptom dimensions can clarify how OCD relates to other disorders. For instance, Baer [3] found that only symmetry and hoarding symptoms were significantly associated with a lifetime history of Tourette's syndrome. Similarly, Eapen *et al* [4] reported that sexual/aggressive obsessions and symmetry/touching compulsions were much more common in Tourette's patients than were cleaning/contamination symptoms. Thus, disorders such as Tourette's syndrome are consistently related to certain types of OCD symptoms (e.g. symmetry/ordering) but not others (e.g. cleaning/washing).

---

[1] *Department of Psychology, University of Iowa, E11 Seashore Hall, Iowa City, IA 52242–1407, USA*

Conversely, disorders of impulse control are most strongly and consistently associated with the obsessions/checking factor and are more weakly related to other OCD symptoms. Indeed, symptoms reflecting poor impulse control (e.g. "fear will steal things", "fear will act on unwanted impulses") loaded significantly on the obsessions/checking factor in the studies by both Leckman *et al* [1] and Summerfeldt *et al* [2]. We have corroborated these results in analyses of two large non-clinical samples, finding that impulse control problems are moderately correlated with symptoms of obsessions and checking, but are essentially unrelated to cleaning, ordering and hoarding.

Finally, syndromes characterized by somatic preoccupation can be linked to both the obsessions/checking and cleaning/washing dimensions. More specifically, syndromes characterized by a preoccupation with physical health (e.g. hypochondriasis) are related to both of these factors. For example, the factor analytic data indicate that symptoms such as "concern with illness and disease" load significantly on the obsession/checking factor, whereas "concerned will get ill because of contaminant" loads on the washing/cleaning dimension [1, 2]. Our own analyses indicate that the washing/cleaning factor is particularly strongly related to the "illness phobia" (i.e. the excessive fear that one might develop a disease) that characterizes many hypochondriacs. In contrast, syndromes involving a preoccupation with bodily appearance (e.g. body dysmorphic disorder, eating disorders) are primarily related to the obsessions/checking factor; for instance, Leckman *et al* [1] and Summerfeldt *et al* [2] both found that an "excessive concern with body part or appearance" loaded significantly on this dimension.

Our analyses also have revealed a fourth type of syndrome that deserves to be added to the taxonomy of OCD spectrum disorders, namely, disorders characterized by disruptions in consciousness, memory and identity (i.e. dissociative disorders). Hollander and Rosen list one of the dissociative disorders—depersonalization disorder—within the somatic preoccupation group, but we believe it is more helpful to treat them as a separate class. Our analyses of non-clinical samples reveal that obsessions (particularly obsessions of doubt) and checking are strongly related to both normal and pathological forms of dissociation (for a discussion of this distinction, see Waller and Ross [5]). In contrast, both forms of dissociation are essentially unrelated to ordering, cleaning and hoarding. On the basis of these data, we suspect that prominent symptoms of both dissociation (e.g. forgetfulness and obliviousness) and OCD (e.g. checking, doubting) may reflect fundamental problems in the regulation of attention.

In conclusion, we agree that OCD can be linked to a broad array of related spectrum conditions. We further agree that these spectrum disorders are phenotypically heterogeneous and can be classified into several broad symptom groups. We encourage researchers to take this approach one step further, however, and to recognize that OCD is itself heterogeneous. Analyses of these replicated symptom dimensions can play an important role in clarifying the nature of the OCD spectrum.

REFERENCES

1. Leckman J.F., Grice D.E., Boardman J., Zhang H., Vitale A., Bondi C., Alsobrook J., Peterson B.S., Cohen D.J., Rasmussen S.A. *et al* (1997) Symptoms of obsessive-compulsive disorder. *Am. J. Psychiatry*, **154**: 911–917.
2. Summerfeldt L.J., Richter M.A., Antony M.M., Swinson R.P. (1999) Symptom structure in obsessive-compulsive disorder: a confirmatory factor-analytic study. *Behav. Res. Ther.*, **37**: 297–311.
3. Baer L. (1994) Factor analysis of symptom subtypes of obsessive compulsive disorder and their relation to personality and tic disorders. *J. Clin. Psychiatry*, **55**: (suppl. 3): 18–23.
4. Eapen V., Robertson M.M., Alsobrook J.P., Pauls D.L. (1997) Obsessive compulsive symptoms in Gilles de le Tourette syndrome and obsessive compulsive disorder: differences by diagnosis and family history. *Am. J. Med. Genet.*, **74**: 432–438.
5. Waller N.G., Ross C.A. (1997) The prevalence and biometric structure of pathological dissociation in the general population: taxometric and behavior genetic findings. *J. Abnorm. Psychol.*, **106**: 499–510.

5.3
Extremes of Impulse Control and Serotonin/Frontal Lobe Pathophysiology

Walter Kaye[1]

Hollander and Rosen's thoughtful review on obsessive-compulsive spectrum disorders (OCSD) links a wide spectrum of behavioural phenomena characterized by substantial impulsivity on one extreme and compulsivity on the other.

Psychiatry attempts, to categorize behavioural disturbances by describing symptoms. In this respect, it may be at a stage that medicine was at in the past, i.e. attempting to distinguish phenomena by clusters of symptoms, as, for example, attempting to identify the type of lung infections by the colour of the sputum (yellow, red, white, etc). As knowledge advanced, it became clear that such symptoms were, in part, related to the underlying

[1] *Department of Psychiatry, University of Pittsburgh Medical Center, 3811 O'Hara Street, Pittsburgh, PA 15213, USA*

pathophysiology and, in part, a non-specific and often state-related response to infection. Unfortunately, the inaccessibility of the brain has made it difficult to associate symptoms with physiological processes. Thus, we still have limited understanding of what symptoms may reflect traits that confer susceptibility. It is also possible that behavioural symptoms are secondary phenomena: for example, humans may have a fairly limited repertoire of behaviours which they use to cope with negative mood states, so that some symptoms may reflect common compensatory pathways.

In their review, Hollander and Rosen have moved beyond merely categorizing symptoms. Rather, they ask the question whether a spectrum of disorders, characterized by extremes of behavioural self-control, are due to alterations of a brain system, perhaps involving serotonin (5-HT) neuronal pathways and the frontal lobes. It may be that different loci of pathology create different impairments in the function of this neuronal network, resulting in poor modulation of impulse control.

There is other evidence that impulsive and compulsive behaviours may be part of a spectrum [1] and that both correlate with prefrontal cortical and/or 5-HT dysfunction. Considerable evidence [2–4] suggests that pathology in the prefrontal cortex, which is directly involved in planning, problem solving and determination of social behaviour, contributes to behavioural under- and over-control. Position emission tomography (PET) studies, using 2-[^{18}F]fluoro-2-deoxy-D-glucose, have found *reduced* prefrontal, and particularly orbital–frontal and adjacent medial–frontal metabolic activity in patients with personality disorders characterized by impulsive aggression [5, 6]. In contrast, a considerable number of imaging studies [7] have shown that people with OCD have orbital/prefrontal cortex abnormalities, with most studies showing *increased* activity on PET or single photon computed tomography (SPECT) imaging.

Similarly, serotonergic function has been implicated in behavioural under- and over-control. In human and non-human primates, many studies [8] have found that indices of reduced 5-HT activity, such as reduced levels of cerebrospinal fluid (CSF) 5-hydroxyindoleacetic acid (5-HIAA), are associated with impulsive, suicidal and aggressive behaviours, whereas increased CSF 5-HIAA may correlate with behavioural inhibition in non-human primates [9]. Recent studies support the speculation that altered 5-HT prefrontal cortical modulation contributes to behavioural extremes of self-control. Siever [10] found evidence of reduced 5-HT modulation of orbital-frontal, ventral medial–frontal and cingulate cortex in people with impulsive, aggressive behaviours.

One other disorder that may fit into OCSD is bulimia nervosa (BN). In this disorder, a number of behaviours, such as feeding and impulse control, are poorly modulated. People with BN have a relentless drive to restrain their food intake and rarely have normal meal patterns. Loss of control with overeating usually occurs intermittently and typically only some time after the onset of dieting behaviour [11]. People with bulimia nervosa tend to have extremes of self-control, so that impulsive and obsessive behaviours [12–14] are common. Finally, recent studies support the possibility that people with BN have persistent disturbances of brain 5-HT activity [15, 16] and orbital frontal lobe activity [17] even after recovery. These clinical observations raise the question of whether extremes of under- and over-control behaviours in women with BN are related to alterations of 5-HT neuronal activity localized to the orbital frontal cortex.

In summary, extremes of impulse control, dysphoric mood, and disordered eating are often comorbid occurrences and frequently benefit from selective serotonin reuptake inhibitors (SSRIs). While it is well accepted that a 5-HT disturbance may contribute to these disorders, the neuronal pathways and mechanisms are poorly understood. Further studies will be needed to define similarities and differences between people with conditions within the OCSD. This spectrum of symptoms may be a consequence of a shared neuronal pathway, but have different pathophysiologic loci. Past studies, which relied upon indirect physiologic measures and pharmacologic response, provided limited insights into neuronal pathway dynamics in humans. Fortunately, we are entering an era in which increasingly powerful tools are available to study the pathophysiology of humans *in vivo*.

REFERENCES

1. Stein D.J., Trestman R.L., Mitropoulou V., Coccaro E.F., Hollander E., Siever L.J. (1996) Impulsivity and serotonergic function in compulsive personality disorder. *J. Neuropsychiat. Clin. Neurosci.*, **8**: 393–398.
2. Damasio A.R., Tranel D., Damasio H. (1990) Individuals with sociopathic behavior caused by frontal damage fail to respond autonomically to social stimuli. *Behav. Brain Res.*, **41**: 81–94.
3. Fuster J.M. (1989), *The Prefrontal Cortex: Anatomy, Physiology and Neuropsychology of the Frontal Lobe*, 2nd edn, Raven Press, New York.
4. Masterman D.L., Cummings J.L. (1997) Frontal-subcortical circuits: the anatomic basis of executive, social and motivated behaviors. *J. Psychopharmacol.*, **11**: 107–114.
5. Raine A., Phil D., Stoddard J., Bihrle S., Buchsbaum M. (1998) Prefrontal glucose deficits in murderers lacking psychosocial deprivation. *Neuropsychiat. Neuropsychol. Behav. Neurol.*, **11**: 1–7.
6. Goyer P.F., Andreason P.J., Semple W.E., Clatyon A.H., King A.C., Compton-Toth B.A., Schulz S.C., Cohen R.M. (1994) Positron-emission tomography and personality disorders. *Neuropsychopharmacology*, **10**: 21–28.
7. Saxena S., Brody A.L., Schwartz J.M., Baxter L.R. (1998) Neuroimaging and frontal-subcortical circuitry in obsessive-compulsive disorder. *Br. J. Psychiatry*, **173** (suppl. 35): 26–37.

8. Higley J.D., Linnoila M. (1997) Low central nervous system serotonergic activity is traitlike and correlates with impulsive behavior: a nonhuman primate model investigating genetic and environmental influences on neurotransmission. *Ann. N.Y. Acad. Sci.*, **836**: 39–56.
9. Fairbanks L.A., McGuire M.T., Melega W.P. (1999) Social impulsivity and serotonin function in vervet monkeys. Presented at the ACNP Annual Meeting, Acapulco, December 12–16.
10. Siever L.J., Buchsbaum M.S., New A.S., Spiegel-Cohen J., Wei T., Hazlett E.A., Sevin E., Nunn M., Mitropoulou V. (1999) d,l-fenfluramine response in impulsive personality disorder assessed with [^{18}F]fluorodeoxyglucose positron emission tomography. *Neuropsychopharmacology*, **20**: 413–423.
11. Weltzin T.E., Hsu L.K., Pollice C., Kaye W.H. (1991) Feeding patterns in bulimia nervosa. *Biol. Psychiatry*, **30**: 1093–1110.
12. Vitousek K. Manke F. (1994) Personality variables and disorders in anorexia nervosa and bulimia nervosa. *J. Abnorm. Psychol.*, **103**: 137–147.
13. Rossiter E.M., Agras W.S., Telch C.F., Schneider J.A. (1993) Cluster B personality disorder characteristics predict outcome in the treatment of bulimia nervosa. *Int. J. Eat. Disord.*, **13**: 349–357.
14. von Ranson K.M., Kaye W.H., Weltzin T.E., Rao R., Matsunaga H. (1999) Obsessive compulsive disorder symptoms before and after recovery from bulimia nervosa. *Am. J. Psychiatry*, **156**: 1703–1708.
15. Kaye W.H., Greeno C.G., Moss H., Fernstrom J., Fernstrom M., Lilenfeld L.R., Weltzin T.E., Mann J.J. (1998) Alterations in serotonin activity and psychiatric symptoms after recovery from bulimia nervosa. *Arch. Gen. Psychiatry*, **55**: 927–935.
16. Smith K.A., Fairburn C.G., Cowen P.J. (1999) Symptomatic relapse in bulimia nervosa following acute tryptophan depletion. *Arch. Gen. Psychiatry*, **56**: 171–176.
17. Kaye W.H., Frank G.K., Meltzer C.C., Price J.C., McConaha C.W., Crossan P.J., Klump K.L., Devlin B. J. Altered serotonin 2a receptor activity after recovery from bulimia nervosa (submitted for publication).

5.4
The Obsessive-Compulsive Spectrum: Fact or Fancy?

Donald W. Black[1]

Hollander and his co-workers have vigorously promoted the concept of a spectrum of disorders related to obsessive-compulsive disorder (OCD) [1]. The spectrum, as they define it, includes a broad array of disorders currently classified in the DSM as impulse control disorders (e.g. trichotillomania, pathological gambling), sexual disorders (e.g. paraphilias), childhood disorders (e.g. Tourette's syndrome), somatoform disorders (e.g. hypochondriasis), dissociative disorders (e.g. depersonalization disorder), personality

[1] *University of Iowa College of Medicine, Psychiatry Research-MEB, Iowa City, IA 52242–1000, USA*

disorders (e.g. borderline personality) and eating disorders. All of the conditions mentioned involve unrestrained, excessive or poorly regulated behaviours that superficially resemble OCD.

The data supporting the obsessive-compulsive spectrum vary considerably. For example, the connection between OCD and tic disorders (especially Tourette's syndrome) has been conclusively demonstrated by Pauls *et al* [2] through careful family studies. Family studies have also demonstrated a clear connection with subsyndromal OCD, although this disorder is rarely mentioned in discussions on the obsessive-compulsive spectrum [2, 3] (subsyndromal OCD is characterized by the presence of obsessions and/or compulsions without evident impairment or distress). A case can probably be made based on clinical, family and treatment data that trichotillomania and body dysmorphic disorder (BDD) are also related to OCD [4, 5]. The evidence supporting the relationship of OCD to the other disorders mentioned above ranges from weak (e.g. pathological gambling) to non-existent (e.g. borderline personality disorder).

One of the innovations introduced by Hollander and co-workers is the emphasis on dimensionality. They view disorders of impulsivity and compulsivity as falling along the three dimensions of certainty–uncertainty, impulsive–compulsive, and motoric–cognitive. BDD, for example, is close to the end of the compulsive spectrum, is somewhat closer to uncertainty than certainty, and is closer to the cognitive end of the spectrum than to the motoric end. These concepts have clinical utility because impulsivity and compulsivity are not either/or phenomena. Many patients have these qualities to differing degrees, and perhaps the idea that they are present along various dimensions is more consonant with clinical reality than is a categorical approach. The tridimensional model has clear heuristic value, and frees us to extend our thinking beyond the artificial divisions created by our current classification schemes.

Of course, Hollander's work raises the issue of whether categorizations in the DSM ought to be based upon descriptive characteristics or perhaps a more fundamental, underlying biological relatedness. The DSM-IV has not been helpful with this dilemma, as some categories contain disorders that have similar symptoms, yet may have different biologic diatheses; other categories clearly seem to be grouped according to their biological relatedness. OCD is itself sufficiently distinctive that experts, including Hollander, have argued that it ought to stand alone, perhaps at the center of a new grouping to recognize what appear to be similar disorders, at least based on descriptive characteristics.

But are these disorders truly related? My own preference is that psychiatric categorization be derived from research showing biological relatedness, and in this regard the jury is still out. Using this standard, the obsessive-compulsive spectrum as described cannot hold up beyond the few disorders cited above. Nonetheless, the concept has considerable value. Looking beyond the strict definition of OCD and drawing comparisons with other disorders has reinvigorated research and has led to new treatment approaches for many patients who have been previously ignored or thought to be treatment-refractory. This, perhaps, is the value of studying these varied conditions, for whether or not an obsessive-compulsive spectrum holds up under scientific scrutiny, we are developing a better understanding of these difficult patients.

REFERENCES

1. Hollander E. (1993) *Obsessive-Compulsive Related Disorders*, American Psychiatric Press, Washington, DC.
2. Pauls D.L., Alsobrook J.P., Goodman W., Rasmussen S., Leckman J.F. (1995) Family study of obsessive-compulsive disorder. *Am. J. Psychiatry*, **142**: 76–84.
3. Black D.W., Noyes R., Goldstein R.B., Blum N. (1992) A family study of obsessive-compulsive disorder. *Arch. Gen. Psychiatry*, **49**: 362–368.
4. Phillips K.A. (1996) *The Broken Mirror: Understanding and Treating Body Dysmorphic Disorder*, Oxford University Press, New York.
5. Schlosser S., Black D.W., Blum N., Goldstein R.B. (1994) The demography, phenomenology, and family history of 22 persons with compulsive hair pulling. *Ann. Clin. Psychiatry*, **6**: 147–152.

5.5
Blurry Spectrum Disorders

Neal R. Swerdlow[1]

Hollander and Rosen put forth a comprehensive and thought-provoking description of the "spectrum" of obsessive-compulsive disorders (OCD). Because the "spectrum" model is a clear departure from existing categorical approaches to the diagnosis of mental disorders, it deserves careful scrutiny. Regarding the "spectrum" of OCD, Hollander and Rosen state, "we have identified other disorders that may share features of OCD". Among these shared features are symptom profile, treatment response, neurobiology, associated features and etiology.

Symptom profile. In a "spectrum" of disorders classified across a common compulsivity/impulsivity (C/I) "dimension" of over- vs. underestimated

[1] *Tourette Syndrome Association, 9525 La Jolla Farms Rd., La Jolla, CA 92037, USA*

harm, some disorders (e.g. depersonalization disorder) seem forced into this dimension, others are notable omissions (e.g. the most dramatic example of impulsivity and underestimated harm must be mania), and some are classified arbitrarily (e.g. anorexics have both overestimated harm—distorted body image—and underestimated harm—lack of insight to starvation). Trichotillomania is listed by Hollander and Rosen on the "compulsive" side of the dimension (see Figure 5.1), but is described in the text ("Symptom clusters") in the impulsive cluster, and later as an "impulse-control" disorder. In truth, all behaviour can be characterized at one or more points on this dimension: the authors acknowledge that both "impulsive and compulsive features may be present at the same time or different times during the same illness". Everyone has his place on this dimension: with universal applicability, it loses clinical utility.

Another argument for a "spectrum" is that symptoms from different disorders form "clusters" of alikeness. But again, the lines are arbitrary. Doesn't attention-deficit/hyperactivity disorder (ADHD) "cluster" with other disorders of impulse control? What of pica? And what makes trichotillomania a disorder of "impulse" rather than "repetitive behaviours"? The symptom of "suicide" is clustered with low monoamine oxidase (MAO) activity and impulsivity. But suicide is the common endpoint for many conditions, for example depression, which is hardly "driven by the desire to obtain pleasure, arousal or gratification" (as Hollander and Rosen define impulsive disorders). In a cluster based on "insight" or a dimensional "ego syntonic/dystonic" continuum, body dysmorphic disorder (BDD) and anorexia might group more with schizophrenia than with OCD.

Treatment responsivity. The notion that the C/I dimension is linked by sensitivity to serotonin reuptake inhibitors (SRIs) is violated in the case of the most impulsive disorder, mania (or hypomania), in which SRIs have devastating consequences. Other "true negatives" include ADHD (stimulants and noradrenergic tricyclics superior to SRIs) and Tourette's syndrome (TS) (SRIs don't reduce tics); "false positives" include depression, panic disorder and premature ejaculation, to name a few (all SRI-sensitive, though hardly C/I disorders). The notion of a treatment-defined spectrum also fails when one considers the utility of exposure and response prevention (ERP) in OCD (it works) vs. paedophilia (it doesn't). Hollander and Rosen acknowledge the differential sensitivity of paraphilias, sexual addictions and obsessions to SRIs, stretching the spectral connections; in truth, SRIs reduce sex drive in the vast majority of patients, regardless of diagnosis. This is not disease-specific pharmacology: increased adult heterosexual preference in paedophilia is precisely what would be predicted on the basis of a left-shift in the "inverted-U" hedonia curve, analogous to a low dose of naloxone in an opiate-tolerant individual.

Neurobiology. Are obsessive-compulsive spectrum disorders (OCSDs) connected across the hypo/hyperfrontal dimension? Virtually all mental illness comes from frontal-connected forebrain circuitry, hardly cause for a "spectrum". And the data? OCD and TS are "compulsive" on the C/I spectrum, but have opposite patterns of forebrain metabolism—hypermetabolic fronto-striatal circuitry in OCD, hypometabolic in TS [1, 2]. Hypofrontality accompanies gambling, schizophrenia, TS and some forms of depression: a spectrum here? Again, we can "hedge" some, claiming that "compulsive disorders and impulsive disorders ... have different dysregulation in the 5-HT pathways". So why a spectrum? With *m*-chlorophenylpiperazine (*m*CPP) responsivity: how can we view the gambler's "high" (like gambling) and the borderline personality disorder (BPD) "high" (like LSD) as evidence for similarity? Tryptophan depletion exacerbates autism and depression (the latter not a C/I disorder), but not OCD [3]. Another paradox: how can tryptophan sensitivity imply OCSD membership, if OCD isn't tryptophan sensitive?

Spectrum "genetics" is perhaps the most concerning "biological" misapplication of this model. Linking these disorders on the guise of a common genetic basis is destructive to patients and science. More than once I have spoken with parents who were certain their child had TS based on bed wetting, fire setting or related behavioural problems. And connecting these disorders (e.g. pathological gambling and ADHD) based on candidate genes contradicts another spectrum "pillar" of SRI responsivity (see above); can we have it both ways?

Associated features. If we link BDD to OCD based on high comorbidity (29%), this means that BDD must have a three-fold closer link to depression (not an OCSD, despite 83% comorbidity). And family history? BDD is again linked more tightly to depression than to OCD. Hollander and Rosen also identify the associated feature of "premonition" to link OCD (obsessions precede compulsions) and TS (sensations precede tics). But aren't all behaviours or cognitions preceded by something? In depression, a sequence might be: negative thoughts–sadness–crying; in PTSD, it might be trigger stimulus–flashback–anxiety; in schizophrenia, it might be hallucination–orienting response. In complex mental processes, events happen in series and in parallel; this is not a feature that distinguishes TS and OCD.

Etiology. Regarding "etiology" Hollander and Rosen offer (for BBD), "head, hands, feet and sexual organs (frequent areas of BDD foci) cover a large area of the somatosensory and motor strips in brain which are involved with self-esteem and social functioning" ... (and for autism), "studies in autism have focused on serotonin, implicated in the regulation of many functions relevant to disorder, such as learning, memory, repetitive behaviours, sensory and motor processes''. Admittedly, our ignorance of etiology is the most valid binding feature of the OCSDs.

We classify mental disorders to facilitate history-taking and hypothesis-testing, improve diagnostic reliability, and predict treatment responsivity, prognosis and, ultimately, pathophysiology and etiology. A careful examination of the five ''shared features'' of the OCSDs reveals that the ''spectrum'' accomplishes none of these goals. The ''spectrum'' model has gained popularity as a unifying approach to complex and often mystifying conditions—a humane alternative to the callous process of categorical diagnostic classification. But the notion of a ''spectrum'' isn't harmless. How can we educate the public that schizophrenia is a brain disorder, when ''experts'' claim that ''road rage'' is part of the mental illness spectrum? Furthermore, by mixing phenocopies, we greatly diminish the likelihood of understanding the genetics of any single disorder. There is a seductive simplicity to unifying explanations for human complexities, that is encouraged by many—including the makers of SRIs—who stand to gain from an abandonment of diagnostic boundaries. As clinicians and scientists, it is our responsibility to look beyond this seductiveness, and to understand human complexities based on systematic and rational thinking.

REFERENCES

1. Eidelberg D., Moeller J.R., Antonini A., Kazumata K., Dhawan V., Budman C., Feigin A. (1997) The metabolic anatomy of Tourette's syndrome. *Neurology*, **48**: 927–934.
2. Baxter L. R., Phelps M.E., Mazziotta J.C., Guze B.H., Schwartz J.M., Selin C.E. (1987) Local cerebral glucose metabolic rates in obsessive-compulsive disorder. *Arch. Gen. Psychiatry*, **44**: 211–218.
3. Barr L.C., Goodman W.K., McDougle C.J., Delgado P.L., Heninger G.R., Charney D.S., Price L.H. (1994) Tryptophan depletion in patients with obsessive-compulsive disorder who respond to serotonin reuptake inhibitors. *Arch. Gen. Psychiatry*, **51**: 309–317.

5.6
Spectrum Disorders: Utilitarian Concepts or Utopian Fantasies?

James W. Jefferson[1]

The concept of spectra of illnesses or treatments has great appeal, because it promises understanding through simplification and a ''one size fits

[1] *Healthcare Technology Systems, 7617 Mineral Point Road, Suite 300, Madison, WI 53717, USA*

all'' approach to therapeutics. Beneath this spectral umbrella, one can hope to be sheltered from the vagaries and uncertainties of categorical classification, diagnostic heterogeneity and pharmacologic unpredictability.

Medical history is replete with the rise and fall of spectrum conceptualizations. In the mid-to-late 1800s, the uric acid diathesis was used as ''an umbrella concept under which to gather a wide range of complaints'', both physical and mental [1]. The full title of the first edition (1892) of Alexander Haig's text, *Uric Acid as a Factor in the Causation of Disease. A Contribution to the Pathology of High Arterial Tension, Headache, Epilepsy, Mental Depression, Gout, Rheumatism, Diabetes, Bright's, and Other Disorders*, illustrates the breadth of this spectrum. The therapeutic glue that held the uric acid diathesis together was lithium—it dissolved uric acid crystals *in vitro* and, therefore, it was assumed to be an effective treatment for all disorders of uric acid metabolism (which, at the time, appeared to be virtually all disorders). As Johnson reported in *The History of Lithium Therapy*, the uric acid diathesis survived well into the twentieth century and then only fell slowly into disrepute [1].

Not too long ago, we entered a similar era that might be referred to, at least in psychiatry, as the serotonin diathesis, in which imbalances of serotonin metabolism are thought to be responsible for a myriad of psychiatric disorders, and potent serotonin reuptake inhibitors (SRIs) are thought to be panaceas for these illnesses. While issues of etiology remain unresolved and the role of serotonin supported primarily by inductive generalizations from therapeutic observations, late twentieth century experimental design has provided considerable support for a spectrum of SRI-responsive disorders.

The obsessive-compulsive spectrum disorders (OCSDs) have been tied to obsessive-compulsive disorder (OCD) by a thread or threads of clinical similarities, therapeutic responsiveness and suggestions of common neurological underpinnings. Of course, it is difficult to adapt the categorical classification system of DSM-IV to the continuum implied by a spectrum. One can see easily that ''concern about harm'' has a dimensionality, but placing impulsiveness and compulsiveness at opposite ends of a spectrum requires that some definitional liberty be taken. It becomes an even more difficult task to superimpose the symptom clusters of DSM-IV disorders along a compulsive–impulsive continuum in a way that suggests that they are all members of a large family with greatly varying degrees of relatedness. Finally, one might wonder whether the term OCSDs is a misnomer (after all, OCD occupies the far right end of the spectrum shown in Figure 5.1 of Hollander and Rosen's review) that might better be replaced by the term ''impulsive-compulsive (or compulsive-impulsive) spectrum disorders''.

That brings us to the central question of whether the OCSD concept would have arisen had it not been for the stimulus supplied by the pharmaceutical industry. In his book *The Antidepressant Era* [2], David Healy points out that depression in the 1950s was a relatively uncommon condition that blossomed into a major mental health hazard in parallel with the discovery, development and marketing of antidepressant drugs. Was depression, in the broad sense we know it today (the mood disorder spectrum), created for pharmaceutical sales purposes or discovered because the availability of effective treatment now justified the search for what was already there but not recognized? Healy put it more succinctly: "Knowledge in psychopharmacology doesn't become knowledge unless it has a certain commercial value" [2]. Personally, I tend to support the "effective treatments led to diagnostic advances" position, although I must acknowledge that the marketing of concepts sometimes outstrips the science to support it.

The emergence of OCD onto center stage after decades of relegation to the "it's so rare who cares" wasteland of psychiatry was initiated, not by industry, but rather by the Epidemiologic Catchment Area (ECA) study finding that it was actually a quite common condition [3]. Industry did follow close behind after calculations of potential sales volumes justified investment in controlled clinical trials, first with clomipramine and eventually with all of the SRIs. The creation and expansion of an obsessive-compulsive spectrum followed close behind. This, in turn, extended the potential uses (and market size) of potent SRIs based on the implied logic of "if OCD responds to SRIs and if OCSDs have similarities to OCD, then OCSDs should respond to SRIs". Despite flaws in this logic, the SRIs have lived up to their spectral promise, especially if certain limits are placed on the boundaries of the OC spectrum. Of course, the broad clinical success of the SRIs suggests a shift from a diagnostic spectrum of disorder (the OCSDs) to a pharmacologic spectrum (the SRI spectrum disorders) that would extend beyond the OC spectrum to include conditions such as depression, panic disorder and premenstrual dysphoric disorder.

Regardless of which spectrum is currently in vogue, it is important that it functions to stimulate scientific thought, advance knowledge, and ultimately extend effective treatment to the greatest number of affected individuals. To become wedded to a spectrum disorder concept without clear recognition of these goals can be only a disservice to the patients we treat. After all, the American view of schizophrenia as a broad spectrum disorder ("even a trace of schizophrenia is schizophrenia" [4]) did little to advance the field of psychiatry. Hollander and Rosen, on the other hand, have approached the OCSD concept with a healthy degree of open-mindedness, recognizing clearly both its certainties and uncertainties.

REFERENCES

1. Johnson F.N. (1984) *The History of Lithium Therapy*, Macmillan, London.
2. Healy D. (1997) *The Antidepressant Era*, Harvard University Press, Cambridge.
3. Robins L.N., Helzer J.E., Weissman M.M., Orvaschel H., Guenberg E., Burke J.D. Jr, Regier D.A. (1984) Lifetime prevalence of specific psychiatric disorders in three sites. *Arch. Gen. Psychiatry*, **43**: 949–958.
4. Lewis N.D.C., Piotrowski Z.A. (1954) Clinical diagnosis of manic-depressive psychosis. In *Depression* (Eds P.H. Hoch, J. Zubin), pp. 25–38, Grune & Stratton, New York.

5.7 Carving Nature at Its Joints: Different Approaches to the Obsessive-Compulsive Spectrum of Disorders

Dan J. Stein[1]

Hollander and colleagues have, over the years, made a seminal contribution by emphasizing a dimensional approach to a range of hypothesized obsessive-compulsive spectrum disorders (OCSDs).

Categorical approaches are, of course, useful for the purposes of reliable clinical diagnosis. However, nosologists have recognized that psychiatric entities are not carved out at the joints by nature, and biological researchers have similarly emphasized the dimensional nature of the neurochemical and neurogenetic underpinnings of these disorders.

Dimensional approaches are, however, not unlikely to be controversial. Perhaps one reason for this is that, in approaching a heterogeneous and complex body of data, several different dimensions can be highlighted, with each emphasis leading to a rather different pattern of focuses. Certainly, a number of different approaches may be taken in exploring the heterogeneity of OCSDs. This commentary deals with some of them.

Neurochemical. Central to the notion of the OCSDs is the finding that not only does OCD respond selectively to serotonin reuptake inhibitors (SRIs), but that clomipramine is more effective than desipramine in a range of other conditions characterized by intrusive repetitive symptoms, including body dysmorphic disorder, trichotillomania, onychophagia, obsessive-compulsive symptoms in autism, and so forth.

There are, however, a number of problems with this paradigm. First, SRIs may be more effective than noradrenergic reuptake inhibitors in a range of

[1] *MRC Research Unit on Anxiety Disorders, Department of Psychiatry, University of Stellenbosch, PO Box 19063, Tygerberg 7505, South Africa*

other disorders, including panic disorder and premenstrual dysphoric disorder. Second, only a subgroup of OCD patients respond to clomipramine. Similarly, only a subgroup of patients with OCD demonstrate exacerbation of symptoms after *m*-chlorophenylpiperazine (*m*CPP) or sumatriptan challenge. Also, OCD patients with comorbid tics are less likely to respond to SRIs, and are more likely to respond to augmentation with a typical neuroleptic.

Interestingly, the combination of a dopamine blocker with a selective serotonin reuptake inhibitor (SSRI) may be useful in Tourette's syndrome, in trichotillomania, and perhaps also in some other putative spectrum disorders [1]. Other biological systems are ultimately also likely to be crucial in understanding the OCSDs. These include immunological mechanisms, hormonal systems, neuropeptides and others. For example, D8/17 is raised in patients with OCD, tics and autism [2], but apparently not in trichotillomania [3].

Ultimately the neurogenetic basis for this heterogeneity will require delineation. This is likely to be complex. For example, an interesting recent finding is of an association between homozygosity for the low activity catechol-*O*-methyltransferase (COMT) allele and OCD in males. However, in a more homogeneous population of OCD patients of Afrikaner background, a rather different pattern of COMT findings was observed [4].

Cognitive. The extent to which putative OCSDs are characterized by a range of different cognitive features has perhaps not been paid sufficient attention. There appear to be both visuomotor integration (e.g. fine motor coordination) and executive function (e.g. set-shifting) abnormalities in OCD. The underlying neuroanatomical and neurochemical substrates of these dysfunctions, and the extent to which similar dysfunctions are present in OCSDs, remain to be fully delineated.

Similarly, brain imaging similarities and differences across the OCSDs require further exploration. For example, there is some suggestion that the volume of the caudate is decreased in OCD, while the putamen is smaller in OCSDs with more motoric symptoms, such as trichotillomania [5], although again this delineation requires further replication [6].

One possibility is that OCD is in fact best conceptualized as an impulse control disorder. However, in OCD there is compensatory suppression of symptoms, whereas in impulse disorders there is not. This may be relevant to aspects of the neurochemical heterogeneity of OCD; for example, in OCD there is both serotonin hypofunction (with blunted prolactin response to *m*CPP), reminiscent of impulsive disorders, and serotonin hyperfunction (with symptom exacerbation after *m*CPP) [7].

Cognitive heterogeneity may be relevant in devising psychotherapeutic interventions for these disorders; exposure therapy may be useful in OCD to decrease intrusions, but in patients with impulsive disorders cognitive restructuring and external limit-setting are more important.

Cultural. A number of authors have explored obsessive-compulsive symptoms across different cultures. Reviews have, however, agreed that in OCD the form of the disorder appears to be universal. For example, although patients from different ethnic groups may have different checking concerns, the nature of the checking is similar.

In the OCSDs, however, cultural variations may play a more significant role. The prevalence of pathological gambling, for example, is directly related to opportunities that populations have for gambling. There seems to be a relationship between certain eating disorders and Western constructs of beauty; similarly, it is not unlikely that complex relationships may exist between body dysmorphic disorder and social constructions of physical attractiveness.

Evolutionary. Given that evolutionary theory lies at the heart of the biological sciences on which medicine and psychiatry is based, it is timely that increased attention is being paid to the relevance of Darwinian constructs for understanding psychiatric disorders. MacLean [8] pointed out that the basal ganglia are repositories for fixed action patterns such as grooming, and several authors have since suggested that dysfunction in such patterns may be relevant to OCD.

This perspective may also be used to explore the heterogeneity of the OCSDs. Hoarding, for example, is also an evolutionarily conserved behaviour that is governed by cortico-striatal circuits. However, dopamine may be more relevant to hoarding than serotonin, so that patients who suffer mainly from this symptom may be relatively refractory to serotonergic interventions.

It is possible that certain fixed action patterns are more relevant to particular species; for example, horses are not unexpectedly more likely to develop locomotory stereotypies than other kinds of stereotypies. In humans, the more abstract stereotypies of rumination, worry and so forth are perhaps the most characteristic, and this may relevant to understanding the broad spectrum of serotonergic medication across not only the OCSDs, but also the mood and anxiety disorders.

Summary. The dimensional constructs proposed by Hollander and colleagues have significant heuristic value for researchers and for clinicians. The heterogeneity and complexity of the OCSDs remains, however, a significant challenge. Indeed, a spectrum of different approaches may itself be useful in approaching these conditions; this will likely include genetic, chemical, imaging, cognitive, sociocultural and evolutionary constructs and methods.

REFERENCES

1. Stein D.J., Bouwer C., Hawkridge S., Emsley R.A. (1997) Risperidone augmentation of serotonin reuptake inhibitors in obsessive-compulsive and related disorders. *J. Clin. Psychiatry*, **58**: 119–122.
2. Hollander E., DelGiudice-Asch G., Simon L., Schmeidler J., Cartwright C., De Caria C.M., Kwon J., Cunningham-Rundles C., Chapman E., Zabriskie J.B. (1999) B lymphoctye antigen D8/17 and repetitive behaviors in autism. *Am. J. Psychiatry*, **156**: 317–320.
3. Niehaus D.J.H., Knowles J.A., van Kradenberg J., du Toit W., Kaminer D., Seedat S., Daniels W., Cotton M., Brink P., Beyers A.D. *et al* (1999) D8/17 in obsessive-compulsive disorder and trichotillomania. *S. Afr. Med. J.*, **89**: 755–756.
4. Niehaus D.J.H., van Kradenberg J., Brink P., Emsley R.A., Knowles J.A., Stein D.J. (1998) Genetics of OCD in the Afrikaner population. Presented at the 3rd International Obsessive-Compulsive Disorder Conference, Madeira, September 11–13.
5. O'Sullivan R.L., Rauch S.L., Breiter H.C., Grachev I.D., Baer L., Kennedy D.N., Keuthen N.J., Savage C.R., Manzo P.A., Caviness V.S. *et al.* (1997) Reduced basal ganglia volumes in trichotillomania measured via morphometric MRI. *Biol. Psychiatry*, **42**: 39–45.
6. Stein D.J., Coetzer R., Lee M., Davids B., Bouwer C. (1997) Magnetic resonance brain imaging in women with obsessive-compulsive disorder and trichotillomania. *Psychiatry Res.*, **74**: 177–182.
7. Stein D.J. (2000) Neurobiology of the obsessive-compulsive spectrum disorders. *Biol. Psychiatry*, in press.
8. MacLean P.D. (1978) Effects of lesions of globus pallidus on species-typical display behavior of squirrel monkeys. *Brain Res.*, **149**: 175–196.

5.8
The Challenge of Deconvolving the Obsessive-Compulsive Disorder Spectrum into Its Component Diseases

Mark George[1]

Hollander and Rosen's thorough and masterful review summarizes the current state of the art of the attractive theory that all (or at least most) neuropsychiatric disorders characterized by obsessive or compulsive behaviour can be understood as a spectrum of disorders—called by the authors the obsessive-compulsive spectrum of disorders (OCSD). According to this reasoning, which is well described in the review, many psychiatric disorders can be conceptualized by obsessions and compulsions (obsessive-compulsive disorder-OCD, body dysmorphic disorder, hypochondriasis,

[1] *Functional Neuroimaging Division, Psychiatry, Medical University of South Carolina, 171 Ashley Avenue, Charleston, SC 29425, USA*

depersonalization disorder and anorexia nervosa) or as problems with impulse control (pathological gambling, paraphilias and sexual addictions). These conditions have some similarities with neuropsychiatric disorders involving repetitive behaviour, such as Tourette's syndrome and autism. The authors skillfully discuss the neurobiology and available treatments of these disorders, and argue that they can be understood on a dimensional scale with an exaggerated sense of harm at the compulsive end and an underestimate of harm at the impulsive end. The review is well written and provides state of the art studies involving neurobiology and comorbidity. Hollander and Rosen's (and others') attempt to understand these disorders along a spectrum of behaviour has been heuristically enormously helpful. The spectrum concept has generated testable hypotheses and has served to counter the limited thinking spawned by the DSM approach to psychiatric diagnoses, where disorders are merely unconnected checklists of symptoms decided upon by committee.

While attractive and compelling, with the dawn of a new century, it is time to critically review the notion of a spectrum of disorders involving compulsive or impulsive behaviour. Unlike the rest of medicine and even some areas of neurology, the main problem with current psychiatric diagnoses is that they lack information about fundamental disease pathophysiology. Currently, with inadequate understanding of fundamental disease pathophysiology, psychiatrists are forced to describe and try to understand diseases from their manifest symptoms. Looking historically at other branches of medicine where we now have better understanding, one can see how limited this type of symptom-based nosology can be. For example, at the beginning of the last century, epilepsy researchers viewed the diseases of epilepsy as a spectrum of behaviour, with some individuals having a single seizure under metabolic or psychological stress, others having intermittent seizures limited to a portion of the body, and still others having whole-body convulsions. Because they shared in common the behaviour of seizing, these conditions were viewed as a spectrum of disorders. They were also grouped together because, by and large, they all responded to treatment with non-specific agents like barbiturates. Today, with advances in brain imaging and full knowledge of the cellular mechanisms behind seizure propagation, we discuss these disorders as "the epilepsies". Each disease has a different cause, pathophysiology and prognosis and responds to different types of anticonvulsants (e.g. focal seizure with secondary generalization due to mesial temporal sclerosis caused by childhood anoxia, or juvenile myoclonic epilepsy). Although they share in common the outward behaviour of a seizure, the brain pathophysiology (genetics, regional anatomy, pharmacology) is markedly different. Thus, with advances in clinical neuroscience, an area that was initially viewed as a "spectrum" is now known to comprise multiple different diseases.

I would argue that with the new century upon us, the OCSD will be similarly deconvolved into its component diseases, much as the epilepsies came to be better understood in the past century. In order for this to occur, there will have to be continued advances in cognitive or affective neuroscience, which is trying to understand the regional brain circuits involved in normal appetitive behaviour, as well as in pathological compulsions and addictions. In addition, we will have to understand better how our brains act to inhibit an action, or how we choose not to act. This functional regional anatomy will have to be integrated with knowledge of pharmacology and neurotransmitters. Finally, the notion of temperament, or of predispositions to act in certain ways, will have to be understood better.

How then will the notion of OCSD be deconvolved? In epilepsy, advances in nosology occurred with the use of the electroencephalogram, direct brain testing during neurosurgery, and pharmacologic knowledge of seizure propagation in animal models. Similarly, the new tools available will help understand the different diseases currently under the OCSD umbrella. Additionally, if one disease within the umbrella can be redefined in terms of pathophysiology, and studied in depth, then the others will follow. For example, if one could understand in its entirety how some individuals, following a streptococcal infection, then develop OCD, with integrated knowledge of host susceptibility (including genetics), neuroanatomy, pharmacology and the change in functioning circuits, then one can begin to deconvolve the entire OCSD group. One can see the early hints of this happening in the studies outlined in Hollander and Rosen's review.

In summary, the notion of an OCSD has been and continues to be an enormously helpful construct for understanding and studying these disorders. However, it is important as we move forward to remember that the OCSD construct is not likely to be the entire or final answer. We should not let its synthetic and organizational charm stand in the way of ultimately understanding these neuropsychiatric diseases in terms of their true discrete pathophysiologies.

5.9
Obsessive-Compulsive Spectrum Disorders: are Opposites Related?

Rocco Crino[1]

Hollander and Rosen argue that certain disorders, characterized by impulsive or compulsive behaviours, are related to obsessive-compulsive disorder

[1] *Clinical Research Unit for Anxiety Disorders, University of New South Wales, 299 Forbes Street, Darlinghurst, New South Wales, 2010, Australia*

(OCD) on the basis of similar phenomenology, clinical features, neurobiology, family history and treatment response. A hypothetical compulsive–impulsive dimension is proposed with an exaggerated sense of harm at one end and an underestimate of harm at the other. The disorders purported to belong to the OCD spectrum are seen to vary along this dimension, with Axis I disorders, such as OCD and body dysmorphic disorder (BDD), at one end, and Axis II disorders, such as antisocial and borderline personality disorder, at the other.

The discussion of spectrum disorders in relation to a single dimension unfortunately implies a relationship which may not be as suggested. The disorders may also vary on the basis of other dimensions, such as whether the essential features are ego-syntonic or ego-dystonic, whether they are unpleasant or gratifying, whether they are resisted or not, whether they are a function of a discrete Axis I syndrome or whether they are the result of maladaptive personality features. As with the compulsive–impulsive dimension, the spectrum disorders would also vary considerably along these other dimensions which, when taken together, would provide important evidence of their essential phenomenological differences rather than similarities. To suggest that disorders are related on the basis of one possible dimensional feature is narrow and denies the many elements that differentiate between these disorders.

Furthermore, many of the phenomenological similarities are based on the behavioural manifestations rather than the cognitive and/or affective components of the disorders. Repetitive behaviours are indeed a function of many of the disorders listed as part of the OCD spectrum. However, there are important differences, in that the repetitive behaviours in OCD are not pleasurable or gratifying, as in impulse control disorders or the paraphilias, are not selectively purposeful, as in dieting disorders, and are not in response to an urge, as in Tourette's syndrome and trichotillomania. With specific reference to the cognitive elements, BDD is proposed to be most like OCD within the spectrum of disorders. However, according to the DSM-IV, in OCD the individual experiences "recurrent and persistent thoughts, impulses, or images... that are intrusive and inappropriate...", while BDD is characterized by "preoccupation with an imagined physical defect in appearance". The ego-dystonic, intrusive unpleasant thought or image in OCD is phenomenologically quite distinct from the ego-syntonic preoccupation with an imagined physical defect experienced in BDD.

To a large extent, ignoring the cognitive mediation of the various disorders is the major failing of the argument in favour of the OCD spectrum. Unless one takes the view that the reasons behind the repetitive behaviours are little more than post-hoc rationalizations, then there are perhaps more differences than similarities between the spectrum disorders. For example, inflated responsibility [1] and thought–action fusion [2] are considered to be cognitive biases specific to OCD and are particularly relevant in compulsive checking and obsessional ruminators, while danger expectancies, rather than responsibility *per se*, has been implicated as a mediating factor in compulsive washing [3]. Treatments aimed at reducing inflated responsibility and reappraising danger expectancies have been shown to be effective (e.g. [4]). Clearly, such cognitive features are specific to OCD and would be irrelevant in the majority of the other spectrum disorders, where totally different cognitive factors may be mediating the problem.

The grouping of disorders on the basis of treatment response is also problematic, particularly when Hollander and Rosen acknowledge that "compulsive and impulsive disorders show differential SRI treatment response, indicating differential biological mechanisms". The differing temporal response rates, maintenance doses, augmentation, etc., as noted in the review, point to differences rather than similarities. In addition, some spectrum disorders do not respond selectively to selective serotonin reuptake inhibitors (SSRIs) (e.g. Tourette's syndrome) and there is insufficient data to suggest that other disorders respond only to SSRIs (e.g. pathological gambling, autism).

Although family history is also suggested to indicate a relationship between the various disorders, little hard data is presented to support this assertion. Studies that have examined disorders in the first-degree relatives of OCD probands (e.g. [5]) tend to indicate a higher rate of anxiety and depressive disorders in relatives of OCD subjects than normal control relatives, suggesting a relationship between OCD and anxiety and depressive disorders in general. Similarly, both epidemiological (e.g. [6]) and clinical comorbidity studies in OCD (e.g. [7]) have suggested high rates of lifetime anxiety and depressive disorders in OCD subjects, and vice versa. Although these findings tend to reinforce the relationship between OCD and anxiety and depressive disorders, anxiety and depressive disorders are not proposed to be part of the spectrum.

In conclusion, Hollander and Rosen propose one way of conceptualizing a group of disorders that may share some features. To some extent, this may be productive, in that it encourages research into the similarities and differences between the conditions. However, at this point it is difficult to argue a relationship between the conditions, when our knowledge of many of the disorders remain in the embryonic stages. From a conceptual point of view, it is difficult to argue the relationship between the unwanted, distressing intrusions concerning harm to self or others, blasphemy or sexually inappropriate thoughts in OCD and the deceitful, aggressive, reckless, remorseless but impulsive behaviour in antisocial personality disorder. Unless, of course, we argue that the opposites are related.

REFERENCES

1. Salkovskis P.M., Kirk J. (1997) Obsessive compulsive disorder. In *Cognitive Behaviour Therapy: Science and Practice*, (Eds D.M. Clark, C.G. Fairburn), pp. 179–208, Oxford University Press, Oxford.
2. Rachman S.J. (1997) A cognitive theory of obsessions. *Behav. Res. Ther.*, **35**: 793–803.
3. Jones M., Menzies R.G. (1997) The cognitive mediation of obsessive handwashing. *Behav. Res. Ther.*, **35**: 843–850.
4. van Oppen P., de Haan E., van Bolkum A.J.L., Spinhoven P., Hoogduin K., van Dyck R. (1995) Cognitive therapy and exposure *in vivo* in the treatment of obsessive compulsive disorder. *Behav. Res. Ther.*, **33**: 379–390.
5. Black D.W., Noyes R., Goldstein R.B., Blum N. (1992) A family study of obsessive compulsive disorder. *Arch. Gen. Psychiatry*, **49**: 362–368.
6. Karno M., Golding J.M., Sorenson S.B., Burnam M.A. (1988) The epidemiology of obsessive compulsive disorder in five US communities. *Arch. Gen. Psychiatry*, **45**: 1049–1099.
7. Crino R., Andrews G. (1996) Obsessive compulsive disorder and axis I comorbidity. *J. Anxiety Disord.*, **10**: 37–46.

5.10
The Spectrum of Obsessive-Compulsive-Related Disorders: State of the Art

Donatella Marazziti[1]

The controversy about the use of categories and dimensions in psychiatric nosology is far from being resolved and represents one of the most intriguing current debates. Undoubtedly, the recognition of discrete diagnostic entities has become very sophisticated and standardized in the DSM system, but the lack of precise etiological models represents the main weakness of the categorical approach. Nevertheless, categories are useful for the classification of patients and the standardization of treatment.

In classifying psychopathology, however, phenomena rarely fit into clear-cut and homogeneous categories, but rather fall on a continuum [1]. For this reason, a dimensional approach appears more flexible and suitable for the recognition of atypical patients or of patients at the borders of classical entities. Furthermore, it is now evident that the multicausality of psychiatric disorders is more in agreement with a dimensional mode.

The categorical and the dimensional approaches are not necessarily incompatible, and the recent emergence of the concept of

[1] *Department of Psychiatry, Neurobiology, Pharmacology and Biotechnologies, University of Pisa, Via Roma 67, 56100 Pisa, Italy*

obsessive-compulsive disorder (OCD)-related or OCD spectrum disorders (OCSDs) proposed by Jenike [2] and Hollander [3] represents an intriguing and serious attempt to overcome this duality.

In their review, Hollander and Rosen describe the rationale behind the proposal of the OCSDs. The starting point was clinical and categorical. The observation that obsessive-compulsive symptoms, despite being the core features of OCD, did not appear to be limited to it, led to considering diagnostic categories along a spectrum that grouped together different disorders, on the basis of shared characteristics, including not only symptomatology, but also family history, age at onset, comorbidity, pathophysiology and pharmacological response. These disorders are characterized by obsessive thoughts or preoccupations with body appearance (body dysmorphic disorder), bodily sensation (depersonalization), body weight (anorexia nervosa), or by stereotyped, ritualistic or driven behaviours, such as tics (Tourette's syndrome), hair pulling (trichotillomania), sexual compulsions, pathological gambling or other impulsive disorders [3].

Apart from these features, the various disorders can be grouped together also according to a dimensional approach. Those dimensions which have so far been proposed include estimation of risk, or risk-aversive (compulsive)/risk-seeking (impulsive), cognitive (obsessional)/motoric (ritualistic), and another one ranging from the obsessive certainty through overvalued ideas to delusional certainty (uncertainty/certainty dimension) [3]. In addition, OCSDs can be also conceptualized as consisting of distinct symptom clusters, including disorders of impulse control, exaggerated preoccupation with appearance, weight or bodily sensations, and neurological disorders with repetitive behaviours.

In their review, Hollander and Rosen focus mainly on impulse control disorders (such as pathological gambling as an example of the impulsive pole and body dysmorphic disorder at the opposite pole), somatoform disorders and neurological disorders with repetitive behaviours, in particular autism. They present neurobiological findings and treatment implications for each of the disorders analysed.

This OCSD model represents only a working hypothesis, which still requires testing but which, however, has provoked an upsurge of interest in disorders that have been neglected by psychiatrists for a long time or for which no treatment option has been available. This is a great merit of the authors, who have attempted to provide dignity to several disorders which are not well defined in the DSM system. However, the proposed neurobiological models appear too simplistic: if several and congruent evidences link a decreased serotonin (5-HT) system functioning to impulsive behaviours, the hypothesis that an increased sensitivity of distinct 5-HT receptors may underlie compulsive behaviours is supported by meagre data. Probably, it seems more appropriate, at this stage, to hypothesize an involvement of the 5-HT system yet to be determined. Following this thought line, we have recently demonstrated that OCD and OCSDs share a common dysfunction at the level of the platelet 5-HT transporter [4]. Clearly, common serotonergic dysfunctions are better explained according to a dimensional rather than a categorical model, as they probably reflect a vulnerability towards the development of symptom clusters common to all conditions, or to shared dimensions which are common to different disorders [5]. Although much research is still required, some authors have already highlighted relationships between the 5-HT transporter and personality traits [6], aggressive features [7] and anxiety traits [8]. We believe that the identification of these common dimensions and of their pathophysiological mechanisms will constitute an extremely fruitful area for future research.

At the therapeutic level, preliminary observations [5, 9], mainly derived from open clinical trials, have shown that patients with different OCSDs respond to drugs inhibiting 5-HT reuptake. However, if these data raise a cautious optimism, large controlled studies need to be carried out urgently, as the authors themselves underline. Only the integration of different research lines might permit to substantiate or reject the spectrum model.

REFERENCES

1. Kendell R.E. (1975) *The Role of Diagnosis in Psychiatry*, Blackwell, Oxford.
2. Jenike M.A. (1990) Illnesses related to obsessive-compulsive disorder. In *Obsessive-compulsive Disorders: Theory and Management* (Eds M.A. Jenike, L.B. Baer, W.E. Minichiello), pp. 39–60, Year Book Medical Publishers, Chicago.
3. Hollander E. (1993) *Obsessive-compulsive Related Disorders*, American Psychiatric Press, Washington DC.
4. Marazziti D., Dell'Osso L., Presta S., Pfanner C., Rossi A., Masala I., Baroni I., Giannaccini G., Lucacchini A., Cassano G.B. (1999) Platelet ^{3}H-paroxetine binding in patients with OCD-related disorders. *Psychiatry Res.*, **89**: 223–228.
5. Hollander E., Wong C.M. (1995) Body dysmorphic disorder, pathological gambling and sexual compulsions. *J. Clin. Psychiatry*, **56** (suppl. 4): 7–12.
6. Lesch K.P., Bengel D., Heils A., Sabol S.Z., Greenberg B.D., Petri S., Benjamin J., Muller C.R., Hamer D.H., Murphy D.L. (1996) Association of anxiety-related traits with a polymorphism in the serotonin transporter gene regulatory region. *Science*, **274**: 1527–1531.
7. Coccaro E.F., Kavoussi R.J., Sheline Y.I., Lish J.D., Csernansky J.C. (1996) Impulsive aggression in personality disorder correlates with tritiated paroxetine binding in the platelets. *Arch. Gen. Psychiatry*, **53**: 531–536.
8. Mazzanti C.M., Lappalainen J., Long J.C., Bengel D., Naukkarinen H., Eggert M., Virkunnen M., Linnoila M., Goldman D. (1998) Role of the serotonin transporter promoter polymorphism in anxiety-related traits. *Arch. Gen. Psychiatry*, **55**: 936–940.

9. Hollander E., DeCaria C.M., Mari E., Wong C.M., Mosovich S., Grossman R., Begaz T. (1998) Short-term single-blind fluvoxamine treatment of pathological gambling. *Am. J. Psychiatry*, **155**: 1781–1783.

CHAPTER

6

Costs of Obsessive-Compulsive Disorder: A Review

Martin Knapp, Juliet Henderson and Anita Patel

London School of Economics and Political Science, Department of Social Policy and Administration, Houghton Street, London WC2A, UK

INTRODUCTION: DEMAND AND SUPPLY

Scarcity

Economics is primarily concerned with how resources are allocated and with what consequences. Most health care systems of the world operate under conditions of scarcity: there are not enough skilled professionals, drug doses, hospital beds or other resources to meet all of the health care needs of the population. From this starting point, many health economic analyses concentrate on how to get the best outcomes for patients (or for the population more generally) from given resources. When the oppressive climate of scarcity is lifted (which happens occasionally), economic analyses might be called upon to suggest how an expanding resource base of provision might obtain the maximum societal benefits in terms of health status and associated outcomes.

Scarcity prompts choice. When there are insufficient health care or other resources available to meet the assessed needs or expressed wants of patients or of the population as a whole, decisions must be taken as to how those resources are deployed. Those decisions could be left to the unchecked forces of the market—the individual with the ability to purchase treatment is free to do so, subject only to finding a suitable therapist willing to provide it—or could be restricted in various ways. Restrictions might be imposed by therapists themselves, by private insurance companies, by those employers who pay health insurance premiums for their staff or by government bodies.

Obsessive-Compulsive Disorder. Edited by Mario Maj, Norman Sartorius, Ahmed Okasha and Joseph Zohar.

Whatever the health care system, and whatever the decision-making procedures within it, those choices and those restrictions have increasingly been influenced by economic considerations. What does that treatment option cost? Is it cost-effective? How much more benefit will follow from a little more spending on this service? Is the high price of this new drug counter-balanced by cost savings elsewhere in the health care system?

These questions seem to be posed with more regularity today than in the past. One reason for this is a more widespread recognition of scarcity, and a more explicit willingness to face up to the need to ration access to treatment, preferably in transparent, rational and fair ways. Another factor in the growth of interest in economic issues has been acknowledgement, not simply that the costs of mental disorders are often substantial and spread widely—falling on those who are ill, their families and the national economy—but also that resources might be better deployed so as to achieve improved outcomes. In the face of scarcity, choices have to be made between alternative uses of the same resource or service, which raises questions about comparative costs and effects.

Macro- and Micro-analyses

Health economists are thus concerned about resource allocation and conduct their analyses at various levels of aggregation. At the highest level are macro-level studies of how health care systems operate. For example, these might examine the consequences of different funding arrangements and organizational incentives for the motivations and behaviour of key 'stakeholders'. In a private health care system that is predominantly reliant on insurance payments—such as in the USA—studies are needed that focus on how different payment mechanisms might influence the behaviour of patients and health care professionals, and how, in turn, they exert effects on service utilization rates, levels of health status and overall system costs and cost-effectiveness. With the rapid spread of "managed care", economists have been busy studying the effects of, for instance, cost containment methods such as utilization reviews, case management and capitated payments.

In a health care system that is much more closely linked to the public sector—such as the state-run National Health Service in the UK—the rationing of access to treatments might take different forms. Macro-level economic studies could usefully look at the consequences of strategic policy decisions (nationally, regionally or locally), and would therefore need to take cognisance of political forces and public administrative processes in seeking to understand how those decisions are reached and with what consequences. Market-inspired reforms to the public sector in the UK at the start of the 1990s stimulated another mixed strand of enquiry, particularly focused on whether quasi-markets achieve fairer or more efficient allocations of health benefits than more centralised, bureaucratic allocation arrangements, whilst still reliant on tax-funded budgets.

Through macro-analyses, economists seek to contribute to the better understanding of how health care systems might improve the utilization of scarce resources to the benefit of patients as a group, and with what effects on the economy as a whole. Micro-level analyses have equivalent aims but are pitched at a much lower level of aggregation, commonly at the practice level of the treatment of individual patients. Typical micro questions address the outcome and cost consequences of alternative care settings (hospital vs. community-based care, for instance), different organizational arrangements (such as intensive case management), new psychopharmacological interventions, and the various psychological therapies. Economists have a range of evaluative tools to apply to these micro questions, notably the techniques of cost-effectiveness, cost-benefit and cost-utility analysis.

Most of the discussion and all of the empirical evidence offered in this review is located at the micro-level. The primary reason for this is because it is at the micro-level that the issues specific to obsessive-compulsive disorder (OCD) get raised and where OCD-specific economics research has been undertaken. However, we should not overlook the relevance of macro-level research for shedding much-needed light on the broader workings of mental health care systems.

Supply Response

Despite the broad potential and undoubted relevance of economic analyses in the mental health field, until quite recently these methods had not been widely deployed at either macro- or micro-levels. Unfortunately, even when economic analyses *are* been carried out, they are sometimes poorly designed, badly executed or inappropriately interpreted [1]. To make matters worse, the distribution of economics studies in the mental health field is also very uneven, with some diagnostic groups, treatment settings, therapeutic modes and regions of the world comparatively well provided with economic evidence, and others poorly served. One of the areas most neglected has been the whole span of anxiety disorders. Consequently, as will soon become clear, there are disappointingly few economics studies of OCD. Moreover, the majority of those that have been completed or published have tended to be more descriptive than evaluative, seeking to gauge the overall "cost burden" of OCD, often in comparison with other mental disorders, rather than to test whether, for example, particular therapeutic interventions are cost-effective.

There is another distributional imbalance: across the full spectrum of mental health disorders, most of the available empirical evidence comes from North America. This is also the case with economics research on OCD. Such a regional concentration may not matter unduly when looking at basic scientific or clinical research, because the evidence generated can usually be applied across national boundaries and cultures. The same is not necessarily true of health services research. Economics evidence in particular may not travel well because health care systems and funding arrangements have such a bearing on the findings: what is a cost-effective service configuration or therapy in one system may not prove to be cost-effective in another. This cautionary note should be borne in mind when assessing the relevance of the empirical material summarized in this review.

Structure of the Review

This review is structured as follows. We start by distinguishing the main resource consequences of OCD, and then look at the overall impact with an account of what economists sometimes call "cost-of-illness" or "burden-of-disease" studies. The next section introduces the main types of evaluation conducted by health economists and how they might be deployed in the OCD field. Sadly, there is not really any evaluative evidence that explicitly includes an economic dimension, but there are a few pointers from clinical studies that can be highlighted. Finally, we summarize the evidence and identify research gaps.

RESOURCE CONSEQUENCES OF OCD

Broad and Long-term Impacts

What are the economic impacts of OCD, and how large are they? Some economic impacts are readily identified, at least at the level of principle, and many are usually quite straightforward to measure in practice. For example, once the disorder has been diagnosed by a clinician there will usually be provision of treatment services. These service inputs could be measured in terms of frequency and intensity of utilization, and could then also be expressed in terms of their costs (however, sufferers may not refer themselves for treatment, and primary care doctors may not diagnose the condition [2]).

By contrast, some of the economic impacts of OCD are rather less obvious or less easily quantified, such as the deleterious consequences of such a debilitating disorder for many domains of a patient's quality of life, and also the consequences for the family. A well-known but rarely measured cost is the effect of OCD on performance at the workplace. And because OCD is a chronic condition, with relatively early manifestation, many of these disabling effects and their associated costs could persist for some years. The evidence on these direct and indirect impacts, which we assemble below, is not voluminous but it helpfully illustrates both the pervasiveness and the persistence of costs.

Health Service Utilization

Mental Health Expenditures

As we have just suggested, the most immediately and frequently measured economic consequences of mental illness are the costs of the various health services—both specialist and generic—used by sufferers. If we look in aggregate at the full spectrum of mental health problems, we can see that they account for large proportions of national health care expenditure in most countries of the world. Two recent calculations illustrate this. Meerding *et al* [3] computed direct (service) costs nationally for the health care system in the Netherlands in 1994, and allocated them by International Classification of Diseases (ICD) code, using prevalence data. Mental disorders accounted for 23.2% of total expenditure. The main components were: learning disability (mental handicap), 8.1%; dementia, 5.6%; depression and anxiety, 2.3%; schizophrenia, 1.4%; alcohol and drug problems, 0.8%; and other mental disorders, 5.0%. These authors also reported that one or both of the two most costly diagnostic groups in each of five age bands used to categorize the population were mental disorders.

The second illustration comes from the 1992/93 program budget of the National Health Service (NHS) in England and Wales, again disaggregated by ICD code [4]. Twenty-two per cent of total national expenditure on inpatient services was accounted for by mental illness compared to less than 4% of primary care expenditure and only 5% of the drugs budget [5]. (This last percentage would be slightly larger today, given the recent pharmacological "revolution" in many areas of psychiatry). The contributions to national expenditure by the neuroses as a group were quite substantial: 0.6% for hospital inpatient services, 2.1% for outpatient services, 1.1% for primary care, 3.1% for pharmaceuticals, 4.8% for community health services and 2.8% for adult social care services.

Moving from measures of global expenditure to indicators of diagnosis-specific expenditure is not straightforward. Although there certainly have been studies of health care spending at a lower level of diagnostic disaggregation, and conducted in a number of countries, two problems tend to dog them. The first is the familiar nosological challenge of identifying and distinguishing different anxiety disorders. The second and related problem is the high rate of comorbidities, which can make it difficult to attribute cause (e.g. [6, 7]). As well as the high rate of comorbid anxiety and affective disorders, alcohol and drug problems are common [8]. By no means every study of service use patterns and costs for people with OCD has been able to overcome these problems adequately.

We now turn to the most important of the services used by people with OCD. We draw on a number of sources, but two nationally-representative surveys appear regularly in the discussion because they provide rich data. Chronologically, the first, and still the largest, epidemiological survey of mental health problems is the Epidemiologic Catchment Area (ECA) survey conducted by the National Institute of Mental Health in the USA [9]. A sample of more than 18 000 non-institutionalized adults and more than 2000 institutionalized adults from five US sites participated in two waves of face-to-face interviews between 1980 and 1985. At least three groups of researchers have used this well-known source to provide quite comprehensive indications of health care utilization patterns, their costs, and indeed of the overall economic impact of OCD.

Although smaller in scale than the ECA, the Psychiatric Morbidity Surveys in the UK, conducted by the Office of Population Censuses and Surveys (OPCS) in 1993–1994, also provide valuable information on, *inter alia*, the services used by people with different mental health problems [10]. Three separate surveys (each drawing upon a national sample) were completed for private households, institutions (including hospitals and residential homes) and the homeless. Each sampled adult (aged 18–65) was given an initial schedule, covering sociodemographic characteristics, general health questions, the Clinical Interview Schedule—Revised (CIS–R) and the Psychosis Screening Questionnaire. Those who scored at or above the threshold of 12 on the CIS–R or screened positive for psychosis were then given a second, more detailed schedule, covering long-standing illness, medication and treatment, use of health, social and voluntary care services, activities of daily living, recent stressful life events, social activities, networks and support, education, employment, finances, smoking and alcohol consumption. Responses were weighted to allow for non-response, sampling of subjects in different-sized households, and the age–sex structure of the national population.

Inpatient Hospitalization

Most countries of the world have experienced quite a noticeable rundown of psychiatric inpatient services over the past two or three decades. There have usually been a number of factors combining to bring about these changes in the locus of care [11], including changes in public attitudes, resource pressures and of course the development of better pharmacological and psychological therapies. In some health care systems there has been a tendency towards specialist OCD treatment units (inpatient and outpatient) in a smaller number of centres. In these settings, costs are necessarily and appropriately quite high (because of the often high need or symptom threshold for admission, and the associated concentration of skilled professionals), and the travelling distances (and costs) for patients and their families can also be great.

Inpatient hospitalization rates are modest for people with OCD compared with some other psychiatric disorders, although hospitalization can contribute significantly to the overall cost of the illness. This is clear from a number of studies. Probably the most reliable basis for examining the extent of inpatient (and all other) service use is the ECA. Using this source, Narrow *et al* [12] described service utilization patterns over a 1-year period for people with mental and addictive disorders (DSM-III diagnostic categories). Statistical weighting devised to deal with the complex multistage sampling procedures allowed extrapolation to the national level. It was estimated that there were 3.34 million people with OCD in the USA [13], 248 000 (17%) of whom had at least one admission to inpatient facilities for mental health reasons during the year. This was 18% of all people with inpatient admissions for mental health reasons.

Of those 248 000 people with recent hospitalization experience, 36% were admitted to general hospitals (psychiatric units and "scatterbeds"), 29% to state and county mental hospitals, 10% to residential supportive units, 11% to private mental hospitals, 21% to Veterans' Affairs hospital psychiatric units, and 14% to alcohol/drug treatment units. Another 1% had been admitted to nursing homes. There were quite wide confidence intervals around these estimates. It is interesting to compare the numbers of OCD cases admitted for inpatient treatment with other diagnostic groups: 295 000 people with schizophrenia/schizophreniform disorder were admitted, 144 000 with any bipolar disorder, 460 000 with unipolar major depression, 430 000 with dysthymia, 567 000 with phobia, 175 000 with panic disorder, 38 000 with somatization disorder, 145 000 with antisocial personality disorder, and 123 000 with (severe) cognitive impairment.

More recent results for the USA come from a postal questionnaire survey of members of the patient-oriented Obsessive Compulsive Foundation (OCF). Hollander [14] reported that 25% of OCD sufferers had experience of inpatient hospitalization at some point in their lives, more than 50% had spent more than one period as an inpatient, and 10% had more than five hospitalizations. The average cost per person in this sample was US$12 500, and lifetime hospitalization costs were estimated to amount to about US$5 billion. The low response rate (27%) from what is already a special group (those people with the illness who have chosen to become members of the OCF) limits the generalizability of these findings, and comorbidities are not discussed, but the effective sample size of 710 sufferers is unusually large in the OCD field.

In the UK, Patel *et al* [15] used the (weighted) subsample of people in private households with OCD who participated in the Psychiatric Morbidity Surveys to examine economic aspects of the illness. Twenty-one per cent of people with OCD had experienced at least one inpatient admission during the 12 months preceding the interview, compared with only 12% for those people in the sample without psychiatric morbidity. The mean number of days spent in hospital by those admitted was 16.4 (the mean was 3.4 across the full sample of people with the disorder). OCD sufferers with a comorbid psychiatric problem were more likely than those without a comorbidity to have been admitted (25% compared to 11%) and spent longer as inpatients (19.8 days compared to 2.7).

Ambulatory Services

Ambulatory care has grown in importance with the pervasive closure of inpatient facilities in most developed countries. Although the ECA data were collected many years ago, and mental health care has undergone quite major changes in the meantime, they still provide clear indications of the scale of utilization of various ambulatory services. For example, for every one individual diagnosed with OCD who had an inpatient admission during the year, six individuals received treatment on an outpatient basis (1.46 million people). This represented 43.7% of all those people with the disorder, which is not far short of the proportion (45.1%) using *any* mental health or addictive service [13]. Narrow *et al* [12] found that, of these 1.46 million ambulatory care users: 6.4% had been to a psychiatric hospital outpatient clinic (mean of 19 visits per year per treated person); 7.2% to a mental health centre outpatient clinic (17 visits); 5.6% to a general hospital outpatient clinic (11 visits); 6.3% to a Veterans' Affairs hospital (eight visits); 4.0% to an alcohol/drug outpatient unit (47 visits); 4.8% to a mental health specialist in their health plan/clinic (11 visits); 28.7% to a mental health specialist in private practice (14 visits); 0.3% to a crisis centre (one visit); 0.7% to a general hospital emergency department (two visits); and 40.4% had seen a general medicine physician during the same one-year period (5 visits).

The term "visit" in the above list refers to a range of contacts, including telephone consultations and discussions. This first report on service use patterns from the ECA contains many useful comparisons between different mental health problems which we cannot attempt to summarize here. The authors point out, however, the striking result that OCD sufferers made significantly fewer "visits to emergency departments (0.7%)... and had the lowest proportion of total visits among the anxiety disorders for the general hospital emergency department (0.1%)" [12].

Working with the first ECA wave of data collection, Leon *et al* [16] described how 17% of men with OCD and 16% of women sought help from the specialist mental health system, compared with around 2% for people without an Axis I disorder. The rates of utilization of the general medical system were also much higher for people with OCD (7% of men, 12% of women) compared to those without any disorder (2% and 4%, respectively). For both specialist and general health care services, OCD patients were lower-frequency and lower-intensity users than people with panic disorders, but generally higher-frequency and higher-intensity users than people with phobias. In contrast, the smaller scale study by McCusker *et al* [17] in Quebec ($n = 235$ anxiety disorder sufferers) found that OCD, compared to other diagnoses, "was associated with a significantly higher rate of high-intensity mental health service utilization".

Primary care doctors are the first port of call for many people with mental health problems in many health care systems, and the ECA findings presented above illustrate the relatively high rates of contact with these professionals. In the British study, general practitioner (GP) contacts were also found to be high: 33% of OCD sufferers had consulted their GP in just the 2 weeks prior to the interview (mean of 1.39 consultations in 2 weeks). The rate was slightly higher for those with a comorbid psychiatric problem (37%) than for those without (26%). Over the longer period of 12 months prior to interview, 57% had attended outpatient services (mean of four visits for each user), 14% had received other counselling or therapy (mean of twelve contacts), and 13% had at least one home visit by a health or social services professional (mean of 30 visits) [15].

Other Formal Care Services

Health services providers do not attempt to meet *all* of the assessed needs of people with mental health problems, and an illness as serious and persistent as OCD can leave sufferers with multiple disabilities and needs. Consequently, they may require not only skilled therapeutic interventions from health care professionals, but also support from a range of other (non-health) individuals and organizations. Indeed, for many people, multi-agency support will be the norm rather than the exception. When looking at the economic consequences of OCD and its treatment, therefore, one should be careful not to overlook these non-health care costs, nor the sometimes difficult boundary and coordination problems that can characterize multi-agency systems [18]. We should also be careful to note that, because systems of care differ from country to country in what they include within (and exclude from) what is recognized and funded as "health care", it can sometimes be difficult to generalize findings, interpretations and recommendations from one setting to another.

Participants in the ECA survey reported their contacts with a number of human services [12]: 1.1% saw a family/social service agency (mean of 19 contacts per user); 12.4% saw a member of the clergy or a religious counsellor (mean of three contacts); 0.3% saw a natural therapist (mean of two contacts); and 11.4% had support from some other human service (mean of 11 contacts). In all, one in four OCD sufferers was getting some support from human services (mean of eight contacts per user over the year). In addition, 6.0% had attended a self-help group (mean of 38 contacts) and 19.6% had received support from a friend or family member. These components of the "voluntary support network" were active for only 24% of sample members with OCD, but in this respect people with the disorder differed little from people with other mental health problems.

Lost Employment and Education

Studies of OCD sufferers have found substantial effects on employment, mirroring findings for most other mental health problems. One of the largest costs associated with psychiatric morbidity is the cost of lost employment and reduced productivity: about a third of all sickness absence from work in the UK has been attributed to common mental disorders [19].

Compared both to people without mental health problems and to people with other anxiety disorders, OCD sufferers have been found to have lower employment rates, lower earnings, lower levels of educational attainment and greater reliance on social security (welfare) payments. The British Psychiatric Morbidity Surveys found that only 48% of people with OCD were in paid employment (compared to 72% of people without any mental health problems), 16% were unemployed (compared to 8%) and 36% were economically inactive (compared to 22%) [20]. The effects of the illness may start even earlier: 3% of the OCD sufferers living in non-institutional settings had *never* worked, although this was almost the same as the equivalent percentage for the psychiatrically well population [15]. Looking at those people who were in paid employment, 49% of those with OCD had taken 14 or more days off work during the past year, whereas 31% of the well population had taken this amount of time off. This same survey found that 39% of OCD sufferers had no educational qualifications at all, compared to 27% of the well population, a finding at variance with that of Henderson and Pollard [21] in St. Louis.

Other research studies in North America have tended to find similar results to these British findings, particularly those which have reanalysed the ECA data [22, 23]. Forty-five per cent of males and 65% of females said they were not currently employed, compared to 21% and 46% of people without Axis I disorder. Unemployment is also long-term for many of these people: 18% of males with OCD and 29% of females had not been employed at all in the previous 5 years, compared to 5% of well males and 24% of well females [16]. Many trials of psychological or pharmacological treatments have assessed workplace functioning and generally report moderate to severe problems (reviewed by Steketee [24]). Dupont *et al* [25] converted these employment effects of OCD into an annual cost figure, based on the "human capital" method of estimation (see below). By their estimate, the annual value of lost productivity to the US economy attributable to OCD was $5.9 billion (at 1990 price levels), equivalent to 71% of the total cost of the disorder. The total amount and percentage contribution are both high, partly because of the disorder's early onset.

These employment difficulties could have a number of corollaries. Those whose illness prevents them from working, or achieving their full potential, may become both economically and socially marginalized ("socially excluded"). If they are compensated through social welfare payments from the state, there will be a cost to taxpayers. If the economy is running close to full employment, there could be productivity losses. Whilst these effects overlap, and double counting should be avoided, they are clearly considerable and fall quite widely.

Family and Caregiver Impacts

Depending on the system of health care finance operating in a country, some of the costs of treatment and support services and some of the burden of lost employment could rest with the families of people with mental health problems. In systems built predominantly on private insurance arrangements, family-borne costs could be quite immediate (and sizeable), taking the form of payments for some treatment services. In public sector or social insurance health care systems, where families generally have to make few out-of-pocket payments for services, a bigger consideration may be the caregiver role. Because marriage/cohabitation rates tend to be lower among people with OCD than the general population (for instance, 45% for OCD and 64% for the psychiatrically well group in Britain; see [15, 24]), other family members may play important roles.

Estimates of the time that families devote to the caregiver role are difficult to obtain, and attaching a cost can be contentious, particularly if caregivers have not given up work to provide support. More relevant, of course, is the fact that the impact of the illness on family members is more than economic. Families live with behaviour that often involves predictability of rituals, bizarre requests, non-communication, withdrawal, obsessive cleanliness or orderliness and checking/storing of everyday objects. They may have to contend with disruptions to established patterns of household living, social embarrassment, demanding behaviour and reduced leisure time. Whilst it is true that many families learn to cope with OCD symptoms competently, the family impact may not be seen as helpful for continuing constructive relationships with children or other family members. Relationships outside the household may also be affected. Many caregivers have ambivalent relationships with mental health professionals, feeling unsupported, uninformed, misinformed and blamed, in turn reinforcing feelings of guilt. The family impact of the disorder, therefore, is a potentially enormous "cost" in colloquial as well as economic terms, with deleterious effects on mental health [26, 27], family life, socialization and leisure activities [28, 29].

Respondents in this last study [29], conducted in India, also reported reductions in holiday times, neglect of other family members, irritation and sleeplessness. Financial loss was reported as a significant problem for the group: 67% said treatment expenses were a problem, 31% found the patient's lost earnings to be difficult, and 30% incurred expenditure due to extra care arrangements. Family burden was greater for married parents, married relatives and housewives of employed patients.

Mortality

Mortality is another effect of OCD which could be expressed in cost terms through its effects on lost productivity, although this is obviously a minor consideration when set beside the huge personal and social losses of premature death. The most thorough attempt to estimate these mortality costs was made by Dupont *et al* [25], who reviewed the largely unpublished evidence on the rate of attempted suicide by people diagnosed with OCD, and consulted an expert panel. They concluded that approximately 2% of all suicides in the US (total of 31 000 in 1990) could be attributed to the disorder (notwithstanding the problem of attribution because of comorbidities). Costs were based on the (lost) expected future stream of earnings (adjusted by age and sex) and an imputed value for unpaid housekeeping activities. These calculations produced an estimated annual mortality cost of $255 million (at 1990 price levels), or 3% of the total estimated cost of OCD.

Transfer Payments

Economists define social security or welfare payments as transfers from one part of society (taxpayers or social insurance fund contributors) to another (recipients of the payments), and they therefore exclude these amounts from calculations of the aggregate costs of an illness. These are "transfer payments" and may double-count other costs. Nevertheless, to taxpayers these social security or welfare payments can represent a sizeable drain on fiscal resources. In England in the mid-1990s, welfare payments to *all* people with mental health problems may have exceeded £7 billion [5]. For those people with OCD included in the Psychiatric Morbidity Survey of private households, mean social security receipts were £1591 annually (1997/98 price levels), compared to £794 for those people without psychiatric morbidity [15]. In the USA, Leon *et al* [16] reported that 23% of males and 13% of females with OCD were receiving disability payments, compared to 5% of males and 4% of females without an Axis I disorder.

THE AGGREGATE COSTS OF OCD

Cost-of-illness Methods

The economic impacts described in the previous section are clearly felt in a variety of areas, by a variety of stakeholders, and can be measured in a variety of ways. It can sometimes be helpful to transform these impacts into a single, cost-based measure. Although not every such impact might easily be cost-weighted in this way, such a summation has been argued to draw helpful attention to the overall consequences of a disorder or illness. It also allows comparisons with similar calculations for other disorders or diagnostic groups. Another use would be to show how different services, organizations or sectors contribute to the overall economic "burden". But there is an obvious danger, which is that such a global measure risks over-simplifying the complexity of the real world, and might also introduce further measurement error into what is already generally only a rough approximation of impacts in some domains. *Cost-of-illness* or *burden-of-disease* studies, as these aggregation exercises are generally termed, can even be somewhat misleading: the extent of service use will be a function not only of the severity and duration of a disorder but also of the nature of the health care and other systems under study, and especially of the availability of key inpatient and ambulatory services. Clearly, such studies do not examine the achievement (or otherwise) of efficiency or equity goals, because they neither combine cost measurement with any indication of outcomes, nor do they look at resource allocation in relation to needs or demands. Cost-of-illness calculations are thus only rather loose indications of impact, and can only ever offer *broad* guidance to decision-makers on how to use resources.

There are basically two approaches to such estimates, one disaggregating national or regional budgets by diagnostic group, and the other building up the cost figures from detailed prevalence or incidence figures. Prevalence-based cost-of-illness studies calculate the economic burden according to the period in which the illness takes place (usually one year), whilst incidence-based studies—which are more difficult and rarer—measure the lifetime costs of an illness from its onset. Most such studies adopt a societal perspective, attempting to measure the widest span of costs in order to reflect the full social costs of a disorder.

Good epidemiological data, together with accurate information on service utilization patterns, are clearly essential for a cost-of-illness calculation. Also important are good "unit cost" measures with which to weight the services and other impacts before aggregation. Ideally, each of these cost weights would be a measure of *opportunity cost*, that is the value forgone by not using the particular resource (service) in its best alternative employment. What this means in practice, usually, is that the costs of treatment and support services, such as hospital inpatient days, outpatient visits and primary care consultations, are based on expenditure figures, probably after minor adjustment [30]. Other costs, such as those associated with lost employment and caregiver support for which there are no ready "market-based" monetary measures, must be built up from first principles or adapted from other studies. They are obviously more difficult to estimate and there are methodological disagreements about what it is legitimate to include and how they are to be valued [31]. For example, some of the costs attached to lost employment have been criticized for being too high, because they make insufficient allowance for labour market adjustments in response to mental ill-health and the prevailing level of unemployment elsewhere in the economy [32]. Similar difficulties often plague estimates of the costs of caregiver time.

Aggregate Cost Estimates

Since OCD can exert a wide range of impacts, it is not surprising that there have been few successful attempts to measure its complete cost. The most useful cost-of-illness exercises have not only sought to estimate the total cost of the disorder, but have also asked questions about service utilization patterns, living circumstances and employment experiences.

The fullest aggregate costing of OCD was conducted by Dupont *et al* [25] in the USA, building on the ECA-based work of Rice and colleagues [33].

These latter authors completed comprehensive cost-of-illness estimates for all mental health and addictive problems. They included the utilization of health care and other services, federal expenses for medical and health services research, training costs, program administration, the net cost for private health insurance, the value of reduced or lost productivity due to morbidity, the costs of premature mortality, victim costs of crime and criminal justice system expenditures, and the value of time spent by family caregivers supporting their relatives. Direct costs were built up from service utilization rates found in the ECA surveys and national expenditure data. Indirect costs were based on the human capital approach: the value of labour at market prices forgone as a direct result of illness, weighted by average incomes. Regression analysis predictions were used to adjust income effects by taking into consideration other socioeconomic variables. In this way, Rice *et al* calculated an aggregate cost of $148 billion (at 1990 prices) for *all* psychiatric disorders. Anxiety disorders were the highest cost group ($47 billion per annum nationally), but schizophrenia ($33 billion), affective disorders ($30 billion) and other disorders ($38 billion) were also clearly having major economic impacts.

From this broader cost-of-illness study, and informed by the work of Narrow *et al* [12], Dupont *et al* [25] estimated the yearly cost of OCD for 1990 as $8.4 billion, which was 5.7% of the estimated $14.8 billion spent on mental illness in the USA. This, the authors contend, is likely to be an underestimate "because of the significant number of individuals who do not seek treatment and are therefore undiagnosed". They cite one US study which found that 3.8% of people with untreated anxiety symptoms were diagnosed with OCD [34]. The Psychiatric Morbidity Survey data revealed that 23% of those people in private households found to have OCD had not seen their GP in the previous 2 weeks and had used no health or social care services in the previous year, and three-quarters of these people had also taken no medication [15]. Another reason for this aggregate cost being somewhat low is that Dupont's indirect cost figures were based on estimates for all anxiety disorders, whilst OCD tends to be more disabling.

The direct costs are broken down as follows: $756 million for specialist institutions, federal and county private psychiatric hospitals, residential treatment and correction facilities and mental health centres; $120 million on short-stay hospital care; $95 million on physicians; $120 million on professional services such as psychologists and social workers; $791 million on nursing homes; $53 million for prescriptive medications; and $199 million for net private health insurance.

Dupont *et al* [25] calculated that lost work days or reduced productivity due to OCD cost the US economy $5.9 billion in 1990, whilst mortality (also reckoned in terms of lost productivity) cost another $0.26 billion. In total, these "productivity" costs were almost three times the direct health care costs. In fact this is a common feature of economic studies of anxiety disorders: the costs of lost productivity due to morbidity tend to dwarf other costs [33]. Other indirect elements included crime costs at $36 million, social welfare administration $8 million, incarceration $12 million and family caregiver burden $15 million.

On average, these calculations suggest annual direct costs per OCD sufferer of $820 (in 1990) and indirect costs (lost productivity mainly) of $1870. Of course, severity of symptoms and degree of disability vary greatly across the population of OCD sufferers, so that averages of this kind hide quite substantial costs incurred by (and partly falling to) those individuals with the most pronounced disorder. Nevertheless, as Dupont and colleagues conclude, OCD is "more common and economically significant than once thought... [and is] a serious economic problem" [25].

ECONOMIC EVALUATION

Principles of Economic Evaluation

The most common reason for commissioning or conducting economic evaluations is to examine the cost-effectiveness of interventions (treatments or policies). An increasingly frequent aim of system-level health care decision-makers is to contain the various expenditures associated with mental illness to improve the patient outcomes that can be achieved from constrained resources. Economists can offer a range of evaluative tools to address policy and practice questions about resources, the best known being cost-effectiveness, cost-benefit and cost-utility analyses. Each of these evaluation modes is concerned with the relationship between costs and outcomes, where the latter are measured in different ways according to the type of evaluation (see below). As we have just seen, economists also conduct so-called burden-of-disease or cost-of-illness studies, which focus exclusively on costs.

Economic evaluation in the mental health field is not intended to replace the expert or experienced judgement of the individual doctor or other treatment professional, neither can it substitute for wider, macro-level decisions by senior executives, boards or politicians in relation to health care systems or state-run services more generally. Policy and practice decisions are made by clinicians, managers and politicians in the light of the information available to them, and evaluative research aims to improve the range, volume and quality of such information.

We noted earlier—and will explain shortly—that measures of the impact or effectiveness of a policy approach, care arrangement or treatment mode vary from one mode of economic evaluation to another. On the other hand, the approach to costing is broadly the same across evaluation types, although there may be disagreements about the *breadth* of costs to measure. Occasionally there will be justification in looking only at the cost to a particular health care funder, or (just) to the health care system, but comprehensive cost measurement is usually seen as desirable. Completeness—or informed premeditated incompleteness—is generally an aim of economic evaluations. Such breadth is of particular pertinence in looking at psychiatric problems: the broad social impact of most mental illnesses, together with the broad societal responsibility often assumed for tackling them, demand it.

Modes of Economic Evaluation

Economic evaluations run from the simple to the complex. On the assumption that an evaluation has been well conducted, one should expect to find a direct correlation between the complexity of analysis and the usefulness of the findings.

The simplest of economic evaluations—cost-offset and cost-minimization analyses—are concerned only with costs. This concentration on the resource side is not because the analysts see outcomes as irrelevant, but because either (a) health and quality of life outcomes have already been established in other research; or (b) they are known to be identical between the options under evaluation; or (c) they are not considered measurable because of conceptual difficulties or research funding limitations. *Cost-minimization analysis* seeks to find which of a number of treatment options has the lowest cost. *Cost-offset analysis* compares the resources expended in delivering a treatment or changing a policy with the costs or resources that are saved as a consequence. That is, it examines the pay-off from a change of practice or policy. A new drug such as a selective serotonin reuptake inhibitor (SSRI) may have a higher acquisition cost (higher price) compared to older drugs with the same indication, but may be more effective in tackling the symptoms of illness and so, in time, may reduce the need for patients to use as many health care services or to take so much time off work.

Cost-effectiveness and *cost-consequences analyses* are more complex but simultaneously much more informative. They use scales to measure outcomes that will be familiar to psychiatrists and other professionals from clinical research, alongside cost measures. Both can help decision makers choose between two or more interventions for specific patient groups. The decision calculus is straightforward: if two care options are of equal cost, which provides the greater effectiveness? Or, if two options are equally effective in terms of improved symptoms, functioning or quality of life, which costs the lower amount? A cost-effectiveness analysis looks at a *single* effectiveness dimension—such as the number of life years saved, the number of symptom-free days or the duration of time to relapse—and then computes and compares the ratio of cost to effectiveness for each of the treatments being evaluated. The option with the lowest cost-effectiveness ratio would be recommended on efficiency grounds. A *cost-consequences analysis* computes total (and component) costs together with measures of change along *every* relevant outcome dimension for each treatment option. The cost and outcome findings are presented without calculation of ratios, and the results can then be reviewed by decision-makers, weighed up informally (and subjectively), and compared with the costs. This makes for a less tidy and more complicated decision calculus than when using cost-effectiveness ratios. On the other hand, decision-makers in health care systems—from strategic policy-makers at macro-level to individual professionals at micro-level—make these kinds of decisions daily.

The drawback of a cost-consequences analysis is that the weighting of the outcomes is implicit, subjective and open to bias, whereas the choice of the single outcome dimension in a cost-effectiveness analysis and the weighting algorithms in the other evaluative modes discussed below are explicit and transparent, and probably less prone to influence from the value positions of key (but not necessarily disinterested) stakeholders. On the other hand, a cost-effectiveness analysis has the weakness of focusing on just a single outcome dimension, which is clearly unrealistic in most contexts.

Some types of economic evaluation attach explicit weights to different outcomes in order to aggregate or conflate them into an unidimensional scale. *Cost-benefit analysis* does this by using monetary weights, and addresses the extent to which a treatment or policy is socially worthwhile in the broadest sense: do the benefits exceed the costs? Because all costs and benefits are now valued in the same (monetary) units, it is possible to ascertain whether benefits exceed costs, in which case the evaluation would support the provision of the treatment, or which of two or more treatments offers the greatest net benefit. Cost-benefit analyses are intrinsically attractive and clearly powerful when undertaken properly, but they are also enormously difficult because of the challenge of valuing outcomes in monetary terms. Recent methodological advances in health economics offer *direct* valuations of health outcomes using "willingness-to-pay" and similar techniques to get individuals to state what they would be prepared to pay (hypothetically) to achieve a given health state or health gain [31].

Cost-utility analysis also seeks to conflate outcomes into a single dimension. It measures and then values the impact of an intervention in terms of improvements in preference-weighted, health-related quality of life. Mental health research has increasingly included patient quality of life as one of the key outcome domains, which has special relevance here given the deleterious consequences of OCD [24, 35, 36]. Cost-consequences evaluations can include this dimension. The difference when looking to undertake a cost-utility analysis is that the quality of life improvement is measured in units of "utility", usually expressed by a combined index of the mortality and quality of life effects of an intervention. The best known such measure is the quality adjusted life year (QALY).

Cost-utility analyses offer a unidimensional measure of impact, a generic metric that allows comparisons to be made across diagnostic or clinical groups, and a transparent methodology for weighting preferences and valuing health states. But these advantages must be weighed against the dangers that the utility measure may be too reductionist, the generic quality of life indicator may not be sufficiently sensitive to the kinds of change expected in mental health treatment, and the transparency of the scale construction paradoxically opens the approach to criticism from those who question the values obtained. Nevertheless, cost-utility analyses avoid the potential ambiguities with multidimensional outcomes in cost-consequences studies and are obviously more general than the single-outcome cost-effectiveness analysis. The result from a cost-utility analysis evaluation is two or more cost-utility ratios (costs per QALY gained), which might have relevance in discussions of health care resource allocation decisions.

These various evaluations are sometimes grouped together under the generic label of "cost-effectiveness" studies, and this is the sense in which we use this term below.

The Evidence Base

Unfortunately, there is no evidence base in the OCD field to match these methods; i.e. the principles of health economics evaluations have not yet been applied in studies of different treatment options or service configurations. There are undoubtedly many reasons for this paucity of economic evidence, some related to the limited supply of economists working in the mental health field, some to constraints on research funding, and some to a reluctance among clinical researchers to include an economics component. What is surprising, however, is that there has not been more demand for such evaluative evidence from health care funding bodies. As we have just seen, the costs of OCD are clearly high and persistent, and it is this kind of cost profile in *other* clinical areas, for example in the treatment of schizophrenia, depression or dementia, which has generated a "funded demand" for cost-effectiveness and similar analyses.

Although inpatient costs are modest for people with OCD—and in other clinical areas where inpatient costs are higher, these have sometimes been the prompt for economic evaluations—the increasing use of drugs such as the SSRIs, with their high acquisition costs (prices), and the development of sometimes quite intensive behavioural or cognitive therapies ought to be stimulating demands for purchasers for cost-effectiveness insights. Such demands have either not been forthcoming, or they have not yet elicited positive responses from the research community.

It is likely that successful treatment, as reported in a number of original studies and meta-analyses (and as reviewed in other chapters of this book), would reduce the medium-to-long-term costs for people with OCD, both by reducing their needs for health care and other services, and by improving their chances of securing paid employment or reducing the rate of absenteeism from work. However, whether these cost reductions would outweigh the costs of the treatments (the SSRIs, behavioural therapy, neurosurgery, etc.) is clearly an empirical question which only well-designed research can answer. If these savings are *not* greater than the treatment costs, there may still be a case on cost-effectiveness grounds for proceeding with the treatment if it is better than the alternative (of doing nothing, or of some other intervention) or if the improved outcomes justify the greater expenditure.

SUMMARY

Consistent Evidence

We have seen that the economic consequences of OCD are wide-ranging, often long-lasting, and sometimes profound. They fall not only to the people with the disorder, but also to their families and—to a much lesser degree—to the wider society. Clearly, the costs of OCD are to be reckoned not simply in terms of treatments received and health services utilized—although these are themselves often sizeable and usually central to the concerns of decision makers—but also by reference to personal income, the ability to work, productive contributions to the national economy, and the impoverishment of quality of life. This broad impact is increasingly being recognized as more and more attention is focused upon the economic consequences of mental health problems by health care decision makers, politicians, the general public and others. OCD has received much less attention than, for example, schizophrenia or depression, but its substantial impact is now beginning to be appreciated.

Although the costs of OCD are high, we do need to keep economic perspectives and issues in context. The computed costs of the disorder tell only part of the story, and they certainly cannot adequately reflect the personal and family pain and impaired quality of life so often associated with OCD.

Incomplete Evidence

The paucity of economic evidence makes it difficult to draw particularly strong conclusions about what is known about OCD, except that the disorder has quite large and wide-ranging costs. Many of these costs may be hidden from view and indirect, because they are not reckoned in terms of health care expenditures but in terms of a greatly reduced inability to work, with immediate consequences for personal income and longer-term implications for the productivity of the economy. Some of the potentially major costs of OCD, such as the impact on the sufferer's family, have not been fully included in these economic descriptions of the impact of the illness. A further limitation is that the available evidence is mainly from the US, and health economics results do not always transfer well from one country to another. Further work is clearly needed to complete the cost picture of OCD in its broadest interpretation.

Areas Still Open to Research

This same paucity of evidence makes it quite difficult to draw conclusions about the cost-effectiveness of different treatment options for OCD, for currently nothing is known. There are substantial gaps—indeed, they are *complete* gaps—in our knowledge about the resource implications of different psychopharmacological and psychological therapies. Yet decision makers in health care systems across the world are increasingly calling for cost-effectiveness and similar evidence to guide their decisions. Effective treatments for OCD are being developed and they are now being more frequently adopted, but they are not inexpensive to deliver. Given the perennial pressures on health care resources, decision makers want to be sure that they are using the budgets, services and time of their staff to best effect. This is why funding bodies in many countries are now encouraging the research community to conduct economic evaluations alongside clinical and similar trials. We would hope that the next few years will witness the initiation of cost-effectiveness evaluations of OCD treatment. However, whilst the pursuit of cost-effectiveness is a laudable aim for any health care system, it is only one of a number of legitimate objectives. Economic evaluative evidence, when it begins to arrive in the OCD field, should therefore also be kept in context.

REFERENCES

1. Knapp M.R.J. (2000) Economic evaluation and mental health: sparse past... fertile future? *J. Ment. Health Policy Economics*, in press.
2. Shahady E.J. (1994) Obsessive compulsive disorder in primary care. *J. Clin. Psychiatry*, **55** (suppl. 10): 79–82.
3. Meerding W.J., Bonneux L, Polder J.J., Koopmanschap MA, van der Mnass P.J. (1998) Demographic and epidemiological determinants of healthcare costs in Netherlands: cost of illness study. *Br. Med. J.*, **317**: 111–115.
4. National Health Service Executive (1996) *Burdens of Disease*, NHSE, Leeds.
5. Patel A., Knapp M.R.J. (1998) Costs of mental illness in England. *Ment. Health Res. Rev.*, **5**: 4–10.
6. Crino R.D. (1999) Obsessive-compulsive spectrum disorders. *Curr. Opin. Psychiatry*, **12**: 151–155.
7. Austin L.S. Lydiard R.B., Fossey M.D. (1990) Panic and phobic disorders in patients with obsessive compulsive and other anxiety disorders. *J. Clin. Psychiatry*, **51**: 456–458.
8. Eisen J.L., Rasmussen S.A. (1989) Coexisting obsessive-compulsive disorder and alcoholism. *J. Clin. Psychiatry*, **50**: 96–98.
9. Regier D.A., Myers J.K., Kramer M. (1984) The NIMH Epidemiologic Catchment Area Program: historical context, major obstacles, and study population characteristics. *Arch. Gen. Psychiatry*, **41**: 934–941.
10. Meltzer H., Gill B., Pettigrew M., Hinds K. (1995) *OPCS Surveys of Psychiatric Morbidity in Great Britain. Report 1: The Prevalence of Psychiatric Morbidity among Adults Living in Private Households*, OPCS, London.
11. Goodwin S. (1997) *Comparative Mental Health Policy: from Institutional to Community Care*, Sage, London.
12. Narrow W.E., Regier D.A., Rae D.S., Manderscheid R.W., Locke B.Z. (1993) Use of services by persons with mental and addictive disorders: findings from the National Institute of Mental Health Epidemiologic Catchment Area Program. *Arch. Gen. Psychiatry*, **50**: 95–107.
13. Regier D.A., Narrow W.E., Rae D.S., Manderscheid R.W., Locke B.Z., Goodwin F.K. (1993) The defacto US mental and addictive disorders service system: epidemiologic catchment area prospective 1-year prevalence rates of disorders and services. *Arch. Gen. Psychiatry*, **50**: 85–94.
14. Hollander E. (1997) Obsessive compulsive disorder: the hidden epidemic. *J. Clin. Psychiatry*, **58**: 3–6.
15. Patel A., Henderson J., Knapp M.R.J. (2000) The costs of obsessive compulsive disorder (submitted for publication).
16. Leon A.C., Porter L., Weissman M.M. (1995) The social costs of anxiety disorders. *Br. J. Psychiatry*, **166**: 19–22.
17. McCusker J., Boulenger J.P., Boyer R., Bellavance F., Miller J.M. (1997) Use of health services for anxiety disorders: a multisite study in Quebec. *Can. J. Psychiatry*, **42**: 730–736.
18. Kavanagh S.M., Knapp M.R.J. (1995) Market rationales, rationing and rationality? Mental health care reform in England. *Health Affairs*, **14**: 260–268.
19. Jenkins R. (1985) Minor psychiatric disorder in employed men and women and its contribution to sickness absence. *Br. J. Industrial Med.*, **42**: 147–154.
20. Foster K., Meltzer H., Gill B., Hinds K. (1996) *Adults with a psychotic disorder living in the community*, OPCS Survey of Psychiatric Morbidity Report 8, HMSO, London.

21. Henderson J.G., Pollard C.A. (1988) Three types of obsessive compulsive disorder in a community sample. *J. Clin. Psychol.*, **44**: 747–752.
22. Steketee G., Grayson J.B., Foa E.B. (1987) A comparison of characteristics of obsessive-compulsive disorder and other anxiety disorders. *J. Anxiety Disord.*, **1**: 325–335.
23. Karno M., Golding J.M., Sorenson S.B., Burnam M.A. (1988) The epidemiology of obsessive-compulsive disorder in five US communities. *Arch. Gen. Psychiatry*, **45**: 1094–1099.
24. Steketee G. (1997) Disability and family burden in obsessive-compulsive disorder. *Can. J. Psychiatry*, **42**: 919–928.
25. Dupont R.L., Rice D.P., Shivaki S., Rowland C.R. (1995) Economic costs of obsessive compulsive disorder. *Medical Interface*, **89**: 102–109.
26. Calvocoressi L., Lewis B., Harris M., Trufan S.J., Goodman W.K., McDougle C.J., Price L.H. (1995) Family accommodation in obsessive compulsive disorder. *Am. J. Psychiatry*, **152**: 441–443.
27. Bellodi L., Sciuto G., Diaferia G., Ronchi P., Smeraldi E. (1992) Psychiatric disorders in the families of patients with obsessive-compulsive disorder. *Psychiatry Res.*, **42**: 111–120.
28. Cooper M. (1996) Obsessive-compulsive disorder: effects on family members. *Am. J. Orthopsychiatry*, **66**: 296–304.
29. Chakrabarti S., Kulhara P., Verma S.K. (1993) The pattern of burden in families of neurotic patients. *Soc. Psychiatry Psychiatr. Epidemiol.*, **28**: 172–177.
30. Netten A., Knight J., Dennett J. (1999) *Unit Costs of Health and Social Care*, PSSRU, University of Kent at Canterbury.
31. Drummond M.F., O'Brien B., Stoddart G.L., Torrance G.W. (1997) *Methods for the Economic Evaluation of Health Care Programmes*, Oxford Medical Publications, Oxford.
32. Koopmanschap M.A., Rutten F.F.H., van Ineveld B.M., van Roijen L. (1995) The friction cost method for measuring indirect costs of disease. *J. Health Economics*, **14**: 171–189.
33. Rice D.P., Kelman S., Miller L.S. (1990) *The Economic Costs of Alcohol and Drug Abuse and Mental Illness: 1985*. Publication No. (ADM) 90-1694, Alcohol, Drug Abuse and Mental Health Administration, Rockville.
34. Fifer S.K., Mathias S.D., Patrick D.L., Mazonson P.D., Lubeck D.P., Buesching D.P. (1994) Untreated anxiety among adult primary care patients in a health maintenance organization. *Arch. Gen. Psychiatry*, **51**: 740–750.
35. Stein D.J., Roberts M., Hollander E., Rowland C., Serebro P. (1996) Quality of life and pharmaco-economic aspects of obsessive-compulsive disorder: a South African study. *South African Med. J.*, **86**: 1579–1585.
36. Hollander E., Kwon J.H., Stein D.J., Broatch J., Rowland C.T., Himelein C.A. (1996) Obsessive-compulsive and spectrum disorders: overview and quality of life issues. *J. Clin. Psychiatry*, **57** (suppl. 8): 3–6.

Commentaries

6.1
Considering the Full Economic Burden

Myrna M. Weissman[1]

The 1990s have brought new information on the economic burden and disability related to mental disorders, including obsessive-compulsive disorder (OCD), worldwide [1]. Moreover, epidemiologic studies show the similarities in rates and patterns of many psychiatric disorders, including OCD, across diverse cultures [2]. The findings of both of these efforts for OCD are useful in considering economic costs.

The World Health Organization (WHO), in collaboration with the World Bank and Harvard University [1], attempted to move from mortality rates, as a traditional outcome of the health status of the population, to measures of the overall economic burden and disability produced by disease. The results suggest that the burden of psychiatric conditions have been heavily underestimated. The key aim of the Global Burden of Disease project was to quantify the combined burden of fatal and non-fatal health outcomes in a single measure, called the "disability-adjusted life year" or DALY. To calculate a DALY due to a disease or an injury in a given year in a population, the researchers added together the years of life lost through all deaths in that year and years of life expected to be lived with the disability for the conditions in that year, summed and weighted for the severity of the condition. Of the 10 leading causes of disability worldwide in 1990, measured as years lived with the disability, five were psychiatric conditions. OCD was tenth on the list, accounting for 2.2% of the total estimate of disability worldwide. Among women aged 15–44, OCD was the fifth of the 10 leading causes of disease, in both developing and developed countries. The rates were higher in developed countries. The predominance of psychiatric disorders, including OCD, in estimates of years lived with a disability, may have to do with the early age of onset and the recurring nature of those disorders.

Separate epidemiologic studies conducted in seven countries (United States, Canada, Puerto Rico, Germany, Taiwan, Korea and New Zealand)

[1] *Division of Clinical and Genetic Epidemiology, New York State Psychiatric Institute, 1051 Riverside Drive – Unit 24, New York, NY 10032, USA*

showed a remarkably consistent lifetime prevalence of OCD, around 2%, with a mean age of onset in the mid to late 20s, and a slightly higher prevalence in females. In all the countries studied, the persons with OCD had a substantially greater than chance risk of also having comorbid depression and other anxiety disorders [2]. Comorbidity is not reflected in the WHO disability estimates. The remarkable consistency in rates, age of onset and comorbidity of OCD across quite diverse cultures further supports the validity of the OCD diagnosis internationally.

A separate analysis of the epidemiologic data from the United States showed that patients with OCD had significantly higher rates of conduct disturbances, adult antisocial personality disorder and suicide attempts, when compared to persons with no disorders [3]. These findings suggest that there is a subgroup of OCD patients who may have impulsive features, including childhood conduct disorder and increased risk of suicide. Again, these findings are not reflected in economic estimates.

The WHO data and the community-based epidemiologic studies show the worldwide burden of OCD, underscore the complexities of estimating economic cost, and suggest that economic projections are probably underestimates. Economic estimates framed as cost offset, demand and supply and disease burden can not be readily translated into patients' lives. Is the true cost of the illness and the human capital loss captured by market earnings alone for the young mother with a psychiatric illness? Human capital loss measured as discounted future earnings does not include the health consequences of her illness on her children. In no other branch of medicine are these questions as important as with mental disorders, where there are few biological measurements to determine patient outcomes. This is not a call to abandon the excellent efforts which have been made to estimate costs, but to realize the limitation of current information. A challenge ahead is to develop economic concepts which capture the full clinical reality of psychiatric illness and its treatment and to put a clinical face on the economic data.

REFERENCES

1. Murray C.L., Lopez A.D. (Eds) (1996) *The Global Burden of Disease*, World Health Organization, Geneva.
2. Weissman M.M., Bland R.C., Canino G.J., Greenwald S., Hwu H.-G., Lee C.K., Newman S.C., Oakley-Browne M.A., Rubio-Stipec M., Wickramaratne P.J. *et al* (1994) The cross national epidemiology of obsessive compulsive disorder. The Cross National Collaborative Group. *J. Clin. Psychiatry*, **55** (suppl. 3): 5–10.
3. Hollander E., Greenwald S., Neville D., Johnson J., Hornig C.D., Weissman M.M. (1996/1997) Uncomplicated and comorbid obsessive-compulsive disorder in an epidemiologic sample. *Depression and Anxiety*, **4**: 111–119.

6.2 The Economics of Obsessive-Compulsive Disorder: Achieving the Potential Benefit

Mark Aveline[1]

Martin Knapp and his colleagues have made the most of a difficult brief. Asked to evaluate the economics of obsessive-compulsive disorder (OCD), they are in the position of proud hosts at a cookery demonstration, eager to show off the latest techniques, demonstrate how succulent, sustaining results can be achieved, and generally give their guests a good time. Sadly, they are unable to set the date for the event itself. The food—the micro-economic studies of therapeutic interventions in OCD, in particular—has not been prepared and there is no certainty about when it will be ready. Faced with this reality, they have written an excellent overview of the methodologies of macro- and micro-economic analyses and their potential benefits. As a commentator, I find myself in the same dilemma about what to write. My resolution, like theirs, is to concentrate on what could be and should be but largely from a clinical perspective.

To suffer from OCD is to live a life of constraint. Simple activities of daily living are rendered fraught by fearful anticipations that disaster will strike unless action is taken to make safe that person's life and the lives of the people who populate it. Obsessive ruminations and compulsive rituals identify respectively the concern and the attempted defence. What should be easy and matter of fact is potentially hazardous and has to be controlled; life slows down. When, as is often the case, the ratchet of anxiety tightens, such a degree of hesitation may so feature in the sufferers' life that they are unable to complete, for example, the simple, first event of the day: getting up and getting dressed. Their day can stop at that point. Inevitably, the family is affected too. Family members may either be tethered by the spider's web of anxiety and control, compromising their freedom through a progressive collusion with the obsessive's demands, or, from a position of incomprehension and frustration, look on impotently and with increasing alienation at strange practices.

Government policy in the UK on mental health by specialist psychiatric providers gives priority to "enduring mental illness", which is largely interpreted as being psychosis, pre-eminently schizophrenia. To my regret, this has led to a neglect of care for those with neurosis. The chronic and handicapping nature of neurosis is not fully recognized by the planners, who are over-influenced by the perception of personal and political risk of harm to the public from psychotics. The macro-analyses presented by Knapp *et al* document the substantial, pervasive and persistent cost of OCD. In a

[1] *Nottingham Psychotherapy Unit, 114 Thorneywood Mount, Nottingham NG3 2PZ, UK*

1-year period in the USA, service utilization was substantial [1]. 17% of people with OCD had a psychiatric admission; they accounted for 18% of all mental health admissions. In general, OCD patients showed an above-average rate of use of primary and secondary health care services [2] and had lower educational achievements and employment rates compared to other mental disorders and those without [3]. Even allowing for difference in practice between nations and the confounding effect of comorbidity, the morbidity highlighted is certainly not trivial, the more so as lesser degrees of OCD are often hidden from view, being contained within single-person and family units, although not without emotional and financial cost. As Knapp *et al* describe, these economic studies, when combined, total the "burden-of-disease" or "cost-of-illness"; the result dramatically quantifies significant cost, which is far more than the direct cost of treatment. In arguing for resources, we, clinicians, need to keep that larger perspective in view.

The dearth of cost–effectiveness, cost–benefit and cost–utility studies in OCD clearly needs to be remedied. I fully agree with Knapp *et al*'s statement, "Economic evaluation in the mental health field is not intended to replace the expert or experienced judgement of the individual doctor", but, when "scarcity prompts choice", economic analysis may suggest how maximum benefit can be achieved for particular expenditures of resource. To achieve this added value from economic analyses, careful attention needs to be given, in my view, to the following parameters:

1. *Explicit diagnostic focus.* OCD constitutes a clearly defined cluster of symptoms, but comorbidity is common. One US survey reported nearly half of people with OCD having a phobic disorder (47%), a third a major depressive disorder (32%) and a quarter substance abuse (24%) [4]. Studies of both the pure condition and, more usefully, the common comorbid patterns, are indicated.
2. *Clinically relevant.* This point follows on from the first. Efficacy outcome studies tend to over-state the effect size for a given treatment and hence are not a good base for policy making. The benchmark should be to test clinical effectiveness, through more naturalistic trials that are close to clinical practice [5]; this is sometimes called representative clinical research [6, 7].
3. *Whose outcome is to be given priority?* In most disorders, the sufferer, the clinician and society (which includes the family) have differing but equally valid perspectives on what constitutes a good outcome. In OCD, is a numerical reduction in checking behaviour a sufficient indicator of improvement? Is there a better marker of function in that person's social group?
4. *Comparisons of the relative effects of various strategies for preventing important health outcomes.* Woolf argues against the current pattern of the

myriad trials which quantify the effects of treatment on selected endpoints [8]. Instead, he ambitiously proposes the establishment of a national bibliographic database and the construction of simulation models of the potential benefits and harms of competing interventions for populations and individuals. I foresee that a marriage of such models with economic analysis would be especially fruitful.

5. *Greater clarity and uniformity in the base used for the economic analysis.* Wolff *et al* [9] calculated unit costs for a hypothetical outpatient service with different assumptions for management, accountant, and economist perspectives. Not surprisingly, there was substantial variation, e.g. the cost of an outpatient hour varying from $108 to $538. No perspective is *per se* best, but clinicians and economists need to debate and agree in the planning stage of the evaluation what the perspective is to be and why.

These parameters are of general relevance with no absolute answers; they are not just for OCD. Their implementation requires close discussion and agreement between clinicians, clinical researchers and economists. Once done, we would be many steps closer to realising the potential benefits of economic analysis.

REFERENCES

1. Regier D.A., Narrow W.E., Rae D.S., Mandersheid R.W., Locke B.Z., Goodwin F.K. (1993) The *de facto* US mental and addictive disorders service system: Epidemiologic Catchment Area prospective 1-year prevalence rates of disorders and services. *Arch. Gen. Psychiatry*, **50**: 85–94.
2. Leon A.C., Porter L., Weissman M.M. (1995) The social costs of anxiety disorders. *Br. J. Psychiatry*, **166**: 19–22.
3. Foster K., Meltzer H., Gill B., Hinds K. (1996) *Adults with a Psychotic Disorder Living in the Community*, OPCS Survey of Psychiatric Morbidity, Report 8, HMSO, London.
4. Karno M., Golding J.M., Sorenson S.B., Burnham M.A. (1988) The epidemiology of OCD in five US communities. *Arch. Gen. Psychiatry*, **45**: 1094–1099.
5. Howard K.I., Orlinsky D.E., Lueger R.J. (1995) The design of clinically relevant outcome research: some considerations and examples. In *Research Foundations for Psychotherapy Practice* (Eds M. Aveline, D. Shapiro) pp. 3–47, Wiley, London.
6. Shadish W.R., Navarro A.M., Crits-Christoph P., Jorm A.F., Nietzl M.T., Robinson L., Svartberg M., Matt G.E., Siegle G., Hazelrigg M.D. *et al* (1997) Evidence that therapy works in clinically representative situations. *J. Consult. Clin. Psychol.*, **55**: 355–365.
7. Weisz J.R., Weiss B., Donenberg E.R. (1992) The lab versus the clinic: effects of child and adolescent psychotherapy. *Am. Psychol.*, **47**: 1578–1585.
8. Woolf S.H. (1999) The need for perspective in evidence-based medicine. *JAMA*, **282**: 2358–2365.

9. Wolff N., Helminiak T.W., Tebes J.K. (1997) Getting the cost right in cost-effectiveness analysis. *Am. J. Psychiatry*, **154**: 736–743.

6.3
In Search of Data on Costs of Obsessive-Compulsive Disorder

Gail Steketee[1]

Knapp *et al* have outlined the remarkable scarcity of information about economic costs associated with obsessive-compulsive disorder (OCD) and the even more surprising absence of significant efforts to evaluate costs and benefits associated with standard treatments that have been available for some time. Most clinicians who regularly treat this condition are very familiar with the extensive costs that many patients with OCD and their family members endure, including direct out-of-pocket expenditures and loss of income. These, of course, are in addition to suffering, impairment in daily activities and family turmoil that cannot easily be counted monetarily. Knapp *et al*'s review points to a number of problems associated with cost accounting, and provides information about OCD and its treatment that is illuminating. A few areas of interest are addressed below.

The authors rightly point to the problem of comorbidity as potentially exaggerating the costs associated with any given disorder. For OCD, comorbidity is substantial, most often encompassing major depression, other anxiety disorders, and personality disorders (especially avoidant and dependent). These disorders may, by themselves, induce sufferers to seek more than usual amounts of health care services. Such comorbid conditions may also interfere with treatment continuation and benefit [1], further complicating cost–benefit analyses of treatments. It is also worth noting that nearly all studies of OCD and its comorbidity typically exclude patients with comorbid psychotic disorders, conditions that can render patients heavy users of mental health services. In addition, in severe forms with somatic obsessions, OCD may co-occur with, or even lead to, medical conditions. In such cases, serious bodily damage can be caused by repeated checking rituals, and repeated contacts with health care providers are common. Thus, comorbidity and special forms of OCD may be responsible for substantially increasing health and mental health care costs associated with the disorder and its treatment. It is hardly surprising that such conditions also add frequency, length and cost to hospital stays.

[1] *264 Bay State Road, Boston, MA 02215, USA*

Among the findings reported by Knapp *et al*, it is interesting to observe the consistency across United States outpatient settings in the average number of visits to mental health settings. These ranged from 14 for private practitioners to 19 for psychiatric hospital outpatient care. Not surprisingly, fewer visits (5–11) occurred in outpatient health care contexts that were equipped to provide repeated care. Interestingly, OCD clients were not heavy users of crisis medical care, but did report regularly to general practitioners. In this regard, findings by Friedman *et al* [2] are useful in identifying OCD clients, especially in minority populations, who have not received a formal diagnosis but who are frequent users of health care. These researchers found that 15% of dermatology clinic patients met diagnostic criteria for OCD, mainly for contamination fears and washing/cleaning rituals. They had not sought mental health treatment, apparently preferring to treat the effects of OCD rather than its source. It is not hard to conclude that other forms of obsessions and rituals (e.g. somatic obsessions, fears of harming others) and related disorders (trichotillomania, body dysmorphic disorder) would lead sufferers to seek repeated medical consultation without coming to the attention of the mental health system.

Another problem that may especially increase service utilization and costs not captured in analyses of health and mental health services is hoarding, which appears to be related to OCD but is distinct from OCD symptoms [3]. Our experience in working with this condition suggests that it occurs with serious consequences in many who never receive an OCD diagnosis, as well as in approximately 20% of those with an OCD diagnosis. For individuals with hoarding problems, costs include not only health and mental health services, but also housing and public health costs and services [4]. In extreme cases, homes are cleaned out and/or demolished at taxpayers' expense. Hoarding appears to be particularly problematic among the elderly, where multiple social service organizations (e.g. protective care, case management, visiting nurse service, homemaker services) become extensively involved in addressing the problem [5]. Such private and public expenditures must also be evaluated in cost analyses of OCD non-hoarders, as well.

Under- or unemployment has obvious direct costs to the individual with OCD, to dependent family members and to the public which pays for disability benefits. Of course, this type of cost accounting does not address the sometimes extensive emotional costs to sufferers and families. Hardships incurred by family members may impair family relationships and undermine important resources for coping. Calvocoressi *et al* [6], as well as others, have highlighted substantial family accommodation to OCD symptoms which is linked to greater family distress and may have family economic costs as well. Further, such family accommodation may adversely influence treatment outcomes, although this has not yet been tested.

Perhaps most importantly, Knapp and colleagues point to the surprising lack of evaluation of the costs and benefits of treatments for OCD using any of several methodologies outlined by these authors. We also drew similar conclusions in reviewing this literature recently [7]. This absence of research is quite surprising, given the substantial costs associated with OCD and debates in mental health circles regarding the most cost effective treatments for this disorder (mainly selective serotonin reuptake inhibitors and cognitive-behavioral psychotherapy). We concur with the authors' call to add cost analyses to our outcome research agenda, with an eye toward determining how best to serve patients, families and the public interest.

REFERENCES

1. Steketee G., Chambless D.L., Tran G. Effects of Axis I and II comorbidity on behavior therapy outcome for obsessive compulsive disorder and agoraphobia (submitted for publication).
2. Friedman S., Hatch M., Paradis C.M., Popkin M., Schalita A.R. (1995) Obsessive compulsive disorders in two black ethnic groups: incidence in an urban dermatology clinic. *J. Anxiety Disord.*, **7**: 343–348.
3. Frost R.O., Steketee G. (1998) Hoarding: clinical aspects and treatment strategies. In *Obsessive-Compulsive Disorders: Practical Management* (Eds M. Jenike, L. Baer, W. Minichiello), pp. 533–554, Mosby, Chicago.
4. Frost R.O., Steketee G., Williams L. Hoarding: a community health problem (submitted for publication).
5. Kim H.-J., Steketee G., Frost R.O. (2000) Hoarding in the elderly. *Health and Social Work*, in press.
6. Calvocoressi L., Mazure C.M., Kasl S.V., Skolnick J., Fisk D., Vegso S.J., Van Noppen B., Price L.H. (1999) Family accommodation of obsessive compulsive symptoms: instrument development and assessment of family behavior. *J. Nerv. Ment. Dis.*, **187**: 636–642.
7. Steketee G., Frost R.O. (1998) Cost-effective behavior therapy for obsessive-compulsive disorder. In *Behavior and Cognitive Therapy Today: Essays in Honor of Hans J. Eysenck* (Ed. E. Sanavio), pp. 289–304, Elsevier, Oxford.

6.4
Obsessive Slowness in Creating a Cost–Effectiveness Evidence Base for Obsessive-Compulsive Disorder

Graham Thornicroft[1]

The current paradigm of evidence-based medicine (EBM) assumes for its successful application a degree of maturity across a field of scientific

[1] *Health Services Research Department, Institute of Psychiatry, De Crespigny Park, London SE5 8AF, UK*

enquiry that in some cases does not in fact exist [1–3]. For its full implementation, this approach requires a series of well-conducted studies, usually randomized controlled trials, which are suitable for systemic review, alongside measures of treatment costs, so that cost–benefit interpretations can be drawn. What is striking about the outstanding review by Knapp *et al* is that while EBM has been successfully applied to many of the major categories of mental disorder, there are also diagnostic hinterlands which are so far largely unexplored. Obsessive-compulsive disorder (OCD) is a clear example of such virgin territory.

Why should we find so little evidence to answer questions on what are cost-effective interventions for OCD? First, until relatively recently OCD was assumed to be rare, and population annual prevalence rates of 0.05% were cited [4]. Better-quality ascertainment procedures have shown more recently that obsessive symptoms are common (prevalence of 7% and 12% for men and women, respectively) as are compulsions (5% and 8%) in the general population [5]. The OCD syndrome is also far more common than previously thought, with the same rate of 1.3% reported for the 1-month prevalence period used in the Epidemiologic Catchment Area (ECA) study [6] and for the British Office of Population Censuses and Surveys (OPCS) National Survey of Psychiatric Morbidity [5]. The first reason for the scientific neglect of this area, therefore, appears to be gross underestimate of the occurrence of the disorder.

Second, the disorder seems to have a low profile in the literature in parallel with its relatively low priority within psychiatric clinical practice. Although common in the general population, the large majority of cases are only ever seen within primary care [7], despite the fact that the outcome is poor in at least a third of cases [8, 9]. In this respect (and in the pattern of early adult onset) OCD mirrors schizophrenia, although perhaps the differences are more illuminating than the similarities. People suffering from the symptoms of OCD may be less likely to arouse concern from family and friends, because the disordered behaviours are different in quantity but not in quality from what is considered normal. Further, sufferers may be housebound by the nature of the condition itself. Third, although distressing to family members, the features of OCD are not usually unpredictable, quite the reverse, and so family members may habituate to the demands of OCD sufferers, rather than seek help on their behalf. In clinical practice it is common to disregard patients presenting with the symptoms of OCD, because they co-occur with other mental disorders to which greater clinical salience is attached. OCD features, for example, may occur in up to one in three cases of unipolar depression [10].

Evidence of treatment effectiveness has been consolidated over the last two decades, and for much of this period has largely emphasized behavioural or cognitive-behavioural psychological treatments [11, 12]. The case for the independent effect of pharmacological treatments, beyond their antidepressant activity, has been established only relatively recently [13], until when there was an associated lack of commercial research and development investment.

Should we now consider the more disabling forms of OCD as types of "severe mental illness" (SMI)? SMI has been applied as category to support research, treatment and policy prioritisation, usually referring to people with psychotic disorders [14]. In fact, many people suffering from non-psychotic disorders are more severely disabled than some who have milder degrees of psychotic illness. A recent population-based study in Verona, Italy, for example, found that annual period prevalence rates of SMI were 1.34/1000 for psychotic and a further 0.98/1000 for non-psychotic disorders, giving a total prevalence rate of SMI of 2.33/1000 for all disorders (where the criterion for disability was a Global Assessment of Functioning (GAF) score of 50 or less and for duration was greater than 2 years). The proportion of all prevalent non-organic psychotic cases which fulfilled the SMI criteria was 40%, whereas, among all non-psychotic cases, 9% fulfilled the criteria for SMI [15].

OCD, therefore, presents an outstanding opportunity for future research into both cost-effective treatments (psychological, pharmacological or combined) and into service delivery systems which offer affordable value-for-money.

REFERENCES

1. Chalmers I., Enkin M., Keirse M.J. (1993) Preparing and updating systematic reviews of randomized controlled trials of health care. *Millbank Quarterly*, **71**: 411–437.
2. Kassirer J.P. (1993) Clinical trials and meta-analysis. What do they do for us? *N. Engl. J. Med.*, **327**: 273–274.
3. Sackett D., Rosenberg W., Muir Gray J., Haynes R., Richardson W. (1996) Evidence based medicine: what it is and what it isn't. *Br. Med. J.*, **312**: 71–72.
4. Black A. (1974) The natural history of obsessional neurosis. In *Obsessional States* (Ed. H. Beech), pp. 79–91, Methuen, London.
5. Melzer H., Gill B., Pettigrew M. (1995) *The Prevalence of Psychiatric Morbidity among Adults Aged 16–64 Living in Private Households in Great Britain*, OPCS Survey of Psychiatric Morbidity in Great Britain. Report No. 1. HMSO, London.
6. Robins L., Regier D. (1991) *Psychiatric Disorders in America: the Epidemiologic Catchment Area Study*, Free Press, New York.
7. Narrow W., Regier D., Rae D., Manderscheid R., Locke B. (1993) Use of services by persons with mental and addictive disorders: findings form the National Institute of Mental Health Epidemiologic Catchment Areas Program. *Arch. Gen. Psychiatry*, **50**: 95–107.
8. Goodwin S., Guze S., Robins E. (1969) Follow-up of mental illness in a total population. In *Psychiatric Epidemiology* (Eds E. Hare, J. Wing), pp. 154–172, Oxford University Press, Oxford.

9. Rasmussen R., Tsuang T. (1986) Clinical characteristics and family history in DSM-III obsessive-compulsive disorder. *Am. J. Psychiatry*, **143**: 469.
10. Coryell W. (1981) Obsessive compulsive disorder and primary unipolar depression. *J. Nerv. Ment. Dis.*, **169**: 220–224.
11. Marks I., O'Sullivan G. (1989) Anti-anxiety drugs and psychological treatment effects in agoraphobia/panic and obsessive-compulsive disorders. In *Psychopharmacology of Anxiety* (Ed. P. Tyrer), pp. 196–242, Oxford University Press, Oxford.
12. Thornicroft G., Colson L., Marks I. (1990) A behavioural psychotherapy unit. Description and audit. *Br. J. Psychiatry*, **158**: 362–367.
13. Mavissakalian M., Turner S., Michelson L., Jacob R. (1985) Tricylic antidepressants in obsessive compulsive disorder: anti-obsessional or anti-depressant agents. *Am. J. Psychiatry*, **142**: 572.
14. Schinnar A.P., Rothbard A.B., Kanter R., Jung Y.S. (1990) An empirical literature review of definitions of severe and persistent mental illness. *Am. J. Psychiatry*, **147**: 1602–1608.
15. Ruggeri M., Leese M., Thornicroft G., Bisoffi G. Tansella G. (2000) The definition and prevalence of severe and persistent mental illness. *Br. J. Psychiatry*, in press.

6.5
Evaluations of Treatments for Obsessive-Compulsive Disorder: the Need for Health Economics Input

Paul McCrone[1]

Obsessive-compulsive disorder (OCD) is a debilitating illness that affects a substantial number of people. In fact, any estimates of the prevalence of the disorder are probably underestimates, because individuals are sometimes reluctant to seek treatment and OCD may go undiagnosed. In their review, Knapp *et al* identify the main economic impacts of OCD. These are: (a) the use of mental health services; (b) the use of other formal care services; (c) lost employment and education; (d) care provided by family and friends; (e) mortality and (f) welfare benefits. They report findings from two large surveys—one in the USA and the other in the UK—which revealed that people with OCD have relatively high levels of service use (inpatient care and ambulatory services), experience adverse effects in their work performance, receive high levels of welfare benefits, and have a relatively high suicide rate. Figures are provided from a study by Dupont *et al* [1] showing that the total cost of OCD to the US economy was $8.4 billion in 1990.

[1] *Health Services Research Department, Institute of Psychiatry, De Crespigny Park, London SE5 8AF, UK*

Although this is less than the $33 billion associated with schizophrenia, it is still substantial.

The authors correctly point out that knowing what the overall cost of an illness is does not indicate whether services are being provided in an ethical and efficient manner, but it does help to focus attention on the fact that OCD is expensive, and this should be a spur for evaluation of different methods of dealing with it. As with most health problems, there are alternative forms of treatment available and it is important to know which forms are most effective and efficient. We live in a world of scarce health care resources, because peoples' desire for health status improvement is generally unlimited, but the money that is available to achieve such improvements is finite. It is therefore crucial that evaluations include an economic component, so that the cost implications of competing services can be observed. Clearly it would be a serious error to focus only on costs. However, it is also wrong to neglect them—to do so would imply that scarcity does not exist. Instead, evaluations of new, or indeed existing but untested, interventions should *combine* cost information with that on effectiveness. Health economics has a number of tools available which enables this process to take place, and Knapp *et al* provide a clear summary of these.

Unfortunately, to date there have been no evaluations of specific services that have included an economic evaluation. This is not because health economics is rarely used in mental health research (although this certainly once was true), but because most studies seem to have focused on specific disorders, notably depression and schizophrenia. The absence of any economic studies in Knapp *et al*'s review mirrors previous reviews [2, 3], and it is a finding which to a greater or lesser extent applies to other conditions such as panic disorder and post-traumatic stress disorder. Why is this so? One reason could be that illnesses such as OCD are often less visible than those like schizophrenia which, although affecting fewer people, attract more attention. Another reason could be that OCD and other anxiety disorders are not seen to be as serious as others, even though in reality their effects can be devastating.

Ironically, there is great potential for utilizing some of the more innovative aspects of health economics in the evaluation of OCD. The use of quality-adjusted life years (QALYs) is a good example. QALYs rely on utility values being attached to different health care states, say before and after treatment, and these values fall within the range 0 (minimum utility) to 1 (maximum utility). Arriving at utility values is a complex procedure and probably unsuitable for use in evaluations of services for patients with psychotic conditions (where many economic evaluations have been performed). On the other hand, it seems that QALYs might work well with people who have non-psychotic conditions like OCD. This might also be the case for valuing treatment outcomes using the contingent valuation approach, where patients are asked to state how much they would hypothetically be willing to pay for a treatment if it resulted in a particular outcome.

To date, health economics has not been used in evaluations of treatments for OCD and this means that health care resources could be being used in an inefficient (even wasteful) way. What then is the way forward? The responsibility of redressing this problem rests with three groups. First, those that fund research—especially governments—must insist that trials of pharmaceutical and psychological services include a health economic component. Second, clinicians and others actually providing treatments should be concerned to know whether their already stretched budgets are being put to the best possible use. Third, health economists themselves must be proactive in pushing forward the techniques that they possess into this area of research. Elsewhere in mental health care this has happened and there is no fundamental reason why OCD should not be next.

REFERENCES

1. Dupont R.L., Rice D.P., Shivaki S., Rowland C.R. (1995) Economic costs of obsessive compulsive disorder. *Med. Interface*, **89**: 102–109.
2. Evers S.M.A.A., van Wijk A.S., Ament A.J.H.A. (1997) Economic evaluation of mental health care interventions. A review. *Health Economics*, **6**: 161–177.
3. McCrone P., Weich S. (1995) Mental health care costs: paucity of measurement. *Soc. Psychiatry Psychiatr. Epidemiol.*, **31**: 70–77.

6.6
Obsessive-Compulsive Disorder: a Psychiatric Disorder in Economic No Man's Land

Peter Tyrer[1]

The review by Knapp *et al* nicely summarizes the importance of economic studies of common mental disorders, of which obsessive-compulsive disorder (OCD), affecting about 2% of the population [1, 2], is one. They give a powerful argument for cost–effectiveness studies at a time in which the notion of rationing in health services is no longer regarded as unacceptable. As Dorothy Warnock [3] has recently put it in connection with the UK National Health Service, "We have to acknowledge that some things cannot be afforded and that, therefore, private as well as public money may have to

[1] *Department of Public Mental Health, Imperial College School of Medicine, Paterson Centre, 20 South Wharf Road, London W2 1PD UK*

be expended on health care provision, with the means test (by a more acceptable name) becoming once again an acceptable phenomenon. Alongside this, we must learn not to throw up our hands in horror when something is described as not being cost-effective''.

Unfortunately, as Knapp *et al* move on to the subject matter of OCD, they look almost in vain for studies that examine the economic aspects of the subject at either the macro- or micro-level. The reason for this seems to be the unusual position of OCD in both the classification of psychiatric disorders and service provision. It is the forgotten outsider, which is embraced by those keen on pharmacological interventions (particularly at present in the war of too many antidepressants) despite limited evidence that they have much effect in the longer term [4], but is generally ignored by epidemiologists, apart from important exceptions [5].

Why should this be so? Knapp *et al* point out the universal problem of comorbidity, an agnostic description of association that makes it impossible to distinguish between what the economist would like to see as primary core conditions and secondary ones which can be viewed as complications of the primary one. OCD is more homogeneous than most non-psychotic disorders, but it still has a marked degree of comorbidity, as the authors point out, particularly with personality disorders (rates of up to 75% [6]), and this comorbidity significantly increases the costs of care [7].

However, this does not account for OCD being so isolated in economic research. I judge that the main problem is that the condition is, as pointed out in the review, a severe one with frequent hospital attendance and yet it is placed with the anxiety disorders in the classification system. At the same time, OCD is not usually judged to be a ''severe mental illness'' (except by epidemiologists who recognize it to be in their discipline [8]) and, unlike conditions such as schizophrenia and bipolar affective disorder, it is still possible to suffer for years without having any contact with psychiatric services.

When Knapp *et al* discuss the ''funded demand'' that forces neglected disorders to the attention of planners of psychiatric services, they acknowledge the importance of collective action which is, in the last resort, political rather than scientific (or in the language of today, needs-led). OCD sufferers are not good at collective action, as they are usually isolated individuals, and each has his own unique pedantry that does not lead to compromise and the force of collective action. So, in spite of the hints from this review that OCD is a condition with high economic costs that might be reduced with more aggressive treatment, I suspect that we will continue to see the subject as like Switzerland in Europe, belonging neither to one group nor the other, having a tendency towards introspection and isolation, and that OCD will continue to be overlooked in the grand scheme of economic assessments, unless we force it to come to our attention.

REFERENCES

1. Kolada J.L., Bland R.C., Newman S.C. (1994) Epidemiology of psychiatric disorders in Edmonton. Obsessive-compulsive disorder. *Acta Psychiatr. Scand*, **89** (suppl. 376): 24–35.
2. Sasson Y., Zohar J., Chopra M., Lustig M., Iancu I., Hendler T. (1997) Epidemiology of obsessive-compulsive disorder: a world view. *J. Clin. Psychiatry*, **58** (suppl. 12): 7–10.
3. Warnock D. (1998) Ethics, ideology and rationing in the NHS. *J. Roy. Coll. Physicians*, **32**: 118–120.
4. O'Sullivan G., Noshirvani H., Marks I., Monteiro W., Lelliott P. (1991) Six-year follow-up after exposure and clomipramine therapy for obsessive compulsive disorder. *J. Clin. Psychiatry*, **52**: 150–155.
5. Nestadt G., Romanoski A.J., Brown C.H., Chahal R., Merchant A., Folstein M.F., Gruenberg E.M., McHugh P.R. (1991) DSM-III compulsive personality disorder: an epidemiological survey. *Psychol. Med.*, **21**: 461–471.
6. Bejerot S., Ekselius L., von Knorring L. (1998) Comorbidity between obsessive-compulsive disorder (OCD) and personality disorders. *Acta Psychiatr. Scand.*, **97**: 398–402.
7. AuBuchon P.G., Malatesta V.J. (1994) Obsessive compulsive patients with comorbid personality disorder: associated problems and response to a comprehensive behavior therapy. *J. Clin. Psychiatry*, **55**: 448–453.
8. Regier D.A., Narrow W.E., Rae D.S., Manderscheid R.W., Locke B.Z., Goodwin F.K. (1993) The *de facto* US mental and addictive disorders service system. Epidemiologic catchment area prospective 1-year prevalence rates of disorders and services. *Arch. Gen. Psychiatry*, **50**: 85–94.

6.7
Not Expensive and Cheap to Treat: New Evidence Leads to Different Conclusions

Gavin Andrews[1]

Some of the data in the Knapp *et al*'s review comes from advocates [1]. If one relies on data from advocates, one runs the risk of obtaining inflated estimates. Knapp *et al*, therefore, tend to rely more on epidemiological data than on that from special interest groups. But even that can lead one astray. Obsessive-compulsive disorder (OCD) was, until treatments were available, regarded as a rare and severe disease, because only severe cases came to specialist attention. The Epidemiological Catchment Area (ECA) studies found that 1.5% of adults reported symptoms in the previous year that met criteria for DSM-III OCD. On the basis of those data it was later

[1] *School of Psychiatry, University of New South Wales at St. Vincent's Hospital, 299 Forbes Street, Darlinghurst, New South Wales 2010, Australia*

reported that while only a quarter had sought medical help the majority of people who did so were hospitalized. In hindsight it is clear that hospitalization was not evidence of severity, but evidence that the doctors at the time knew of no appropriate remedies and therefore hospitalization was a strategy of dispair. Appropriate remedies now exist and our specialist clinic has not hospitalized anyone with OCD for 15 years. Thus, old data cannot always be used for costing estimates, simply because practice changes. The UK population survey used a symptom check list to ascertain the prevalence of anxiety and depressive symptoms and, on the basis of those symptoms, but not on the basis of whether those symptoms satisfied the ICD or DSM diagnostic criteria, arbitrarily allocated people to a diagnosis. Thus, even quite recent epidemiogical data should sometimes be viewed with caution.

The 1990 Burden of Disease project [2] is maybe a better guide. After all, it was established to provide data to replace advocacy with epidemiology and, by careful reconciliation of data, not to double-count causes of death, even though they made no allowance for comorbidity overestimating years lived with disability [3]. Comorbidity is common in OCD and any disability is as likely to be due to the comorbid condition as to the OCD. In the Burden of Disease project, prevalence was based on the ECA estimates of 1.5% of the adult population being affected in any 12-month period. Disability-adjusted life years (DALYs) lost due to OCD in established market economies like the UK and the USA were 5% of the burden due to mental disorders and 1.5% of the total burden of disease, similar to the burden attributed to drug use.

One of the advantages of writing a commentary is that the authors define the subject area and quote their findings. Commentators are then free to use more recent data to put the findings in perspective. Andrews *et al* [4] have recently reported on the results of the Australian National Survey of Mental Health and Well-being, in which OCD was identified by a structured diagnostic interview that covered the diagnostic criteria in detail. Mathers *et al* [5] used these data and published a revised burden of disease calculation for Australia that dispensed with the controversial age weighting used in the Burden of Disease project, that overestimated the burden of disorders like OCD, and controlled the overestimate due to comorbidity by dividing the disability weight by the number of conditions present. They found that mental disorders (not including dementia) accounted for 13.3% of the total burden of disease, the proportion being lower than in the Burden of Disease project because of these changes in method. OCD accounted for 1.4% of the mental disorder burden. This was similar in magnitude to the burden attributed to panic disorder or agoraphobia. Thus, on these data, OCD accounts for only 0.2% of the total burden of disease in Australia. It does not rank among the top 75 leading causes of burden. Burden is in part an estimate of the costs to society of a disease. As the burden is small, OCD is unlikely to be a disease of great cost.

Mathers *et al* also provide direct cost data from the year 1993–94 for the various types of mental disorders. The anxiety disorders accounted for 7.9% of the total expenditure associated with mental disorders. On a pro rata basis, and there is little reason to see OCD as more expensive than the other anxiety disorders, OCD would account for 0.9% of the total expended on mental disorders. In the Australian context it accounts for 0.004% of the Gross Domestic Product. In Australia the direct costs of OCD are not great.

Present expenditure is a poor guide to need [6]. Of more interest is the return on investment—just what does it cost to gain one quality adjusted life year (QALY) or avert one DALY? There are a number of league tables that show the cost per QALY for various treatments and disease pairings. $30 000 per QALY is a shadow price for a treatment that is likely to appeal to a health planner. What then is the cost of treating OCD? Twelve consultations with a specialist plus a selective serotonin reuptake inhibitor (SSRI) cost some $3000 per year. A course of cognitive-behavioural therapy (CBT) costs no more, the advantage of CBT being that in many cases the 1 year treatment cost is the total cost. Just how many QALYs the industry standard 15-point drop in the Yale–Brown Obsessive Compulsive scale (Y-BOCS) score equates to, needs to be worked out, but the cost-effectiveness of either CBT or an SSRI seems unlikely to exceed the shadow price. Knapp *et al* say that the costs of OCD are "high" and the cost of treatment is "not inexpensive". This commentator has tendered evidence that in Australia the costs are not high and that treatment is relatively inexpensive.

REFERENCES

1. Hollander E. (1997) Obsessive compulsive disorder: the hidden epidemic. *J. Clin. Psychiatry*, **58**: 3–6.
2. Murray C.J.L., Lopez A.D. (1996) *The Global Burden of Disease*, Harvard University Press, Cambridge.
3. Andrews G., Sanderson K., Beard J. (1998) Burden of disease: methods of calculating the disability from mental disorder. *Br. J. Psychiatry*, **173**: 123–131.
4. Andrews G., Hall W., Teesson M., Henderson S. (1999) *The Mental Health of Australians*, Commonwealth Department of Health and Aged Care, Canberra.
5. Mathers C., Vos T., Stevenson C. (1999) *The Burden of Disease and Injury in Australia*, Australian Institute of Health and Welfare, Canberra.
6. Andrews G., Henderson S. (2000) *Unmet Need in Psychiatry*, Cambridge University Press, Cambridge.

6.8
Economics of Obsessive-Compulsive Disorder: on Safe Grounds?

Wulf Rössler[1]

Once obsessive-compulsive disorder (OCD) was regarded as a very rare disease. Newer surveys based on standardized classification procedures reported rates of 2–3% of the general population to be affected. Although still not *very* common, OCD is acknowledged as a relevant public health problem: current epidemiological evidence tells us that it is a chronic and disabling disease with an early age of onset. Furthermore, OCD seems to impose a considerable burden on the families of affected persons and on the economy as well.

As such, it seems reasonable to ask for the costs of OCD. Prof. Knapp and colleagues have tried to answer this question. From their extensive and thorough review, they conclude that the economic consequences of OCD are wide-ranging, often long-lasting and sometimes profound. But, aside from costs of illness studies, which give us an overall impression of the total costs of an illness, more specified cost evaluations of OCD are missing. The authors complain of the paucity of in-depth economic evidence and express their hope that in the coming years further economic evaluations on OCD will be initiated. One tends to support their assessment. But first we should discuss some of the presumptions forming the basis of economic evaluations of OCD today.

Methodological problems. Assessing comparable disease rates with standardized classification methods is primarily an indicator of the reliability of our current classification systems, but not of the validity of diagnostic entities. According to Angst [1], a valid case definition of OCD remains a problem, as "there is little doubt to the existence of a spectrum of OCD manifestations, ranging from transitional symptoms through sub-clinical mild transient syndromes with a good prognosis to clinical non-recurrent, recurrent and even chronic cases". In the Zurich cohort, for example, the 10-year prevalence rate of sub-clinical OCD amounts to 5.7%, which significantly surmounts the lifetime prevalence rates of most studies on OCD [2].

Additionally, we should discuss some cultural aspects in the epidemiology of OCD. Studies performed with a comparable methodology revealed considerable differences between countries, i.e. lower lifetime prevalence rates in Asia [3, 4] compared to industrialized countries, but also to other developing countries like Egypt [5].

Last but not least, there is a solid body of evidence that OCD is linked with a broad range of other disorders (somatoform disorders,

[1] *Psychiatric University Hospital, Militärstrasse 8, PO Box 1930, 8021 Zürich, Switzerland*

eating disorders, impulse control disorders and personality disorders, to name just a few). Crino [6] discusses the question if such co-occurrence indicates a vulnerability to anxiety and depressive disorders in general.

Need and utilization. In a recent lecture, Wittchen [7] stated that diagnosis in itself cannot answer appropriately questions about needs for care and service utilization, and epidemiological studies from the past two decades fail to provide coherent and comprehensive information about these important issues. Furthermore, our current epidemiological database is largely deficient concerning help-seeking behaviour, which links the affected persons' perceptions of their needs for care with their decisions for service utilization. This refers not only to individual help-seeking behaviour but also to transcultural aspects of help-seeking behaviour, influenced by culture-bound attitudes toward the disorder [5].

There is also not enough information on how different service provider models determine utilization with respect to the availability of services and the access to services. For example, proximity to services as an inverse relationship between distance to and utilization of services is a decisive factor for utilization known for more than a century [8].

Cost calculation under uncertainty. Summarizing the arguments so far, it seems that the current economic knowledge concerning the costs of OCD is not on very safe grounds.

The current case definition of OCD is probably too restrictive. Health care-relevant subclinical cases with a better prognosis are excluded. Furthermore, our transcultural knowledge concerning classification and course of OCD is insufficient. As such, the current classification, on which cost evaluations are grounded, is not very representative for the disorder.

There is a tendency in psychiatric research to restrict diagnostic classification to core psychopathological processes. This might be useful in identifying homogenous study populations but is not useful from a public health perspective, where psychiatric conditions are best described as continua [9] related to measures of role performance. As Wittchen [7] points out, "... the exclusive reliance on categorical threshold diagnoses carries substantial risks of artifactual explanation (such as in comorbidity analyses) and fails to acknowledge the dimensional nature of most expressions of psychopathology". The dimensional view allows us to look for variation instead of homogeneity—variation with respect to individual, socioeconomic, societal and finally cultural variables. In the same way, variation in costs would possibly permit us to take a more differentiated look at the economic aspects of mental disorders.

REFERENCES

1. Angst J. (1994) The epidemiology of obsessive compulsive disorder. In *Current Insights in Obsessive-Compulsive Disorder* (Eds E. Hollander, J. Zohar, D. Marazziti, B. Olivier), pp. 93–104, Wiley, Chichester.
2. Degonda M., Wyss M., Angst J. (1993) The Zurich Study. XVIII. Obsessive-compulsive disorders and syndromes in the general population. *Eur. Arch. Psychiatry Clin. Neurosci.*, **243**: 16–22.
3. Yeh E.K., Hwu H.G., Chang L.Y., Yeh Y.L. (1985) Mental disorder in a Chinese metropolis: symptoms, diagnosis and lifetime prevalence. *Seishin Shinkeigaku Zasshi*, **87**: 318–324.
4. Khanna S., Gururay G., Sriram T.G. (1993) Epidemiology of obsessive-compulsive disorder in India. Presented at the First International Obsessive-Compulsive Disorder Congress, Capri, March 9–12.
5. Okasha A., Saad A., Khalil A.H., El Dawla A.S., Yehia N. (1994) Phenomenology of OCD. A transcultural study. *Compr. Psychiatry*, **25**: 191–197.
6. Crino R.D. (1999) Obsessive-compulsive spectrum disorders. *Curr. Opin. Psychiatry*, **12**: 151–155.
7. Wittchen H.U. (2000) Epidemiological research in mental disorders: lessons for the next decade of research. *Acta Psychiatr. Scand.*, **101**: 2–10.
8. Meise U., Kemmler G., Rössler W. (1993) Psychiatric community care—a matter of distance? *Fort. Neurol. Psychiatr.*, **61** (suppl. 1): 7.
9. Lewis G. (1996) Depression and public health. *Int. Rev. Psychiatry*, **8**: 289–294.

6.9
Obsessive-Compulsive Disorder: the Hidden Costs of a Hidden Epidemic

Luis Salvador-Carulla[1]

Epidemiological studies have shown that obsessive-compulsive disorder (OCD) may be at least twice as common as once thought. Over 2% of the general population may suffer from this condition [1], which is the fourth most prevalent psychiatric disorder in the USA. Knapp *et al* have reviewed the existing evidence, which indicates that OCD is associated with high rates of service utilization, lost productivity, and both personal and family burden. Hidden psychiatric morbidity is also high, because many patients do not seek psychiatric treatment, and often present first to other medical professionals. Nearly half of OCD patients are misdiagnosed as having depression or generalized anxiety [2]. Apart from misdiagnosis, comorbidity with other disorders facilitates diagnostic overshadowing of OCD: a significant number of psychiatric and neurological diseases, e.g. Tourette's syndrome or Sydenham's chorea, may coexist with this disorder.

[1] *Department of Psychiatry, University of Cadiz, Spain*

OCD symptoms may then simply be attributed to the other condition, and remain unexplored.

Non-diagnosed psychiatric patients make high use of inefficient health services. This utilization decreases dramatically when proper diagnosis and treatment are provided (a shift in the health service utilization pattern known as the "offset effect"). Direct and indirect costs of non-diagnosed patients are significant in depression [3] and panic disorder [4]. They may be even higher in the case of OCD. Hollander *et al* [2] found a 17-year delay between the onset of the illness and prescription of adequate treatment. To my knowledge, this is the longest gap reported in the literature for any psychiatric disorder. In this study, the average age at which respondents first experienced OCD symptoms was 14.5 years; however, they did not seek professional help until an average of 10 years later. In the average case, an additional lag of 6 years occured before OCD was diagnosed, and adequate treatment was begun 12 months later.

Personal and societal costs of non-diagnosis are often overlooked in mental health economics. In spite of their limitations, naturalistic cost-offset studies do provide useful information for macro-economic analysis and modelling. Their contribution may be particularly relevant in the case of OCD; however, there is no information available on this issue. Information is also scarce on the cost-effectiveness of OCD's treatment alternatives, and both macro- and micro-economic studies in this area are insufficient and limited. Knapp *et al* highlight the problems of inadequate use of cost-of-illness information from a single top-down study, as well as the fact that its results cannot be generalized. Apart from broad epidemiological studies and administrative registers, bottom-up data on OCD costs come from surveys conducted in patients' organizations using self-report questionnaires [2, 5]. Illustrative as they may be, such data should complement future cost–incidence and prevalence studies, rather than serve as the sole support for resource allocation. The existing data on key health economics topics (e.g. quality of life) are also far behind those data available for other, more high-profile psychiatric disorders, such as schizophrenia and depression [6].

Several factors may explain the current lack of information on OCD economics. First, mental health professionals have not been aware of OCD's heavy societal burden until very recently. Second, many aspects of its nosology and assessment remain unresolved. Even the assignment of OCD to the anxiety grouping is in question: ICD-10 classifies it as a separate category, and both clinical and biological data suggest that OCD is closely related to a variety of other spectrum disorders, including Axis I and II disorders, risk-aversive/impulsive behaviours and neurological diseases [7]. Up to 10% of the population may suffer from an OCD spectrum disorder, making its overall societal burden even higher. On the other hand, the OCD assessment procedures used in several major epidemiological studies have been challenged. OCD was not included in the economic analysis of anxiety disorders in the National Comorbidity Survey (NCS) [8]. Third, cost analysis of OCD may be hindered by other methodological complications, including the assessment of hidden costs related to misdiagnosis and comorbidity.

In spite of the scarce data, Knapp *et al*'s paper clearly states that OCD constitutes a major health problem and deserves special attention from health decision-makers and planners. In this case, cost data may not only be a tool for resource allocation, but also a valuable means of tackling this problem's true magnitude.

REFERENCES

1. Sasson Y., Zohar J., Chopra M., Lustig M., Iancu I., Hendler T. (1997) Epidemiology of obsessive-compulsive disorder. *J. Clin. Psychiatry*, **58** (suppl. 12): 7–10.
2. Hollander E., Kwon J.H., Stein D.J., Broatch J., Rowland C.T., Himelein C.A. (1996) Obsessive-compulsive and spectrum disorders: overview and quality of life issues. *J. Clin. Psychiatry*, **57** (suppl. 8): 3–6.
3. Rupp A. (1995) The economic consequences of not treating depression. *Br. J. Psychiatry*, **166** (suppl. 27): 29–33.
4. Salvador-Carulla L., Seguí J., Fernandez-Cano P., Canet J. (1995) Costs and offset effect in panic disorders. *Br. J. Psychiatry*, **166** (suppl. 27): 23–28.
5. Stein D.J., Roberts M., Hollander E., Rowland C., Serebro P. (1996) Quality of life and pharmaco-economic aspects of obsessive-compulsive disorder. A South African survey. *S. Afr. Med. J*, **86** (suppl. 12): 1582–1585.
6. Schneier F.R. (1997) Quality of life in anxiety disorders. In *Quality of Life in Mental Disorders* (Eds. H. Katschnig, H. Freeman, N. Sartorius), pp. 149–163, Wiley, Chichester.
7. Hollander E. (1997) Obsessive-compulsive disorder: the hidden epidemic. *J. Clin. Psychiatry*, **58** (suppl. 12): 3–6.
8. Greenberg P.E., Sisitsky T. Kessler R.C., Finkelstein S.N., Berndt E.R., Davidson J.R.T., Ballenger J.C., Fyer A.J. (1999) The economic burden of anxiety disorders in the 1990s. *J. Clin. Psychiatry*, **60**: 427–435.

6.10
Obsessive-Compulsive Disorder: an Underestimated Disorder

Mathias Berger[1], Ulrich Voderholzer[1] and Fritz Hohagen[2]

Obsessive-compulsive disorder (OCD) is one of the four most common psychiatric disorders, with a lifetime prevalence of about 2–3% [1]. Knapp

[1] *Department of Psychiatry and Psychotherapy, University Clinic, Albert-Ludwigs-University, Freiburg, Germany;* [2] *Department of Psychiatry, University Clinic, Ratzeburger Allee 160, Lübeck, Germany*

et al's review is a detailed and thorough report on all economic aspects of this disorder. Generally, it is very difficult to estimate the costs of any psychiatric disorder, which is true for both the direct costs caused by the utilization of the health care system and for the indirect costs due to unemployment and reduced productivity, consequences for the family and for the society. Many studies dealing with this issue are methodologically insufficient. Some economic aspects may also essentially differ from country to country and therefore conclusions from studies performed in the United States or the United Kingdom, where most reports are coming from, cannot be generalized to the worldwide situation.

In the case of OCD, it, seems even more difficult to estimate the economic impact. In the whole field of anxiety disorders, there are fewer studies aiming at economic questions compared with depression and schizophrenia. There is also a high comorbidity between OCD and major depression and between OCD and personality disorders.

Knapp *et al* emphasize that the paucity of economic evidence makes it difficult to draw particularly strong conclusions about what is known about OCD, except that the disorder has quite large and wide-ranging costs. As a consequence, it is not possible to state whether or not treatment options for OCD are cost-effective.

From our experience over the past years, we can underline many aspects of the review. In a large proportion of our OCD patients, there has been a time-lag of many years between onset of symptoms and seeking treatment. In most of them the onset is during adolescence, with a chronic course and a low tendency for spontaneous remission. In a substantial proportion of the patients, the disease is debilitating, with a severely reduced life quality.

It has repeatedly been mentioned that the prevalence of OCD has been underestimated in the past. Moreover, there is evidence that the frequency of OCD is still underestimated today. Hohagen *et al* recently performed a screening of 2265 patients in psychiatric practices in the area of Freiburg, by using a standardized diagnostic interview (unpublished data). 11% of the patients were found to have OCD, frequently in association with other psychiatric disorders. Surprisingly, in only a quarter of patients meeting the criteria for OCD had the disorder been diagnosed by the psychiatrist. This may be explained by the well-known tendency of OCD patients to hide their symptoms, with the consequence that even the specialist may overlook the disorder. This further supports Knapp *et al*'s conclusion that the economic impact of the disorder has been underestimated.

Whereas for a long time the disorder was assumed to be refractory to therapy in most cases, cognitive-behavioural therapy (CBT), including exposure and response prevention, and serotonin reuptake inhibitors have been shown to be effective in a large number of studies. We have shown that the combination of CBT and a selective serotonin reuptake inhibitor (SSRI) is more effective than CBT and placebo and is currently the most effective treatment strategy for OCD [2], with a response rate as high as 87% in terms of an at least 35% reduction of the Yale-Brown Obsessive Compulsive Scale (Y-BOCS) score. A follow-up after 2 years demonstrated a stable improvement in most of the patients. However, improvement is rarely a full remission and many secondary consequences of the disorder are not resolved. In our experience, CBT with exposure in OCD patients is a time-consuming, and therefore costly, therapy requiring much training for the therapist and it is not generally part of the psychotherapy training, at least in our country. Many of the OCD patients referred to our department had been treated with unspecific psychotherapy but not with CBT and exposure.

Regarding pharmacological treatment, dosages of serotonin reuptake inhibitors for OCD are twice as high as those needed for depression, which further indicates that an effective treatment of OCD is costly. However, with regard to the disabling character of OCD and all the consequences for social relationships, employment, work performance and other aspects, we are strongly convinced that current treatment options, such as CBT and SSRIs, may not only improve life quality but will be also cost-effective in the economic sense. For a further clarification, long-term follow-up studies including measures of life quality are mandatory.

Our survey in psychiatric practices showed that about 50% of the OCD patients who had been diagnosed by the psychiatrist (a quarter of 11%) had already received an effective treatment, i.e. CBT and/or SSRIs or clomipramine. Only a small proportion had received the combination of both treatments. Considering also the fact that many OCD patients do not seek psychiatric help, one can conclude that most OCD patients in our society do not receive adequate treatment.

REFERENCES

1. Angst J. (1994) The epidemiology of obsessive compulsive disorder. In *Current Insights in Obsessive-Compulsive Disorder* (Eds. E. Hollander, J. Zohar, D. Marazziti, B. Olivier), pp. 93–104, Wiley, Chichester.
2. Hohagen F., Winkelmann G., Rasche-Räuchle H., Hand I., König A., Münchau N., Hiss H., Geiger-Kabisch C., Kappler C., Schramm P. *et al* (1998) Combination of behaviour therapy with fluvoxamine in comparison with behaviour therapy and placebo. Results of a multicentre study. *Br. J. Psychiatry*, **35** (suppl. 73): 71–78.

Acknowledgements

The Editors would like to thank Drs Paola Bucci, Umberto Volpe, Andrea Dell'Acqua, Andrea Fiorillo, Francesco Perris, Massimo Lanzaro, Vincenzo Scarallo, Giuseppe Piegari, Mariangela Masella, Pasquale Saviano and Enrico Tresca, of the Department of Psychiatry of the University of Naples, for their help in the processing of manuscripts.

The publication has been supported by an unrestricted educational grant from Ravizza Farmaceutici, which is hereby gratefully acknowledged.

Index

Note: Obsessive-compulsive disorder is abbreviated to OCD

adolescence, OCD in *see* child and adolescent OCD
adult-onset 27
age of onset 2, 27
ambulatory services 260–1
anorexia nervosa 154–5, 156, 213
antidepressants 44
  in combination with cognitive behavioural therapy 125–8
antigen D8/17 160–1
antiobsessional medications 44
  side effects 48
anxiety disorders, comorbidity 25
arachnoid cysts 27
Asperger's syndrome 156, 195, 196, 205, 215
assessment 22–4
assessment tools 11–13
attention-deficit/hyperactivity disorder (ADHD) 155, 188
augmentation 52, 57, 64, 85
autism 153, 156, 195, 205, 215, 216–17
averaged evoked response (ARE), somatosensory 14
aversion therapy 94, 95

bare attention 140–1
Barrett–Lennard Relationship Questionnaire (BLRQ) 120
basal ganglia diseases 21
Beck Depression Inventory (BDI) 102
behavioural therapy 37, 62, 129–30
  amount of therapist contact 116
  in combination with clomipramine 116–17, 137–8
  in combination with fluvoxamine 138
  in spectrum disorders 205–6
benzodiazepines 62, 66
beta-hemolytic streptococcus, group A (GABHS) 30, 51, 64, 160
body dysmorphic disorder 38, 87, 156, 213–14, 225, 226–7
borderline personality disorder 10
brain derived neurotrophic factor (BDNF) 70
brain injury 27
Brown Assessment of Beliefs Scale (BABS) 13, 35
BT STEPS ™ 117–18, 135
bulimia nervosa 156, 213–14
burden-of-disease studies 265–6, 279
buspirone 52, 53, 62

carbamazepine 77
carers, impact on 263–4
catechol-*O*-methyltransferase (COMT) allele 40, 242
challenge studies 84–5
child and adolescent OCD 27
  age and developmental effects 152
  age at onset 151, 188
  chronicity 186
  classification 151
  clinical characteristics 149–56
  comorbidity 154–5, 186, 188, 197, 200
  developmental perspectives 187–9
  diagnosis 151
  diagnostic assessment and rating instruments 153–4
  differential diagnosis 153
  etiology of compulsions 191
  etiopathogenesis 156–61
    autoimmune factors 160–1
    biochemical factors 157–8
    frontal–subcortical circuit dysfunction 159
    genetic factors 158
    psychogenetic factors 156–7
  in Guatemala 198–200
  history 147, 191–2
  onset 150, 193

child and adolescent OCD *(Cont.)*
outcome 167–73
prospective follow-up studies 169–72
retrospective follow-up studies 167–9
risk and prognostic factors 172–3
prevalence 147–9, 188, 193
sex ratio 151–2
spectrum disorders 155–6, 195–6
symptoms 149–50, 199
theoretical and clinical implications 184–6
treatment 161–7
cognitive-behavioural treatment (CBT) 164, 165, 166, 193
family psychopathology 166
milieu therapy 166
psychodynamic psychotherapy 164
psychopharmacological 161–3
treatment guidelines 166–7
choreiform movements 159
citalopram 44, 46
in child and adolescent OCD 163
classification 2–7
cleanliness, ritualistic 9
Clinical Global Impression (CGI) scales 13, 39, 210
clomipramine (CMI) 30, 37, 43, 44, 55, 62
augmentation 74–5
augmentation with SSRIs 53
in child and adolescent OCD 161–3, 166
effectiveness 73, 86
intravenous 54
long-term approach 49
prospective follow-up studies 169–72
side effects 161–3, 166
switching to SSRIs 52
clonazepam 55
clonidine 55–6, 189
clozapine 54
cognitive behavioural therapy 136
antidepressants in combination with 125–8
in child and adolescent OCD 164, 165, 193, 197
drop-out 120
enhancing effects of 119–21
individualized treatment 120
new approaches 131–3
patient/therapist relationship 119–20
relapse 120–1
cognitive compulsions 5
cognitive restructuring 132–3
cognitive therapy 124, 129–30, 142–4
comorbidity 8–9
anxiety 25
in child and adolescent OCD 154–5, 186, 188, 197, 200
costs and 281
personality disorder 119
schizophrenia 8–9, 11, 50–1, 58, 64, 153
Comprehensive Psychopathological Rating Scale (CPRS) 12
compulsions
recognition as senseless 6
relationship between obsessions and 5
compulsive-impulsive dimensional models 203–4
compulsivity 203–4
computed tomography (CT) 159
contamination obsessions 10
corticosteroids 69
cost–benefit analysis 270, 279
cost–consequences analyses 269, 270, 271
cost–effectiveness analysis 269–70, 273, 279
cost-minimization analysis 269
cost-offset analysis 269
cost-of-illness studies 265–6, 279
cost–utility analysis 270–1, 279
costs
aggregate 265–8
comorbidity and 281
dearth of studies 279–80, 281–3, 283–5, 288–9
direct 267, 292
economic evaluation 268–72
estimates 266–8
hidden 295–7
mental health expenditure 257–8
productivity 267–8
underestimation of disease 297–9
welfare 265
worldwide 276–7
course 7–8

D8/17 antigen 160–1
demographic features 2
depersonalization disorder 205, 229
depression 10, 130, 237
desensitization, systematic 94
desipramine (DMI) 43
  in child and adolescent OCD 161
dexamethasone suppression test (DST) 13
diagnosis 29–31
  biological aspects in 13–14, 37–8
  difficulties in 4
  by etiology 20–2
  in Latin America 39–40
  psychological approaches to limitations 35–6
  questions used in 4–5
  symptoms and implications for treatment 32–3
  transcultural aspects 9–10
Diagnostic Interview Schedule (DIS) 2
differential diagnosis 10–11
Disability Adjusted Life Years (DALYs) 14, 276, 291, 292
DSM-IV 2–4, 36
  comparison of ICD-10 and 6–7
dysmorphophobia 78

eating disorders 213–15
  see also anorexia nervosa; bulimia nervosa
economic evaluation 268–72
  cost calculation under uncertainty 294
  evidence base 271–2
  methodological problems 293–4
  models 269–71
  need and utilization 294
  principles 268–9
economic impacts 256–7
education 262–3
electric shock 66, 94, 95
employment 262–3, 267–8, 282
encephalitis lethargica 21
eosinophilia–myalgia syndrome 54
evidence-based medicine 283–4
exposure 94
exposure and ritual prevention (EX/RP) 95–7
  availability 117–18, 134
  centers of expertise 109
  in combination with SRIs 137
  current practice 131–2
  decreasing session frequency 109
  failure of uptake 117
  family involvement in 123
  family involvement vs EX/RP treatment 100–1
  individual vs. group EX/RP 101–2
  integrated approach 132–3
  multi-modal, systematic-strategic behavioural approach to 122–5
  patient refusal 109
  patient self-help 117–18, 135, 137, 139–41
  predictors of treatment outcome 106–8, 110
    expectancy of outcome 107
    motivation and compliance with BT 108
    personality disorders (PD) 107
    pretreatment depression 106–7
    pretreatment OCD severity 107
  refusal 137
  scarcity of trained therapists 134–5
  treatment variables 97–100
    duration of exposure 98–9
    exposure vs. ritual prevention vs. EX/RP 97
    frequency of exposure sessions 97
    gradual vs. abrupt exposures 99
    implementation of ritual prevention 100
    therapist-assisted vs. self-exposure 98
    use of imaginal exposure 99–100
  vs. cognitive therapies 102–5, 124
  vs. pharmacotherapy 105–6, 124
Eysenck Personality Questionnaire (EPQ) 207

family, impact on 263–4
family psychopathology 166
fenfluramine 52, 53
fluoxetine 44, 45, 47, 52, 55, 62
  in child and adolescent OCD 163
fluvoxamine 44, 45, 47, 52, 55, 62, 76
  in child and adolescent OCD 163

gambling, pathological 208–10
gender-related differences 27

Greenberg Sexual Preference Fantasy Scale 212–13
group A beta-hemolytic streptococci (GABHS) 30, 51, 64, 160
growth hormone 14
guanfacine 189

hallucinogens 69
haloperidol 50
Hamilton Rating Scale for Depression (HAM-D) 210
health care
  ambulatory services 260–1
  broad and long-term impacts 256–7
  distributional imbalance 256
  family and carers 263–4
  formal care 261–2
  inpatient hospitalization 258–60
  macro- and micro-analyses 254–5
  scarcity of resources 253–4
  supply 255–6
  utilization 257–61, 282
homovanillic acid 158
Hopkins Symptoms Checklist (HSCL) 11, 23
Huntington's disease 159
5–hydroxyindoleacetic acid (HIAA) 37, 157, 158, 207
5–hydroxytryptophan 83, 230–2
5–HT2 agonists 68–70
hypochondriasis 78, 205, 213
hypomanic episodes, drug-induced 77

ICD-10 4, 36
  comparison of DSM-IV and 6–7
imipramine 43, 71
impulse-control disorders 207–13
impulsivity 204
inositol 55
inpatient hospitalization 258–60
insight 34–5, 38, 78

juvenile OCD *see* child and adolescent OCD

learning theory 93
Leyton Obsessional Inventory (LOI) 11, 23
  Child Version (LOI-CV) 154
lithium 52, 53, 77
L-triodothyronine 54
L-tryptophan (LTRY) 83
lysergic acid diethylamide (LSD) 69

magnetic resonance imaging (MRI) 159
management 22–4
manic episodes, drug-induced 76–7
Maudsley Obsessive Compulsive Inventory (MOCI) 11, 23, 90
m-chlorophenylpiperazine (*m*-CPP) 84, 206–7
mental retardation 153
mescaline 69
3–methoxy-4–hydroxyphenylglycol (MHPG) 158, 209
milieu therapy 166
mindfulness-based cognitive therapy (MBCT) 140–1
monoamine oxidase (MAO) activity 207
monoamine oxidase inhibitors (MAOIs) 33, 55, 62
mood disorders, link with 13
mortality 264

National Institute of Mental Health (NIMH)–Global Obsessive Compulsive Scale (GOCS) 13, 39
nefazodone 72
neuroimaging 84
neurological disorders 215–17
neurosurgery 57
nortriptyline 43
nosology 2–7

obsessions
  recognition as senseless 6
  relationship between compulsions and 5
obsessive-compulsive personality disorder (OCPD) 20–1, 23, 25
  antidepressants in 89–91
  pharmacological treatment 89–90
  as predictor of outcome in OCD 90
obsessive-compulsive spectrum disorders 21, 87–8
  associated features 237
  categorical approaches 241
  cognitive perspective 242–3
  cultural perspective 243
  deconvolving into component diseases 244–6
  dimensional approaches 241

emergence of concept 240
etiology 237–8
evolutionary perspective 243
four-factor model 228–30
impulse-control disorders 207–13
limitations of concept 225–6, 238, 247–8
neurobiological models 206–7, 237, 250–1
neurochemical perspective 231–2
neurological disorders 215–17
response to treatment 205–6, 236
somatoform and eating disorders cluster 213–15
symptom clusters 204–5, 235–6
treatment grouping 248
treatment response 205–6, 236
usefulness of 233–5, 235–8, 239–40
olanzapine 52, 54, 64
onychophagia 156
opportunity cost 266
overvalued ideas 38
Overvalued Ideas Scale (OVIS) 13, 35

PANDAS 191, 225
panic attacks 10
paradoxical intention 94
paraphilias 211–13
Parkinson's disease 27, 159
paroxetine 44, 46, 47, 62
pathological gambling (PG) 208–10
genetics 208–9
neurobiology 209
treatment 210
pediatric autoimmune neuropsychiatric disorders associated with streptococcal infections (PANDAS) 191, 225
Personality Diagnostic Questionnaire (PDQ) 23
personality disorder comorbidity 119
positron emission tomography (PET) 159, 231
pharmacotherapy
augmentation and combination treatment 72–3
in child and adolescent OCD 193–4
choice of drugs 71, 83, 86–8
cross-response 63
dose 47, 72, 80
effectiveness 83
future studies 79–81
improvement 87
long-term treatment 80
response time 80
switching 71–2
phenelzine 55
pimozide 50
pindolol 52–3, 64, 76, 85
placebo effect 83
post-streptococcal autoimmunity 51
pregnancy
pharmacotherapy and 83
SSRIs in 74
prevalence 1–2, 276–7
prolactin response 206–7
psilocybin 69
psychedelic drugs 69
psychodynamic treatment 144–6
psychoeducation 101
psychological approaches to diagnosis, limitations of 35–6
psychosocial treatments, early 93–5
"pure" OCD 27–8

quality adjusted life year (QALY) 271, 287–8, 292

rapid eye movement (REM) 14
rater-administered scales 12–13
Rational Emotive Therapy (RET) 102–3, 104, 142–4
recurrence of symptoms 138
reinforcement procedures 95
repetitive behaviours 5
reward deficiency syndrome 208–9
rheumatic fever 30, 160
risperidone 50, 52, 64
ritual purity 9
ruminations 33

schizophrenia 195, 196
pharmacotherapy 87–8
schizophrenia comorbidity 8–9, 50–1, 58, 64
in children and adolescents 153
SCL-90 11–12
segregation analysis 40
selective serotonin reuptake inhibitors (SSRIs) 43, 44–7, 55, 62, 63
augmentation with CMI 53

selective serotonin reuptake inhibitors *(Cont.)*
in child and adolescent OCD 189
choice among 46–7
dosage 47, 166–7
effectiveness 71, 73, 74, 84, 86
long-term approach 49
safety 74
side effects 74, 163
switching among 71–2
switching to CMI 52
Self-instructional Training 102, 142
Self-rated Scale for Obsessive Compulsive Disorder 11, 12
self-rating scales 11–12
self-treatment 117–18, 135, 137, 139–41
Sensation Seeking Scale (Zuckerman) 207
serotonin hypothesis 37, 84
serotonin reuptake inhibitors (SRIs) 7–8, 30, 31, 33, 37, 43
advantages 64–5
in combination with behavioural therapy 137–8
effectiveness 86
response to 66–7
in spectrum disorders 205
serotonin transporter protein gene (SLC6A4) 67
sertraline 44, 45–6, 47, 52, 55, 62, 74
in child and adolescent OCD 163
in paraphilias 211–13
sexual addictions 211–13
single photon emission tomography (SPECT) 30, 159, 231
somatoform disorders 213–15
South Oaks Gambling Screen (SOGS) 210
spontaneous decay 132
streptococcal infections 21
Structured Clinical Interview for (DSM-III-R SCID)-II 119
Structured Interview for Personality Disorders 23
subtypes 25–6, 26–8
diagnosis 29–31
pharmacotherapy and 58
suicide 264
sumatriptan 85
Sydenham's chorea 27, 30, 51, 160, 186, 205, 215
symptom clusters 204–5

Therapist Client Rating Scale (TCRS) 120
thought–action fusion (TAF) 36
thought-stopping 95
thyroid hormones 52, 54
tic-related OCD 25, 28, 49–50
childhood onset 155
tics 25, 29, 64, 159
Tourette's syndrome 21, 27, 29, 30, 49, 55, 64, 159, 185–6, 188, 196, 197, 205, 226, 228
transfer payments 265
trazodone 52, 53
treatment-resistant OCD 51–6
treatment response, onset of 48–9
trichotillomania 10, 87, 156, 226
tricyclic antidepressants 44, 48, 62
Tridimensional Personality Questionnaire (TPQ) 207
tryptophan 52, 54
tryptophan 2,3–dioxygenase gene (TD02) 209
twin studies 40

Yale–Brown Obsessive Compulsive Scale (Y-BOCS) 12, 13, 20, 30, 39, 76, 84, 87, 90, 104, 154, 157, 210
CY-BOCS 154, 187
PG-YBOCS 210

zolmitriptan 85

Index compiled by Annette Musker